Leveraging the Law

Teaching Texts in Law and Politics

David A. Schultz
General Editor

Vol. 3

PETER LANG
New York • Washington, D.C./Baltimore • Boston
Bern • Frankfurt am Main • Berlin • Vienna • Paris

Leveraging the Law

Using the Courts to Achieve Social Change

David A. Schultz,
Editor

PETER LANG
New York • Washington, D.C./Baltimore • Boston
Bern • Frankfurt am Main • Berlin • Vienna • Paris

Library of Congress Cataloging-in-Publication Data
Leveraging the law: using the courts
to achieve social change/ David A. Schultz (editor).
p. cm. — (Teaching texts in law and politics; v. 3)
Includes bibliographical references and index.
1. Judge-made law—United States. 2. Social change—United States.
I. Schultz, David A. (David Andrew). II. Series: Teaching texts
in law and politics (New York, N.Y.); v. 3.
KF8700.L47   340′.115′0973—dc21   96-39624
ISBN 0-8204-3492-2
ISSN 1083-3447

Die Deutsche Bibliothek-CIP-Einheitsaufnahme
Leveraging the law:
using the courts to achieve social change/ David A. Schultz. (Ed
—New York; Washington, D.C./Baltimore; Boston; Bern;
Frankfurt am Main; Berlin; Vienna; Paris: Lang.
(Teaching texts in law and politics; Vol. 3)
NE: Schultz, David A. [Hrsg]; GT
ISBN 0-8204-3492-2

Cover design by James F. Brisson.

The paper in this book meets the guidelines for permanence and durability
of the Committee on Production Guidelines for Book Longevity
of the Council of Library Resources.

© 1998 Peter Lang Publishing, Inc., New York

All rights reserved.
Reprint or reproduction, even partially, in all forms such as microfilm,
xerography, microfiche, microcard, and offset strictly prohibited.

Printed in the United States of America.

To Nate Hakman and Emilo Roma, they taught me well.

Acknowledgments

There are many more people than I can think of to thank and acknowledge. First, all of the contributors to this volume deserve special thanks for their chapters and for stimulating my thoughts on this subject. In particular, Steve Gottlieb was very helpful in developing many of my ideas in Chapter Four as well as in designing this book.

The many participants at a 1995 American Political Science Association panel on the courts and social change were also influential in helping to frame ideas for this book as well as the issues that should be addressed in any serious discussion of this topic. Moreover, colleagues at Trinity University, and others, including Christopher Smith, Nancy Kassop, Bruce Auerbach, John Shockley, Dan Lowenstein, Thomas Sullivan, and Jim Chen also stimulated many of my ideas for this book, and I am ever grateful.

Contents

Introduction   Courts and Law in American Society   1
                David Schultz

Chapter 1   One Voice Among Many:
                The Supreme Court's Influence
                On Attentiveness to Issues in the
                United States, 1947–1992
                John Bohte, Roy B. Flemming, B. Dan Wood   21

Chapter 2   The Politics of Rights Revisited:
                Rosenberg, McCann, and the
                New Institutionalism
                Michael Paris, Kevin J. McMahon   63

Chapter 3   The Pro-Choice Legal Mobilization
                  and Decline of Clinic Blockades
                Robert Van Dyk   135

Chapter 4   Legal Functionalism and Social Change:
                A Reassessment of Rosenberg's
                The Hollow Hope
                David Schultz, Stephen E. Gottlieb   169

Chapter 5   The Supreme Court and Policy Reform:
                The Hollow Hope Revisited
                Bradley C. Canon   215

Contents

Chapter 6   Knowledge and Desire:
                Thinking about Courts and Social Change
                Gerald N. Rosenberg
                251

Chapter 7   Juricide
                Marvin Zalman
                293

Chapter 8   Law and Political Struggles for Social
                Change: Puzzles, Paradoxes, and
                Promises in Future Research   319
                Michael W. McCann

About the Authors   351

Index   355

Introduction

Courts and Law in American Society

David Schultz

Do courts and the law matter? Can legal institutions significantly affect public opinion, encourage political mobilization, or influence the functioning and operations of social institutions? Do legal norms constrain behavior or are political preferences more important in controlling the choices of judges and political actors? Much of the politics and political activity in the United States in the last fifty years assumed an affirmative answer to these questions. However, in an era when some wonder how far we have come in desegregating our schools or in reforming our prisons after all these years, it is not so clear that the conventional wisdom and answers are correct. Hence, asking if courts and the law are institutionally and politically efficacious forms the theme for this book, building upon a series of debates surrounding the efficacy and legitimacy of the courts and the law to effect social change in American society.

Federal Courts and American Politics

Disagreement over the role of the courts in American society dates back to the days of the constitutional framers, who debated what role the federal courts should have vis-à-vis the executive and legislative branches. In 1787, delegates to the Constitutional Convention debated whether the judiciary would have the power to "set aside the law" or whether the court should have a veto over the legislature (Farrend 1966, 298–299). In addition, delegates probed the jurisdictional limits of judicial power, asking what impact the court might have upon states or how it would affect the president and Congress (Madison 1966, 46, 537, 538–539). Similarly, in the debates on the ratification of the Constitution that occurred in 1787–1788, individuals such as Elbridge Gerry claimed that the proposed judicial system was too powerful while others such as James Wilson argued that judicial review was a necessary and important check upon the legislature (Gerry, Wilson 1993. 232, 823). Yet perhaps the most famous statement on what role the federal judiciary should have in the new constitutional order was found in Alexander Hamilton's views in *Federalist* 78.

Federalist 78 posited several claims addressing the scope of power of the new national judiciary. First, Hamilton states that upon being appointed, judges should have life tenure to insulate them from politics and to situate them above public opinion "to secure a steady, upright, and impartial administration of the laws" (Hamilton 1937, 503). Second the job of the courts "must be to declare all acts contrary to the manifest tenor of the Constitution void" (Hamilton 1937, 505). Such a power seems overwhelming, but does it create a serious problem or threat of tyranny? Hamilton argued no, contending that the judiciary would have neither "FORCE nor WILL, but merely judgment" (Hamilton 1937, 504). Hence, the Supreme Court, and all of the federal courts, would have to rely upon other branches of government for funds and the enforcement of their decisions. Hamilton also argued that to "avoid an arbitrary discretion in the courts, it is indispensable that they should be bound down by strict rules and precedents, which serve to define and point out their duty in every particular case that comes before them" (Hamilton 1937, 510). In short, for Hamilton, the "Constitution is, in fact, and must be regarded by the judges, as fundamental law" (Hamilton 1937, 506). Limitations upon the judiciary's ability to enforce its decisions and upon how it would decide cases would ensure that the courts would not be powerful political institutions, but instead would be the "least dangerous" branch of the government (Hamilton 1937, 504).

The vision of judicial power suggested in *Federalist* 78 was quite limited. Courts were to be above politics; presumably this meant that the judiciary should not formulate policy. Second, consistent with the overall vision of separation of powers and checks and balances delimited in the Constitution and the *Federalist Papers*, no branch of the federal government, and especially the judiciary, was to have too much political power on its own to be able to effect significant or quick and easy change in social policy (Dahl 1963).[1] Instead, one of the overarching goals of the new constitutional order was to constrain political power, limit majoritarian preferences, and to force the different branches of government to work together to effect any type of major policy or social change. At least under one reading of how our constitutional system is supposed to operate, the federal courts have neither the capacity nor the legitimacy to effect social change; instead they must defer or at least be a junior party to Congress, the presidency, and perhaps the states in making social policy.

However, in actual operation, the courts have seemingly departed from the vision articulated in *Federalist* 78 and the constitutional debates. Reasons for this expansion of judicial power are many. Perhaps from the start, America has had a tradition of judicial activism, or perhaps institutional necessity forced the courts to become involved to reconcile conflicts between the state and national government or among the other branches of the federal government (Choper 1980). Or perhaps Alexis DeTocqueville was correct when he noted in 1840 in *Democracy in America*: "There is hardly a political question in the United States which does not sooner or later turn into a judicial one. Consequently the language of everyday party-political controversy has to be borrowed from legal phraseology and conceptions" (DeTocqueville 1969, 370). Because of trends to resolve all political issues into matters for the courts, DeTocqueville argued that "Americans have given their courts immense political power" (DeTocqueville 1969, 102). Sooner or later because of the close association between politics and law in America, all disputes in our society come to be addressed by the courts, and trends in America suggest the judiciary will continue to assume this political role in the future, often articulating important decisions that at least in theory have made social policy and affected society in some way. Whatever the reasons, decisions such as *Dred Scott v. Sanford* (604 U.S. 393 [1856]); *Hammer v. Dagenhart* (247 U.S. 251 [1918]); the first and second New Deal cases;[2] *Baker v. Carr* (369 U.S. 186 [1962]); *Miranda v. Arizona* (384 U.S. 43 [1966]); and *Roe v. Wade* (410 U.S. 113 [1973]) just to name a few cases, have all been controversial in their time, often striking down major pieces of legislation or perhaps setting into motion a series of political events that would place the Court either in conflict with other branches of the government or public opinion.

The Legacy of *Brown*

Perhaps the single most controversial opinion articulated by the Court in the last fifty years was *Brown v. Board of Education* (347 U.S. 483 [1954]). In reversing its 1896 *Plessy v. Ferguson* (163 U.S. 537

[1896]) decision, the Warren Court invalidated the separate but equal education doctrine that had segregated racial minorities from whites. With *Brown*, and its progeny, such as *Bolling v. Sharpe* 347 U.S. 497 [1954]) and subsequently a series of other decisions that ordered the forced integration of public schools throughout the United States, but especially in the South, the federal courts launched a significant enterprise in challenging the political status quo and in seeking to change social attitudes. While many lauded *Brown*, others, especially in the South, fought its implementation.[3] While part of the challenge to *Brown* resided in its frontal assault on segregation or its implications for educational equality, others questioned the legitimacy and perhaps the wisdom of the Court to make that decision.

From almost the day *Brown* was decided it was criticized by those who questioned the legitimacy of the Court to render this decision. Troubled by the *Brown* decision, Herbert Wechsler evaluated the legitimacy of judicial review in terms of the right of the Court to operate as a "naked political organ" to enact its policy preferences (Wechsler 1959, 12). Wechsler's disagreement with *Brown* resided not in the "ultimate holding" that outlawed racial segregation, but in the reasoning of the opinion, which looked to be a policy prescription more legislative in nature than anything else (Wechsler 1959, 33). To constrain the Court's ability simply to push its policy preferences, Wechsler contended that the legitimacy of judicial decisions must reside in the articulation of general and neutral principles of law that are not simply the applied to the case at hand but to an entire category of cases (Wechsler 1959, 33).

Similarly, Alexander Bickel endorsed the result in *Brown* but also questioned the reasoning of the decision, suggesting that it was ad hoc and political (Bickel 1962, 58). What disturbed Bickel in *Brown* and other similar types of decisions where the Court employed judicial review was that the use of court power often carried counter-majoritarian tendencies. By that, the Court, an unelected, appointed-for-life body articulated policy preferences that upset or contradicted the will of the majority as well as electorally accountable, policy-making branches of the government (Bickel 1962, 16). To alleviate the capacity for its tendency to render political decisions that might be counter-majoritarian, Bickel advocated, among other remedies, that the judiciary be constrained in its decisions by basing them upon general neutral principles of law. Like Wechsler, Bickel believed such an appeal to general principles of law would sharply limit the overstepping of the courts into policy making.

Like the other two advocates of neutral principles, Robert Bork also had difficulty with the *Brown* opinion, stating that while it "was a great and correct decision . . . it was supported by a very weak opinion" (Bork 1990, 75). While originally Bork advocated that the Court's opinion should have rested upon neutral principles to be legitimate, later on he argued that the opinion had to reside in the original understanding of the Fourteenth Amendment to be legitimate. Yet such an original understanding, while perhaps available to salvage *Brown*, was not similarly available to *Bolling v. Sharpe* and other opinions, leaving the legitimacy of many of the Court's recent segregation and race opinions of dubious legacy (Bork 1990, 82).

Conversely, other scholars have sought to defend the legitimacy of *Brown*, arguing, for example, that it was consistent with a theory of judicial review that the Court first advocated in footnote four of *United States v. Carolene Products* (304 U.S. 144 [1938]). In *Democracy and Distrust*, John Hart Ely (1980) elaborates upon the implications of *Carolene Products* for defining a role for the courts in American society. He defended the Warren Court's activism by arguing that the role of the Supreme Court should be to keep the channels of political change open and to facilitate the representation of minorities in the political process. Relying upon Justice Stone's famous footnote number four in *Carolene Products*, Ely describes the job of the courts not as second guessing the substance of legislation, but as helping discrete and insular minorities protect their interests in the political process (Ely 1980, 75–76).

Ely described the Constitution as a process-orientated document (Ely 1980, 92). Among the processes deemed important in the Constitution is representation where different individuals and groups compete to influence legislative deliberations (Ely 1980, 103). When certain interests are denied access to the political process, or when the representative system ignores or fails to represent a minority out of prejudice, hostility, or an incompatibility of interests, the political process has "malfunctioned" (Ely 1980, 102–103). The role of the judiciary is not to substitute a legislature's policy judgment with its own, but to take steps to ensure that unrepresented and unprotected interests and groups receive a fair and adequate opportunity to be heard in the political process. The court's role is broadening and strengthening the democratic political process by striking down legislation that limits the access or ability of certain groups to protect themselves.

In addition to Ely, numerous other scholars have also sought to legitimize the role of the federal courts to make social policy.[4] In various ways, these arguments have contended that the courts have as much legitimacy to make these type of policy decisions other branches of the federal government (Chaynes 1976, 1281).

While the *Brown* decision, busing for integration, and the legacy of Warren Court judicial activism prompted debates over the legitimacy of the courts to make social policy, another line of research and criticism has addressed the capacity of the courts to achieve social change. By that line, the courts are institutionally inferior to make policy when compared to the other branches of the government, in terms of both their inability to secure compliance with their decisions and their institutional capacity to undertake the functions necessary for effective policy implementation and oversight.

In *The Courts and Social Policy*, Donald Horowitz (1977) provides several case studies of judicial intervention to reform police behavior, juvenile justice, school financing, and citizen participation plans. In critiquing the impact that the Court had in these cases, three sets of claims are made. First, the courts, as an adversarial resolution body, lack the structure, resources, and capacity to engage in policy making because courts are ill suited to gather social facts. Second, courts are passive and reactive institutions that get a skewed set of facts that many not be representative of a policy area. This means that a single case may make the rule for an entire policy area when the policy area is more diffuse or when the case at hand is not characteristic of the entire policy domain. Hence, the policy that the courts make is too ad hoc and not comprehensive. Three, courts treat policy areas as homogeneous and cannot differentiate among different cases or situations. Fourth, courts can not oversee implementation and therefore follow up on their orders or otherwise monitor enforcement. Overall, courts have moved from performing a grievance-answering to problem-solving function in seeking to bring about social or institutional reform, and this type of function is ill-suited or inapplicable to the structure of the courts and the adjudicative process (Fuller 1978, 355).[5]

In addition, others contend that judicial policy making or structural reform litigation preempts the authority of electorally accountable decisionmaking local governments or coordinate branches of the national government by making policy or political decisions that they ought to make (Nagel 1984; Glazer 1975). In other cases, the claim is that judicial activism is the product of a liberal interventionist court giving judges fairly wide discretion to hear cases and fashion remedies. For example, Jeremy Rabkin (1989) contends that the Court should abandon the legal legacy of the 1960s because such a legacy has corrupted administrative and constitutional law, executive authority, and responsible government that is accountable to the people government.

According to Rabkin, the legal legacy of the 1960s had its roots in two sources: the logic of footnote four of *Carolene Products*; and second, *Brown v. Board of Education* and the Warren Court's judicial activism. The impact of these influences has resulted in the judicial legitimization of interest group politics, and such politics has produced the privatizing of public power such that "contemporary administrative law extends the policy leverage of particular interest groups or advocacy groups and ends up, in this way, aggravating the maladies of interest group politics" (Rabkin 1989, 243). In sum, the legal legacy of the 1960s grants interest groups special access to public power, resulting in the distorting of policy making and the capacity of public institutions to stimulate policy innovation and change. The legal legacy of the 60s has resulted not in social change but interestgroup gridlock that prevents the president from bringing about change.

Drawing upon Theodore Lowi's (1969) critique of interest group liberalism and the effect such politics had upon the policy process, Rabkin contends that Court rulings in the 1960s made it easier for groups to challenge administrative rulings and determinations. The result has been the expansion of standing by judicial determination and legislative enactment and the legalization of bureaucratic policies with law and allowing interest groups to challenge administrative regulations and have their own construction of the congressional law (and not the administrative interpretation of it) accepted if the court found this more persuasive. Thus, courts incorrectly treat bureaucratic decisions as law, and this results in the making of policy more of a litigious or legal issue than a question of executive policy making.

Overall, judicial expansion has incorrectly transformed policy making into lawmaking; given judges excessive control over federal regulation making; and forced politically unaccountable judges to serve organized interests. This means that the judiciary aggravates the maladies of interest group liberalism that results in the franchising of public power into private hands and the excluding of public accountability from the law. Hence, as opposed to making the courts a superior means of achieving social change, interest group activity in the judiciary makes policy making resistant to change because interest groups are all conservative in nature.

While much of the academic literature has criticized either the capacity or the legitimacy of the federal courts to effect social change, others have offered at least a qualified endorsement of the judiciary's ability to act and make critical distinctions in the policy arena. Phillip Cooper in *Hard Judicial Choices* (1988) examines hundreds of examples of judicial policy making in the 1970s and 1980s and argues against the three claims that many critics of the courts make. Cooper first demonstrates that many conservative judges engaged in policy making and, when interviewed, they suggested that they did not out of a desire to intervene but because the party presented a justiciable claims involving a bonafide judicial claim. Second, Cooper shows how cases are triggers to devise a core remedy but that the remedy does not always treat a policy area as homogeneous. Moreover, courts do demonstrate capacity to adapt to make policy and discern differences in environment. Overall, case studies from 1970s and 1980s suggest the Court has learned much from earlier failures and that, compared to Congress and other policy bodies, the Court appears to be no better or worse in its ability to recognize diverse policy environments, formulate policies, and eventually oversee their implementation.

In sum, in evaluating the legacy, legitimacy, and efficacy of the courts to effect social change since *Brown*, the verdict is still out. For some, the federal courts have proven to be trusted allies in furthering the cause of social reform, performing its function of protecting discrete and insular minorities and otherwise policing the political process to keep the channels of representation open. For others, the federal courts have proven themselves either to be clumsy agents at producing lasting social change or usurpers of political power rightly lodged in the states or with Congress and the President.

Courts and Social Change: Contemporary Debates

Debates over the legitimacy and the capacity of the courts to effect social change persist into the 1990s and remain salient even today. Publication of Gerald Rosenberg's *The Hollow Hope: Can Courts Bring About Social Change?* in 1991 reignited debate over the capacity of the courts to achieve social change. In arguing that the Court's efficacy to affect public opinion or integrate schools as a result of *Brown* was marginal, especially in comparison to that of Congress, Rosenberg stimulated discussion about whether it made sense for social activists to turn to the judiciary or to the statehouses if they wanted to secure political change. His conclusion was that a more "constrained" model of judicial efficacy was more realistic in describing when the courts could secure social change, and perhaps social reformers and activists would be better served by reconsidering how much hope was placed upon working through the courts versus investing more time to win critical victories thorough the political process.

Hollow Hope was greeted with significant response, both critical and laudatory, and among the books deemed to be a "rejoinder" was Michael McCann's *Rights at Work*. McCann's book, an analysis of the pay equity movement, adopted contrasting methodologies and assumptions about the law to assess what impact it had upon political mobilization and social consciousness. Moreover, McCann argued that reformers were able to use litigation along with other political tactics to further causes and that court decisions, either furthering or impeding a group's objectives, were critically important as rally points to galvanize political action and social change. Hence, McCann's *Rights at Work* was seen as a rejoinder and alternative assessment to Rosenberg's *Hollow Hope* in providing an alternative perspective, methodology, and set of assumptions about how the courts do and can effect social reform.

The Rosenberg/McCann debate has occupied much ink in the field of law and politics and it is unnecessary to review that debate here or otherwise to assess the accuracy of the scholarship exploring either of the works.[6] Instead, the essays in this volume speak for themselves in how they engage the debate of the role of the courts in articulating social reform. The diverse chapters in this volume in part grow out of the issues raised by the Rosenberg/McCann debates, but they are even broader than that. Many of the chapters originally were prepared for a 1995 American Political Science Association Convention panel on the courts and social change. These original papers have been significantly expanded and modified since then. In addition, many of the chapters of this book were written especially for this volume, seeking in a variety of ways to explore ways one can assess judicial behavior, social reform, and the impact of legal norms upon society. The essays that make up this volume are multifaceted in that they employ a wide scope of methodological techniques, ranging from sophisticated statistical analysis to case studies, and they look at the issue of social reform from the perspective of action on the national and local level. Furthermore, as will be apparent from reading some chapters, some of the contributions offer metacritiques on where the public law discipline and research is directed and the types of assumptions that imbue that research.

Assessing the Courts: About this Book

Chapter 1 explores media coverage and attention to Supreme Court decisions from 1947 to1990. John Bohte, Roy B. Flemming, and B. Dan Wood begin by asking if the United States Supreme Court influences the national agenda by placing certain issues and items on the national agenda. For the authors, Rosenberg's *Hollow Hope* offers the controversial conclusion that landmark decisions like *Brown v. Board of Education* or *Roe v. Wade* had little discernible impact on the national agenda. If the Supreme Court is unable to influence media coverage or attention to issues, then the Court's effectiveness in producing legal change is seriously diminished. Hence, an important aspect of legal change is the mobilization of public opinion through the information and perspectives provided by newspapers, magazines, and television. The media thus links the Supreme Court to the public. If media elites fail to publicize important Court decisions and broaden their coverage to the relevant issue area, the public awareness and debate that are a necessary precondition for Court directed legal change are absent. In this chapter the authors question the methodological and analytical grounds for Rosenberg's skepticism and present analyses that indicate the Supreme Court can re-direct media attention and thus shape the national or systemic agenda. They place this discussion in the broader context of institutional, top-down influences on agenda-setting processes in America and how these processes are linked to legal change. Their empirical analyses rest on careful counts of article references in the *Readers' Guide to Periodical Literature* to three issue areas in which the Court has been active since the end of the World War II—racial integration of public schools, freedom of speech and obscenity questions, and church-state issues centering on establishment matters. Over 8,179 references across all three policy domains were identified, and the three policy areas are modeled using sophisticated quantitative time series methods. The findings of these analyses reveal that a handful of the Supreme Court's decisions (including *Brown v. Board of Education*) produced marked increases in media attention and that this heightened level of attentiveness persisted over time. The impact of these decisions, however, depends on the political response to the decisions; media attention rose with the amount of controversy and with whether the decisions attracted "macropolitical intrusions" from Congress or the president. The chapter concludes with a discussion of these findings, contending that the dynamics of media attention to social problems is a competitive process for limited space on the systemic agenda where media rules allocate agenda space according to what the media consider to be newsworthy. One irony from this study is that the Supreme Court is most likely to influence agenda setting in the United States when the conditions Rosenberg identifies as necessary for successful Court-induced legal change do not exist.

Chapter 2 by Michael Paris and Kevin McMahon uses two cases studies, the Montgomery bus boycott and education finance reform in New Jersey in an attempt to clarify the methods and approaches used by McCann and Rosenberg to study social change. The authors argues that while Rosenberg's approach obfuscates the potential of the law and the courts in oppositional change, McCann's framework promises to yield better normative and descriptive insights. The first section of the chapter briefly reviews the terms of the Rosenberg/McCann debate. The second section reexamines the events surrounding the Montgomery bus boycott in light of this debate. Here the chapter argues that Rosenberg's view obfuscates the potential role of law and courts in oppositional and reform projects, and that McCann's framework promises to yield better descriptive and normative insights. The third and concluding section raises some questions for scholars interested in building upon McCann's work. Specifically, the authors suggest that McCann's legal mobilization approach might be usefully modified through incorporation of themes and concepts found in new institutionalist analysis of social policy.

Chapter 3 by Robert Van Dyk explores the role of prochoice groups in seeking to use the law to counteract the blockade of abortion providers by Operation Rescue. In first providing an analysis of how Operation Rescue successfully used a variety of prayer actions, sitins, and other acts of civil disobedience to shut down facilities where abortions were performed, Van Dyk takes the reader through the variety of means used by prochoice advocates, such as the Klan Acts, RICO laws, and state statutes, to respond to Operation Rescue. As a result, the chapter indicates not only that litigation by prochoice groups had an impact on keeping clinics open but that the threat of criminal penalty significantly influenced the political consciousness and mobilization of both the prolife and prochoice forces. Van Dyk concludes his chapter with some observations on how the prochoice legal mobilization strategy fits into the dynamic of social change and efficacy proposed by Rosenberg and McCann.

Schultz and Gottlieb argue in chapter 4 that functionalism has been fundamental to American law since 1787. Noting that while there is a long academic and policy tradition committed to legal functionalism, Gerald Rosenberg's *The Hollow Hope* challenges functional claims about the law, specifically assertions that the Supreme and lower federal courts are able to effect significant social change. This chapter examines Rosenberg's claims by placing his book and arguments in terms of the broader questions regarding legal functionalism. The chapter clarifies the functionalist issue by asserting three claims: law matters; but intentions do go awry; and it is not clear that law without intent would achieve similar or better results. The authors argue that the power of legal norms is concealed by Rosenberg's methodology and standards of proof and causality ascribed to the courts but not other institutions. Overall, Schultz and Gottlieb contend that Rosenberg misunderstands the nature of judicial policymaking as well as the impact of the courts and law upon American society. Schultz and Gottlieb contend that the courts and the law define or redefine structures, institutions, and expectations, and that this capacity to redefine agendas may be the most important but generally misunderstood function that the judiciary undertakes. In the end, the chapter offers a broader view on how to understand and study judicial behavior and social change by asserting that the functionalist perspective is integrated into the fabric of how our political institutions operate and how we think about the law.

In chapter 5 Bradley Canon focuses specifically upon the diverse impacts that Supreme Court decisions can have. In situating the issue of the courts and social reform in the context of many of the assertions made by Rosenberg in *Hollow Hope*, Canon begins his chapter by stratifying the issue of judicial impact, looking at the topic from the macro and micro levels as well as from the point of how decisions change expectations in terms of inspiring action. In looking at the different constraints on the Court noted by Rosenberg, Canon indicates that one first needs to look at a variety of questions regarding the type of implementation required and whether the impact by the Court is direct or more inspirational. Examining issues as diverse as criminal justice, desegregation, reapportionment, abortion, and the advertising of sexually oriented materials, among other topics, Canon notes how the impact of the Courts in some areas was significant, either directly or inspirationally in terms of changing attitudes, often in cases when some of the constraints on the courts noted by Rosenberg were present. The chapter concludes with a final assessment of the efficacy of the Supreme Court to make policy, suggesting that its power is vastly underrated.

In chapter 6 Gerald Rosenberg responses to many of the critics in this volume and implicitly in the public law field, contending that often their claims about judicial efficacy are based more upon hope and desire for such efficacy than upon hardcore evidence supporting their conclusions. The strength of this chapter lies not so much in the tit-for-tat discussion found between Rosenberg and critics in this volume. Instead, this chapter reveals some deeper and more interesting debates concerning the way social scientists view the courts and politics, the issue of causation, and the dynamics of how one assesses judicial behavior. While clearly lawyers and political scientists, as good academics, disagree over many points, the chapter reveals that there is a common fascination among many over the role of the courts in society and how social reformers should think about using their resources in seeking to secure their goals. Hence, for any plaintiff considering the litigation option, Rosenberg forces a careful consideration of that option, and for any academic asserting that the courts have an impact upon social change, Rosenberg also forces a careful articulation of that claim.

Chapter 7 by Marvin Zalman looks at the death of law and legal norms, or "juricide," in contemporary legal scholarship. For Zalman, the development of "political jurisprudence," the analysis of judicial decision and policy making and the empirical study of legal mobilization and impact, has added immeasurably to social understanding of the legal enterprise. Yet certain works of political scientists move to a position that, in a manner of speaking, negates the existence of law, a phenomena the author labels as "juricide." For Zalman, examples of this include Gerald Rosenberg's position that major Supreme Court cases have had no impact on social policy, Jeffrey Segal and Harold Spaeth's view that only political attitudes influence the outcome of cases, and some postmodernist writing that views law as violence. Although these views have been highly touted, they do not represent a majority of the work of political scientists. This chapter shows that these juricide positions are untenable, that, as Epstein and Kobylka have stated, "law matters," and that this is a politically important datum. This chapter asserts the value of doctrinal analysis as the only way that any legal system in the western tradition can develop and operate. The chapter concludes by comparing the juricide phenomena in political jurisprudence to a similar slant in legal jurisprudence that has been detected in legal realism and critical legal studies, and speculating on the forces that generate ideas that appear to be far outside from the normative center of thought in the disciplines.

Finally the book concludes with Michael McCann offering a forward-looking chapter that discusses new directions and possible future trends in public law scholarship. Its focus is on the decentered, constitutive perspectives on law and change. The chapter analyzes the differences between positivist/constitutive paradigms, focusing on how we define law, its role in a social context, and where law fits into issues of social power, resistance, change, and consciousness. The focus in this chapter is really upon assessing scholarly trends upon legal behavior in the United States and elsewhere, concluding that greater comparative analysis of the law in a variety of social contexts could help clarify many issues raised in this book and in the scholarship McCann identifies.

Overall, the chapters in this book offers several important conclusions regarding the study of courts and social change. First, all too often scholars focus on the capacity of the Supreme Court to effect social change or political mobilization at the expense of looking at state and federal district courts for the real sources of change. Much in the same way that students of policy evaluation know that one needs to look to streetlevel bureaucrats to see how and where real implementation occurs, one needs to look not to the Supreme Court but to the lower courts to see where the real change occurs. It is here that the real battles regarding *Brown* occurred. Books like *58 Lonely Men* (Peltason 1971) document that battle while other books such as, *Our Town: Race, Housing, and the Soul of Suburbia* (Kirp, Dwyer, and Rosenthal 1995), and *Suburbs under Seize* (Haar 1996), as well as the growing field studying state judicial federalism, offer interesting discussions of the efficacy of the state courts in addressing segregation issues.[7] Hence, we need to view the issue of judicial capacity and mobilization from the perspective of the lower courts and local struggles.

A second issue to keep in mind is that too often academics look for "grand" social change in terms of lots of people or many changes in percentage points when it comes to voting, attitudes, etc. We should not expect courts to have any greater influence on public opinion that any other institution in American politics. Robert Dahl has taught us that we live in a nation where political or numerical minorities carry the balance of power. We need to look to the courts to see how they have more micro influences that alter small constituencies and then perhaps how those groups may have important regional or national influence.

Third, we should not forget what Lon Fuller once said, i.e., the courts are primarily a grievance-addressing body. Public law scholars often forget this point, instead expecting the courts to act like Congress or evaluating it in terms of how we would evaluate legislative policy-making institutions. Again, such an evaluation may not be appropriate. Moreover, when examining the impact of the court, we should not confuse the goals of the plaintiffs with the goals of the Court versus the goals we have assigned to a specific opinion over time. All of these issues or goals are different and we need to be attentive to them. In particular, we need to be especially attentive to what the plaintiffs sought and ask what was the nature of their litigation when evaluating court decisions and efficacy.

Fourth, when discussing the efficacy of the courts to achieve social change scholars often view the judiciary in isolation from other political institutions and actors in our political process. Such an isolation may lend the impression that courts and judges are autonomous when, in fact, they are not. Courts and judges are clearly constrained in the choices they make by other institutions and choices made by other political actors. Similarly, the courts are also constrained by their own previous choices and by numerous other political factors that public law scholars are only beginning to describe. The importance of the "new institutionalism" scholarship to the public law field is to help clarify the constraints the courts face, thereby helping to define the arenas in which the courts can make social policy.[8]

Fifth, public law scholars need to be more attentive to the methods they use when examining impact. Perhaps Gerald Rosenberg's single most important contribution to the study of the courts in *Hollow Hope* and in his chapter in this book is that we need to be careful in how we study the courts, less we let our hopes or desires blind us to the facts. The chapters in this volume demonstrate the nuances in evaluating the courts, and perhaps understanding social change lies in plowing the fine lines of causation and measurement. Moreover, when evaluating judicial efficacy, we are often really addressing issues of historical change and causation yet we use regression analysis and other quantitative tools of analysis illsuited for historical explanation. Historians have a much richer understanding of causation than most of us political scientists and we need to profit from their skills.

Finally, the essays in this volume reach two last conclusions. First, there is a diversity of approaches to studying the courts and social change and it is to be hoped that public law and legal fields can mutually profit from the work the other has performed. Often those of different methodological bents ignore the research of those employing alternative techniques, and perhaps the diversity of conclusions and perspectives in this book show the need to engage the divergent perspectives if we are to enrich our knowledge of the courts. Second, as the chapters in this book reveal, the courts and the legal process continue to fascinate us all. As an institution partly above politics and enmeshed in political controversy, the federal and state courts remain important institutions in our society. The task of public law scholarship is to recognize that courts "are only one of many authoritative agencies of government in a position to articulate goals for the polity" (Scheingold 1978, 116), and that clarifying the myth versus the reality of how effective the judiciary is in making social policy is critical to understanding how the American political process works.

Notes

1. Dahl develops this line of argument, contending that the Framers sought to place limits upon political change in order to limit majority factions and prevent any one branch or group from tyrannizing another.

2. Among other cases, *Carter v. Carter Coal*, (298 U.S. 238 [1936]); *Panama Refining Co. v. Ryan*, (293 U.S. 388 [1935]), and *Schechter Poultry Corp. v. United States*, (295 U.S. 495 [1935]) constitute the core of the first New Deal cases while, *NLRB v. Jones & Laughlin*, (301 U.S. 1 [1937]); *U.S. v. Darby*, 312 U.S. 100 [1941]); *Wickard v. Filburn*, (317 U.S. 111 [1942]); *Mulford v. Smith*, (307 U.S. 38 [1939]); and *Steward Machine v. Davis* (301 U.S. 548 [1937]) are the second New Deal cases and for the most part overrule the first New Deal cases.

3. J.W. Peltason's 1971 work *58 Angry Men: Southern Federal Judges and School Desegregation* offers a good picture of the battle for desegregation in the south.

4. The literature on this topic is voluminous but includes Perry 1982; Dworkin 1977; and Fiss 1982.

5. Fuller 1978, 353 compare elections, contracts, and adjudication as different forms of dispute resolution and asks whether adjudication is a viable way to address certain social issues. His conclusion is that social issues are "polycentric" and he wonders if adjudication can handle this. While he says these types of problems are not part of the "proper" role for the judiciary, courts are not necessarily unsuited to do this and they can adapt to meet these new demands.

6. Two of the exchanges between McCann and Rosenberg are found in Rosenberg 1992, McCann 1992 and Rosenberg 1996 and McCann 1996.

7. The literature on state courts and judicial federalism is large and growing rapidly. Good general studies on this topic include: Stumpf 1992; Tarr 1988; and Tarr 1996.

8. Gillman 1996 offers a good review of the significance of the new institutionalism scholarship for the field of public law.

Works Cited

Bickel, Alexander. 1962. *The Least Dangerous Branch: The Supreme Court at the Bar of Politics*. New Haven: Yale University Press.

Bork, Robert. 1990. *The Tempting of America: The Political Seduction of the Law*. New York: Touchstone Books, 1990.

Chayes, Abram. 1976. "The Role of the Judge in Public Law Litigation." *Harvard Law Review* 89: 1281.

Choper, Jesse. 1980. *Judicial Review and the National Political Process: A Functionalist Reconsideration of the Supreme Court*. Chicago: University of Chicago Press.

Cooper, Phillip J. 1988. *Hard Judicial Choices: Federal District Court Judges and State and Local Officials*. New York: Oxford University Press.

Dahl, Robert A. 1963. *A Preface to Democratic Theory*. Chicago: University of Chicago Press

DeTocqueville, Alexis. 1969. *Democracy in America*, New York: Anchor Books.

Dworkin, Ronald. 1977. *Taking Rights Seriously*. Cambridge: Harvard University Press.

Ely, John Hart. 1980. *Democracy and Distrust: A Theory of Judicial Review*. Cambridge: Harvard University Press.

Farrand, Max. ed. 1966. *The Records of the Federal Convention of 1787*, vol. 2. New Haven: Yale University Press.

Fiss, Owen M. 1982. "The Social and Political Foundations of Adjudication." *Law and Human Behavior* 6: 121.

Fuller, Lon. 1978. "The Forms and Limits of Adjudication." *Harvard Law Review* 92: 353.

Gerry, Elbridge. 1993. Elbridge Gerry to the Massachusetts General Court, and Wilson, James, James Wilson Replies to Findley" in *The Debate on the Constitution: Federalist and Antifederalist Speeches, Articles, and Letters During the Struggle over Ratification*, part I, New York: The Library of America.

Gillman, Howard. 1996-97. "The New Institutionalism, Part I." *Law and Courts: Newsletter of the Law and Courts Section of the American Political Science Association* 7: 6.

Glazer, Nathan. 1975. "Towards an Imperial Judiciary." *The Public Interest* 41: 104. 104.

Haar, Charles M. 1996. *Suburbs Under Seize: Race, Space, and Audacious Judges*. Princeton: Princeton University Press.

Hamilton, Alexander. 1937. *The Federalist*. New York: The Modern Library.

Horowitz, Donald L. 1977. *The Courts and Social Policy*. Washington, D.C.: The Brookings Institution.

Kirp, David L., John P. Dwyer, and Larry A. Rosenthal. 1995. *Our Town: Race, Housing, and the Soul of Suburbia*. New Brunswick: Rutgers University Press.

Lowi, Theodore J. 1969. *The End of Liberalism: Ideology, Policy, and the Crisis of Public Authority*. New York: W.W. Norton & Company, Inc.

Madison, James. 1966. *Notes of Debates in the Federal Convention of 1787 Reported by James Madison*. New York: W.W. Norton & Company.

McCann, Michael. 1992. "Reform Litigation on Trial." *Law & Social Inquiry* 17: 715 (Fall).

McCann, Michael. 1996. Causal versus Constitutive Explanations (or, On the Difficulty of Being so Positive . . .)." *Law & Social Inquiry* 21: 457 (Fall).

Nagel, Robert F. 1984. "Controlling the Structural Injunction." *Harvard Journal of Law and Public Policy* 7: 395.

Peltason, J.W. 1971. *58 Angry Men: Southern Federal Judges and School Desegregation*. Urbana: University of Illinois Press.

Perry, Michael J. 1982. *The Constitution, The Courts, and Human Rights*, New Haven: Yale University Press.

Rabkin, Jeremy. 1989. *Judicial Compulsions: How Public Law Distorts Public Policy*. New York: Basic Books.

Rosenberg, Gerald. 1992. "Hollow Hopes and Other Aspirations: A Reply to Feeley and McCann." *Law & Social Inquiry* 17: 761 (Fall).

Rosenberg, Gerald. 1996. "Positivism, Interpretivism, and the Study of Law." *Law & Social Inquiry* 21: 455 (Spring).

Scheingold, Stuart A. 1978. *The Politics of Rights: Lawyers, Public Policy, and Political Change*. New Haven: Yale University Press.

Stumpf, Harry P., & John H. Culver. 1992. *The Politics of State Courts*. White Plains: Longman Publishing Group.

Tarr, G. Alan, ed. 1996. *Constitutional Politics in the States: Contemporary Controversies and Historical Patterns*. WestPort: Greenwood Press.

Tarr, G. Alan, & Mary Cornella Aldis Porter. 1988. *State Supreme Courts in State and Nation*. New Haven: Yale University Press.

Weschler, Herbert. 1959. "Toward Neutral Principles of Constitutional Law." *Harvard Law Review* 75: 1.

Chapter 1

One Voice Among Many: the Supreme Court's Influence On Attentiveness to Issues in the United States, 1947-1992

Roy B. Flemming
John Bohte
B. Dan Wood

Introduction

Schattschneider's (1960, 68) declaration that the definition of alternatives is the "supreme instrument of power" pointed to the importance of agendas in politics. Of equal political significance, if only because it precedes the specification of alternatives, is the ability to draw attention to particular problems or issues. Since political attention to issues is limited by a law of scarcity, attentiveness to one problem is often purchased at the expense of ignoring others. The bias of attention thus becomes an important concern for political science, one at the center of research on problem identification, and agenda setting processes more generally (Cobb and Elder 1972; Kingdon 1984; Baumgartner and Jones 1993; Rochefort and Cobb 1994). These processes are not static, of course. Attention to issues changes over time. Rising and falling attention correspond with changes in the visibility of issues and thus in Schattschneider's terms expand or contract the scope of conflict in policy arenas. Shifts in attention also activate different preferences which introduce further instability and change into democratic politics (Jones 1994).

In this study we focus on the US Supreme Court as a bellwether of systemic attention to policy issues. In Federalist 78, Hamilton offered his by now famous and often repeated opinion that the Court would be "the least dangerous branch." Without the power of the sword or purse at its disposal, the Court's authority in American politics would ultimately depend its ability to persuade and convince. The Supreme Court, however, may be more effective in drawing attention to issues and identifying problems than in changing preferences about them (cf. Franklin and Kosaki 1989; Hoekstra 1995). Its decisions and the cases heard by the Court address questions that often attract media interest, and the media by publishing or broadcasting stories about these issues links the Court's actions to the contents of the systemic and institutional agendas (Cobb and Elder 1972). The Supreme Court, therefore, may influence the agenda-setting process in the United States, and in doing so constitute an institutional source of change in American public policy and politics.

The Supreme Court has largely been ignored as a precursor of attention in the general literature on agenda setting. This study marks the first effort at modeling the Supreme Court's impact on systemic attention to policy domains in which the Court is especially active. To determine whether the Supreme Court influences the national agenda over time, we look at clearly defined, active issue areas for which reliable and appropriate time series data are available. We examine three specific issues that have been important components of the Court's civil rights and civil liberties policy domains over the past four decades—school desegregation, church-state relations centering primarily on establishment questions, and freedom of speech and obscenity matters. The Supreme Court's involvement in these issues reflects broader changes in the Court's institutional agenda and its policy emphases.

In the years following the New Deal and World War II, the Court turned away from such traditional matters as economic and business regulation and shifted its focus to address questions dealing with civil rights and civil liberties that it had largely ignored (Pacelle 1991, 1995). Evidence of this shift is revealed by changes in the Court's docket. At the height of the New Deal, First Amendment issues made up only 1.2 percent of the cases heard by the Court; cases raising equality questions under the Fourteenth Amendment were only slightly higher at 1.4 percent. By the mid-eighties, the two proportions had reached 10.7 percent and 16.6 percent respectively (Pacelle 1991, 56). After World War II, the Court opened up new policy domains for itself where it could play a vigorous policy making role through decisions like *Sweat v. Painter* (1950) and *McLaurin v. Oklahoma* (1950) dealing with the separate but equal doctrine in education, *Everson v. Board of Education of Ewing Township* (1947) questioning government support of parochial education, and *Roth v. United States* (1957) regarding obscenity.

The Supreme Court did not cut these issues from whole cloth. Public debates over racially segregated schools, censorship, and government support of religion were all part of the national discourse prior to the Court's involvement. The intensity of the debate waxed and waned with events, public opinion, or media attention, and these dialogues continued after the Court began to express its views. Interest groups, acting both as a stimulus to these changes as well as a response to the Court's evolving role, increasingly appeared before the justices as sponsors of cases and as amicus curiae in these policy areas (Tushnet 1987; Kluger 1975; Sorauf 1976; Kobylka 1991, 1995). Litigating groups also courted the media and reporters assigned to the Supreme Court in hopes of drawing attention to the group's positions (Davis 1994). The Court, it should be noted, does not have unlimited authority over the evolution of issue domains. It competes with other political and social institutions for influence over the law, and its involvement in these issues frequently ran against the grain of public opinion or the preferences of entrenched interests.

In sum, the Supreme Court chose to participate in the national dialogue over school desegregation, separation of church and state, and freedom of speech. But to what degree has it been a dominant voice? One way of answering this question would be to trace the ebbs and flows in public opinion in relationship to the Court's decisions. Unlike comparable research on the president's ability to shape the national agenda (Cohen 1995), this option with a few notable exceptions like abortion (e.g., Franklin and Kosaki 1989; Wliezen and Goggin 1993) is not available for understanding the Court's agenda setting influence in most of the issue areas in which it has been active. Continuous, regularly collected public opinion data over extended periods of time with regard to the three issue areas in this study either do not exist or are inadequate.[1]

An alternative solution is to follow media attention to issues. Relations between the media and the public are obviously reciprocal in nature. The media faces market incentives to follow events and develop stories that attract audiences. At the same time, public concerns over issues reflect in part the media's coverage (Neuman *et al* 1992).

Many issues move on and off the systemic agenda according to media priorities and definitions of what is news and what deserves coverage. As a consequence citizens' assessments of the importance of issues vary in part with the amount of coverage the issues receive from the media (Iyengar and Kinder 1987). This is particularly true in the instance of the Supreme Court where press and television attention greatly influence popular knowledge of Court decisions (Franklin and Kosaki 1995). Controversy over school prayer or flag burning may well exist on the systemic agenda without drawing the interest of the media, but the visibility of these controversies and their perceived importance to the public will rise if the press or television publicize the matter or turn the spotlight on Court decisions dealing with the conflict. Still, media coverage of the Court and its decisions, when compared to the presidency and Congress and their actions, is episodic, selective, and less intense (Graber 1993, 290–291; Danielian and Page 1994, 1063–1065).

The media, therefore, provide the Court with an unreliable link to the public, which presumably weakens the Court's ability to redirect or to affect the intensity of national concerns. If newspapers or television outlets pay limited attention to the Court, it is unlikely the Supreme Court's decisions will dominate what the public views as important. Indeed, Rosenberg (1991), upon analyzing media coverage of civil rights and abortion issues, raised fundamental questions about the Court's ability to shape national debates over important issues. He argued that the Supreme Court's ability to lead public opinion and thus the direction of legal change pales in significance when compared to the pervasive, more powerful influences of the events and incidents that make up what he calls the "tide of history." Rosenberg's challenge is especially sharp in light of the fact that the media concentrate their limited coverage of the Court to decisions dealing with civil rights and First Amendment questions (O'Gallaghan and Dukes 1992; Danielian and Page 1994, 1074; Franklin and Kosaki 1995), the two policy domains where the Court has been especially active over the past 45 years or so.

Media attention, then, offers a surrogate indicator of what issues the public is likely to believe are important. Filtered by media coverage, there are reasons to expect that the Supreme Court has a weak hand in moving issues onto the systemic agenda and holding them there. Media attention to Court decisions is less intense and more irregular than attention to the presidency and Congress. This means that the Court's concerns are unlikely to arouse the public to the same degree as presidential pronouncements or congressional activities. It is also possible, as Rosenberg argues, that the Court's voice regarding major controversies cannot be heard over the rush of history. Whatever the reason, the Supreme Court may be less able to shape public dialogues over issues of national concern. These reservations are an advantage to this research since the answer to the question about the Court's influence over the systemic agenda is not preordained and the issue remains problematic. In effect they establish the grounds for an initial null expectation that no relationship exists between the Supreme Court's decisions and changes in issue attentiveness by the media and system.

Measuring "Issue Attentiveness" in American Politics

Recent research on agendas in American politics has relied on *The Readers' Guide to Periodical Literature* to develop quantitative measures of the printed media's coverage of issues over long periods of time in order to track the dynamics of issue attention (e.g., Rosenberg 1991; Baumgartner and Jones 1992; Flemming *et al* 1995). These measures can stand alone as indicators of issue attentiveness by the print media or they can be used profitably as surrogate indicators of trends in the systemic agenda. As Baumgartner and Jones (1992, 253–266) explain, indicators of long-term trends in the visibility of issues using the *Readers' Guide* are valid, reliable measures that correlate highly with changes in attention to issues more generally.[2] The *Readers' Guide* surveys a wide assortment of general interest and specialized publications that have a combined readership far greater than the circulation of any single elite or regionally prominent newspaper like the *New York Times* or the *St. Louis Post-Dispatch* or even newsweeklies like *Time* or *Newsweek*. Because of the size and diversity of the markets served by the periodicals included in the *Readers' Guide*, the combined editorial emphases of the general interest magazines and more specialized journals can be presumed to be as representative of concerns on the systemic agenda as measures resting on narrow, selective samples of the print or electronic media.

We developed three indicators of attention based on the number of references to articles listed in the *Readers' Guide* dealing respectively with school desegregation and church/state issues for the period from 1947–1990, and freedom of speech/censorship for the period from

1947–1992.³ It is important to keep in mind that we defined these issue areas in broad terms. We are not concerned with case-specific media coverage of Supreme Court decisions, but with whether the Court can shift or redirect trends in national attentiveness to broader issues over time. The question we seek to answer is whether the Court's decisions dealing with these issues affect these trends and shape the national dialogue about school desegregation and First Amendment controversies.

The *Reader's Guide* keywords we used for school desegregation were: Negroes in America, Education; Negroes in America, Segregation; and Public Schools, Desegregation.⁴ For the freedom of speech policy domain, the following keywords were used: Freedom of Speech; Censorship; Immoral Literature; Obscenity; and Obscenity, Trials. For the third policy domain, church/state relations, the keywords were: Church and State; Prayer in Schools; Public Schools and Religion; and Taxation, Exemption. These keywords are consistent with the issue categories listed in the *Supreme Court Judicial Database* (Spaeth 1993), but more important they also appear regularly in the *Readers' Guide* for the entire study period. The *Readers' Guide* frequently listed other keywords but their stays were usually brief and their references to articles generally overlapped those under the permanent keywords. Each article reference under a keyword was recorded on a spreadsheet listing the day (when appropriate), month, and year when the article was published, the leading page number, and the periodical in which it appeared. This time-consuming procedure enabled us to preclude double-counting articles that might be listed under more than one keyword, and also allowed us to preserve the option of aggregating the data by different time periods.

These coding procedures offered us the option of aggregating or disaggregating the data. This is a critically important advantage over survey data since the timing and intervals between polls often depend on reasons or purposes unrelated to later research questions. In this study we selected the month as the temporal unit of analysis for several reasons. First, most of the periodicals listed in the *Readers' Guide* are published on a weekly or monthly basis; a monthly unit of analysis is consistent with the publishing cycle of many of the periodicals. At the same time, this unit of analysis avoids the problem of too many zeroes and excessive noise that shorter temporal spans like a week would create.⁵ The second reason is both methodological and analytical. Discrete time series data aggregated on the basis of longer time spans would reflect the combined influence of many events and activities during these periods making it very difficult to identify or evaluate the effects of any one event. The longer the time period the greater the number of potentially confounding influences we can expect to find surrounding the time of particular Supreme Court decisions.

This is the problem Rosenberg (1991) encountered when he relied on annual data to examine the impact of *Brown v. Board of Education* (1954) on the national agenda regarding civil rights. Expecting to find an increase in media attention in the years after *Brown,* Rosenberg discovered instead that he was unable to determine the decision's effects because they could not be disentangled from the competing impacts on media attention of the Montgomery bus boycott, violent racial incidents elsewhere in the South, and the 1956 presidential election (Rosenberg 1991, 111–116). The Montgomery bus boycott, for example, began six months after *Brown I.* Annual measures of turbulent policy domains where one event after another follows rapidly on the heels of others will not be sufficiently sensitive to isolate the Court's influence on media coverage. By shortening our temporal unit of analysis as much as possible, we are better able to check for threats to the internal validity of our analyses. It is much easier to determine if other events or incidents occurred close to the time of a Court decision that may be alternative explanations of a decision's apparent impact when the temporal unit of analysis is short rather than long. In this way we avoid the problem Rosenberg faced, and we can be more confident of the validity of our findings.

A third advantage of monthly data is that by increasing the number of observations and degrees of freedom needed for statistical modeling, we avoid the hazards of depending on subjective judgments while enhancing the robustness of the findings. Larger numbers of observations decrease the likelihood of making Type II error when there are several or many alternative factors hypothesized to be statistically significant influences on the time series. Finally, shorter temporal measures facilitate the inclusion of lagged relationships in the statistical models that are consistent with the underlying dynamics of the time series. For all these reasons, we disaggregated the data to create monthly measures of media attention.

For our measure of media attention, we identified a total of 8179 references in the *Readers' Guide* to articles dealing with the three issue areas. It should be stressed that these are references to all articles pertaining to the particular policy domain. Our measures are thus not limited to references to the Supreme Court's decisions. References to these decisions are part of the count but they were not the exclusive or even primary focus. The total number of articles pertaining to school desegregation was 2700; for freedom of speech/censorship, the number was 3075; and for church/state issues, the total was 2024. Figures 1 through 3 display the data with the raw monthly frequencies recalculated for visual acuity as three month moving averages.

Media coverage of school desegregation issues rises from the late 1940s and peaks in the latter half of the 1950s. There are scattered spurts in attention during the ensuing decades but they are short-lived. Attention to this aspect of the civil rights policy domain generally traces a downward trend in the years after a peak in the fifties. The time series dealing with censorship and free speech follows a different trajectory. Over the entire 44 year period, the frequency with which the media published stories dealing with these matters remains relatively constant, although there is considerable fluctuation from month to month, and the level of attention falls off somewhat during the seventies and early 1980s. One "spike" is obviously evident toward the end of the period. The overall frequency of articles dealing with church-state issues tends to be lower than for the other two issue areas over the course of the study period. Two sharp increases clearly disrupt this time series and give it a cyclical pattern. The first appears during the early 1960s and the second occurs in the early part of the 1980s. These three time series describe fairly different levels and patterns of media attention to the three issue domains over four decades.

Identifying "Politically Significant" Supreme Court Decisions

If the Supreme Court is America's "schoolmaster" on constitutional questions and an important agent in leading legal change, then its decisions ought to influence in a clear, decisive manner the nation's dialogues about these questions (Franklin and Kosaki 1989). Not all of the Court's decisions, however, can be expected to have this impact; too many of them address narrow issues, straighten out technical details, clarify previous opinions, or settle lower court conflicts to influence dramatically the country's constitutional discourse. In contrast, decisions that overturn longstanding precedents, create new precedents or establish new rights, push the Court into new areas of

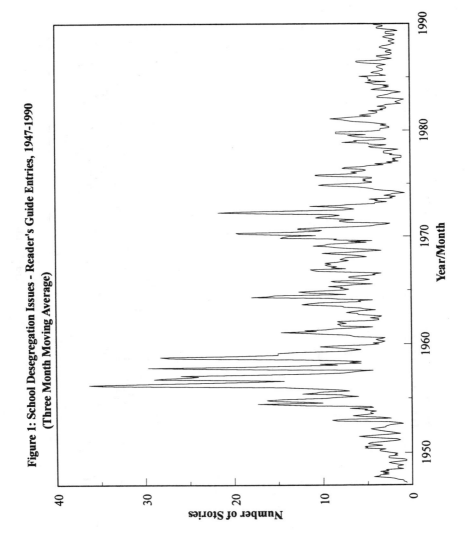

Figure 1: School Desegregation Issues - Reader's Guide Entries, 1947-1990 (Three Month Moving Average)

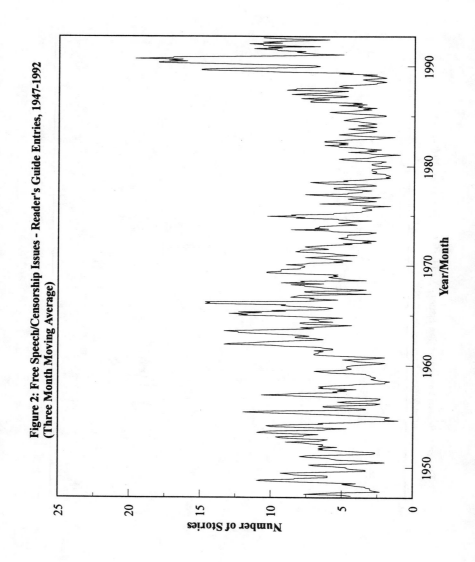

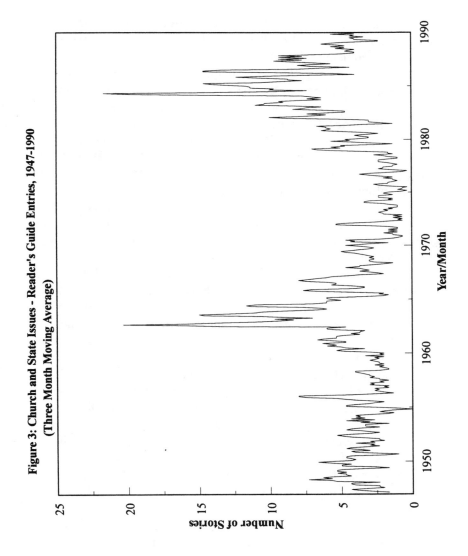

Figure 3: Church and State Issues - Reader's Guide Entries, 1947-1990 (Three Month Moving Average)

constitutional law, or alter political relationships between individuals or institutions are the kinds of decisions that presumably reshape constitutional dialogues. These distinctions are easily made in the abstract. Other than such obvious cases as *Brown vs. Board of Education* (1954), however, judicial scholars do not agree on the criteria and procedures that might reliably identify "major," "important," or "politically significant" decisions (Cook 1993).

Bickel and Schmidt (1984, 85) suggested that decisions that touch "with particular immediacy the main question of the day" are important. This means that the importance of decisions varies with the context of the time when the Court issues them. To borrow Lippman's famous metaphor, such decisions focus more intently the beacon of the press or the media's spotlight on current controversies and give them greater visibility, thus altering the priorities of the systemic agenda. Court opinions also might draw attention to issues on the fringes of the systemic agenda or perhaps occasionally bring new issues into the limelight. In either case, we would argue these decisions are politically significant; they at least establish a necessary precondition for legal change even if the odds of change depend on many other factors and the actual impact occurs much later (Johnson and Canon 1984). However, this also means that the political significance of any decision depends on the contemporary context and reactions of the day. Hindsight, of course, easily reveals the latent importance of an opinion. At the time the original decision was rendered, however, it may go unnoticed and have little impact on the systemic agenda. The historical importance of decisions, then, must not be confused with, nor should it be allowed to overshadow contemporary appraisals of which opinions were significant and which ones were not.[6] The identification of contemporaneous politically significant cases raises various difficulties, not all of which can be satisfactorily resolved (Cook 1993). For the purposes of this study the chief concern is a tautological operationalization that depends on media attention. At the same time, it should be recognized that complete solutions to this problem are hard to find.

The cases for this analysis were drawn from *Congressional Quarterly*'s list of "major decisions" published in the *CQ Guide to the US Supreme Court* (Witt 1979, 1990). Cook (1993) shows that this list is a valid, reliable, and simple way of identifying politically significant decisions. When compared to other compilations of landmark cases (e.g., Epstein *et al* 1994, 81–94), the *Congressional Quar-*

terly list includes fewer decisions. The value of *CQ*'s short list is that it reduces the obvious statistical risks of searching for an impact of numerous Supreme Court decisions; the greater the number of possible interventions in the time-series the greater the likelihood of falsely rejecting the null hypothesis. The list also is more contemporaneous than relying on compilations based on casebooks, and it emphasizes the political as opposed to legal significance of Court opinions (Cook 1993). As a result, the *CQ* list sometimes includes decisions that authors of legal textbooks ignore or treat in minor ways later on. By the same token, the list occasionally excludes opinions that eventually appear in casebooks. For example, the list does not include *Abington School District v. Schempp* (1963) which forbade bible reading in public schools. The *CQ* list does not eliminate the problem of a tautological operationalization, but it at least reduces the bias of selecting decisions through hindsight. The decisions used in this analysis are shown in Table 1.

In two instances, we had to prune the *CQ* lists to include only those opinions that were relevant to or consistent with the policy domains. For the civil rights list, all cases involving school desegregation, particularly busing, were retained. Other cases less directly linked to this issue domain were dropped, such as *Bob Jones University v. United States* (1983) which is arguably a decision involving free exercise of religion questions (Epstein and Walker 1995, 97–98). We also edited the list pertaining to freedom of speech decisions. We excluded opinions dealing with the Smith Act and the Communist Party (i.e., *Dennis v. United States* (1951) and *Yates v. United States* (1957)) because the *Readers' Guide* did not catalog articles dealing with these decisions under the rubrics used to measure attention to free speech issues. The final list includes cases dealing with free speech in public forums, symbolic speech, freedom of expression, and obscenity. No cases were dropped from *CQ*'s freedom of religion list because all decisions dealt in one way or another with establishment questions, the dominant issue of the church-state policy domain during the past five decades.

Speculating about the Supreme Court's Impact on Issue Attentiveness: Three Hypotheses

The vast majority of Supreme Court decisions receive little or no attention from the print or electronic media because the decisions are

TABLE 1: Supreme Court Decisions Used in Analysis

Issue Area	Decision	Date
School Desegregation:	Sweatt v. Painter	June, 1950
	McLaurin v. Oklahoma	June 1950
	Brown v. Board of Education of Topeka	May 1954
	Brown v. Board of Education of Topeka	May 1955
	Cooper v. Aaron	Sept. 1958
	Griffin v. County School Board of Prince Edward County	May 1964
	Green v. County School Board of New Kent County Va.	May 1968
	Swann v. Charlotte-Mecklenburg County Bd of Education	April 1971
	Keyes v. Denver School District No. 1	June 1973
	Milliken v. Bradley	July 1974
	Runyon. McCrary, Fairfax-Brewster School, Inc. v. Gonzales Southern Independent School Association	June 1976
	Pasadena City Board of Education v. Spangler	June 1976
	Columbus Bd of Education v. Penick, Dayton Bd of Education v. Brinkman	July 1979
Freedom of Speech:	Terminiello v. Chicago	May 1949
	Kunz v. New York	January 1951
	Feiner v. New York	January 1951
	Edwards v. South Carolina	Feb. 1963
	Tinker v. Des Moines Independent Community School District	June 1969
Freedom of Expression:	Bd of Education, Island Trees Union Free School District #26 v. Pico	July 1982
	Texas v. Johnson	June 1989
Obscenity:	Roth v. United States, Alberts v. California	June 1957
	Miller v. California	June 1973
Church-State:	Illinois ex. re. McCollum v. Board of Education	March 1948
	Engel v. Vitale	June 1962
	Lemon v. Kurtzman	June 1971
	Mueller v. Allen	June 1983
	Lynch v. Donnelly	March 1984
	Wallace v. Jaffree	June 1985
	Aquilar v. Felton	July 1985
	Edwards v. Aguillard	June 1987
	Allegheny County v. ACLU, Greater Pittsburgh Chapter	July 1989

Source: *CQ Guide to the US Supreme Court*

not deemed newsworthy. Some decisions, of course, pass the media's muster and receive correspondingly greater coverage. When stories about Supreme Court decisions such as *Brown v. Board of Education* or *Roe v. Wade* appear on the front pages of newspapers, the covers of newsweeklies, and on the evening television news, the casual observer might argue that such decisions draw the media's attention to the issue and lead to greater and expanded coverage. However, Rosenberg (1991) argues that appearances can be deceiving. He claims that larger, more powerful social and political forces either cancel out and overwhelm the Court's voice in national dialogues about controversial topics, or that the Court's influence at most is marginal, temporary, and short-lived compared to the impact of history on the nation's concerns. Moreover, the issues placed before the Supreme Court do not emerge from within a litigious cocoon; they often grow out of social and political processes that identify them as social problems and push them onto government's institutional or decisional agendas. The Court's actions thus become redundant since it is simply ratifying a historically-driven process that has already selected issues for attention. Finally, it also can be argued, that even under the best of circumstances the Court's weaknesses as a political institution hamper its ability to single-handedly focus or redirect the national agenda's attention on particular issues.

Because the Court's decisions are only one of many influences affecting the content and priorities of the systemic agenda, its opinions may fail to alter the media's attention to the issues addressed by these decisions. This hypothesis of no influence by the Court warrants serious consideration, because media coverage of the Court's *decisions* is not synonymous with the media's attention to the *policy domains*. The latter subsumes the former as the Court's opinions are only one of the many ingredients that make up media coverage of the domain. The media often single out particular decisions for extensive coverage, but this enhanced coverage may not lead to greater coverage of the underlying issues or the related policy domain. A competitive news environment and limited news capacity force the media to ration its news coverage. Thus, attention to a Court decision may be offset by temporary reductions in the coverage of related events in the particular policy domain or the activities of other participants involved in the issue area. Attention to the issue area remains the same even though attention to the Court's decision increases, because the media make compensatory adjustments. This stability reflects at any moment much broader decisions about the relative importance of competing issues pressing on the media's allocation of limited news space. In other words, a time series of media attention to any particular issue or policy domain reflects the homeostatic tendencies arising from the collective response of the media to the competitive forces demanding its attention. A politically significant Court decision, this first hypothesis suggests, produces no significant expansion in media coverage of the policy domain, even though the media publicize the decision when the Court announces it.

On the other hand, major Supreme Court decisions may influence the national agenda by boosting media attention to the issues raised by the decisions, but the impacts may be short-lived. Wlezien and Goggin (1993) find support for this second hypothesis by showing that increases in "court activities" on current abortion policies temporarily raised public support for existing abortion policies, but this effect soon fell off. Likewise, Franklin and Kosaki (1995) show that coverage of five important Court decisions by the *St. Louis Post-Dispatch* and a local affiliate of a national television network rose at the time the decisions were announced. This coverage quickly disappeared after a day or two unless a decision became controversial in which case the coverage lingered for a while before fading away. Franklin and Kosaki, like virtually all researchers in this area, used short-term measures based on counts of articles or reports dealing specifically with the Court and particular decisions. Rosenberg's measures were more broadly conceived and covered longer periods of time, and thus his findings are more relevant to the second hypothesis. Rosenberg (1991, 114–115) found an abrupt jump in civil rights coverage in the year the Supreme Court ruled in *Brown v. Board of Education*, but this attention then dropped the following year before it rose again, he claims for other reasons.[7] This second hypothesis, then, suggests that media coverage may "spike" as a result of important Court decisions, but media attention soon fades away.

Why would media attention increase temporarily and then decline? Is there any reason to expect a "pulse" effect in a time series measuring media coverage? At first glance it seems these temporary spurts of interest reflect nothing more than the normal routine of producing the news. The Court is an important governmental institution and reporting what it does is part of the everyday production of political news (Gans 1980; Davis 1994). Stories about significant or interesting decisions will appear in the press or on television and afterward about reactions to the decisions. This coverage is brief and soon dies out, because it is unlikely the Court's decisions by themselves will alter the media's newsmaking routines sufficiently to sustain this enhanced coverage. The problem with this explanation is that it is too closely tied to the media's coverage of the Court's decisions, rather than to its coverage of the policy domains of which the decisions are just one part.

A more satisfactory explanation is that rises and falls in media coverage prompted by Supreme Court decisions may resemble the dynamics of "issue attention cycles" in public arenas (Downs 1972; Hilgartner and Bosk 1988), and possibly follow the boom and bust patterns typical of "cascades" in attention (Bikhchandani, Hirshleifer, and Welch 1992). From these perspectives, the media are seen as rushing in to publicize decisions related to preexisting social problems that have drawn its attention in the past or that highlight a social problem previously ignored or overlooked by other governmental or public institutions. The Court's decisions either add new drama to an ongoing story or introduce a fresh new story for the media to develop. The media's initial enthusiasm pushes competing stories on other issues to the sidelines for a while and results in net increases in attention. At some point, the popularity of the issue begins to wane. As its hold on the media or public weakens, other social problems arising in other public arenas gain a competitive edge and begin to encroach on the attention the aging issue receives from the media. Scarce attention results in a decline in attention to the issue area.

The rise and fall in attention may also resemble a "cascade" because the media use similar criteria to identify newsworthy events and often follow each others' lead. When one member of the media, a reputable newspaper or a widely circulated newsweekly, picks up a Court decision and highlights the issues raised by it, the rest of the media follow suit. During this process the media's focus broadens beyond the decision's immediate legal substance to include its larger political implications. As this redefinition or reframing of the decision proceeds, the issues involved in the decision attract the attention of organized or newly mobilized interests, and thus further media attention. The result is a sudden upsurge of stories pertaining to the issue across the media that squeezes out other stories, producing a net increase in issue attention, but at the expense of attention to other issues. This attention quickly collapses, however, producing a short-lived boom or "pulse" in issue attention.

Can Supreme Court decisions produce more enduring changes in the national agenda? Are there grounds for a third hypothesis that Supreme Court decisions produce media and systemic attention that persists for long periods of time? Conflict and controversy are key contextual conditions for expecting Supreme Court decisions to reshape the national agenda. Intense and continuing conflict or opposition to a decision by the public, organized interests, the president, or Congress will supply stories that fuel media attention and sustain its attention beyond what Supreme Court decisions normally receive. Immediate political opposition creates what at first glance appears to be a spurt of media attention, but this heightened level of attention persists over time because the Court's decision is seen in terms of fundamental cleavages or national values around which there are established interests or around which political interests mobilize and then polarize. Long-term agenda change may occur when landmark decisions "hit the nation like a fire alarm in the middle of the night" (Johnson and Canon 1984, 257).

For many observers *Brown v. Board of Education* offers the quintessential illustration of this phenomenon (e.g., Kluger 1975). Too often, however, the argument for *Brown* is grounded in anecdotal evidence and the historical narrative teeters precariously close to the *post hoc, propter hoc* fallacy as key events in the civil rights movement and subsequent federal legislation in the 1960s are attributed in whole or in part to this landmark decision. Rosenberg's skepticism that *Brown* actually had an impact on the nation's agenda arises from his reading of the quantitative indicators he developed to measure agenda attention over a lengthy period of time. His controversial conclusions, however, rest on a visual interpretation of these data; he does not use rigorous statistical methods or models to analyze his data. Because he could not rule out alternative explanations to *Brown* for the media's shifting attention to civil rights, he was forced to conclude that the turbulence of the civil rights era, rather than *Brown*, redirected the national agenda. This does not mean that *Brown* had no impact on the national agenda; it means only that Rosenberg could not single out the relative importance of *Brown v. Board of Education* compared to the other influences that impinged on the media's attention to civil rights.

Because the Court's history is marked by many cases like *Brown*, it is difficult to dismiss lightly the prospect that a few Supreme Court decisions produce enduring impacts on the national agenda if they happen to rearrange the ecology of public issues. Such decisions should produce a "step" effect in media attention. When compared to the "pulse" effects of the second hypothesis, the third hypothesis postulates that some decisions lead to abrupt and enduring shifts in media coverage of the issue area. Instead of quickly fading away, this coverage remains at a higher level because of the political controversy that arises in the wake of the decisions. The overall impact is a change in the systemic agenda that persists for a long period of time.

Method of Analysis and Findings

How do politically significant Supreme Court decisions affect media attention to particular issues through time? Media attention is a socially organized process with its own dynamic qualities. We do not attempt to explicitly model this process since the primary concern is focused simply on whether Supreme Court decisions produce either temporary or permanent changes in media attention through time. Rather, we model the impact of the Supreme Court's decisions using Box-Tiao (1975) impact assessment methods. The Court's opinions are thus treated as interventions capable of disrupting and changing the series dynamic of media coverage. The statistical model takes the following form:

$$Y_t = f(I_t) + N_t$$

where:
- Y_t = time series for media coverage
- I_t = intervention event(s) [Court decision(s)] at time t
- N_t = ARIMA noise model for stochastic processes and trends

The impact assessment design differs from the typical regression design in that there is less concern for specifying all covariates of the dependent series. One is purely interested in determining whether an event at some time t produced change in the dependent series at time t or t+n (n being the number of periods into the future). Campbell and Stanley (1963), in assessing the strengths and weaknesses of various research designs, conclude that the impact assessment design has only one threat to internal validity, history. "[T]he rival hypothesis exists that not X but some more or less simultaneous event produced the shift" (Campbell and Stanley 1963, 37). Thus, as long as one incorporates adequate controls for history, this quasi-experimental design is extremely powerful.

The histories associated with the media series are undoubtedly driven by inertia, as well as various extraneous events that produce temporary changes through time in media coverage.[8] Box-Tiao (1975) impact assessment methods deal with problems of history through the prior construction of Box-Jenkins (1976) ARIMA models (N_t above). ARIMA models explicitly control for stochastic fluctuations in a dependent series by identifying and estimating autoregressive and moving average components. Because ARIMA models are dynamic, relative to the typical regression model they account for much larger proportions of series variance, provide stronger statistical control, and also track extremely well through time even without interventions. The assessment of hypothesized interventions takes place only after these historical effects have been identified and fully modeled. In time series jargon, the dependent series must be "white noise" prior to hypothesis testing.

We developed an appropriate ARIMA model for each of the three series. In order to satisfy the time series assumptions of variance stationarity, each series was also logged prior to testing. We then represented each Supreme Court decision as a binary (0–1) variable with a switch in level occurring in the month the decision was announced, the point of intervention in the time series. Pulse variables were coded as "on" for the month of the intervention and "off" for all other months; step variables were coded "off" for all months prior to the intervention, and "on" for all months after. We used transfer functions to assess the impact of the interventions on the dependent series. Transfer functions provide flexibility for testing the three hypotheses outlined earlier in that they account for both abrupt and gradual changes in various functional forms (e.g., see McCleary and Hay 1980, 172 for examples). As required by the theoretical discussion above, short-term effects can be modeled as pulses while long-term effects can be modeled as steps, with dynamic transference from the interventions determined empirically through the model estimates.

The effect of each major decision was then evaluated for temporary and permanent changes in media attention through time. Since the data on media coverage are monthly, consideration was restricted to current and one month lagged effects. A one month lag was consistent with the fact that Court decisions are announced at any time during a month and because of the schedules of many publications. If lagged effects were not considered, the impact of opinions released late in the month would not be captured by the model nor would the model take into account the coverage of many periodicals published on a monthly basis. We restricted consideration to no more than a one month lag to remain conservative in hypothesis testing. Longer lags could bias the analyses in favor of rejecting the null hypothesis even though other events or incidents occurring after the decision account for the apparent changes in media attentiveness. Thus, restricting the analysis to no more than a one month lagged effect is an added control for history and the threat to validity discussed by Campbell and Stanley (1963).

We considered for inclusion in the models all decisions listed by *CQ* that were relevant to the issue areas discussed above. Because including all decisions in a single model would be cumbersome, we report final models constructed from only those decisions that resulted in model improvement using an information criterion approach. We used Schwarz's (1978) Bayesian Criterion in choosing between lagged and unlagged specifications, as well as whether a Supreme Court decision belonged in the final model. Schwarz's Criterion converges to the "true" model more often than any other dimension reducing criterion (Geweke and Meese 1981).[9] The following sections present results of hypothesis tests concerning how the remaining Supreme Court decisions affected media coverage of issue attentiveness in the three policy domains. For each issue area, the final model is presented in both tabular and graphical form. The graphical presentation offers a visual analysis of the statistical models and affirms with an ocular test that the reported interventions actually occurred.

School Desegregation

The final model for school desegregation which is reported in Table 2 and Figure 4 includes three cases—*Brown v. Board of Education* (1954), *Cooper v. Aaron* (1958), and *Griffin v. County School Board of Prince Edward County* (1964). Given the overarching importance of *Brown* to the final model, the statistical analysis disclaims Rosenberg's skepticism about the impact of *Brown* on systemic attention to civil rights issues. *Brown* was the only one of the three cases having a permanent effect on media attention. With logged data we can obtain a percent change due to the first order intervention using the transformation

TABLE 2 : The Impact of Supreme Court Decisions on Media Coverage of School Desegregation Issues

Model Component[a]	Parameter	Estimate	t statistic
Brown I (I_{t1-1})	ω_{01}	0.55	3.11
	δ_{11}	−0.58	−1.80
Cooper (I_{t2})	ω_{02}	0.53	2.62
	δ_{12}	0.86	7.28
Griffin (I_{t3-1})	ω_{03}	0.53	2.18
First Order Moving Average	θ_1	0.74	17.03
First Order Autoregressive	φ_1	0.94	46.11
Seasonal Autoregressive	φ_{12}	0.06	1.50
Mean	μ	0.30	3.61

Measures of fit: residual mean square (noise only), .084; residual mean square (full model), .0652; autocorrelation of residuals, Q=24.62 with 21 degrees of freedom. N=528.

[a] *Brown* was modeled as a step input. *Cooper* and *Griffin* were modeled as pulse inputs.

$$\% \text{ Change} = 100 \left[\exp\left(\frac{\omega_0}{1 - \delta_1}\right) - 1 \right]$$

McCleary and Hay 1980, 174). Thus, Brown produced a lasting impact on media coverage of school desegregation issues, raising it by about a 41 percent over the long term. A large spike occurred immediately after *Brown*, reflecting contemporaneous media attention to the decision, but while attention to school desegregation issues then receded somewhat it remained significantly higher than during the pre-intervention portion of the series. The negative first-order transfer function denominator for *Brown* ($d_1 = -0.58$) suggests some oscillation in media coverage before it reached a new equilibrium.

In contrast to *Brown's* enduring effect, the other two decisions were best modeled as temporary changes, producing only transitory shifts in media attention to school desegregation issues. *Cooper v. Aaron* and *Griffin v. County School Board of Prince Edward County* each produced temporary shifts equivalent to about 70 percent increases in media coverage. *Cooper* was best modeled as a first order transfer function, indicating some persistence through time, while *Griffin* was best modeled as a zero order transfer function, indicating only a one month shift. Tracking out the dynamics of *Cooper* mathematically reveals that media coverage declined exponentially after the initial shock to about half the peak coverage after about 5 months, to about one fourth after ten months, and to very near the preintervention level after about 15 months.[10] Thus, *Cooper* appeared to focus systemic attention to school desegregation issues for a longer period and more intensely than *Griffin*.

Figure 4 shows graphically the step effect in media attention after the first *Brown* decision in May 1954 and the two transitory changes in media coverage associated with *Cooper v. Aaron* in September 1958 and *Griffin v. Consolidated School Board of Prince Edward County* in May 1964. The story of *Brown I* is sufficiently well-known that a detailed reprise is unnecessary here. Its impact on media attention to school desegregation was substantial and prolonged. The decision itself overturned the "separate but equal" doctrine established by *Plessy v. Ferguson* (1896) and laid the groundwork for challenging Jim Crow laws in the South and Border states. The reaction to the decision, of course, kept the issue of school desegregation in the limelight. Although a Gallup poll at the time of *Brown I* showed a majority of Americans (54 percent) supported the Court's decision (Epstein et al 1994, 593), resistance to desegregation quickly surfaced in the Deep South. Reactions ranged from state activities to preserve all-white schools, the formation of white Citizens' Councils, a revival of the Klu Klux Klan, economic reprisals against those who challenged segregation, plus violence (Nieman 1991, 154–155). A year after *Brown I* the Court released *Brown II* mandating that desegregation proceed with all deliberate speed. In March 1956, southern members of Congress issued the "Southern Manifesto" pledging to reverse the Court's desegregation decisions.

Although in the years immediately following *Brown I* the Court proceeded to strike down other aspects of racial segregation, it made no further rulings involving school desegregation until *Cooper v. Aaron* in September 1958. This case arose out of the Little Rock high school crisis in September 1957 and the resistance to integration led by Arkansas' governor Orville Faubus. On September 25 President

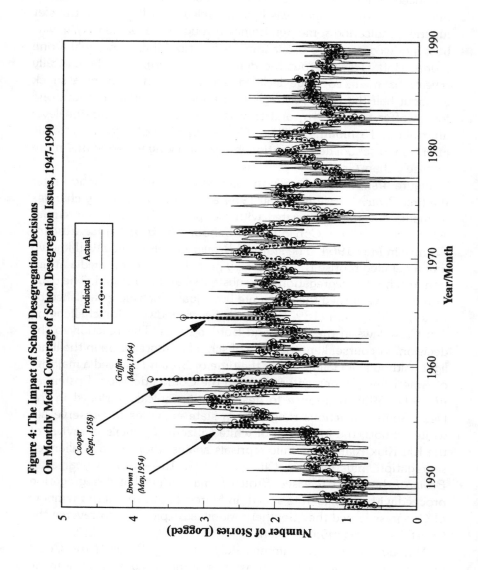

Figure 4: The Impact of School Desegregation Decisions On Monthly Media Coverage of School Desegregation Issues, 1947-1990

Eisenhower sent federal troops to Little Rock to enforce a lower court order requiring admission of black students to the school. In February 1958 a federal district court agreed to postpone further desegregation efforts. At the start of the 1958 school year, on September 12, the Supreme Court issued a *per curium* opinion in *Cooper* affirming an appellate court reversal of the lower court. In reaction, Arkansas closed the four high schools in Little Rock. On September 29 the Court, sharply rebuking the governor and state legislature for their obstructionism, issued a unanimous formal opinion which in a break with tradition was individually signed by each of the nine justices. The timing of the events involved in *Cooper* is such that it appears the decision independently prompted additional media coverage of school desegregation.

The influence of *Griffin* seems more questionable when put into historical context. In *Griffin* the Supreme Court ruled that Virginia could not close its public schools and replace them with all-white private academies to avoid integration. The decision was announced on May 25, 1964 during a time of high political drama and conflict. Southern Democrats, trying to block a vote in the Senate on the Civil Rights Act of 1964, conducted a record-breaking filibuster that was finally cut off on June 10. Roughly ten days later, the president signed the bill into law. The act was linked to the issue of school desegregation through Title 4 which gave the government and courts additional powers to implement school integration orders. The title's language regarding transportation to achieve racial balance in schools would later figure prominently in the 1971 busing case, *Swann v. Charlotte-Mecklenburg* (Graham 1992, 174–179). Most constitutional law textbooks give *Griffin* short shrift (e.g., O'Brien 1991, 1299; Abraham and Perry 1994, 238; Epstein and Walker 1995, 730). In this instance hindsight may provide the best assessment of the decision's importance. It is quite possible that the one month pulse effect associated with *Griffin* reflected the politics surrounding the 1964 Civil Rights Act.[11]

Free Speech and Censorship

The free speech and censorship policy domain includes several notable Supreme Court cases that are commonly considered to be among its most controversial. However, the final time series model includes only *Texas v. Johnson* (1989) in which the Court ruled 5–4 that the First Amendment precludes states from punishing individuals for desecrating the American flag. In *Texas v. Johnson* a member of the Revolutionary Communist Youth Brigade soaked an American flag with kerosene and set it aflame outside the convention hall in Dallas where the 1984 Republican Convention was being held. As the model and figure indicate, the Supreme Court's opinion in *Texas v. Johnson* produced an enduring effect on media attentiveness in this policy domain. Results of the analysis are reported in Table 3 and Figure 5.

The Court's "flag burning" decision and the political reaction sparked by it produced a step effect in media attention. Beginning in June 1989, the month of the Supreme Court decision, coverage of issues in this policy domain rose by about 43 percent and remained at this new level for the 42 remaining months of the series. Figure 5 shows the sharp change due to *Johnson* and the model's predicted values. It bears noting that in contrast to *Brown* where the effect was gradual but enduring, the effect of *Johnson* was immediate, suggesting the extreme public outrage over the issue. In this case the Supreme Court was a catalyst, sparking system-wide concern over an issue that previously was not under active consideration by other institutions. The Court mobilized the media and a concerned public, which in turn resulted in increased attention both by the president and Congress.

TABLE 3 : The Impact of Supreme Court Decisions on Media Attention to Free Speech and Censorship Issues

Model Component[a]	Parameter	Estimate	t statistic
Texas v. Johnson (I_{t1})	ω_{01}	0.36	3.07
First Order Moving Average	θ_1	0.58	5.17
First Order Autoregressive	φ_1	0.75	8.38
Sixth Order Autoregressive	φ_2	0.08	2.02
Mean	μ	0.64	16.89

Measures of fit: residual mean square (noise only), .333; residual mean square (full model), .0331; autocorrelation of residuals, Q=25.48 with 21 degrees of freedom. N=570.

[a] *Texas v. Johnson* was modeled as a step input.

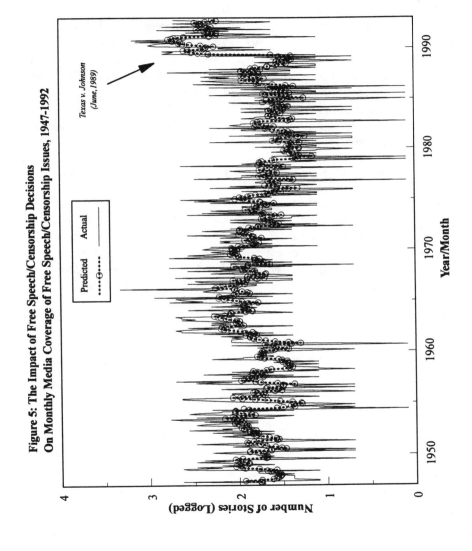

Figure 5: The Impact of Free Speech/Censorship Decisions
On Monthly Media Coverage of Free Speech/Censorship Issues, 1947-1992

The Court's surprising and unexpected decision caused an immediate uproar that ignited demands for federal action. Public opinion polls showed a 3 to 1 majority in favor of a constitutional amendment overturning the decision (Baum 1995, 151). President Bush and members of Congress promptly condemned the Court's ruling. On the heels of the decision, Congress passed and the president signed into law the Flag Protection Act of 1989. Within a year, however, the Court struck down the act in *United States v. Eichman* (1990) on the same constitutional grounds it used in *Texas v. Johnson* which fueled further and continuing controversy. *Eichman* met with no more favor than *Johnson*, and during the ensuing years various constitutional amendments were proposed by members of Congress intended to overturn these decisions.

Freedom of Religion and Establishment Questions

Church and state cases involve questions about aid to parochial schools, prayer in public schools, and religious symbols in public settings. The final model for this issue area includes three cases dealing in various ways with each of these questions: *Illinois ex. rel. McCollum v. Board of Education* (1948), *Engel v. Vitale* (1962), and *Lynch v. Donnelly* (1984). Table 4 and Figure 6 present results for this model.

TABLE 4 : The Impact of the Supreme Court on Media Attention to Church and State Issues

Model Component [a]	Parameter	Estimate	t statistic
McCollum (I_{t1})	ω_{01}	0.29	2.37
Engel (I_{t2-1})	ω_{02}	0.38	3.15
Lynch (I_{t3})	ω_{03}	0.52	2.27
	δ_{13}	0.31	1.69
First Order Moving Average	θ_2	0.88	41.09
Mean	μ	0.00	−0.71

Measures of fit: residual mean square (noise only), 0.0616; residual mean square (full model), 0.0598; autocorrelation of residuals, Q=25.16 with 24 degrees of freedom. N=528.

[a] *McCollum* and *Engel* were modeled as step inputs. *Lynch* was modeled as a pulse input.

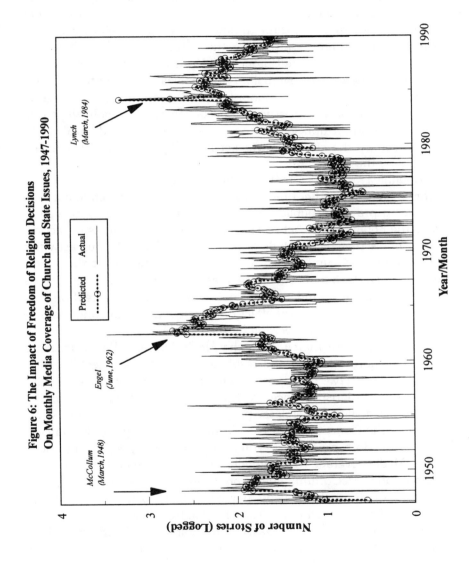

Figure 6: The Impact of Freedom of Religion Decisions
On Monthly Media Coverage of Church and State Issues, 1947-1990

Of the three decisions, *Lynch* was modeled as a temporary effect, while *McCollum* and *Engel* were modeled as abrupt, permanent shifts. Following *Lynch*, media attention jumped immediately by about 110 percent, but it quickly subsided. Tracking the dynamics of the *Lynch* decision mathematically through time shows that the effect was virtually negligible three months after the initial impact. This March 5, 1984 decision by the late Burger Court was one of three decisions in two years where a narrow majority of justices that emerged after the appointment of Justice O'Connor took an "accommodationist" stance regarding establishment issues (Koblyka 1995). In *Lynch*, the Court by a 5–4 margin upheld the constitutionality of including a crèche purchased by the city of Pawtucket in a Christmas display partially funded by the city.

Roughly two weeks after the Court handed down *Lynch*, Congress, after failing yet another time to pass a constitutional amendment reintroducing prayer in public schools, gathered the majority needed to pass the Equal Access Act of 1984 which allowed students in secondary schools that receive federal funds to conduct religious activities under certain circumstances. The coincidental timing of the *Lynch* decision and the Senate vote raise questions as to whether the Court's decision exerted an independent quickening in media attention.[12] It may be that the temporary effect of *Lynch* was due to congressional action, rather than the decision by the Court.

In contrast with *Lynch*, both the *McCollum* and *Engel* decisions attracted more attention and resulted in a more persistent systemic reaction. These two decisions reflected the "separationist" tendencies of the Court's jurisprudence. With *McCollum* the Court for the first time struck down a time-release program for religious instruction, while in *Engel* the Court declared New York's school prayer policy unconstitutional. Both precedent-setting opinions were greeted with much furor. Media coverage rose immediately and permanently by about 49 percent after *McCollum*, while *Engel* caused a permanent long-term increase of approximately 54 percent. Figure 6 shows the abrupt changes that occurred as a result of these two decisions.

The Supreme Court's released time opinion in 1948 and school prayer decision in 1962 set off intense national debates. As Sorauf (1976, 5) noted, "Only the furor over desegregation and the rights of racial minorities rivaled the intensity of feeling on prayer in the public schools, or public aid to private religious schools." *McCollum* generated a backlash that prompted Justice Black, the author of the opinion, to write shortly afterward in a related case that "Probably few opinions from this Court in recent years have attracted more attention or stirred wider debate" (quoted in Sorauf 1976, 21). According to Reichley (1985, 147), however, "The wave of condemnation raised against *Engel* made the criticisms . . . directed at *McCollum* . . . seem like a summer squall."

The political response to *Engel*'s school prayer decision was immediate and enduring. Two days after the decision, on June 25, 1962, a senator introduced a constitutional amendment to overturn the decision, the first of 56 similar amendments filed during that year. A survey the following year revealed that 70 percent of the public opposed the Court's decision (Stanley and Neimi 1992, 21). In 1966 the Senate Judiciary Committee conducted hearings on a voluntary prayer amendment proposed by Senate Minority Leader Everett Dirksen. In September the amendment, although supported by a vote of 49 to 37, failed to muster the required two-thirds majority. Congressional enthusiasm for a school prayer amendment waned until 1971 when a congressman at the urging of a grass roots organization managed to bring a bill similar to the Dirksen amendment to a vote in the House. The bill again won a sizable majority, but it fell short of the two-thirds needed for passage. Congress' inability to pass these amendments led to an effort in 1974 to curtail the federal court system's jurisdiction over school prayer.

With the rise of the conservative Christian movement, motivated in part by the Court's decisions dealing with religion, and the 1980 election of Ronald Reagan and a Republican majority in the Senate came new efforts to overturn the Court's prayer and related decisions (Moen 1989, 1992). By 1987 congressional efforts aimed at restoring prayer or devotional services in public schools totaled more than 600 constitutional amendments and 45 jurisdictional statutes curbing the Court's authority with regard to this issue (Keynes 1989, 174). Efforts to restore school prayer continue to the present time.

Discussion and Conclusions

This research has attempted for the first time to chart through systematic analysis the extent to which the Supreme Court focuses attention to issues in the US system. Attentiveness to issues does not rhythmically rise and fall with the tempo set by the announcement of Supreme Court opinions. To expect covariation of this kind is tantamount to constructing a strawman; it demands too much of the Court's ability to dominate public policy discourse in the United States. Conversely, to expect no covariation at all is equally unrealistic and counterintuitive in light of the history of the Court's impact on American politics over the past two centuries. Between these two extremes lies a great deal of unmapped middle ground.

Over a period stretching from 1947 through 1992, four extremely controversial and reputedly important decisions prompted the media to increase its coverage of the issues raised by these cases and to sustain this heightened level of attention. Three other decisions produced temporary jumps in media coverage, although in two of these instances the shifts potentially reflect other events occurring at the same time. In two of the three issue areas we examined—school desegregation and church-state relations—the Court's decisions were especially important in drawing attention to problems and policy alternatives that reshaped the political ecologies of these policy domains. The Court's actions in the area of free speech and censorship were less influential except for its "flag burning" opinion.

The non-finding that most of the *CQ* "important" decisions failed to produce discernible changes in media attention over time does not necessarily mean that the system ignored the Supreme Court. One of the problems motivating this study was the apparent contradiction between the obvious fact that some Supreme Court decisions are reputedly significant and Rosenberg's (1991) strong assertion that two of the Court's most politically charged decisions in the past 50 years (*Brown* and *Roe v. Wade*) had no impact on media coverage of civil rights and abortion. Given the results of our analysis, it is unlikely that when the Court speaks in cases involving important questions of the day that its voice is routinely ignored or goes unheard. Instead it may mean that as one of many voices calling for the media's attention, the media temporarily make room for the Court's views by substituting stories about the decisions for related competing stories, only to have them replaced shortly afterward by subsequent events. The attention allocated to the issue area would thus remain stable even as the composition and source of stories change over time. Competition for the media's attention and its limited capacity to construct and produce news stories, as well as its rules for determining the newsworthiness of events, thus, operate as sources of negative feedback that foster homeostatic or equilibrating tendencies in issue attention.

It is clear from the analyses presented here, however, that these periods of stasis or equilibrium can be upset or disturbed by Supreme

Court decisions. In a sense, the Court "punctuates" the equilibrium (Jones 1994) by interjecting new or rediscovered social problems or policy alternatives into the national dialogue. It is not the decisions *per se* that set off cascades of attention in the media or that propel it to reapportion its attention to issue areas, although a necessary characteristic of these decisions may be that they overturn precedents, create new law, or rearrange political opportunities for groups. Instead it is the magnitude or scale of the political opposition to the decisions and the issues they raise that matters most. Conflict expansion and reactions by the public, Congress, and president create the positive feedback needed to overcome the homeostatic tendencies of issue attention in the media.

For the most controversial of decisions, the Supreme Court's voice in the national dialogue is obviously heard, and its views shift the focus of national discourse. The dynamics of agenda setting in the United States thus reflects an important top-down influence in which a major governmental institution, the Supreme Court, influences the attentiveness of the media and through the media to some extent the attentiveness of the public and other institutions to particular issues. The media's news rules guarantee the publication of stories that evoke controversy, and as these stories appear they help to expand the scope of conflict, mobilize groups, and rearrange the competitive balance among social problems on the system agenda.

This view of the Supreme Court's ability to direct national attention to issues strikes a contrast with Rosenberg's depiction of the conditions under which courts can be "effective producers of significant social reform" (Rosenberg 1991, 36). Rosenberg claims that several conditions must exist simultaneously in order for the Court's actions to have an impact. There must be ample legal precedent for the change, substantial Congressional and presidential support, either support from citizens or lows levels of opposition, and an effective, reliable means available for implementing the change. Only when all of these conditions prevail, Rosenberg argues, are legal decisions likely to lead to "significant" social reform. A moment's reflection, however, makes one wonder if the Supreme Court's voice would be heard over this chorus of consensus on the need for legal change. With conflict and dissensus removed from a federal system of separated powers that normally offers many opportunities to block change, a Court decision under these conditions does little more than ratify what society and its politics already want. In many respects the Court's voice would be superfluous since it would be indistinguishable from many others. The

Supreme Court of the United States, ironically, may influence constitutional dialogues more effectively and alter legal rights discourse more substantially, although with greater uncertainty of the final outcome, when it risks its authority by speaking out against the reigning consensus or if it gambles on its legitimacy by expressing views that could shift the terms of debate in unsettled, highly charged areas of America's politics.

Notes

1 For a review of polling data relevant to Supreme Court decisions in various issue areas that illustrates the problem of selective attention, short time-series, and irregular polling intervals, see Epstein *et al* (1995, 587–609)

2 Baumgarter and Jones (1993, 257–259) report the results of several studies indicating high correlations among indexes based on newspaper, magazine, and electronic media For example they found a correlation of .88 in the trends between their *Readers' Guide* index measuring attention to child abuse and a similar index based on the *New York Times*. In turn they also note the high correlations between major newspaper coverage of issues and television attention to this issues..

3 The freedom of speech/censorship series is longer than the other two series because a critical Supreme Court decision, *Texas v Johnson* (1989), occurred late in the series. In order to have sufficient observations for statistical analysis we extended this series for two additional years.

4 Rosenberg (1991), using an article count references under the *Reader's Guide* keyword, "Negroes in the United States", reaches the surprising conclusion that *Brown v Board of Education* had no easily or readily identifiable impact on media coverage of civil rights. One reason his analysis may have reached this null conclusion is the inclusiveness of the measure. This keyword includes 16 different subcategories. Virtually all the stories dealing with school desegregation during 1952–1956, however, are located under just two subcategories, "Negroes in America—Education" and "Negroes in America—Segregation." Rosenberg's inclusive operationalization creates a heterogeneous measure that is consistent with arguments that *Brown I* was a critical moment in mobilizing the civil rights movement. At the same time, however, the measure's heterogeneity reduces its sensitivity to events directly affecting school desegregation. Thus, an independent count of the 926 stories under the general "Negroes in the United States" keyword for 1952–1956 found that only 306 dealt with the topic of race and education. Sizable shifts in media attention to this topic could occur without producing noticeable changes in this inclusive measure. In addition to this problem, Rosenberg may have undercounted media attention regarding school desegregation because he overlooked or ignored a related, highly relevant *Reader's Guide* category. Under the heading "Public Schools in America" there is a subcategory entitled "Public Schools—Desegregation." Over time, this subcategory grows so large that it swamps the number of articles in the two school-related subcategories from the "Negroes in America" category. In short, most stories on school desegregation in the *Reader's Guide* are found under a heading that Rosenberg does not include in his analysis.

5   Although shorter temporal units may provide more sensitive indicators, they still cannot overcome the problem that arises if the interventions occur simultaneously This is not an infrequent occurrence on the Supreme Court because as Table 1 indicates the Court often combines and hears cases raising similar or common substantive questions. For example, the Court issued opinions in *Kunz v. New York* and in *Feiner v. New York*, two major free speech cases, on the same day in January 1951. An earlier example occurred in *Sweatt v. Painter* and in *McLaurin v. Oklahoma State Regents* which were handed down on the same day in 1950, and, of course, *Brown v. Board of Education of Topeka* was accompanied by *Bolling v. Sharpe* when the Court made its momentous announcement on May 17, 1954 declaring public school segregation unconstitutional. Although this analysis indicates the first two pairs of decisions did not produce statistically significant changes in media attention, simultaneous announcements require close scrutiny of how the media reported the decisions if one of them is considered by authorities to be more influential than its twin. In the instance of the two sets of *Brown* decisions, each set is simply referred to by the name of lead case and most of the time are treated collectively as one decision.

6   An interesting and intriguing illustration of how contemporary and historical perspectives differ as to the significance of Supreme Court cases can be found in Chief Justice Warren's ranking of *Brown* as ranking second in importance to *Baker v Carr* (1962). Warren at the time of his retirement in 1969 thought the reapportionment decision was "the most important case we decided in my time" (Abraham and Perry 1994, 20).

7   It is worth noting that this short-lived jump in media attention at the time of *Brown* was not duplicated in Rosenberg's data for *Roe v Wade*. Indeed, media coverage increased in the two years preceding *Roe* only to drop the year the Court handed down the decision (Rosenberg 1991, 230–231).

8   Indeed, Rosenberg (1991) claims that the tide of history is the motivating force behind media attention to civil rights issues and associated changes

9   Schwarz's Bayesian Criterion is given:

$SBC = \ln(L) - 5K\ln(T)$

where SBC = Schwarz's Criterion
L = the likelihood function
K = the number of variables
T = the number of time points.

Schwarz (1978) showed mathematically that his criterion leads to the true model asymptotically with unit probability. However, other model selection critieria can also be shown to lead to the true model. For a survey of the available criteria, see Judge et al. (1985, 870–75).

10 The intervention is tracked out recursively to produce these numbers At any particular time period the series level is computed:

$$y_t = \delta_1 y_{t-1} + \omega_0 I_t$$

where: y_t = series level
I_t = the intervention series
ω_0 = transfer function numerator
δ_1 = transfer function denominator

11 It appears based on a visual inspection of the publication dates of the article references before and after *Griffin* and for the period following passage of the Civil Rights Act that the media's attention rose after this law was enacted The jump in attentiveness to this issue area does not seem to be due to the Court's actions.

12 Visual inspection of the article references for the days preceding and following the Court's decision in *Lynch* and for the period around Congress' vote on the Equal Access Act of 1984 while not conclusive suggests that media's heightened attentiveness to this issue area was prompted by the passage of this law

Works Cited

Abraham, Henry J., and Barbara A. Perry. 1994. *Freedom and the Court: Civil Rights and Liberties in the United States.* 6th ed. New York: Oxford University Press.

Baum, Lawrence. 1995. *The Supreme Court.* 5th ed. Washington, D.C.: CQ Press.

Baumgartner, Frank R., and Bryan D. Jones. 1993. *Agendas and Instability in American Politics.* Chicago: University of Chicago Press.

Bickel, Alexander M., and Benno C. Schmidt, Jr. 1984. *The Judiciary and Responsible Government, 1910–1921.* New York: Macmillan.

Bikhchandani, Shushil, David Hirshleifer, and Ivo Welch. 1992. "A Theory of Fads, Fashion, Custom, and Cultural Change as Information Cascades." *Journal of Political Economy.* 100:992–1026.

Box, G.E.P. and G.M. Jenkins. 1976. *Time Series Analysis: Forecasting and Control.* New York: Holden Day.

Box, G.E.P. and G.C. Tiao. 1975. Intervention Analysis with Applications to Economic and Environmental Problems. *Journal of the American Statistical Association.* 70: 70–79.

Campbell and Stanley. 1963. *Experimental and Quasi-Experimental Designs for Research.* Chicago: Rand-McNally.

Cobb, Roger W., and Charles D. Elder. 1972. *Participation in American Politics: The Dynamics of Agenda-Building.* Baltimore: Johns Hopkins Press.

Cohen, Jeffrey E. 1995. "Presidential Rhetoric and the Public Agenda." *American Journal of Political Science.* 39:87–107.

Cook, Beverly B. 1993. "Measuring the Significance of US Supreme Court Decisions." *Journal of Politics.* 55:1127–1139.

Danielian, Lucig H., and Benjamin I. Page. 1994. "The Heavenly Chorus: Interest Group Voices on TV News." *American Journal of Political Science.* 38:1056–1078.

Davis, Richard. 1994. *Decisions and Images: The Supreme Court and the Press.* Englewood Cliffs, NJ: Prentice Hall.

Downs, Anthony. 1972. "Up and Down with Ecology—The 'Issue-Attention Cycle." *The Public Interest.* 28:38–50.

Epstein, Lee, Jeffrey A. Segal, Harold J. Spaeth, and Thomas G. Walker. 1994. *The Supreme Court Compendium: Data, Decisions, and Developments.* Washington, D.C.: CQ Press.

Epstein, Lee, and Thomas J. Walker. 1995. *Constitutional Law for a Changing America: Rights, Liberties, and Justice.* 2nd ed. Washington, D.C.: CQ Press.

Flemming, Roy B., B. Dan Wood, and John Bohte. 1995. "Policy Attention in a System of Separated Powers: An Inquiry into the Dynamics of American Agenda Setting." Presented at the annual meeting of the Midwest Political Science Association, Chicago.

Franklin, Charles H., and Liane C. Kosaki. 1989. "Republican Schoolmaster: The US Supreme Court, Public Opinion, and Abortion." *American Political Science Review.* 83:751–771.

Franklin, Charles H., and Liane C. Kosaki. 1995. "Media, Knowledge, and Public Evaluations of the Supreme Court." In *Contemplating Courts,* ed. Lee Epstein. Washington, D.C.: CQ Press.

Gans, Herbert J. 1980. Deciding What's News. New York: Random House.

Geweke, John and Richard Meese. 1981. Estimating Regression Models of Finite but Unknown Order. *International Economic Review.* 22: 55–70.

Graber, Doris A. 1993. *Mass Media and American Politics.* 4th ed. Washington, D.C.: CQ Press.

Graham, Hugh Davis. 1992. *Civil Rights and the Presidency.* New York: Oxford University Press.

Hilgartner, Stephen, and Bosk, Charles L. 1988. "The Rise and Fall of Social Problems: A Public Arenas Model." *American Journal of Sociology.* 94:53–78.

Hoekstra, Valerie J. 1995. "The Supreme Court and Opinion Change: An Experimental Study of the Court's Ability to Change Opinion." *American Politics Quarterly.* 23:109–129.

Iyengar, Shanto, and Donald R. Kinder. 1987. *News That Matters.* Chicago: University of Chicago Press.

Johnson, Charles A., and Bradley C. Canon. 1984. *Judicial Policies: Implementation and Impact.* Washington, D.C.: CQ Press.

Jones, Bryan D. 1994. *Reconceiving Decision-Making in Democratic Politics: Attention, Choice, and Public Policy.* Chicago: University of Chicago Press.

Judge, George G., W.E. Griffiths, R. Carter Hill, Helmut Lutkepohl, and Tsoung-Chao Lee. 1985. *The Theory and Practice of Econometrics.* 2d ed. New York: Wiley.

Keynes, Edward. 1989. *The Court vs. Congress: Prayer, Busing, and Abortion.* Durham, NC: Duke University Press.

Kingdon, John W. 1984. *Agendas, Alternatives, and Public Policies.* Boston: Little, Brown and Company,

Kobylka, Joseph F. 1991. *The Politics of Obscenity: Group Legimation in a Time of Legal Change*. New York: Greenwood Press.

Kobylka, Joseph F. 1995. "The Mysterious Case of Establishment Clause Litigation: How Organized Litigants Foiled Legal Change." In *Contemplating Courts*, ed. Lee Epstein. Washington, D.C.: CQ Press.

Kluger, Richard. 1975. *Simple Justice*. New York: Random House.

McCleary, Richard and Richard A. Hay. 1980. *Applied Time Series Analysis for the Social Sciences*. Beverly Hills: Sage Publications.

Moen, Matthew C. 1989. *The Christian Right and Congress*. Tuscaloosa, AL: University of Alabama Press.

Moen, Matthew C. 1992. *The Transformation of the Christian Right*. Tuscaloosa, AL: University of Alabama Press.

Neuman, W. Russell, Marion R. Just, and Ann N. Crigler. 1992. *Common Knowledge: News and the Construction of Political Meaning*. Chicago: University of Chicago Press.

Nieman, Donald G. 1991. *Promises to Keep: African-Americans and the Constitutional Order, 1776 to the Present*. New York: Oxford University Press.

O'Brien, David M. 1991. Civil Rights and Civil Liberties. Vol. 2 of *Constitutional Law and Politics*. New York: W.W. Norton.

O'Gallaghan, Jerome, and James O. Dukes. 1992. "Media Coverage of the Supreme Court's Caseload." *Journalism Quarterly*. 69:195–203.

Pacelle, Richard L., Jr. 1991. *The Transformation of the Supreme Court's Agenda*. Boulder, CO: Westview Press.

Pacelle, Richard L., Jr. 1995. "The Dynamics and Determinants of Agenda Change in the Rehnquist Court." In *Contemplating Courts*, ed. Lee Epstein. Washington, D.C.: CQ Press.

Reichley, A. James. 1985. *Religion in American Public Life*. Washington, D.C.: Brookings Institution.

Rochefort, David A., and Roger W. Cobb, eds. 1994. *The Politics of Problem Definition: Shaping the Policy Agenda*. Lawrence, KS: University of Kansas.

Rosenberg, Gerald N. 1991. *The Hollow Hope*. Chicago: University of Chicago Press.

Schattschneider, E.E. 1960. *The Semisovereign People*. New York: Holt, Rinehart and Winston.

Schwarz, Gabriel. 1978. Estimating the Dimension of a Model. *Annals of Statistics*. 6: 461–64.

Sorauf, Frank J. 1976. *The Wall of Separation: The Constitutional Politics of Church and State.* Princeton: Princeton University Press.

Spaeth, Harold J. 1993. *United States Supreme Court Database, 1953-1991.* Ann Arbor: Interuniversity Consortium for Political and Social Research.

Stanley, Harold W., and Richard G. Niemi. 1992. *Vital Statistics on American Politics.* 3rd ed. Washington, D.C.: CQ Press.

Tushnet, Mark V. 1987. *The NAACP's Legal Strategy against Segregated Education, 1925-1950.* Chapel Hill, NC: University of North Carolina Press.

Witt, Elder (ed.). 1979. *CQ Guide to the US Supreme Court.* 1990. Washington, D.C.: CQ Press.

Witt, Elder (ed.). 1990. *CQ Guide to the US Supreme Court.* 1990. Washington, D.C.: CQ Press.

Wlezien, Christopher B., and Malcolm L. Goggin. 1993. "The Courts, Interest Groups, and Public Opinion about Abortion." *Political Behavior.* 15:381-405.

Chapter 2

The Politics of Rights Revisited: Rosenberg, McCann, and the New Institutionalism

Kevin J. McMahon
Michael Paris

Introduction

Gerald Rosenberg's *The Hollow Hope* (1991) has sparked renewed debate about the role of law and courts in oppositional or reform projects. "To what degree, and under what conditions," Rosenberg asks, "can judicial processes be used to produce political and social change?" After examining the effects of court decisions across several policy areas, he concludes that courts (alone) cannot bring about "significant social change." Courts, then, "act as 'flypaper' for social reformers who succumb to the 'lure of litigation'." In this view, would-be reformers would do well to direct their energies elsewhere—in the legislative arena or, even better, in the streets. Thus, Rosenberg sees himself a critic of the use of courts "from the left." He wants to convince us that his inquiry proceeds from a hardheaded, realistic concern for the intended beneficiaries of the causes he studies.[1] A thoughtful critic of Rosenberg identified with the left has been Michael McCann. McCann has provided a detailed review and critique of *The Hollow Hope*, and has recently brought out his own empirical study elaborating an alternative "legal mobilization" approach (McCann, 1992; 1994).

This chapter seeks to shed some light on the dispute between Rosenberg and McCann over approaches and methods in the study of law and social change. In what follows (two separately authored case studies and a co-authored concluding section), we argue that Rosenberg's view obfuscates the potential role of law and courts in oppositional and reform projects, and that McCann's framework promises to yield better descriptive and normative insights. We also suggest that elements of McCann's perspective can be usefully adapted to the study of moderate, elite-dominated reform projects—that is, legal efforts not characterized by coordination with social movement activities. Here, we explore possibilities for integrating McCann's view of law and change, on one hand, and themes and concepts found in "new institutionalist" analyses of social policy, on the other.[2]

We proceed as follows. A section below briefly reviews McCann's critique of Rosenberg and sets forth the basic terms of his alternative approach.[3] We then offer two case studies, or illustrative discussions, to help us explicate our claims. The first (written by Kevin McMahon) examines Rosenberg's argument about the role of *Brown v. Board* in the Montgomery bus boycott. A close review of Rosenberg's rendition of Montgomery not only demonstrates that his claim about a lack of connection between *Brown* and the bus boycott misses the mark, but also highlights what is to be gained from attention to McCann's alternative view. The second (written by Michael Paris) examines the role of law and courts in a state-level conflict. It draws upon certain elements of McCann's model to explore the interplay of law and politics in a struggle over the meaning of "equal educational opportunity" in relation to school finance policy in New Jersey. This second discussion both illustrates the practical utility of McCann's perspective and attempts to demonstrate how it might be adapted to elite-dominated reform efforts and synthesized with liberal-institutionalist themes and concepts.[4] Finally, a co-authored concluding section raises a few general questions for scholars interested in building upon McCann's framework. Here, we argue that the construction of thick "conflict and policy narratives," guided by McCann's model, might lead to some new insights, particularly with respect to (1) "cause lawyering" and political mobilization, and (2) the role and status of law and courts *as institutions* in a "decentered," legal mobilization approach.

The Politics of Rights Revisited: Rosenberg and McCann

The Rosenberg-McCann debate represents the latest development in a line of public law inquiry that began with Stuart Scheingold's *The Politics of Rights* (1974).[5] Indeed, Rosenberg and McCann's competing perspectives can be seen as different responses to a tension at the heart of Scheingold's original conceptual outline. On one hand,

Scheingold's view was characterized by strong traces of legal realism and political jurisprudence, combined with the left's traditional suspicion of liberal legalism. The talk of "ideologists" inside the legal world (that is, on the "law" side of the "law/politics boundary," so conceived) is approached as largely epiphenomenal. Thus, in Scheingold we find little attention to the choices lawyer-reformer or other activists make in framing and constructing legal challenges, and little attention to the content and character of legal arguments or judicial opinion. These things are not the real stuff of politics and power relations. On the other hand, Scheingold's perceptive attention to the cultural resonance of rights claims in American politics and their potentially legitimizing and mobilizing effects at least implicitly pointed toward the social construction of reality, and the role that legal forms and institutions might play in this construction.

Rosenberg's *The Hollow Hope* develops the dominant neorealist outlook of Scheingold's work. It offers an elegant analytical framework for examining propositions about possible causal links between court decisions and social change, and a relentless search for empirical evidence. Like Scheingold before him, Rosenberg takes aim at law reformers embracing "the myth of rights" (1991, 3, 12). What has been most controversial about Rosenberg's work, however, is that he denies the empirical validity of the sorts of claims usually made for a "politics of rights." His analysis, he argues, demonstrates that courts are a "particularly poor tool for changing opinions and for mobilization," and this fact "makes dubious any claims for important extrajudicial effects of court actions" (338–39).[6]

For his part, McCann agrees with Scheingold and Rosenberg in their respective critiques of the myth of rights. However, drawing upon various strands of critical social and legal theory, McCann develops a far different understanding of the potential role of legal forms and institutions in social and political conflict. Compared to Scheingold and Rosenberg, McCann proposes an alternative notion of the very meaning of "indirect effects" and the research stance required to grasp them. Thus, his view explores the conceptual and methodological implications of the submerged, "cultural" side of Scheingold's argument.

McCann's critique of Rosenberg begins with a basic point about possible "standpoints." He contrasts "court-centered, top-down" models of law and politics with "decentered, bottom-up models." Court-centered models like Rosenberg's cannot tell us anything about "how or why people litigate and deploy legal tactics." With "courts at the center" of analysis, we gain no insight into "the intentions, understandings, and tactical designs of those who engage in such practices." McCann continues:

> If judges are the legal agents and aspiring producers of change to be scrutinized, the reactions of target citizens (masses and official elites) are the primary measure of how effective such actions are. Causality is presumed to initiate at the top in a discrete judicial source, and trickles down unidirectionally *on* society, if at all. This impact . . . can be either direct (coercion) or indirect (moral persuasion). In both forms of impact, however, the primary standard of effective change is *compliance* with, or affirmative action (inspired) toward, the goals of the court by target populations (1992, 731).

Dispute-centered views, by contrast, begin from the standpoint of nonjudicial individuals or group actors engaged in conflicts. With "social struggles" at the center of inquiry, "nonjudicial actors are viewed as practical legal agents rather than as simply reactors to judicial commands." McCann's legal mobilization perspective, then, seeks to understand "how legal strategies shape personal aspirations, structure the terms of conflict, and advance or impede reform goals" (718).[7]

In our view, the use of McCann's model yields more accurate descriptions of the role that law, courts, and judicial decisions play in reform conflicts. In the two chapters that follow, we focus on nonjudicial actors in two distinct reform efforts, but do so with an eye toward understanding the judiciary's independent impact on strategies and politics outside the courtroom. In other words, the "decentered" approach not only uncovers "mobilization of the law," but also allows for a better understanding of how institutions condition social group activity, and in turn shape political understandings and conflicts.

Did the Federal Judiciary Help Spark the Civil Rights Movement?
Brown, Courts, and the Montgomery Bus Boycott

Kevin J. McMahon

Introduction

Imagine that it is now 1938. You are taking part in a strategy session at the NAACP's headquarters in New York. To your left sits Charles Houston, to your right Thurgood Marshall. They are discussing recent events concerning the advancement of civil rights for African-Americans. Assuming that you have 1997 knowledge, what would you advise them to do?[8]

For Gerald Rosenberg, the answer seems clear. Reliance upon the courts would needlessly divert valuable resources and in the end provide little, if any, significant support toward advancing the goals of the civil rights cause. In *The Hollow Hope*, Rosenberg's claim about the irrelevance of *Brown v. Board* in producing change stands as the initial and most striking exhibit in his case against the courts. Rosenberg makes this argument about *Brown* by posing two basic questions: First, what "direct effects" did *Brown* have on segregated schools in the South? Second, did *Brown* have any "indirect effects" on the emergence of the civil rights movement? The answer to the first question is clear and indisputable. Meaningful reform did not arrive in southern schools until after the Congress passed and President Johnson signed the Civil Rights Act of 1964. More noteworthy, Rosenberg's search for alternative evidence concerning the Court's indirect impact leads him to the same conclusion. The answer to the second question is also no. Others factors, he asserts, such as "economic change, black migration and the concentration of black voters in key electoral states, international awareness, and, in general, a changing society" were the crucial factors in the success of the civil rights movement. By themselves "courts were of limited relevance to the actual progress of civil rights in America" (Rosenberg 1991, 157).

By reexamining the events surrounding the Montgomery bus boycott, however, I show how Rosenberg's reliance on the court-centered approach leads him to misrepresent the significance of *Brown* and the federal judiciary in shaping the strategy of the boycott and in producing its victorious outcome. Montgomery is important to Rosenberg's overall argument on civil rights and to understanding the role *Brown* and the courts had in igniting the civil rights movement for the following three reasons. First, according to most accounts the movement "began" in Montgomery just eighteen months after *Brown* was handed down. Second, as Rosenberg points out, the bus boycott "is mentioned by . . . many civil rights activists [as the inspiration for their participation in the movement], and because it launched both Dr. King's and Reverend Abernathy's civil rights careers" (135). And third, given that Montgomery occurred so soon after *Brown*, many assumed that it provoked Montgomery's African-American community into action. Thus, if I can show that *Brown* and courts had a much larger role in

Montgomery than Rosenberg suggests, his central claim about courts and civil rights is significantly weakened.

In accordance with Michael McCann's approach, then, I begin by attempting to stand in the shoes of the boycott's leaders and participants. From this standpoint, I explore the significance of *Brown* and the importance of courts in the boycott. The outline of this inquiry is a bit different than the one pursued by Rosenberg in his analysis of Montgomery. He asks what impact *Brown* had on Montgomery and on the civil rights movement in general. Finding none, he concludes that *courts* were not very significant in the advancement of civil rights in America. Thus, Rosenberg blurs the line between decisions and institutions. I separate *Brown* as a decision from the federal judiciary as an institution by asking two distinct questions. First, what role did *Brown* play in inspiring the leaders (and to a lesser extent all the participants) of the boycott? Second, what role the did the courts play in shaping the strategy of the boycott and in producing its successful outcome? I suggest, moreover, that the answer to the second question helps to answer the first as well. In other words, if *Brown* had no impact on the boycott, and if King, as Rosenberg alleges, "rejected litigation as a major tool of struggle (Rosenberg 1991, 139)," then we would expect to find the boycott's leaders avoiding the litigation trap. Why pursue a costly campaign in the courts, if there was nothing to be gained? On the other hand, if there was belief in the prospect of *Brown*, then we would expect to find a legal attempt to expand the "separate is inherently unequal" doctrine into the area of transportation. And if this attempt was successful, we would further expect to find an effort to implement the expanded scope of this doctrine by riding desegregated buses.

The story that follows, then, is a reinterpretation of the Montgomery bus boycott in relation to *Brown* and the courts. It builds on the work of those scholars who have examined the boycott or who have reviewed *The Hollow Hope,* and at times attempts to draw out points made by other reviewers of Rosenberg. It also draws heavily on the speeches, articles, books, and memories of the activists in Montgomery.

In offering competing approaches, McCann and Rosenberg have disputed over "source selection," "data interpretation," and "interpreting sources and understanding history" (Rosenberg 1992, 769–774). Specifically, McCann criticizes Rosenberg for relying on "selective quotations" which support his argument but end up leaving the reader "unsatisfied." As McCann notes, "one could easily fill many pages with quotes" from individual activists who emphasize the significance of *Brown* and courts in the emergence of the civil rights movement (McCann1992, 722). In his response, however, Rosenberg stresses that "the major question... is not whether any activist ever mentioned *Brown* or the Court, but rather the importance of the decision for the movement as a whole" (Rosenberg 1992, 767–768).[9] He then points out that McCann's own selection of a quote by Bayard Rustin was made "30 years after the event" and reminds us of the general unreliability of oral histories. In attempting to convey the thought of the time, I rely almost exclusively on the accounts published around the time of the boycott. In addition, given the importance of Ralph Abernathy and Martin Luther King, Jr. to the leadership of the civil rights movement, I pay particular attention to their interpretation of *Brown's* significance in the bus boycott.[10] While one might expect them to downplay the role of *Brown* and the courts in order to escalate their own roles in the victory at Montgomery, I find the opposite to be true. I note that *Brown* figures prominently in their discussions of why the bus boycott took place in 1955–56, as does the federal judiciary in their (especially King's) accounts of the events surrounding the busing campaign. This narrative, however, is not limited to personal accounts of the boycott. Rather, it examines the details of the event with particular attention to how *Brown* and *the courts* affected the participants' actions and the final result. I rely on the activists' stories simply to confirm my claims.

Did Brown Inspire the Leaders of the Bus Boycott?

As Rosenberg points out, a bus boycott had been threatened before the *Brown* decision was handed down on May 17, 1954. Nevertheless, before *Brown*, the Montgomery African–American community sought a negotiated settlement to alter the seating policy on buses. Tensions rose, however, following a meeting in March, 1954, in which city leaders rejected a list of demands put forth by African–American leaders—citing their inconsistency with Alabama's segregation statutes.[11] As Rosenberg writes, "several days later an angry Mrs. [Jo Ann] Robinson," the leader of Women's Political Council—"the most militant and uncompromising organ of the black community"—lashed out at Mayor W.A. Gayle during a phone conversation. As the Mayor recalled, she said "they were going to show me, they were going in the front door and sitting wherever they pleased." Yet, in the following days, no boycott was called and no violations of the Alabama's segregation code were noted in Montgomery. On May 21, 1954, just four days after *Brown*, Jo Ann Robinson renewed her threat in a letter to the Mayor, stating that "even now plans are being made to ride less, or not at all, on our buses."[12] But despite this apparent eagerness to implement *Brown,* the boycott would not begin until eighteen months after the Court announced its decision.

Finding a Test Case

Why did Montgomery's African-American activists wait until December 5, 1955, to call the boycott? The answer lies in the nature of their campaign. Aware of the difficulty of organizing and maintaining mass political action in the South, they waited for the right moment to institute the boycott. The evidence shows that they were not prepared to call a boycott until a test case, challenging the constitutionality of Alabama's segregation statutes, was found to accompany it and to rally the African-American citizens of Montgomery around the overall effort. Indeed, the boycott did not begin until an appropriate test case was found and continued until the U.S. Supreme Court delivered its *per curiam* decision *Browder v. Gayle*, which extended the *Brown* doctrine into the area of transportation by upholding a lower court's ruling striking down Alabama's Jim Crow laws. At this point, November 13, 1956, the boycott was effectively over. It did not officially end for another month when all of the city's legal means were finally exhausted and it became possible to implement *Browder v. Gayle.* The bus boycott, then, was a dual campaign, one in the streets and one in the courts. In other words, it was a campaign to press for the fulfillment of *Brown's* promise by bringing a test case to court and confronting white leaders with the reality of the Court's landmark decision. As Ralph Abernathy wrote in his 1958 masters' thesis:

> The Supreme Court decision of 1954 declaring segregation in the public schools unconstitutional deepened the dissatisfaction of both white and Negro individuals over the state of affairs in their city. Generally, Negroes began to seek a way to implement the decision, and most whites, particularly the political leaders, started to look around for ways and means to circumvent, nullify or resist the court decrees (Garrow 1989, 109).[13]

The first possible test case involved a March 2, 1955, incident in which Claudette Colvin, a fifteen year-old African-American girl, was dragged from a city bus by the police for refusing to give up her seat to newly-boarding white passengers. Following her arrest, African-American leaders acted immediately. Rosa Parks, a longtime member of the NAACP and a NAACP Youth Council advisor to Colvin, began raising funds for her legal defense. E.D. Nixon, president of the Montgomery chapter of the NAACP, and Jo Ann Robinson began interviewing Colvin with the intention of using her case to challenge the constitutionality of Montgomery's bus seating practices. Nixon also consulted privately with Clifford Durr, a liberal white lawyer who had worked in the Franklin Roosevelt administration and who was a sponsor of a controversial integrated school in Tennessee and was a relative through marriage of Justice Hugo Black. (According to Taylor Branch, Durr's defense of the Highlander Folk School as a "sensible, patriotic experiment in racial democracy . . . during the passions of the Joseph McCarthy hearings and the *Brown* case" landed him, his wife, and some of the school's other sponsors before James Eastland's Senate Internal Security Subcommittee. As Branch writes, the Mississippi senator's characterization of Highlander as "freakish, mongrelized, and basically Communist" infuriated Durr so much that, on television, he challenged Eastland to a fist fight. Not surprisingly, this confrontation did little to stimulate Durr's Montgomery law practice.) Also involved in the discussions was Fred Gray, a young black lawyer and part-time preacher, who agreed to represent Colvin. Durr had been advising Gray on the "eccentricities of the Montgomery courts, and now they weighed the prospects of turning the Colvin defense into an attack on segregation." In the end, the group concluded that Colvin's immaturity—she was "prone to breakdowns and outbursts of profanity"—and present condition—she was pregnant and not married—prevented her from becoming the representative of the boycott. "Even if Montgomery Negroes were willing to rally behind an unwed pregnant teenager—which they were not—her circumstances would make her an extremely vulnerable standard-bearer" (Branch 1988, 121–123).

In October, 1955, another arrest was made for a violation of the bus seating policy. Once again, African-American activists prepared themselves for action. Soon after the arrest, however, Nixon decided that Mary Louise Smith "was no better suited to stand at the rallying point than was Claudette Colvin." Smith was a country girl living in a "see-though clapboard shack" with an alcoholic father. The Smith family, Nixon concluded, would fare poorly in newspaper interviews about the case. As he put it, "we wouldn't have a leg to stand on." Asserting that the principle of the case outweighed Smith's shortcomings, leaders of the Women's Political Council (WPC) objected to this decision. But in the end, Smith paid the fine and the effort to find a test case continued (Branch 1988, 121–127). Apparently, Nixon's NAACP training had a clear and dominant impact on the leaders' strategy and the delay of the boycott.

When Rosa Parks was arrested two months later (December 1, 1955), the situation was different. As a respected member of the community, Parks was thought to be the perfect person to represent the legal challenge. Although she had not been "planted" for a test case by the NAACP as many thought, her connections to this organization—she was a former secretary at the local branch—and to Nixon made it difficult to put these rumors to rest.[14] On the day of the arrest, before Nixon went to the jail to secure her release, he picked up Clifford Durr and his wife, Virginia Durr. Mrs. Durr had known Parks, both through her work as seamstress and her activities with the NAACP. She had also recommended that Parks spend a week at the Highlander School to attend an interracial workshop. "Parks had done so, returning to say that her eyes had been opened to new possibilities of harmony between the races." Once at the jail, Mr. Durr and Nixon began discussing Parks' case. It was Durr's opinion that despite the fact that they would first have to go to state court, this was the case they had been waiting for. Nixon then asked Parks if she was willing to put herself and her family through such an ordeal. Although her husband objected, pleading "the white folks will kill you, Rosa," Parks decided that she would go forward with the case (Branch 1988, 130–31).

The Boycott Begins

That night, Jo Ann Robinson and other members of the WPC worked into the morning hours on a letter of protest. At three o'clock in the morning Robinson called Nixon and discussed the idea of a one-day bus boycott to coincide with Parks' appearance in court on the following Monday. Nixon agreed and told her "that he planned to summon Montgomery's leading Negroes to a planning meeting the very next day, at which both the legal defense and the boycott would be organized." At five in the morning Nixon made calls to Abernathy and King. The meeting was held in Nixon's absence (as a train porter, he was working the Montgomery-Atlanta run), in the basement of King's

Dexter Street Church, which, ironically, sat just across the street from Alabama's capitol building. After much discussion, this "disorderly" group of fifty leading black citizens basically agreed to Nixon's proposed plans. And in the following days, a massive effort was made to inform Montgomery's African–American community of the upcoming boycott. Sermons, leaflets, and word of mouth did the job, for on the morning of December 5th, the buses were nearly empty. The Montgomery bus boycott had begun on an impressive note (Branch, 1988, 132–35).

Later that morning Parks was convicted and fined ten dollars and court costs (four dollars). According to King's account in *Stride Toward Freedom*, Parks's arrest and conviction "had a twofold impact: it was a precipitating factor to arouse the Negroes to positive action; and it was a test of the validity of the segregation law itself."[15] That night, when the 26-year-old King, now head of the newly formed Montgomery Improvement Association (MIA), spoke to an overflowing crowd of 5,000 that had gathered at the Holt Street Church, he alluded to their connection with *Brown* and the Court. "If we're wrong, the Supreme Court is wrong. If we're wrong, the Constitution is wrong. If we're wrong, God Almighty is wrong" (Garrow 1986, 15). King explained in *Stride Toward Freedom,* during the days between the arrest and beginning of the boycott, he struggled with the notion that Montgomery blacks were preparing to use tactics similar to those of the White Citizens Councils. As he writes, these councils " had their birth in Mississippi a few months after the Supreme Court's school decision," and were designed to "preserve segregation." How did he reconcile this conflict?:

> I had to recognize that the boycott method could be used to unethical and unchristian ends. I had to concede, further, that this was the method used so often by the White Citizens Councils to deprive many Negroes, as well as white persons of good will, of the basic necessities of life. But certainly, I said to myself, our pending actions could not be interpreted in this light. . . .We would use this method to give birth to justice and freedom, and also to urge men to *comply with the law of the land;* The White Citizens Councils used it to perpetuate the reign of injustice and human servitude, and urged men *to defy the law of the land* (1958, 50–51; 55, emphasis added).

King also made the distinction in his Holt Street Church address on the night of December 5th by noting that "there will be no crosses burned at any bus stops in Montgomery. There will be no white persons pulled out of their homes and taken out to some distant road and murdered. There will be nobody among us who will stand up and defy the Constitution. We only assemble here because of our desire to see right exist."[16]

Abernathy, King, and *Brown*

Other evidence points to an even more direct link between *Brown*, the Court, and the bus boycott. Admittedly, as Rosenberg points out (quoting Branch), "there were no street celebrations in Negro communities" following the Court's 1954 decision. He continues by quoting Abernathy's *And The Walls Came Tumbling Down* (1989). Abernathy wrote that "most blacks in the Deep South states looked with curiosity at what was going on in the high courts, shrugged their shoulders, and went back to their day-to-day lives. . . . After all, they had waited a lifetime and seen no change at all." Through the use of these ellipses, however, Rosenberg leaves out "not necessarily disbelieving the changes that people said were about to occur, but not necessarily believing them either." Moreover, in the following sentence (overlooked by Rosenberg), Abernathy specifically addresses *Brown's* impact on the elites in the African–American community: "But among the educated blacks, and particularly among the clergy, there was talk—lots of talk—and with each subtle shift in the political landscape we eyed the new situation and calculated our chances of forcing the issues, of bringing about our freedom more quickly." Abernathy goes on to note the generational division within the clergy over the pace of social reform efforts. Here he states: "So even though Topeka, Kansas, was a long way from Montgomery, Alabama—and even though many blacks were still not ready to risk their lives for their freedom—something was in the air, an invigorating feeling, like the first chill of autumn" (Abernathy 1989, 114–116). Ten pages later, he writes of a meeting before the boycott between himself, King, and King's predecessor at the Dexter Street Church, Vernon Johns, in which the three agreed that *Brown* "had altered forever the conditions on which the continuing struggle would be predicated. No longer was the law unambiguously on the side of Jim Crow. It now appeared as if the law was on our side, that the federal government might eventually be pressed into service in our fight for freedom" (1989, 126).[17] In addition, according to the editors of the King's papers, "following the *Brown* decision, [Abernathy] chaired the state Sunday School and Baptist Training Union Congress committee to assess the ruling. In September 1954, this committee issued a report (titled "The Report of the Committee on the Recent Supreme Court Ruling on Segregation in Public Education") insisting that Christians should struggle against injustice." Abernathy "then urged the ministers to 'return to their respective communities to fight this evil [of segregation] until Black Men of Alabama are privileged to enjoy every God-given opportunity as any other man'" (Luker, Russel, and Holloran, 1994, 35).

King also alluded to the "new feeling" and altered conditions brought on by the Court's desegregation decision before the boycott began.[18] Eight months after the decision was handed down, the new pastor of Montgomery's Dexter Avenue Baptist Church, "blasted away at apathy among church leaders in the field of civil rights," by calling for "a realistic approach to progress in race relations." As the *Birmingham World* reported, this approach incorporated three methods: (1) "getting the ballot," since King believed "a voteless people is a powerless people"; (2) "joining the NAACP and putting some big money into the freedom fight;" and (3) "using the courts more to obtain unjustly denied rights." According to this account, King "called for an immediate start toward the implementation of the May 17 U.S. Supreme Court decision banning the segregated school system." This call to "implement" *Brown* was similar one the King had made a few weeks earlier in an address to the Montgomery branch of the NAACP and its women's auxiliary. According to notes taken by none other than branch secretary Rosa Parks, King told the members: "We have come a long way, but still have a long way to go. We owe a debt of gratitude to those [who] made possible the Supreme Court decision of May 17." In making these stirring statements, King may have taken a cue from his politically active father. Indeed, in June 1954, just a few weeks after the decision, King, Sr., gave "rousing address to ten thousand Baptists gathered in Birmingham for the National Sunday School and Baptist Training Union Congress. Directing his ire at the city's mayor and superintendent of schools in the audience," he declared that "we have learned the way to the Supreme Court and we will call upon it again and again for those rights guaranteed by the Constitution. It took the highest court eighty-nine years to interpret a law that was already on the statute books; now, how long will it take for the law to be enforced?"[19]

Near the boycott's end, King Jr., again spoke of the significance of *Brown*. He began an address, delivered to the First Annual Institute on Non-Violence and Social Change (taking place in Montgomery) by explaining the "international aspect" of the long history of oppression against peoples of color. He then emphasized the tragedies of American slavery through an analysis of *Dred Scott*, before moving on to a discussion of *Plessy v. Ferguson*. Clearly, he thought the Court's previous actions had a direct impact on the lives on African-Americans for many years. From this point, he examined the development of the "New Negro" which he understood as related to economic change, the general weariness of the African American community, the decline of illiteracy, and the power of religion. Next, he spoke about the impact of *Brown*:

> Along with the emergence of a "New Negro," with a new sense of dignity and destiny, came that memorable decision of May 17, 1954. In this decision the Supreme Court of this nation unanimously affirmed that the old Plessy Doctrine must go. This decision came as a legal and sociological death blow to an evil that had occupied the throne of American life for several decades. It affirmed in no uncertain terms that separate facilities are inherently unequal and that to segregate a child because of his race is to deny him equal protection of the law. With the coming of this great decision we could gradually see the old order of segregation and discrimination passing away, and the new order of freedom and justice coming into being. Let nobody fool you, all of the loud noises that you hear today from the legislative halls of the South in terms of "interposition" and nullification," and of outlawing the NAACP are merely the death groans from a dying system. The older order is passing away, and the new order is coming into being. We are witnessing in our day the birth of a new age, with a new structure of freedom and justice (King, 1956).[20]

As these words and this review of the events surrounding the beginning of the Montgomery bus boycott clearly show, the Court's decision had a significant impact on the thinking of the city's African-American leaders. In sum, they viewed the Court as their ally. They understood that absent the power of the sword the federal judiciary could not implement *Brown* by itself. By continuously challenging the southern status quo, however, they could force the other institutions to act. With *Brown*, there was now reason to expect that their great efforts and sacrifices would not go unnoticed. For King, of course, the ultimate responsibility for action still lay with African-Americans themselves, but they could now see light at the end of the tunnel. To attain integration, many methods of action would be required to force compliance with *Brown*, and to finally destroy Jim Crow. Few people, including the justices of the Court, expected otherwise. As King put it in an address to the annual convention of the NAACP seven months into the boycott:

[The boycott is] a new and creative method which might be added to the several methods which we must use to make integration a reality. We must continue the struggle though legislation. No one should underestimate the power of this method. We must continue to gain the ballot, *and urge the executive and legislative branches of our Government to follow the example so courageously set by the judicial branch.* Also, we must depend on the growing group of white liberals, both North and South, who are still willing to take a stand for justice. But, in the final analysis, the problem of obtaining full equality is a problem for which the Negro himself must assume the primary responsibility. Integration will not be some lavish dish that the white man will pass out on a silver platter. If integration is to be a reality, we must be willing to work hard for it, sacrifice for it, and even die for it if necessary. I have no doubt that by 1963 we will have won the legal battle. *On May 17, 1954, segregation confronted its legal death. But after the legal battle is won, there is the great problem of lifting the noble precepts of our Constitution from the dusty files of unimplemented court decisions. The problem of implementation will be carried out mainly by the Negro's refusal to cooperate with segregation* (1956, emphasis added).

King and the Use of Litigation

In his analysis of Martin Luther King's views, Rosenberg claims that King rejected legal effort as a major tool in the struggle (Rosenberg 1991, 138). To be sure, following the NAACP's victory in *Brown,* King likely felt that the NAACP needed to be reminded of the fact that court decisions would not implement themselves, and that a more complex and realistic approach would be required to achieve integration. But King *did* believe that a litigation strategy was part of this approach. As King put it in his keynote address in front of Lincoln Memorial during the "Prayer Pilgrimage for Freedom," on 17 May 1957, celebrating the third anniversary of the Supreme Court's *Brown* decision (a rally he played a significant role in organizing): "In our nation, under the guidance of the superb legal staff of the NAACP, we have been able, through the courts, to remove the legal basis of segregation. This is by far one of the most marvelous achievements of our generation. Every person of good will is profoundly indebted to the NAACP for its noble work." He continued by noting:

We must not, however, remain satisfied with a court 'victory' over our white brothers. We must respond to every decision with an understanding of those who have opposed us and with an appreciation of the difficult adjustments that the court orders pose for them. We must act in such a way as to make possible a coming-together of white people and colored people on the basis of a real harmony of interest and understanding" (King 1986, 197–200).

Thus, in the final analysis, I tend to agree with King's assessment of the *Brown's* impact on the boycott:

> Many will inevitably raise the question, why did this event take place in Montgomery, Alabama, in 1955? Some have suggested that the Supreme Court decision, handed down less than two years before, had given new hope of eventual justice to Negroes everywhere, and fired them with the necessary spark of encouragement to rise against their oppression. But although this might help to explain why the protest occurred when it did, it cannot explain why it happened in Montgomery.[21]

My purpose, however, has not been to explain what made Montgomery special. Rather, I have tried to show the link between *Brown* and the boycott. Despite an incentive to downplay the decision in an attempt to inspire African Americans through religious appeals expounding upon the "divine dimension," King clearly articulated a belief that the Court's decision had a significant role igniting the movement. In the conclusion of *Stride Toward Freedom*, he returns to this issue through a discussion of the inconsistency between democracy and Christianity, on one hand, and segregation and discrimination on the other:

> This contradiction has disturbed the consciences of whites both North and South, and has caused many of them to see that segregation is basically evil. Climaxing this process was the Supreme Court's decision outlawing segregation in the public schools. For all men of good will May 17, 1954, marked a joyous end to the long night of enforced segregation. In unequivocal language the Court affirmed that "separate but equal" facilities are inherently unequal, and that to segregate a child on the basis of his race is to deny that child equal protection of the law. *This decision brought hope to millions of disinherited Negroes who had formerly dared only to dream of freedom. It further enhanced the Negro's sense of dignity and gave him even greater determination to achieve justice* (1958, 191, emphasis added).

For King, then, the movement began "when the most sublime principles of American democracy—imperfectly realized for almost two centuries—began fulfilling themselves and met with the brutal resistance of forces seeking to contract and repress freedom's growth." It was "not produced by outside agitators, NAACP'ers, Montgomery Protesters, or even the Supreme Court." However, these individuals and institutions revealed the racial "cleavage" in American society and sparked the "massive resistance" to integration which in turn further catalyzed the movement (1958, 192).[22]

Assessing the Importance of Courts in the Bus Boycott

Despite this substantial evidence about the impact *Brown* had on the boycott's leaders, one (i.e. Rosenberg) might still argue that these words were simply rhetoric designed to appeal to a wider audience and therefore had little effect on the movement's beginnings in Montgomery. If so, we would expect King and the boycott leaders to avoid taking their fight to court.[23] Yet, once again, we find the opposite to be true. As Robert Jerome Glennon writes, "The legal system—more accurately federal law and federal judges—played a pivotal, indeed controlling, role in integrating Montgomery's buses." It is true that most accounts of Montgomery do not emphasize the role of the legal system in the strategy and success of the boycott. Fortunately, the recent work of Glennon (and in a different fashion, Randall Kennedy), have filled this gap in the literature. Given that their work provides a full picture of the connection between the courts and the boycott, a brief synthesis here is sufficient (Glennon 1991; Kennedy 1989).

As already noted above, the boycott did not begin until a suitable test case was found. Parks's case, however, was not the one that eventually reached the Supreme Court. Following the arrest of King on January 26, 1956, for speeding (thirty miles an hour in a twenty-five mile an hour zone), Durr, Gray, and a second African-American lawyer Charles Langford, began considering a suggestion made to them by the NAACP's Robert Carter. Carter had advised the MIA to take the legal offensive by filing a separate case in federal court explicitly challenging Alabama's segregation codes.[24] Reluctant to move beyond its initial list of three demands—"first-come first-served seating, courteous treatment, and considering employment of African-American drivers"—the MIA leadership decided against the maneuver. Then, four days later, with his wife Coretta at home with their infant daughter, a bomb exploded on King's front porch. After this incident and the violence that nearly erupted following it (eased only by a nonviolent plea from King), the MIA leadership changed its mind. Relying on *Brown*, Gray and Langford filed *Browder v. Gayle* on February 1, 1956. The suit sought an "injunction against further segregated seating on the buses . . . and against police harassment of the car pool" which had been set up by the MIA to take the place of the boycotted buses (Glennon 1991, 68-69).[25]

Carter, who had worked on a similar case in South Carolina, further assisted MIA lawyers as they prepared for the case. The South

Carolina case involved a suit for damages (but not injunctive relief) by Sarah Mae Flemming, who had been elbowed in the stomach by a bus driver for sitting in the front section and attempting to exit through the front door. After the federal district court dismissed the case, stating that *Brown* had been limited to the area of education, Carter worked on the appeal with the local counsel. On July 14, 1955, four and a half months before the beginning of the boycott, the U.S. Court of Appeals for the Fourth Circuit "reversed and remanded the case for further proceedings" by reasoning "that *Brown* had significantly undermined the continuing validity of *Plessy* and, although the Supreme Court had not explicitly overruled *Plessy,* that the Supreme Court probably intended the principle of *Brown* to apply to transportation." Significantly, "the fourth circuit's decision made headlines in Montgomery" (Glennon, 70).

When the Supreme Court dismissed the South Carolina's bus company's appeal in *Flemming* on procedural grounds in a *per curiam* decision on April 23, 1956, Montgomery's bus company (along with those in twenty one other southern cities) attempted to end the boycott by itself desegregating the buses. In doing so, it instructed its drivers:

> We have been advised that today Monday, April 23, 1956, the Supreme Court of the United States rendered a decision the effect of which is to hold unconstitutional segregation of races on buses. Under the circumstances The Company has *no choice* except to discontinue the practice of segregation of passengers on account of race and drivers will no longer assign seats to passengers by reason of their race (Glennon 1991, 74).

Not surprisingly, city leaders objected strenuously and successfully enjoined the company from implementing the policy. Indeed, the Supreme Court had rejected the *Flemming* appeal because it was premature, and therefore, had not explicitly overruled *Plessy.* Still, when the city sought an injunction against the bus company to comply with the state and city segregation codes, Judge Walter B. Jones of the Montgomery Circuit Court could have read the writing on the wall by following the trend set out in *Flemming* or by extending the *Brown* doctrine to transportation. He didn't. Instead, he "insisted that neither the Congress nor the Supreme Court could regulate segregation on intrastate buses because the Constitution does not include a textual provision explicitly granting this power to the federal government;"

thereby repudiating, "in one sweep . . . the idea of implied or inferred powers, a concept embedded in our constitutional heritage since 1819" (Glennon, 74, 77).

At this point, the MIA leadership continued to assert that the boycott would end if the original demands were granted. Yet, city officials felt as always that such a concession would escalate the African–American community's desire for equal status. As the attorney for the bus company noted at the start of the boycott: "If we granted the Negroes these demands, they would go about boasting of a victory that they had won over the white people; and this we will not stand for" (Glennon, 65). As King concluded, the fate of the boycott now rested in the hands of federal judges and the outcome of *Browder v. Gayle* (Glennon, 77).[26] On May 11, 1956, a three-judge federal district court held an evidentiary hearing. In *Stride Toward Freedom,* King recounted how he felt at that moment:

> It was a great relief to be in a federal court. Here the atmosphere of justice prevailed. No one can understand the feeling that comes to a Southern Negro on entering a federal court unless he sees with his own eyes and feels with his own soul the tragic sabotage of justice in the city and state courts of the South. The Negro goes into these courts knowing that the cards are stacked against him. Here he is virtually certain to face a prejudiced jury or a biased judge, and is openly robbed with little hope of redress. But the Southern Negro goes into the federal court with a feeling that he has an honest chance of justice before the law (1958, 151–52).

According to King, Carter's argument was "brilliant," as he relied on *Brown* to attack Alabama's still valid transportation statutes (1958, 153). As the judges took the case under consideration, state officials took action to end the boycott. On June 1, Alabama's attorney general sought to bar the NAACP from operating in the state. Once again, the case came before Montgomery's Judge Jones. On that same day, Jones enjoined the organization from performing its activities in the state and demanded that it turn over all relevant materials, including documents pertaining the *Browder* case and a complete list of its Alabama members. In what became a virtual tug of war between Alabama judges and federal judges, four days later (June 5) the federal district reached its decision in *Browder.* By a vote of 2–1, the court declared the Jim Crow laws of the state and the city's bus seating policy unconstitutional. As King put it, "The battle was not yet won.

We would have to walk and sacrifice for several more months, while the city appealed the case. But at least we could walk with new hope. Now it was only a matter of time" (1958, 153).

It would take six more months before the city's appeals were concluded. Moreover, as the boycott dragged on into November, city officials moved to enjoin the MIA from operating its car pool. The hearing in the car pool case was scheduled for November 13, 1956; and it was to be heard by the same judge who had convicted Parks and King (for violating the antiboycotting law). For King, the evening before the hearing was "the darkest hour just before dawn" (1958, 158). Without the car pool, thousands would have to walk to and from work if the boycott was to survive. During the hearing, however, word came from Washington that the Supreme Court had upheld the lower court's ruling in *Browder*. "Citing *Brown* and two other summary affirmances involving segregation in public beaches," the Court issued its one-sentence *per curiam* opinion effectively overturning *Plessy* without even citing it (Glennon 1991, 84).

Unlike the reaction after *Brown,* following *Browder* Montgomery's African–American community was said to be "naturally jubilant." King hailed the ruling as a "glorious day-break" in the "long night of enforced segregation," and a bystander rejoiced: "God Almighty has spoken from Washington D.C." On the night of November 14, "the eight thousand men and women who crowded in and around [two of Montgomery's] churches were in high spirits" (King, 1958, 160). George Barrett of *The New York Times,* reported in a December 12, 1956 article that "as the new test period now unfolds, the mood of Montgomery, the mood of the emerging Southern Negro here who has seen the Supreme Court back up his right, the mood of the white Southerner here who still bitterly resents and opposes the Supreme Court stand on desegregation can all be put into two words—watching and waiting." Mayor Gayle noted that "the federal court is the real key to what will probably happen here in Montgomery. Nobody is fixin' to go to the Federal pen." For his part, Barrett thought the words of a mother of six summed upon the feeling among Montgomery's African Americans: "We know, now, that we're free citizens of the United States. Now we are aiming to become free citizens of Alabama. Our state motto, you know is 'We Dare Defend Our Rights.' It says nothing about just white rights" (Barrett, 48–50). On December 20, 1956, with the city's legal maneuvers exhausted, the boycott ended as members of the MIA leadership boarded a bus and sat in the front.

Legal Mobilization and Reform: School Finance Litigation in New Jersey, 1970–1985

Michael Paris

Introduction

The New Jersey Constitution states that "The Legislature shall provide for the maintenance and support of a thorough and efficient system of free public schools for the instruction of all children between the ages of five and eighteen" (*New Jersey Constitution*, art. 8, sec. 4). Since the early 1970s, education finance reformers based in the Garden State's urban centers have won a series of increasingly favorable interpretations of this "thorough and efficient" clause from New Jersey courts. From the beginning, the New Jersey Supreme Court accepted reformers' invitation to see an individual right to "equality of educational opportunity" in the mandate to "provide . . . a thorough and efficient system" (*Robinson v. Cahill*, 303 A.2d 273 [1973]). This doctrinal transformation, in turn, has sparked an ongoing conflict over the meaning of "equal educational opportunity" in relation to school finance policy.

Who were these education finance reformers? What were they trying to accomplish, and how did they organize their project? Did their central reliance upon law and courts help shape ideas, mobilize interests, and influence political institutions and behaviors? What constraints and opportunities did they face along the way? Did they succeed or fail?

The New Jersey school finance controversy encompasses two related cases at state constitutional law, *Robinson v. Cahill* (1970–1976), and *Abbott v. Burke* (1981–1996). This discussion offers an interpretive account of the origins and development of reformers' efforts, covering the period from 1970 through 1985. It will also provide a brief summary of events in *Abbott* since then. In telling this story, I rely upon interviews with attorneys and other reformers, and upon analysis of various secondary sources and public documents.[27]

In approaching these materials, I draw upon certain elements of Michael McCann's model. Specifically, this case study focuses on the self-understandings of reformers, highlighting: their moral vision and political goals with respect to public education and school finance; the choices that they made in framing and constructing their legal challenges; and how they themselves understood the relationship between law and politics in what they were doing. This case study also views legal discourse and judicial opinions as potentially effective in shaping political processes and policy outcomes, albeit not in any simple or direct way. And, finally, it seeks to examine the role of law and courts in changing the context for political action *over time*.

Through this case study, I hope to demonstrate the utility of McCann's model and to explore possibilities for building upon it.

Education Finance and Reform Litigation Generally

Historically, the basic problem in American school finance, as one court put it, has been that "the property rich [school] districts can tax low and spend high while the property poor districts must tax high merely to spend low" (*Edgewood Ind. Sch. Dist. v. Kirby*, 777 S.W.2d 391 [Texas, 1989]).[28] Legal challenges to state school finance systems began in the late 1960s. In several states, reformers relied upon federal equal protection claims in attacking school finance systems.[29] As is well-known, the United States Supreme Court rejected these claims in *San Antonio v. Rodriguez* (1973). However, shortly after *Rodriguez* came down, the New Jersey Supreme Court decided in favor of plaintiffs in *Robinson v. Cahill* on state constitutional grounds. Since then, finance reform litigation has occurred in the state courts of over half of the states.[30]

New Jersey: Contextual Considerations

Before going into the details of reformers' efforts in New Jersey, I note three interrelated points about the social and political context in which they have operated. First, reformers face a tradition of intense localism. New Jersey's 7.8 million inhabitants reside in 567 municipalities and 614 local school districts. New Jersey has more municipalities per square mile than any other state. Until very recently, this tradition of localism was reflected in the weakness of state-level political institutions.[31]

Second, the state-local tension overlaps with a more modern one between urban and suburban areas. Sandwiched between Philadelphia and New York City, New Jersey has a long-standing identity as a "suburban state." It is now, as Barbara G. Salmore and Stephen A. Salmore have put it, a suburban state in an era in which "suburban politics has come of age." The economic boom and massive demographic shifts of the post-World War II era hit New Jersey with particular force, as the expansion of affluent white suburbs went hand in hand with the increasing spatial and social isolation of blacks and, more recently, Hispanics, in impoverished urban centers. The racial disorders across northern New Jersey in 1967 only fueled this pattern of separation. Today, more than half the residents of Newark, Camden, and Trenton are black, and there are large concentrations of minorities in East Orange, Elizabeth, Irvington, Jersey City, Paterson, and Plainfield as well.[32]

Third, the adoption of a new constitution in 1947 and the United States Supreme Court's reapportionment decisions in the 1960s laid the groundwork for the emergence of state-level politics and the development of state institutions. The 1947 charter dramatically altered the institutional bases for the exercise of state executive and judicial power. The new constitution made the office of the governor "among the strongest in the nation,"[33] and entirely restructured the state's archaic judicial system.

On the judicial front, the leading "good government" reformer was Arthur T. Vanderbilt. Vanderbilt combined Hamiltonian ideas about judicial independence and integrity with a penchant for the activist strand of the "sociological jurisprudence" characteristic of the Progressive Era. He was the primary architect of the new system, and also served as Chief Justice between 1948 and 1957. In his opinions and extrajudicial writings, Vanderbilt "categorically rejected the standard canons of judicial restraint." Looking back over Vanderbilt's reform legacy, former Chief Justice Robert N. Wilentz (1979–1996) stated that "the experience still moves us" in that "it produced a refusal to accept rules that bear no present relationship to the needs of society and a willingness to subject legal doctrine to a more penetrating analysis based on the social realities of the time." In short, New Jersey's unique legal culture and political structures have tended to favor independent judicial action in politics. Or, as another former justice put it in the mid-1970s, "no thicket was too political for us."[34]

Robinson v. Cahill and the Public School Education Act of 1975

The school finance controversy in the Garden State began in 1970 when an attorney in private practice in Jersey City (Harry Ruvoldt, Jr.) filed suit on behalf of municipal officials and school children. Just before trial in late 1971, the Newark chapters of the American Civil Liberties Union (ACLU) and the National Association for the Advancement of Colored People (NAACP) sought and were granted amicus status. Jointly, they were represented by Rutgers law professor Paul Tractenberg. Whereas Ruvoldt sought to replicate the federal equal protection arguments that had recently succeeded in California (*Serrano*), Tractenberg focused his attention on the state constitution's education (or "thorough and efficient") clause, which, he argued, implied state assurance of an "adequate education" for all children, as well as the level of funding sufficient to secure this right. Neither attorney gave much thought to the relationship between law and politics, or to broader mobilizations or alliances of any sort. Thus, this reform effort was "politically thin" at the outset and would remain so throughout *Robinson*. As Scheingold, Rosenberg, and McCann would lead us to suspect, the immediate result of this litigation would be disappointing. But, as the transition from *Robinson* to *Abbott* illustrates, judicial opinions and even modest legislative reforms can have important "feedback" or "radiating effects."[35]

In 1972, a state trial court struck down the existing school finance system, resting primarily on plaintiffs' federal equal protection claims. The New Jersey Supreme Court heard arguments in the case in January 1973; in April, it rendered a unanimous decision in favor of reformers.[36]

Writing for the court in *Robinson I*, Chief Justice Weintraub did not pause over the trial court's findings of fact. There were vast disparities in educational expenditures across school districts; these disparities were substantially related to district wealth; and "the quality of educational opportunity" did "depend in substantial measure upon the number of dollars invested, notwithstanding that the impact upon students may be unequal because of other factors, natural or environmental." The court, however, based its decision solely upon the state constitution's education clause. Following Tractenberg's lead, Chief Justice Weintraub undertook a brief review of the origins and development of New Jersey's public school system during the late nineteenth century, and then located the adoption of the education clause in 1875 within this history. Although absolute equality in expenditures per pupil was clearly not required, the court wrote, "we do not doubt that an equal educational opportunity for children was precisely in mind" (294). What, then, could this "equal educational opportunity" possibly mean?

To answer this question, the court turned to an 1895 case interpreting the thorough and efficient (T & E) clause. In *Landis v. Ashworth*, plaintiffs had invoked the T & E clause to challenge a state law requiring state education taxes to be returned to the county of origin. Although the *Landis* court rejected the challenge, Chief Justice Weintraub wrote, it did hold that the T & E clause "required equality within the intended range of that amendment, permitting local decisions only above and beyond that mandated education" (294). Thus, the T & E clause required provision of some adequate minimum level of "educational opportunity." The court then elaborated upon the meaning of this "adequate minimum," in four ways. In the long run, its interpretive methods would turn out to be as important as its vague substantive commentary.

First, and most importantly, the court looked to *Landis* in arguing that the attributes of this individual right to (some) "adequate minimum" had to be understood as "evolving" over time. Secondary education, for example, was not part of the constitutional mandate in 1895, but today it certainly was. Second, the court then anchored this notion of evolution over time to modern conceptions of the functions of public education in the United States: "The Constitution's guarantee must be understood to embrace that educational opportunity which is needed *in the contemporary setting* to equip a child for his role as a citizen and as a competitor in the labor market" (295, emphasis added).

Third, Chief Justice Weintraub emphasized that, whatever this "constitutional mandate" meant, it was the state's duty to ensure that all children would have the benefit of it: "Whether the state acts directly or imposes the role upon local government, the end product must be what the Constitution commands" (294, 297). Now this might seem an obvious thing to say about a state constitutional provision. However, it is worth noting because it strikes hard against the web of "local control" justifications for existing finance arrangements. Although institutionally entrenched and widely endorsed, "local control" does not have constitutional status in *Robinson*. Rather, it is rendered as one possible means to a more important, constitutionally mandated end.[37]

Finally, the court turned to the ultimate question at hand—did the current finance system meet this standard? In holding that it did not, however, it pointed in two seemingly different directions. This tension would structure further conflict as other actors attempted to interpret and respond to *Robinson*. On one hand, Chief Justice Weintraub endorsed the trial court's finding of unconstitutionality on the basis of "discrepancies in dollar input per pupil." Dollar inputs were "plainly relevant," and the current funding scheme had "no apparent relation to the mandate for equal educational opportunity" (296). On the other hand, the Court expressed reservations about using dollar inputs as its sole standard, and complained that "the State has never spelled out the content of the educational opportunity the Constitution requires" (295).

The court's opinion, then, was not a model of clarity. For example, it was difficult to tell whether compliance would amount to reducing dollar disparities (and if so, by how much), or simply "raising the floor," or some combination of these. Nor was it easy to discern whether the locus of the problem was really in the state's failure to define and regulate, thereby implying that the adequacy of a future funding scheme would have to be evaluated in these (as yet undefined) terms. In any event, the court gave the legislature until December 31, 1974 to enact a new school finance system (*Robinson II*, 306 A.2d 65 [1973]).

As Richard Lehne puts it, over the next three years, *Robinson* "involved all of the state's institutions in a protracted minuet of pronouncements, proposals, and rejections" (1978, 19). For the most part, the reform attorneys who initiated the suit would play the role of wallflower, while state officials and established educational interest groups would occupy center stage at the dance.

In 1974, a newly elected Democratic Governor (Brendan Byrne) proposed an ambitious reform package. However, the governor's plan ultimately failed when the state senate refused to go along, and 1974 ended without the legislative action required by the court.[38] Rebuffed by the legislature, the governor then adopted the stance of lead plaintiff. In January 1975, he submitted to the court a "motion for an order in aid of judgment" in which he urged the justices to take strong remedial action. However, the court declined to intervene. It set a new deadline of October 1, 1975, and set forth a provisional remedy to take effect in the event that the legislature failed to act. On September 29, 1975, the legislature finally passed the Public School Education Act (also known as "Chapter 212"). The governor promptly signed the bill and then submitted it to the court for review.[39]

Given its origins in the court's decision in *Robinson I*, it is not surprising that the Public School Education Act of 1975 ("Chapter 212") was a complicated piece of legislation. The court's hand can be seen in its basic structure, if not in its overall spirit. Precatory language in Chapter 212 tracked the court's crucial departure in acknowledging that "the sufficiency of education" was "a growing and evolving concept." Beyond this, the law contained two basic components mirroring the tension between regulation and finance in the court's opinion. Article II of the act stated "goals," and set forth "standards" and "guidelines" for administrative evaluation and enforcement. Article III contained the new finance provisions setting up a modified guaranteed tax base system.

Article II defined the goal of "a thorough and efficient system" as providing "all children in New Jersey, regardless of socioeconomic status or geographic location, [with] the educational opportunity which will prepare them to function politically, economically and socially in a democratic society." It then set forth ten elements of a "T & E system":

a. establishment of educational goals at both the state and local levels;
b. encouragement of public involvement in the establishment of educational goals;
c. Instruction intended to produce the attainment of reasonable levels of proficiency in the basic communication and computational skills;
d. a breadth of program offerings designed to develop the individual talents and abilities of pupils;
e. programs and supportive services for all pupils, especially those who are educationally disadvantaged or who have special educational needs;
f. adequately equipped, sanitary and secure physical facilities and adequate materials and supplies;
g. qualified instructional and other personnel;
h. efficient administrative procedures;
i. an adequate State program of research and development; and
j. evaluation and monitoring programs at both the State and local levels.

These provisions were followed in Article II with a sweeping delegation of power to the state education department.[40]

The finance provisions of Chapter 212 (Article III of the act) set up a *modified* guaranteed tax base (GTB) system. The basic thrust of a "pure" GTB system is "equal tax yield for equal tax effort." In New Jersey, the potentially high costs of equalizing tax yield were limited in various ways. The law set up various categories of state aid to education. Only the first, "equalization aid," embraced the GTB theory, and limits were placed on how much aid would be provided, even within this category. As the statute operated over the years ahead, about half of all state aid dollars would be allocated as equalization aid.[41]

According to Lehne, the public interest lawyers and other "urban reformers" who had joined them

> objected strenuously to the program the legislature had just enacted. They complained that the state had not defined its constitutional obligation in any discernible way . . .; they pointed out that the new financial provisions were unrelated to the educational need of students; and they protested that the hard-pressed urban areas, which had brought the suit in the first place, were not notably better off under this plan than under the one that had been declared unconstitutional in 1973 (1978, 149).

With the governor and the legislature now defending their new measure and public interest lawyers attacking it, a badly divided court rendered a decision upholding the facial validity of the Act (*Robinson V*, 355 A.2d 129 [1976]). In many ways, the court punctuated its per curiam opinion in *Robinson V* with doubts, reservations, and hints of openness to future challenges. The opinion begins with an expression of reluctance to review the statute without the benefit of a trial or evidentiary hearing. However, as if to say "we are weary of the fight," the court acknowledged the "desirability of reaching a speedy decision as to [the Act's] constitutionality—at least when examined facially." "Parenthetically," the court noted, "whether [the Act] may or may not pass muster as applied in the future to any individual school district at any particular time, must quite obviously await the event. Only in the factual context then presented and in the light of circumstances as they then appear could such a determination be made" (131). These themes of reluctance and lack of closure set the tone for the rest of the court's opinion.

Why, then, was Chapter 212 constitutional in light of *Robinson I*? The court pointed to two related factors. First, the legislature had endorsed the notion (at the heart of *Robinson I*) that "the sufficiency of education" was an "evolving concept." Thus, the Court said, the legislature had acknowledged "that what seems sufficient today may be proved inadequate tomorrow, and even more importantly that only in the light of experience can one ever come to know that a particular program is achieving a desired end" (133). Second, the court highlighted the potential for educational improvements under the regulatory provisions in Article II of the Act. Its assessment of the financial components of the law relied heavily upon this optimism about future state regulation: "The fiscal provisions of the Act are to be judged as adequate or inadequate depending upon whether they do or do not afford sufficient financial support for the system of public education that will emerge from the implementation of the plan set forth in the statute" (136).

While plaintiffs' various objections were not entirely without merit, Chapter 212 "had taken a positive step to more nearly equalize per pupil tax resources . . ." and "to eliminate gross disparities in per pupil expenditures. . . ." Only "actual experience" would "demonstrate whether it adequately serves the purpose intended" (137, 138). Thus, the court concluded, "we cannot say that . . . the dollar input per pupil, keeping in mind that there may be and probably are legitimate differences between and among districts and students, will not be sufficient to offer each pupil an equal educational opportunity as required by the Constitution" (137).

In a separate concurring opinion, Chief Justice Hughes added his own further, even more strongly worded, reservations. The reformers and his dissenting brethren had indeed raised many constitutional problems with Chapter 212. In crafting this new system, the legislature had failed to come to terms with the unavoidable common-sense view of the causal linkages involved. Problems flowed from inadequate local tax bases, and Chapter 212 had not gone far enough to remedy this root defect (141–42). However, the chief justice wrote, "the exigencies of government" had led him to conclude that the court should "not now" strike down the Act. However, he warned,

> if perchance in the reasonably near future there should be no effective step toward equalization, and it were to be established by proofs that such failures caused to continue to fester the invidious discordancies of tax resources destructive of meeting the constitutional goal, I would feel constrained to then determine the unconstitutionality in application of the 1975 Act (143).

Finally, two justices each submitted long dissenting opinions chronicling reformers' legal and factual contentions.[42]

Thus, reform-oriented attorneys had initiated *Robinson* in order to channel educational resources to New Jersey's beleaguered cities. At the end of the day, however, they had little to show for their efforts. Throughout the process, these reformers lacked the political resources—such as, organizations with constituencies; money; policy expertise; and group alliances—required for effective participation in state legislative and administrative arenas. They watched from the sidelines while Governor Byrne took up the mantle of reform, only to be disappointed when the legislative process beat back his proposal. As reform attorney Steve Eisdorfer (a law clerk to Justice Pashman who joined the Education Law Center in 1975) put it, "in *Robinson*, we had won a ticket to the game, but we hadn't played much" (Eisdorfer Interview, 8/24/94).[43]

On the other hand, *Robinson V* itself threw open the courthouse doors for another legal challenge. But it was also clear from the court's opinions that this future challenge would have to wait for the accumulation of "actual experience" under Chapter 212. Tractenberg, Eisdorfer, and their colleagues began thinking about the next case virtually the day after the court upheld the facial validity of the act. Their new deliberations would proceed in an interest group and institutional context remade by *Robinson* and Chapter 212.

"Feedback Effects" After *Robinson* and Chapter 212: Changes in the Interest Group and Institutional Context

The *Robinson* litigation and Chapter 212 changed the interest group and institutional context of the conflict in several related ways. I make four points here.

(1) *A foundation-funded law firm.* Over the late 1960s and early 70s, a loose national network developed among lawyers, activists, and researchers concerned with school finance reform. Coming as it did just a few days after *Rodriguez*, the original *Robinson* decision naturally focused the attention of these reformers upon the situation in New Jersey.[44] This attention helped Paul Tractenberg obtain a grant from the Ford Foundation to establish the Education Law Center (ELC) in 1975. At the time, Ford was pouring money into the burgeoning "public interest law movement" and was also backing projects focused on the problems of urban education.[45] Tractenberg proposed public interest law centers in Newark and Philadelphia to work not only on school finance, but also on desegregation, special education, and students' due process rights. The center in Newark became the hub of school finance reform activity in New Jersey. Work at the Newark

ELC would overlap with other developments traceable to the new law, thereby creating an expanded network of pro-reform forces standing behind reformers' next challenge in *Abbott*.

Tractenberg took a leave from Rutgers Law School to serve as the ELC's executive director from 1975 to 1978. Steve Eisdorfer was hired as a staff attorney there in the Fall of 1975, and served as interim director for a year before moving on to New Jersey's Office of Public Advocate in September 1979. Along with other lawyers and education activists, Tractenberg and Eisdorfer held a series of meetings to coordinate monitoring activities under the new law and to map out future litigation strategy.[46] In 1979, the ELC hired Marilyn Morheuser as its executive director. Although the working group of Newark attorneys and reformers had arrived at some conclusions about the next challenge, *Abbott v. Burke* would be Morheuser's case. The personal stamp that she would put upon it reflected her experiences in the civil rights struggles of the 1960s (Interviews with Tractenberg, 6/20/94; Morheuser, 6/22/94; and Eisdorfer, 8/24/94).[47]

These reform-oriented attorneys and their allies shared a "vision" of public schooling. This vision involved both empirical claims and understandings—as in "a way of seeing" political reality—and normative values and ends—as in "an ideal image" of what schooling should be like and what it should do.[48] Their moral outlook took race and class inequality to be fundamental features of American political life. America had become "two nations, two societies," and nowhere was this more evident than in New Jersey (Interviews with Tractenberg; Morheuser). The footrace metaphor undergirding 1960s debates over "equality of educational opportunity" guided reformers' thinking and strategies. Public schooling in America in fact functioned to reinforce systematic inequalities, whereas it could and should be a primary remedial force. A fair system would seek to "filter out" unfair initial advantages. If the schools allowed for a fair contest, educational success and failure would not be so highly correlated with original race- and class-based positions. Christopher Jencks has described the basic distributive principle at work in this "compensatory view" of equal educational opportunity: "Educational resources should go disproportionately to the disadvantaged" (1988, 527).[49]

In framing and constructing *Abbott*, the lawyers would face the problem of translating these views into legal claims and arguments. Here, they confronted a tension between the doctrinal legacy of *Robinson*, on one hand, and their own moral vision and political goals, on the other. Reformers also would have to negotiate certain tensions between the legal and political components of their overall effort. In these endeavors, they benefited from some other changes in the political environment brought about by Chapter 212 itself as well as further support from their friends at the Ford Foundation.

(2) *School Finance Research Monitoring the Fiscal Impact of Chapter 212.* Between 1974 and 1979, a local school-finance research community emerged in New Jersey to follow the consequences of the new finance system. On the whole, these researchers sympathized with the cause of reform, and some of them would serve as expert witnesses for plaintiffs in *Abbott v. Burke*.[50]

(3) *Increased State-Level Regulation and Citizen's Groups.* The regulatory side of Chapter 212 (concerned with the substance of education as opposed to finance) also generated new forms of interest group activity. With some of the money coming from the Ford Foundation, in 1977, business, civic, and religious groups established a coalition called "Schoolwatch." The ELC attorneys became active participants in this coalition.[51]

(4) *Allies Within the State Education Bureaucracy.* Finally, within the state education bureaucracy itself, a conflict developed over the nature of the regulatory system that would be put in place under the delegated authority of Chapter 212. Some of the officials on the losing side of this conflict would ally themselves with the reformers, providing information and expert testimony in *Abbott*.[52]

From Minimum Adequacy to Relative Needs: Framing and Constructing *Abbott v. Burke*

As the decade ended, then, reform attorneys at the ELC were in a much different position than they had been just four years earlier. They had clearly failed to achieve their goals in *Robinson*, but there were reasons for hope in the form of new resources and new allies. What lessons had they learned from their experiences? How would they go about framing and building their next challenge? How did they think about the relationship between law and politics? What opportunities and constraints did they face? What choices did they make, and why?

By 1979, reformers had reached a consensus on some basic lessons from *Robinson*. First, as one lawyer put it, "we all agreed that the next case would have to be much more fact specific." He continued: "The record in *Robinson* consisted entirely of statistical data and expert testimony. It was OK, as far as it went, but between 1972 and 1975 this record had gotten very cold and dry indeed. . . . There were bare statistics without any sense of the meaning for teachers and students in classrooms"(Eisdorfer Interview, 8/24/94).[53] Second, some way had to be found to keep the spotlight on the needs and interests of urban, minority, poor school children—their needs had faded into the background as *Robinson* progressed. Yet, this strong desire "to go with the urban, minority poor," as Morheuser put it, posed several problems, both legal and political in nature.

The path of least resistance in terms of doctrine would have involved an appeal to the "adequate level of education" standard in *Robinson*, combined with a factual presentation of inadequacy in the urban centers, in terms of both dollars and programs. It would then be the state's responsibility to provide more resources to remedy deficiencies. Reform attorneys gave serious thought to this approach—they called it "the basketcase case"—but rejected it because it might focus too much attention on local administrative deficiencies and not enough on overall finance equity. Thus, they resisted a mechanical stance toward the doctrinal legacy of *Robinson* because it did not do the work they wanted it to do. For a time, this tension between a traditional school finance focus (overall tax and expenditure data) and a developed presentation of "the facts" of education in the poorer urban districts was left unresolved (Eisdorfer Interview, 8/24/94).[54]

The reform attorneys also considered a related issue, this one involving a tension between winning in court and mobilizing in politics. A potentially useful strategy in mobilizing their natural constituency would have been to involve the urban school districts and other advocacy groups as equal partners and plaintiffs in the case.[55] However, the reformers rejected this strategy, for two related reasons. First, just as in "the basketcase case," making the urban districts parties to the suit would facilitate an attack on their administrative practices. These were "big, messy districts," and the ELC did not want to be in the position of defending them. Second, looking across the Hudson to school-finance litigation in New York State, reformers feared the implications of expanding the scope of the conflict *prior to* a definitive judicial resolution (Interviews with Eisdorfer; Morheuser).[56] Thus, fearing the consequences of broadening the scope of the conflict and losing control of the litigation, the attorneys decided that "their clients" would be school children from a selected, geographically representative range of poor, urban school districts. They would enjoy the moral authority of "speaking for the children," and would not have to worry about school districts or other advocacy groups determining their litigation strategies. "We wanted their help," Morheuser said, "but we did not want them in as parties." The reform attorneys did not believe that a judicial victory would easily translate into political reform. However, they did think that the right kind of judicial decision was a necessary pre-condition for redistributive change, and that the available options for broader attention or political alliances would do more harm than good (Interview with Morheuser).[57]

The problem of the precise legal theory of the case remained when Morheuser arrived at the ELC in late 1979. The most plausible reading of *Robinson* was that it had endorsed the concept of some sufficient level of educational opportunity, beyond which local districts were free to tax and spend at higher levels. Yet, reformers believed that disadvantaged children needed greater resources, not the same or less, than children in the suburbs. Morheuser's response to this challenge provides some interesting insights into the way that creative, specifically legal practices can "drive" the evolution and development of official legal doctrine. The simplest way to describe Morheuser's legal approach is that she let her basic moral outlook—her focus upon "relative needs, and resources available to meet those needs"—guide and structure her more specific stance toward and work with the materials available from *Robinson*. In turn, going through plausible steps authorized by *Robinson* would provide a way to pin down and factually explicate the meaning of "relative needs" (Interview with Morheuser).

In its reluctant decision in *Robinson V*, the court expressed an expectation that Chapter 212 would narrow "gross disparities" in tax capacity and expenditure per pupil. As of 1980, under the new law the overall floor had been raised, property tax rate disparities had narrowed somewhat (thus, much of the extra state money went to local property tax relief, other things being equal), and there had been some expenditure equalization among the districts below the "guaranteed tax base" level (the bottom two-thirds of the distribution). However, tax and expenditure disparities between the poorest and the wealthiest districts had actually widened. Thus, *Robinson* provided an easy "first step" in making a factual case. The point would be to show strong correlations between district wealth and per pupil expenditures as well as Chapter 212's failure to reduce disparities over time, with the usual emphasis upon the numbers at the low and high ends. The finance data would be the resting place of the factual case, with other claims spinning out from there.

But it was not clear from *Robinson* whether tax and expenditure disparities would be a sufficient basis for striking down the law. While expenditures were "plainly relevant," the court had said, money was not all that mattered in the constitutional analysis. Thus, *Robinson* also highlighted a possible and potentially difficult "second step" in the "factual" case. If plaintiffs could show that tax and expenditure disparities "caused" inadequate (or perhaps inequitable) educational opportunity, then their case would be a much stronger (Interview with Margaret Goertz, 8/3/94). Moreover, *Robinson* held that an adequate education was one that equipped a child for citizenship and the labor market "in the contemporary setting." This language opened up space for debate about what kind of information is relevant in constructing an account of the "contemporary setting."

Morheuser pursued this second step through the lenses of "relative needs." She paired poorer urban districts with nearby, wealthy suburban ones, and then gathered evidence for detailed, "point-by-point" comparisons in terms of specific educational programs, practices and outcomes. These presentations would also include information about background social conditions. In this way, amorphous notions of "adequacy" and "need" would be given content and meaning through a detailed "re-presentation" of educational experiences in rich and poor districts. The "needs" of urban school children would be explicated in two ways: first, against the backdrop of their own impoverished environment and, second, by reference to the resources available to already advantaged children in the wealthiest districts.[58]

This strategy was not without its risks, however, for a plausible response—one that state defendants did in fact make—was that proofs at the extremes were entirely beside the point. The constitutional standard called for a debate about "adequacy," and the fact that some districts had more and better was not relevant to this discussion. Indeed, just before trial in 1983, the superior court (the trial-level court) dismissed the ELC's case on precisely these grounds. So, to put it another way, Morheuser opted for a "fact-driven" strategy in order to "refigure" the very meaning of "adequacy." When she was done, "adequacy" for school children in the poor urban centers would mean "equality" with children in New Jersey's wealthiest suburbs—that is, at least this is what it would mean at the level of state constitutional doctrine.[59]

Abbott v. Burke, 1981–1985

The ELC attorneys decided upon four poor urban school districts from which to draw children as plaintiffs: Camden, East Orange, Irvington, and Jersey City. They filed *Abbott v. Burke* in February, 1981. Their complaint attacked the constitutionality of Chapter 212's finance components as violative of the education clause, state and federal equal protection clauses, and the State Law Against Discrimination.

In the gubernatorial election in November 1981, Republican Thomas Kean edged out Democrat James Florio by less than 2,000 votes. In July 1982, the governor appointed Saul Cooperman as his commissioner of education. Kean and Cooperman were early and vigorous supporters of the "educational excellence" reform movement mobilized by business and conservative elites during the early 1980s, and they constructed the state's defense in *Abbott* accordingly. In their view, the ELC's focus upon "equity" diverted attention from the true building blocks of education: strict discipline and quality teaching of the "basic curriculum," enforced by high standards for all. Moreover, reformers were seeking more money "to do the same things that [hadn't] worked."[60]

In responding to the ELC's suit, the state set up a factual defense advancing two main claims. First, a large body of social science research had destroyed the notion that there was a simple relationship between increased expenditures or resources and improvements in educational achievement. Second, to the extent that certain districts were not providing the constitutionally adequate level of education, the cause of any such deficiencies was not insufficient resources, but "mismanagement, waste, and corruption" in the local school districts and municipalities. Here, plaintiffs had available to them Chapter 212's existing system of regulation to remedy any local district problems. On the law, the state argued that the court had upheld the constitutionality of the existing system and that reformers were misconstruing the operative constitutional standards. Finally, the state argued that Chapter 212's finance arrangements secured important constitutional values by providing institutional space for local participation and control.

The ELC and the state spent 1982 and the better part of 1983 engaged in pretrial motions and discovery. The ELC's "plaintiffs" were certified as a class representing all school children in the four original districts. In addition to working with her experts and sifting through documents, Morheuser interviewed hundreds of potential witnesses, from both poor and rich districts—school board members, administrators, teachers—in the process of building her case. The court set a trial date for December 1983.[61]

In September 1983, the state moved for summary judgment, arguing that plaintiffs' complaint should in the first instance go to the commissioner of education for administrative review. In November, the trial court granted the state's motion to dismiss for "failure to exhaust administrative remedies." The trial judge reasoned that *Robinson V* had resolved all doubts about the facial constitutionality of the act, and that the commissioner was empowered to hear complaints arising under the school laws. If administrative remedies led to the correction of local problems, then the constitutional issue raised by plaintiffs would not have to be faced.[62]

The ELC and its supporters viewed this dismissal as nearly fatal to their entire project. In rejecting as premature plaintiffs' facial attack upon the entire finance system and relegating them to administrative proceedings focused solely upon deficiencies in particular districts, the trial judge had placed them upon precisely the terrain they had sought to avoid. Moreover, as a practical matter, the ELC was left with the prospects of an administrative proceeding in which the state would be both defendant and judge. The ELC could appeal to the courts from any adverse administrative resolution, but it was impossible to know how long this would take or what shape the record would be in when it was over. Morheuser appealed; and, it should be noted, she did so armed with an extensively developed factual case that was "trial ready" at the time it was bounced out of court.

In May 1984, the appellate division reversed the trial court's order.[63] The state then appealed to the New Jersey Supreme Court. The court heard arguments in November, 1984.

On July 23, 1985, in an unanimous decision, the court handed reformers a major victory disguised as a procedural setback (*Abbott v. Burke*, 496 A.2d 376 [1985]). On the surface of things in *Abbott I*, the court seemed to agree with the state: Plaintiffs would have to go through a presumably longer and more cumbersome administrative law process. But, at the same time, Justice Alan Handler's opinion for the court managed to work a doctrinal transformation—one muted, to be sure, by its studied ambiguity and lack of immediate practical effects—but one clearly discernible nonetheless. This transformation would prove to be highly "productive" in shaping the subsequent course of the litigation as well as the future politics of educational reform in New Jersey.

Justice Handler begins by proposing a broad definition of the court's task in deciding the case. Although it is true that this appeal presents "only one narrow issue" and that "the ultimate merits of the constitutional claims and defenses are not before" the court, Handler noted, "the merits...cannot be ignored, because the nature and scope of the necessary factual inquiry and legal analysis influence the procedural course to be taken by this litigation." (p. 380–81). We can restate Justice Handler's initial move here as follows: The "narrow issue" for decision is, which tribunal shall hear this case? In order to answer that question, we cannot avoid looking into "the merits" (that is, the factual and legal claims on both sides) so that we may determine what it is that the chosen tribunal will be asked to do ("the nature and scope of the factual inquiry") and how it should do it (the "legal analysis").

These elements—facts, law, and the future course of the litigation—set the basic terms for a long excursion in which Justice Handler would swing back and forth between prior law and current factual and legal claims and defenses. In this fashion, the opinion takes on a synergistic quality. At the end of the journey, we arrive at a point very far from where we began.

Justice Handler states the court's basic holding early on: "The parties claims should initially be presented to an administrative tribunal." However, in the very next line, he rejects the trial court's rationale for this conclusion and substitutes another. The administrative route is preferred not because plaintiffs' claims lack "constitutional dimensions," but because the case presents the need for "the creation of an administrative record sufficient to guide the adjudication of the constitutional issues on any future appeal" (381).

Justice Handler then reviewed the history of the *Robinson* litigation and Chapter 212, highlighting the lack of closure there and noting that the present case "must be understood and related to the antecedent litigation" (382–83). Insofar as it defined goals and standards, Chapter 212 was indeed "constitutional on its face." The broad question presented was, as Justice Handler framed it, "whether the operative terms of the 1975 Act in fact assure that all the state's children receive their due" (383). Instead of turning directly to what it would mean for children to "receive their due," Justice Handler rendered 14 consecutive paragraphs going over the factual claims on both sides (8 for plaintiffs and 6 for defendants) (383–87). The exhaustive review of the ELC's claims was punctuated with language indicating that reformers should be allowed to make their case as they had framed it.

The Politics of Rights Revisited

The crucial section of Justice Handler's opinion disclaims definitive resolution of constitutional issues, but then goes on to provide guidance on plaintiffs' education clause and equal protection arguments. "The constitutional issues must be gauged in light of the facts that the parties are prepared to marshal," Handler wrote.

In 1975, the legislature itself had established that "the sufficiency of education" was "a growing and evolving concept." "This evolving standard," Handler stated,

> will influence judicial evaluation of documented differences in either educational achievement or program offerings. If, for example, significant numbers of students in plaintiffs' school districts fail to receive an effective secondary education by reason of the 1975 Act's operation, then the Act fails to provide equal educational opportunity. . . . Similarly, the 1975 Act may fail to provide equal educational opportunity by allowing equivalently-qualified students to attend schools providing significantly disparate program offerings. See *Robinson V* . . . (disparities in tax bases may show inadequate available resources) (388).

From this passage, it seems that the standard is rapidly evolving as Justice Handler writes. Justice Handler seems to know this, for he immediately moves to qualify the quoted passage with a nod to the language in *Robinson I* holding that the state could authorize local governments "to go further" above the constitutionally mandated level, "provided that such authorization does not become a device for diluting the State's mandated responsibility."

But then Justice Handler again turns away from *Robinson*. He elides the background assumption of "*minimum* adequacy" that grounded this notion of an authorization "to go further" by moving his focal point back to "*the state's responsibility*." He states:

> In evaluating whether the 1975 Act satisfies *the State's responsibility*, a measure of local educational expenditures in terms of "dollar input per pupil . . . is plainly relevant." [quoting *Robinson I*]. Dollars pay for current operating expenses and capital expenditures, and judicial notice has been taken that differences in area costs as well as qualities of students may result in different levels of spending required to achieve the same educational opportunity in different districts. Further, in some cases for disadvantaged students to receive a thorough and efficient education, the students will require above-average access to educational resources (388, emphasis added).

At the very least, relative need has now taken its place along side minimum adequacy as a viable competitor for the title of evolving constitutional standard under the education clause.

After another two pages of asserting here, qualifying there, Justice Handler noted that plaintiffs claims under the education and equal protection clauses would necessarily overlap. Then, in the most important passage in the opinion, he wrote that "both claims" would

> turn on proof that plaintiffs *suffer* educational *inequities* and that these inequities derive, in significant part, from the funding provisions of the 1975 Act. The claims may differ, however, in that the thorough and efficient education issues call for proofs that *after comparing the education received by children in property-poor districts, it appears that the disadvantaged children will not be able to compete in, and contribute to, the society entered by the relatively advantaged children*. The equal protection issues, on the other hand, call for proofs that, even if all children receive a minimally thorough and efficient education, the financing scheme engenders more inequality than is required by any other State interest (390, emphases added).

In the end, Justice Handler chooses the term "inequities" (unfairness) to describe what it is that plaintiffs "suffer." And, as the rest of the passage makes clear, deciding what is fair will involve an inquiry into relative needs.[64]

Abbott v. Burke, 1985-1996: A Summary Overview

The trial in *Abbott* was held over the course of late 1986 and early 1987. It took up 95 trial days, with a total of 99 witnesses testifying and approximately 700 documents admitted into evidence. In August 1988, administrative law judge Steven Lefelt rendered a 607-page decision in favor of plaintiffs. "Based upon all the evidence presented," he wrote,

> I have determined that plaintiffs proved there are unmet educational needs in poor urban districts and vast program and expenditure disparities between property rich suburban and property poor urban school districts. The expenditure disparities are in some cases greater now than before Chapter 212 was enacted. I have concluded that the funding law contains systemic defects which contribute to continued inequity.[65]

The commissioner of education rejected Lefelt's recommendations in 1989, and plaintiffs appealed to the Supreme Court. In *Abbott II*, decided in June 1990, a unanimous Supreme Court struck down Chapter 212 as applied to 28 poorer urban school districts. The court wrote:

> The students of Newark and Trenton are no less citizens than their friends in Milburn or Princeton. They are entitled to be treated equally, to begin at the

same starting line. Today the disadvantaged are doubly mistreated: first, by the accident of their environment and, second, by the disadvantage added by an inadequate education. The State has compounded the wrong and must right it.

Accordingly, the court held that expenditures for the regular educational budget in these poorer urban districts must be brought up to the average level among the 108 wealthiest districts (*Abbott II*, 575 A.2d 359 [1990]).

At the behest of newly elected governor Jim Florio, the legislature passed the Quality Education Act (or QEA I) in July 1990. Part of a larger tax reform package (raising taxes by $2.8 billion over two years), the act set up a new "high foundation" school finance system funneling considerably more state education aid to poor urban areas. The QEA was to go into effect for the 1991–92 school year. However, over the course of 1990, popular counter-mobilizations among citizens opposed to the tax hikes as well as to the school funding law led to the amendment of the QEA (QEA II) in March, 1991. Much of the money originally targeted to go to the urban districts was diverted to general property tax relief. The ELC returned to the Supreme Court in June 1991, arguing that the amended act violated the court's holding in *Abbott II*. The court remanded the case for trial on whether, as amended, the QEA conformed to its decision in *Abbott II*. In November 1991, the Republicans won-veto proof majorities in both houses of the legislature.

In 1992, Republican leaders sought further reversal of the redistributive thrust of reformers' efforts in *Abbott*. They floated a proposal to amend the constitution and, when this failed, sought ordinary legislation to blunt the effects of *Abbott*. Also in 1992, during trial in *Abbott* upon the court's remand, reform attorneys agreed to give up a prong of their case challenging state payment of teacher pensions in order to form an alliance with educational establishment groups. In turn, this new coalition—the New Jersey Association for Public Schools (NJAPS)—was strong enough to win one-year compromise legislation at the end of 1992. Here, the Republicans, the governor, and NJAPS all agreed to the formation of a bi-partisan commission to examine the school finance question. Through NJAPS, the Education Law Center joined forces with leaders from education groups (e.g. the teachers union) and some wealthier school districts, most of whom initially mobilized against the QEA.

In September 1993, the trial judge adopted reformers' position and struck down the QEA, as amended. In November, Republican Christine Todd Whitman defeated Florio in the gubernatorial election. In *Abbott III* (July 1994) the Supreme Court affirmed the trial court's ruling and reaffirmed and clarified its holding in *Abbott II*. It set a new deadline (September, 1996) for full compliance with *Abbott II*. As this deadline approached, the ELC returned to the Supreme Court again. In *Abbott IV*, the court extended the deadline for passage of a new measure to January 1, 1997. In December, 1996, the legislature passed and Governor Whitman signed the Comprehensive School Improvement and Financing Act. As of this writing (January 1997), plaintiffs have once again returned to the Supreme Court, alleging that the new measure does not fulfill the court's mandate in *Abbott II* to equalize spending between the poorest and richest districts.

Abbott v. Burke: Concluding Remarks

In evaluating the results of law reform efforts, much will depend upon our time frame and upon how we define and measure success or failure. A number of "on the one hand, on the other hand" statements about the New Jersey controversy are possible. In the protracted nature of the controversy and the "counter-mobilization" that followed reformers' eventual legal victory in *Abbott II*, critics of the use of courts to secure social reform could find a good deal of evidence to support their claims.

However, by focusing upon the self-understandings of lawyers and paying attention to the transition from *Robinson* to *Abbott*, this study provides a more complicated picture of the role lawyers and litigation in this liberal reform effort. After *Robinson*, reformers took stock of lessons learned and then slowly went about organizing an expanded reform network and mobilizing resources to support it. They also worked hard with the materials at hand to translate their moral vision into plausible legal claims and arguments. They went to court and carefully managed their litigation not because they believed in "myths" about rights, but because they believed that the courts would be their only springboard to politics, and that an effort at broader mobilization would have been counterproductive. Whether this judgment was warranted or not, it cannot be denied that this network of reformers has been fairly successful in using law and courts to project a strongly compensatory notion of distributive justice onto the political agenda. By all accounts, the current debate over "equality of educational opportunity" and school finance policy in New Jersey now takes place in terms largely defined by *Abbott*. Since 1990, moreover, urban school districts have enjoyed a significant redistribution of state education dollars in their favor, although they are still a long way from parity with the wealthiest districts in one of the nation's wealthiest states.

Had this study continued the story through the aftermath of *Abbott II*, it would have possible to show that the case not only shaped debate, but also structured the actual organization of educational reform politics. School districts, for example, organized for action in politics in the "three tiered" pattern of the court's opinion—high wealth, low wealth, and the middle districts. Here, perhaps, we find some grounds for criticizing what reformers have done. First, as noted above, reformers' single-minded focus on a victory in court may have resulted in some missed opportunities for organizing and mobilizing a broader political constituency to support their efforts. A second, related issue to consider has to do with reformers' "race and poverty" framing of their case. The court's eager endorsement of this "race and poverty" rhetoric in *Abbott II* helped fuel a racially charged counter-mobilization, with many citizens inveighing against "throwing money down the rat hole." But reformers did adjust to the right-populist upheaval that followed *Abbott II* and the QEA in 1990. By using their ongoing litigation to leverage a move from outsiders to pragmatic insiders, reformers have formed new alliances and won "a seat at the table." Although the conflict is not over, it is going to be hard for state officials to avoid minimal compliance with *Abbott III* (Firestone, et al., [1994]; Goertz [1994, 6]).

Conclusion: Another Plea for Narrative

Michael Paris
Kevin J. McMahon

In his review of *The Hollow Hope*, Jonathan Simon highlights the narrow pluralist and neolegal realist assumptions undergirding Rosenberg's explanatory framework. For Rosenberg, political changes are best explained by broad social and economic forces ("the current of history," as he puts it) flowing into the political system. Simon argues that "the risk in Rosenberg's approach is treating institutions, including courts, as little more than black boxes through which some kind of exogenous social energy passes.... It is only through exploring the black boxes and the structures, ideologies, and agendas that operate there that we can begin to delineate the ways in which change is articulated in its historical specificity" (Simon 1992).[66] Thus, Rosenberg neglects the potential significance of legal rhetoric for activists, ignores the importance of what courts say in understanding what courts do, and in general, discounts courts as effective institutions shaping political action. In the preceding two sections, we have tried to illustrate the pitfalls of Rosenberg's perspective as well as the utility of McCann's alternative approach.

Kevin McMahon's review of the role of law and courts in the Montgomery bus boycott demonstrates that Rosenberg's claims about a lack of connection between *Brown* (and the courts) and Montgomery are largely unfounded. Legal concepts and categories (e.g., definitions, understandings, moral aspirations) "inscribed social circumstances" (to borrow Simon's words again) and helped define the terms of social conflict and oppositional politics. Legal institutions, both state and federal, were integral parts of this epic struggle. In short, law and courts "mattered" in precisely that way that McCann has claimed that they might.[67] Rosenberg, however, sees political action in Montgomery as somehow separate from *Brown* and the courts. In this, it is worth noting, his interpretations are also at odds with those of the boycott's primary leaders.

Michael Paris's study of education finance reform litigation in one state sought to illustrate how McCann's view might be adapted to a different sort of reform effort, one not characterized by social movement organizations and activities. Sensitivity to McCann's central themes facilitated an analysis exploring both elite reformers' creative mobilization of the law and avoidance of a broader democratic politics, as well as the independent stamp that the state courts placed upon political processes and policy outcomes.[68]

In both illustrative discussions, we made use of McCann's model to construct detailed narrative accounts of the interplay of law and politics in particular conflicts. Based upon our work here, we conclude with some questions and comments for scholars interested in building upon McCann's legal mobilization perspective.

Upon reading McCann's *Rights At Work*, we not only came to similar conclusions about the book's many virtues, but also agreed upon the root source of what was most unsatisfying. Simply put, we found ourselves wanting "whole stories rather than excerpts from stories" (Gordon 1988, 18). At first blush, this seems to be a rather trivial point about nothing more than how McCann chose to present his research. McCann studied twenty-four cases of pay-equity conflicts. He then organized his presentation according to his four-stage model of movement activity.[70] In other words, McCann marshals excerpts from his case studies ("data") to support his general, theoretical propositions about how rights work in practice at various stages of conflict.[71] As a result, the reader is unable to follow any one conflict from "start" to "finish." We do not mean to say that McCann should have written a different book. Rather, we merely want to pose some questions about what is lost in McCann's presentation and what might be gained by an effort to tell "whole stories" guided by his approach to law, politics, and group conflict. We suggest that there is a good deal more at stake here than simply the tension between the particular and the general.[72]

The main problem with McCann's presentation of bits and pieces of various conflicts is that, for all of the talk about "the context-specific experiences of individuals" and "situational rationality and local knowledge" (18–19), there are not many choices or actions discussed in *Rights At Work* that can really be understood "in context." The construction of "whole stories," we suggest, would facilitate building upon McCann's view in at least the following two ways.

Cause Lawyering: Legal Framing, the Articulation Between Law and Politics, and Reflexivity

McCann pays close attention to the self-understandings of lawyers and other activists about the role of law and courts in reform projects. From McCann, for example, we learn that labor and feminist attorneys in pay-equity conflicts had a sophisticated, political understanding of what litigation might do to serve broader organizational goals; that lawyers and activists often self-consciously used lawsuits themselves as vehicles to increase rank and file participation (e.g., formulating legal strategy, gathering information and evidence, giving testimony); and, finally, that these actors often evidenced a "dual consciousness" about legal claims and arguments, a consciousness at once skeptical about reliance upon law and courts, yet hopeful about the aspirational side of rights discourse and its "resonance" with women in the workplace. Indeed, it is as if these lawyers (and many of the activists) had read and readily accepted Stuart Scheingold's argument in *The Politics of Rights (1974)*.[73]

We think that telling whole stories in light of McCann's view would do a good deal more work in exploring questions about lawyer consciousness and cause lawyering.[74] First, and most obviously, thicker narratives would allow us to gain a better sense of who these lawyers are and how they have come to hold the views that they do.[75] Second, and more importantly, narration would allow researchers and readers alike to come closer to standing in the cause lawyer's shoes. McCann's account does provide a vivid sense of how pay-equity lawyers were "disciplined" by their active participation in broader political organizations and by the activism of "flesh and blood clients."[76] Not only would thicker narrative provide access to more of the details of these lawyer-client relations; it would also require the provisional adoption of an "internal" perspective on legal practice—that is, the perspective of cause lawyers situated before a particular set of legal materials, legal and political institutions, and legal and political adversaries.

Now, with McCann, we agree that this situated legal sense in "the law space" is not the most important part of the story. Rather, what matters most is the relationship between this situated location and what lawyers make of it, on one hand, and broader mobilization, political conflict, and structural constraints, on the other. And, as McCann shows, this relationship between legal action and reform projects is only partly instrumental; it is only partly a matter of strategic leverage. At least potentially, it also has to do with the content and character of legal arguments (or legal rhetoric) and their "resonance" with potential change agents or in the organization of politics generally (McCann 1994, 133–35). We would add that lawyers sometimes have a range of choices in framing and constructing legal challenges, and that the (specifically legal) choices they make will be an important part of how the legal and political dimensions of reform efforts "articulate" with each other. These choices and their possible significance, we think, can only be grasped through whole stories attentive to lawyer consciousness and the details of legal practice.

We have used the word "choices" here, but obviously there may be options and opportunities that are not conceptualized as such by lawyers and activists, for a variety of reasons. In order to make such a claim—a claim about a disjunction between an actor's consciousness and what was "really" possible or really going on—the researcher must stake out and defend some ground upon which to stand. This is precisely what Scheingold (1974) did in making claims about "ideology" (the myth of rights) and reality (the politics of rights). And, in 1974, not surprisingly, Scheingold's own ground was legal realism. In turn, we suggest, the emergence of "constitutive" perspectives like McCann's opens up the possibility of understanding and criticizing "realist" practices in new and potentially useful ways.[77] This brings us to our final point about cause lawyering, which involves the notion of reflexivity.

Sociologist Anthony Giddens has characterized what he calls a "model of reflexivity" as follows:

> The relation between sociology and its subject matter—the actions of human beings in conditions of modernity—has to be understood . . . in terms of the "double hermeneutic." The development of sociological knowledge is parasitical upon lay agents' concepts; on the other hand, notions coined in the meta-languages of the social sciences routinely reenter the universe of actions they were initially formulated to describe and account for. But it does not lead in a direct way to a transparent social world. *Sociological knowledge spirals in and out of the universe of social life, reconstructing both itself and that universe as an integral part of that process* (Giddens 1990, 15–16, emphasis in original).

Applied to cause lawyering and the study of law and reform more generally, Giddens's observation might lead researchers to be more self-conscious about reflexivity–about the porous boundaries among observers, political actors, and readers. McCann himself points in this direction when he describes how he and his research associates learned a great deal about law and politics from "generating dialogue" through "active interviews" with informants (McCann 1994, 18).[78] As noted above, the lawyers and activists with whom McCann spoke seemed to embrace realist understandings of law and politics. What would it mean, then, for lawyers and activists to reflect upon "constitutive" perspectives like McCann's? It might mean that those who mobilize the law would become more self-conscious about the potentially constitutive capacity of law and its fit (or lack of fit) with a broader political project. And, again, we suggest that there is something different to be learned from the construction of whole stories-from the effort to reflect, as much as possible, lives as lived—as opposed to the more general view and personal "distancing" that come with McCann's excerpts from stories.[79]

Institutionalism, Law, and Courts

Finally, our illustrative discussions lead us to ask whether researchers making use of McCann's insights in other contexts shouldn't give some thought to the status of law and courts *as institutions* in a "decentered," mobilization approach. Admittedly, there is a great deal of institutionalism in McCann's work, and law and courts are very much in the picture. However, when it comes to the role of law (especially doctrine and the framing and construction of legal cases) and courts in particular conflicts, McCann seems to slide into a realist view concerned with political leverage and legal and political results. In other words, he deemphasizes the role of courts as independent actors in shaping social conflict and policy outcomes while emphasizing how lawyers and activists employed courts in the pursuit of social change. New institutionalist perspectives, by contrast, pay attention to how institutions affect political action. As James G. March and Johan P. Olsen explain:

> The organization of political life makes a difference, and institutions affect the flow of history. . . . Actions taken within and by political institutions change the distribution of political interests, resources, and rules by creating new actors and identities, by providing actors with criteria of success and failure, by constructing rules for appropriate behavior, and by endowing some individuals, rather than others, with authority and other types of resources. Institutions affect the ways in which individuals and groups become activated within and outside established institutions, the level of trust among citizens and leaders, the common aspirations of political community, the shared language, understanding, and norms of the community, and the meaning of concepts like democracy, justice, liberty, and equality (1989, 159, 164; Putnam 1993, 17; Skocpol 1992, 41–42).

With such insights in mind, our question about McCann's view asks whether there is a need for more "recentering" after the "decentering"—a need for more attention to the details of judicial processes and to the interactions among courts, other institutions, and the organization of politics, even though the researcher provisionally adopts the standpoint of agents who mobilize the law. In the Montgomery case study above, McMahon sought to show how the leaders of the boycott were influenced by *Brown* and guided toward a path that highlighted the federal courts due to the relatively sympathetic position of the federal judiciary. In the New Jersey case study above, Paris sought to demonstrate the compatibility between elements of McCann's framework and an "institutional" treatment of law and courts. By institutionalism in public law, we mean simply attention to (1) the historical evolution of bodies of doctrine and particular courts, viewed both internally and in relation to other political institutions (e.g., separation of powers, federalism, party systems), and (2) the feedback effects of prior doctrinal and policy developments upon the subsequent organization of politics, broadly understood.[80]

The telling of whole stories in light of McCann's framework would yield a certain kind of "institutional" perspective, one that highlights *political* institutions and arrangements, as opposed to broader social structural and economic forces. This is an institutionalism that would keep the focus upon political agents, and upon political-institutional opportunities and constraints that might reasonably fall within the purview of political agents. The goal here would be descriptive accounts providing as much nuance and detail as possible about linkages between reform-minded mobilization of the law, on one hand, and the institutional processes through which policies are made and remade, on the other.[81] In this approach "to the study of politics, institutions are expected to shape the interests, resources, and ultimately the conduct of political actors, such as judges, governmental officials generally, party or interest-group leaders, and other identifiable persons. The actions of such persons are in turn expected to reshape those institutions more or less extensively" (Smith 1988, 91). Activists, lawyers, and scholars interested in the efforts of those who mobilize the law need good, detailed knowledge of these institutional processes; hence, our suggestion that some "recentering" might be in order.

Concluding Thought

There are many standard criteria for evaluation of theories or frameworks in social inquiry—for example, congruence with social reality, cogency, internal coherence, parsimony, and, given some purpose(s), practical utility. Our suggestions about what might be gained from the construction of thick narratives guided by McCann's approach follows from viewing practical utility as the most important criterion. If the central point of a McCann-like mobilization perspective is to understand and evaluate action in context, then the construction of whole stories would seem to be a promising avenue to pursue.

Notes

1. Recognition of Rosenberg's self-avowed left orientation is important for understanding his case. For example, one common response among reviewers has been that Rosenberg neglects the significant role that courts actually do play in policy making—consider, for example, the role of the Court in defining the precise terms of school desegregation policy between 1968 and 1974— (see, e.g., Schuck 1993). However, given his claim to stand with the proponents of significant change, Rosenberg has an easy response to such objections. He can say that the actual role of courts in shaping public policy is not his concern, *unless* courts can be shown to be the primary or motor force behind successful reform efforts.

2. See, for example, Skocpol (1992) and Pierson (1993, 595). Our primary reference point for the application of the new institutionalism to the study of law and courts is Smith (1989). We are concerned with Smith's general notion that a focus upon ideas and "cognitive structures" as embedded in institutions (in their historical trajectories or current practices) can aid researchers in (1) treating the content of legal ideas and categories as important in their own right, and (2) trying to discern lines between structural constraint and individual or group choice. We leave aside Smith's more specific proposal for packaging this departure in the language of positive social science (e.g. "independent" and "dependent variables").

3. Rosenberg's book has been thoroughly reviewed by a broad array of impressive scholars. In addition to McCann, see, for example, Feeley (1992); Simon (1992); and Schuck (1993).

4. The reader may be wondering about the logic of "case selection" here (the Montgomery bus boycott and school finance litigation in one state). We have no large justification to offer. These illustrative discussions stem from our separate work, and converge at the point of rejecting Rosenberg's model.

5. Other prominent examples of work in this line of research include Handler (1978); Gambitta, May, and Foster (1981); Olson (1984).

6. We assume that readers are familiar with Rosenberg's basic framework—e.g. his "constrained" and "dynamic court" views, and his hypotheses about paths of causation. For a critique of Rosenberg's conceptualizations of "causation," see, in addition to McCann, Simon (1992). Simon agrees with McCann in concluding that Rosenberg's "analysis of the effects of courts suffers from his commitment to a narrowly positivist tradition of social science that overvalues quantitative data and deals uncomfortably with historical and narrative material" (925).

7. In *Rights At Work*, McCann applies a "constitutive, dispute-centered" perspective in an analysis of feminist/labor struggles for pay equity during the

late 1970s and 1980s. "Legal mobilization" simply refers to the translation of a desire, want, or goal into a demand articulated as an assertion of rights. "Law as social practice" sees law as "constitutive" in two general senses. First, "inherited legal conventions shape the very terms of citizen understanding, aspiration, and interaction with others." Second, "these inherited legal symbols and discourses provide relatively malleable resources that are routinely reconstructed as citizens seek to advance their interests and designs . . . ." Rights discourse, for example, allows actors to "refigure the terms of past settlements" and express aspirations for new entitlement and power relationships (McCann 1994, 6–7). McCann's rendition of this "constitutive" approach goes hand-in-hand with a broader "skeptical position regarding traditional social scientific goals of defining clear causal relations and developing strong predictive capacities" (15). The constitutive perspective calls for research methods capable of informing persuasive accounts of self-understandings and actions in specific contexts.

8   See, for example, Tushnet (1987). Rosenberg cites Tushnet at several points in *The Hollow Hope*. It is odd that he doesn't view Tushnet's treatment of the interplay of law and politics (particularly its internal, organizational significance for the NAACP) as a challenge to some of his more sweeping claims about courts and social change

9   Nevertheless, given Rosenberg's own tendency to count things in order to show *Brown's* ineffectiveness and his commenting upon the number of references to the decision in a book on the black press (133), this point is at least a minor concession.

10 Michael J. Klarman, who largely agrees with Rosenberg on *Brown*, also writes that "testimonials by participants in the civil rights movement" are not " particularly convincing evidence of the inspirational impact" of the decision. He contends that other "similar statements were made, perhaps even in roughly equal numbers, about the motivational forces of the lynching of Emmett Till in the Mississippi Delta in 1955 (and the subsequent acquittal of his killers), the Montgomery bus boycott, and the rapid decolonization of Africa." He continues by pondering that "maybe what these testimonials show is that participants in social movements, when asked to articulate their inspiration, identify concrete, highly salient events such as court decisions, boycotts, and lynchings. It seems unrealistic to expect them to attribute causal significance to deep-seated but intangible forces such as urbanization and industrialization, demographic shifts, political realignments, economic advances, and the rising literacy rates" (Klarman, 1994, 91).
In their 1958 accounts of the Montgomery bus boycott, however, Ralph Abernathy ("The Natural History of a Social Movement," Masters' thesis) and Martin Luther King, Jr., (*Stride Toward Freedom*) do attempt to take such forces into account. For instance, besides stressing the importance of *Brown*, Abernathy discusses such factors as the growing population of Montgomery, the impact of World War II on race relations in the city, the role of class in the African-American community, and "the dominant psychological moods of the participants" in his study on the boycott (108–9, 139).

11 The March meeting did produce some results. The policy of having buses only stop at alternate blocks in black areas of the city was changed. The principal demand of the Women's Political Committee (WPC), however, concerned the seating policy. The members of the WPC wanted the city leaders to alter the policy so that African–Americans could sit in "whites only" seats when they were vacant, and so that they did not have to give up their seats to whites on overcrowded buses. See Garrow, (1989, 621).

12 Rosenberg (1991, 136); Robinson (1987).

13 Unfortunately, Rosenberg only relies on Abernathy's 1989 *And the Walls Came Tumbling Down* for the account of the events at Montgomery.

14 As King (1958) writes, "many people in the white community argued that [Rosa Parks] had been 'planted' by the NAACP in order to lay the groundwork for a test case, and at first glance that explanation seemed plausible, since she was a former secretary of the local branch of the NAACP" (43–4). Parks had not been planted by the NAACP, but as King notes, "so persistent and persuasive was this argument that it convinced many reporters from all over the country. Later on, when I was having press conferences three times a week—in order to accommodate the reporters and journalists who came to Montgomery from all over the world—the invariable first question was: 'Did the NAACP start the bus boycott?'"

15 According to King, "this was one of the first clear-cut instances in which a Negro had been convicted of disobeying the segregation law. In the past, either cases like this had been dismissed or the people involved had been charged with disorderly conduct" (55).

16 In a later meeting during the boycott, King again made this distinction. According to Abernathy, he stated that "there had not been and would not be any cross burning; lynchings; defying of the Constitution of the nation; violence; and attacks on the United States Supreme Court" (King 1958, 958, 148).

17 These words, moreover, are consistent with his 1958 account quoted above, provided that the earlier statements are understood as referring to the attitudes of leaders in the African–American community. After all, the 1958 study was about the Montgomery Improvement Association.

18 King wrote about his role as a leader of the local branch of the NAACP: "As an expression of my concern with [racial] problems . . . one of the first committees that I set up in my church was designed to keep the congregation intelligently informed on the social, political, and economic situations. The duties of the Social and Political Action Committee were, among others, to keep before the congregation the importance of the NAACP and the necessity of being registered voters, and—during state and national election-to sponsor forums and mass meetings to discuss the major issues. . . . By November 1955, in my annual report to the [church] membership, I was able to say that 'the work of this committee has been superb, and every member of Dex-

ter has felt its influence. [In June 1955, the committee gave a "special briefing" on *Brown II* entitled 'The NAACP and the Supreme Court'.] Through the work of this committee many persons have become registered voters, and Dexter has led all other churches in Montgomery in contributions to the NAACP. After having started the program of the church on its way, I joined the local branch of the NAACP and began to take an active interest in implementing its program in the community itself. Besides raising money through my church, I made several speeches for the NAACP in Montgomery and elsewhere. Less than a year after I joined the branch I was elected to the executive committee. By attending most of the monthly meetings I was brought face to face with some of the racial problems that plagued the community, especially those involving the [state and local] courts" (King 1958, 30-31); On the special briefing, see, Luker, Russell, and Holloran (1994, 34).

19 Luker, Russel, and Holloran (1994, 330-331). The remaining quotations in this paragraph either appear in or are from the introduction of this volume of King, Jr.'s papers (35, 20, respectively).

20 See also King 1958, 191-92. At Yale University on January 14, 1959, King also explained that "broadly speaking, there have been three distinct periods in the history of race relations in this nation." The first period (1619-1863) was "the era of slavery." The second period (1863-1954) "the period of restricted emancipation. . . . *The third period in the development of race relations in America had its beginning on May 17, 1954.* This is the period of constructive integration. It is the period in which men seek to rise to the level of genuine intergroup and interpersonal living. The Supreme Court's decision which came to give legal and constitutional validity to the dominant thought patterns of this period stated that the old Plessy doctrine must go, that separate facilities were inherently unequal, and that to segregate a child on the basis of his race is to deny that child equal protection of the law. *As a result of this decision we find ourselves standing on the threshold of the most creative period in the development of race relations in the history of our nation.* To state it figuratively in biblical language: We have broken loose from the Egypt of slavery; we have moved through the wilderness of "separate but equal"; and now we stand on the border of the promised land of integration" (emphasis added).

21 Rosenberg uses part of this quote, but unfortunately his "selective quotation" leads him to misstate King's point. In *The Hollow Hope,* the last three sentences of Rosenberg's section on Montgomery reads as follows: "Finally, King specifically addressed the influence of *Brown* on the boycott. It was clear, he said, that *Brown* 'cannot explain why it happened in Montgomery' and that the 'crisis was not produced by . . . even the Supreme Court' (King 1958, 64, 191-92). Although Montgomery may have inspired blacks, there does not appear to be much evidence that the Court inspired Montgomery" (1991, 132).

22 As King emphasized: "The present crisis in race relations has characteristics that come to the forefront in any period of social transition. The guardians of

the status quo lash out with denunciation against the person or organization that they consider most responsible for the emergence of the new order. (Often this denunciation against the person or organization that they consider most responsible for the emergence of the new order.) Often this denunciation rises to major proportions. In the transition from slavery to restricted emancipation Abraham Lincoln was assassinated. In the present transition from segregation to desegregation the Supreme Court is castigated and the NAACP is maligned and subjected to extra-legal reprisals. As in other social crises the defenders of the status quo in the South argue that they were gradually solving their own problems until external pressure was brought to bear upon them. The familiar complaint in the South today is that the Supreme Court's decision on education has set us back a generation in race relations, that people of different races who had long lived at peace have now been turned against one another. But this is a misinterpretation of what is taking place. When a subject people moves toward freedom, they are not creating a cleavage, but are revealing the cleavage which apologists of the old order have sought to conceal" (1958, 193).

23   In *Stride Toward Freedom,* Kings writes about the impact of law and courts in the following terms: "The law itself is a form of education. The words of the Supreme Court, of Congress, and of the Constitution are eloquent instructors. In fact, it would be a mistake to minimize the impact upon the South of the federal court orders and legislative and executive acts already in effect. Desegregation of the armed services, for instance, has already had an immense, incalculable impact. Federal court decrees have altered transportation patterns, teachers' salaries, the use of recreational facilities, and myriad other matters. The habits if not the hearts of people have been and are being altered every day by federal action" (1958, 199).

24   As Glennon writes, the difficulties with the Parks case were as follows: "First, her appeal through the Alabama state court system might consume years before reaching the Supreme Court, particularly if court clerks and judges acted dilatorily. Second, on the peculiar facts of her case, because no other seat was available to her, an Alabama court might avoid the constitutional issue of separate-but-equal by ruling that the statute did not apply to these specific facts. Third, because Mrs. Parks was convicted of violating the state bus segregation statute, the Alabama appellate courts would not explicitly address the constitutionality of the Montgomery ordinances. Of course, a ruling on the state statutes might have implications for the continuing validity (or invalidity) of the Montgomery ordinances but, in an uncooperative legal climate, further litigation would be required. Finally, the Alabama courts might resolve her appeal based on a question of Alabama law rather than federal law. . . . As a consequence, although Mrs. Parks's appeal squarely presented a constitutional question, it might not reach the Supreme Court in a timely fashion or in a form proper for resolution" (67–68).

25   Along with this NAACP assistance, the organization's president Roy Wilkins announced it would pay for most of the legal costs of the Parks' case, *Browder*

v. Gayle, and the defense of over a hundred boycotters (including King) who had been indicted for violating an antiboycotting law.

26 According to Branch (1988, 153), earlier in the boycott King told a reporter that "although as MIA leader he was seeking concessions within segregation, he was personally for "immediate integration" because as a minister of the gospel he believed segregation to be evil."

27 This discussion of finance reform litigation in New Jersey is a compressed summary of a much longer case study. I use notes to elaborate upon the summary presented here; these notes are there for the reader to take or leave. In this summary, I cover only about half of this controversy, ending the narrative in 1985 with the New Jersey Supreme Court's first decision in *Abbott (Abbott I). Abbott I* remanded the matter for trial. The New Jersey Supreme Court did not decide the case on the merits until 1990 (*Abbott II*). Because it does not go into much detail about developments after 1985, this study will not address "the impact" side of reformers' efforts much beyond this point, although it does offer a few speculative remarks.

28 For a journalist's account of the problem and its significance, see Kozol (1991). School finance arrangements reflect American traditions of federalism and local control over public schooling. Public education has long been viewed as a state-level function. As states developed common school systems over the course of the nineteenth century, they delegated most fiscal responsibility down to a large number of small school districts. Here, the vast majority of revenue for schools have come from *ad valorem* taxes levied upon real property within each district. Thus, the amount of money a local district could raise for schools depended upon two main factors: (1) the locally-decided upon tax rate, and (2) the valuation of taxable property within the district or municipality. In response to inequities, by the late 1930s most states had adopted some form of intergovernmental grant mechanism to provide "state aid" to local districts. For an overview, see Coons, Clune, and Sugarman (1970, 39–95).

29 These initial suits were a product of their times, invoking the legacy of *Brown* and the civil rights movement, and appealing to a body of federal equal protection doctrine in a state of flux. Reformers' first victory came in August, 1971, in *Serrano v. Priest.* Here, the California Supreme Court endorsed plaintiffs' claim that "education" was a fundamental right and "wealth" a suspect classification under the federal equal protection clause. Soon thereafter, a three-judge panel in Texas adopted the California court's reasoning, the state appealed to the United States Supreme Court, and the result was *San Antonio v. Rodriguez.*

30 For overviews, see Taylor and Piche (1990); and Underwood (1994).

31 Prior to the World War II, the legislature dominated state politics, and local, county-based political machines and business interests (particularly the railroads) dominated the legislature. See Salmore and Salmore (1993).

32 In 1930, the six largest cities housed 30% of the state's residents; today the figure is 8%. Loss of manufacturing jobs, tax revenues and political power accompanied this decline in population. Salmore and Salmore (1993, 52–57); Sternlieb and Hughes, in Pomper (1986, 56–84); *National Advisory Commission on Civil Disorders* (1968, 56–84).

33 Whereas the prior constitution limited the governor to one 3-year term, the new one extended the term to 4 years and permitted reelection for one additional term. The governor is the only official in New Jersey elected statewide, a trait New Jersey shares with only two other states. He or she can issue executive orders, has line-item and conditional vetoes, appoints and removes cabinet members, and controls about 500 additional high level appointments. While, as always in politics, formal powers are only part of the story, since the mid-1960s the Governor has come to play the dominant agenda-setting and policy-initiating role in state politics. Salmore and Salmore (1993, 128, and 127–143).

34 I rely here upon Tarr and Porter (1988, 193–197; and 64–66, 184–236). Tarr and Porter tell the story of "the legacy of reform" in considerable detail. Vanderbilt's new judicial article in the 1947 charter "eliminate[d] the [prior] division of law and equity, consolidate[d] judicial structures, create[d] a seven member supreme court, and centralize[d] managerial authority in the Chief Justice's hands" (191). An intermediate appellate court handles routine appeals, leaving the high Court free to control its docket. Popular elections play no role in judicial selection in New Jersey. Judges and justices are nominated by the governor and confirmed by the 40-member state Senate. After a seven year probationary period, judges and justices then have life tenure until a mandatory retirement age of 70. See also, Salmore and Salmore (1993, 182–200); Lehne (1978, 43).

35 McCann uses the term "radiating effects." (1994, 10). He in turn borrows it from Marc Galanter (1983).

36 See *Robinson v. Cahill (*118 N.J. Super. 223; 287 A.2d 187 [1972] [Botter, J.S.C.]; *Robinson v. Cahill* (62 N.J. 473; 303 A.2d 273 [1973]. Further citations in text, to *Atlantic Reporter.*

37 Lehne's study shows that the state-level officials responsible for defending *Robinson* over these years were not all that opposed to the broad objectives of the suit. Their defense paid more attention to relative institutional capacity (the court was not the proper place to do policy reform, and not that reform should not take place), and only weakly resisted on the substantive merits (Lehne, 32–33). It is unlikely that the Court would have been persuaded by a more vigorous defense developed to defend "local control." Still, it bears mentioning that "local control" did not get a hearing before the court, and that the court's treatment of this issue would set up an ongoing tension between legal ideals and concepts and deeply entrenched political and institutional practices. I say that "local control" represents a "web of justifications" because arguments for local control vary in emphases and empirical grounding. Pro-

ponents typically focus on the values enhanced by decentralization of fiscal responsibility, decision-making authority, and public administration. Here, some highlight the purported link between fiscal and political responsibility, on one hand, and participatory democracy, on the other. Others point to "diversity" in local community norms and/or the availability of market-like choices among school districts. Still others focus less on the benefits of decentralization than on the dangers of centralized authority and regulation.

38 The governor endorsed a guaranteed tax base program, assuring each district of a tax base per pupil equal to twice the state average tax base. At a time when the total state budget was $3 billion, Byrne's plan called for an increase of $550 million in state education aid, thereby raising the state's share of the total from 30 to 50%. Byrne also proposed a state income tax as "the only equitable way to raise the revenue needed for this program. . . ." For Byrne's proposal, see Lehne, 107–115. The reform attorneys were unhappy with the "guaranteed tax base" (or GTB) form because even a generous GTB plan like Byrne's still left much to local discretion-e.g., the trade-off between property tax relief and more money for education. Moreover, under the plan Byrne proposed-a plan that the legislature would not accept-middle- and lower-wealth suburban districts stood to gain more than increasingly pressed urban areas.

39 See Lehne (1978, 132); *Robinson III* (335 A.2d 6 [1975]; *Robinson IV* (339 A.2d 193 [1975]. Between 1971 and 1974, there was a turnover of 6 justices on the 7 member court. In late 1973, Governor Cahill nominated his Democratic gubernatorial predecessor, Richard Hughes, for the position of chief justice. On the whole, according to Tarr and Porter, the new group "shared . . . a generally positive assessment of the Warren Court's rulings." Hughes would serve as chief justice until his retirement in 1979, whereupon Governor Byrne nominated the late Robert N. Wilentz for the position (Tarr and Porter, 204–05). The leading dissenter favoring reformers' views in the *Robinson* cases was one of the newcomers, Justice Morris Pashman. One of Pashman's law clerks at the time was a young Harvard Law School graduate named Stephen Eisdorfer. After his clerkship, Eisdorfer joined the Education Law Center as a staff attorney and later served as its interim executive director. He was one of the architects of reformers' second-round challenge in *Abbott*, and continued to play a role in the case from his position in the State's Office of Public Advocate over the course of the 1980s and 90s (Eisdorfer Interview, 8/24/94).

40 Article II of the act continued: "For the purpose of evaluating the thoroughness and efficiency of all the public schools of the state, the Commissioner [of Education], with the approval of the State Board and after review by the [Legislature's] Joint Committee on the Public Schools, shall develop and administer a uniform, statewide system for evaluating the performance of each school" (*New Jersey Statutes Annotated*, 18A: 7A-4; 7A-5). The statutory provisions are discussed in great detail in the various opinions in *Robinson V*. To be sure, the legislature's ten elements "defining" a "thorough and efficient system" (with words like "adequate," "efficient," "qualified," and "encourage-

ment") can be viewed as empty rhetoric intended to satisfy the Court. Given the huge delegation of legislative authority to the state education department which followed here, this may well have been the "legislative intent." However, these goals and characterizations expressed ideals and structured expectations for various players in educational reform politics. There would be ongoing conflict over the meaning of these and other provisions, but these were terms (or "discursive resources") to which future reformers would appeal in order to advance their claims.

41 A second component of Article III, "minimum aid," continued to provide at least some state aid to the wealthier districts with equalized assessed valuations per pupil above the guaranteed level. The third component, "categorical aid" operated as a flat-grant mechanism, with weights for additional cost factors. These "categoricals" were special education; bilingual education; compensatory education; vocational education; and transportation aid. A final major component of state aid to education, the Teachers Pension and Annuity Fund (TPAF), existed entirely outside of Chapter 212. Since the mid-1960s, the state has through annual appropriations picked up the full costs of teacher pensions and the employers' share of Social Security. See Reock (1993).

42 Justice Conford and Justice Pashman, respectively. Justice Conford argued that finance reform would have to go at least as far as Governor Byrne's original proposal. Although Chapter 212 had raised the GTB to about $80,000 per pupil, the many districts (more than 200 of them) above the cut-off point had assessed valuations in the "hundreds of thousands of dollars . . ." (148). These "favored districts" would continue to enjoy greater resources combined with lower tax rates, compared to the others. Justice Pashman's dissent, as things turned out, did much to map out the terrain of future debate. There would be strong echoes of his opinion in reformers' future claims and the court's opinions in *Abbott v. Burke*. Justice Pashman organized his opinion according to "plaintiffs' and amici's objections to the 1975 Act." The majority, Pashman claimed, had "not even acknowledg[ed]" most of these objections (170). The thematic focus of his opinion is the possible meanings of the Act's regulatory and finance provision for children in poorer districts.

Although the court had upheld the facial validity of Chapter 212, the *Robinson* saga was not quite over. In passing the new law, the legislature had deferred action on revenue measures to cover its costs. In *Robinson V*, the Court proceeded on the assumption that the act would be fully funded, and retained jurisdiction to ensure compliance. In May 1976, after the legislature failed to fund the measure, the court held that "on or after July 1 . . . every public officer, state county or municipal," would be "enjoined from expending any funds for the support of any free public school." And, after legislators still could not agree on a revenue bill, the schools in fact closed on July 1, 1976 (there were about 100,000 students in summer session). On July 9, the Legislature passed a new state income tax, thereby bringing the *Robinson* litigation to a close (*Robinson VI*, 358 A.2d 457 [1976], at 459).

43 On the weakness of "urban-based reformers" in legislative politics during *Robinson*, see also Lehne (1978, 100–101).

44 This attention generated effects even as the *Robinson* litigation proceeded. In 1973, the National Urban Coalition provided money and staff to begin organizing efforts in Newark to support reform. Other national network channels organized around the Lawyers Committee for Civil Rights Under Law (Washington, D.C.) and school finance research conducted at Syracuse University's Maxwell School of Citizenship and Public Affairs, also became involved in supporting the New Jersey case. Local reform attorneys began taking steps to create their own institutional bases and to mobilize broader interest group support for their project.

45 For a discussion of the Ford Foundation's vast support of the public interest law movement in the mid-1970s, see Rabin (1976, 228–29).

46 Among the other lawyers was David C. Long of the Lawyers Committee for Civil Rights Under Law. Long would later assist lead attorney Marilyn Morheuser in trying *Abbott v. Burke*. An important activist was Herbert T. Green, Executive Director of "Schoolwatch" (see below).

47 See also "Coalition Plans Legal Action in Attempt to Overturn 'T & E'," *Newark Star-Ledger*, 11/4/79. Morheuser's experiences as a political activist began in Milwaukee in the early 1960s. At the time, she was a member of the Sisters of Loretto, a religious order of Catholic nuns. After the assassination of Medgar Evers, she was drawn into civil rights activities there, and soon left the Sisters of Loretto. After stints with a local black newspaper (she is white) and a settlement house involved in community organizing, she took a job as a researcher with the Milwaukee chapter of the NAACP. As a member of the NAACP's paid staff, she was in charge of factual research supporting a school desegregation suit brought by a local coalition and backed by the NAACP. She stated that, working closely with Robert L. Carter, she gathered data, interviewed potential witnesses, and negotiated the local chapter's relationship with other local groups. Then, in 1970, at the age of 46, Morheuser entered Rutgers Law School. After graduation, jobs as a public defender and then as a staff attorney with the ACLU preceded her move to the ELC in 1979. Interview with Morheuser, 6/20/94; DePalma, 1990; McLaurin, 1994.

48 I have borrowed the dual sense of "vision" from McCann (1986, 21).

49 The terms "filter out" and "compensatory view" are also taken from Jencks. Jencks' piece provides a useful sketch of some of the different meanings of "equality of educational opportunity." The New Jersey reformers also adopted what we might call a liberal, humane culture-of-poverty stance toward the place of education in structuring life chances and alleviating other social problems, such as poverty and crime. One can find statements similar to their outlook in the National Advisory Commission (Kerner) Report (424–56); and Schorr (1988, vii-xxix, 1–22, and 215–255).

50 In 1974, the Education Testing Service (ETS) in Princeton established a research institute and hired Syracuse professor and school finance expert Joel Berke to coordinate its activities. After the passage of Chapter 212, the Ford Foundation provided ETS with a grant to follow and report upon the fiscal impacts of the new law. Berke then hired his former student, Margaret Goertz, to supervise this Chapter 212 project. Goertz's research and data analysis took place over 1977 and early 1978. ETS released its report, titled "Money and Education: Where Did the 400 Million Dollars Go?," in March, 1978. The Report's central conclusion was that "[t]he basic distribution pattern for aid was unchanged...The new plan had no impact on disparities among districts in per pupil expenditures. In fact, the dollar gap between districts spending at the low 5th percentile and districts spending at the high 95th percentile widened. . . ." ETS circulated copies of its study to the media, and to citizens and advocacy groups (Interview with Margaret Goertz, 8/3/94). Goertz was a professor at Trenton State College when she joined her mentor at ETS. The ETS report took its background assumptions about what the new law should do from *Robinson I*, citing this case five times. It did not discuss *Robinson V* (Braun, 1978). In 1979, two other studies highlighted Chapter 212's failure to reduce tax and expenditure disparities across districts. The first, commissioned by the legislature's Joint Committee on Public Schools, was authored by Ernest Reock. Reock, a school finance specialist with the Rutgers University Bureau of Government Research, concluded that Chapter 212's "impact on fiscal equity" had "run its course." Wealthier communities still had the capacity to outpace others in expenditure increases, a trend being exacerbated by shifts in property values. "The major urban centers," on the other hand, were "heavily disadvantaged by the fiscal system." The second, a closer study of twenty districts by Rutgers professor Lawrence Rubin, concluded that "the educational disparities between poor and rich districts noted by the Court" had "actually worsened in almost all respects" (Braun, 1979; Zarate, 1979).

51 Schoolwatch had enough funding to set up an office with a small staff. The civic leaders who gathered the funding hired an education activist from Plainfield (Herbert Green) as the group's executive director. Schoolwatch's "Statement of Organizational Objectives" set forth the following goals: (1) to encourage and facilitate public participation in all levels of decision-making affecting public education; (2) to publicize the opportunities for and importance of citizen participation; (3) to research and analyze public education issues; (4) to disseminate research and analysis of public education issues and programs and recommendations for school improvement; and (5) to review implementation of the Public School Education Act of 1975, with specific emphasis on the role of the State Department of Education *(Interview with Herbert T. Green, 9/24/94).*

52 In this internal conflict, a proposal, backed primarily by Tom Corcoran (the education department's director of evaluation), to develop educational program and content standards was defeated in favor of "a process model—essentially, the state required local school districts to plan to plan." Tom Corcoran met Paul Tractenberg and Herbert Green through the Schoolwatch network.

He assisted reformers in *Abbott* and later served as Governor Jim Florio's education advisor (*Interview with Tom Corcoran, 9/29/94*).

53   As a former law clerk for New Jersey Supreme Court Justice Pashman, Eisdorfer was at least in a position to know what the record looked like to the Court over the course of *Robinson*.

54   That this issue was left unresolved is corroborated by the content of a *Newark Star-Ledger* article by Braun (1979b). The article notes differences in the desired approaches of the Newark Urban Coalition and the Education Law Center, with Eisdorfer emphasizing "the finance side" of the claims. *Abbott* was not actually filed until February, 1981. In addition to further development of the legal theory of the case and gathering evidence, the delay was also the result of continued conflict between the (white-led) ELC and the (minority-led) Urban Coalition. The Urban Coalition and Newark officials filed their own suit in 1980, but were soon persuaded to withdraw their challenge and to support the ELC's case. As it turned out, the state's primary defense in *Abbott* would be that any educational deficiencies in urban districts stemmed not from Chapter 212's finance scheme, but from "mismanagement, waste, and corruption" in local school districts.

55   In other states, school finance reform efforts evidence different "lawyer-client" patterns and related thinking about the relationship between law and politics. In Kentucky, for example, the reform effort began within the state education bureaucracy, and gradually spread out to local school districts. A political organization ("The Council for Better Education, Inc.") became the client in the lawsuit, and the lawsuit became part of a much broader political effort. Dove (1991).

56   In New York, after 27 property poor suburban districts initiated a challenge to the finance system, the 4 largest, property-rich (but allegedly "municipally overburdened") urban districts successfully intervened as additional plaintiffs. Later, 85 relatively property-rich districts successfully intervened in order to join the state in defending the existing system. The New Jersey reformers believed that the New York suit had become unwieldy—with too much attention paid to too many different issues and interests—thereby replicating in the judicial realm "the very majoritarian balance of power that reformers go to court to avoid," as Eisdorfer put it. On the New York case, *Board of Education v. Nyquist*, 57 N.Y.2d 27, 439 N.E.2d 359 (N.Y. Court of Appeals, 1982) (New York's highest court rejects challenge to school finance law), see Kaden (1983) and Berke, et al. (1984).

57   Maintaining good relationships with "constituents" thus held at arms length would be a delicate operation. Although the relationship between local district personnel and the ELC was at first "uneasy and ambivalent" (*Green Interview*), over the course of *Abbott*, Morheuser's talents as an advocate and perseverance as an activist increasingly won her the respect and admiration of this constituency. It helped that Morheuser adopted what she called an "agnostic" stance on the question of administrative practices (mismanage-

ment, corruption) in the local districts. It would be naive not to see something of a *quid pro quo* in this tacit bargain between the ELC and the urban school districts. Another point worth noting is the significance of foundation support in allowing the ELC to become a player in the complicated terrain of education reform politics. None of these strategic moves would have been possible without an independent resource base. Over the course of the 1980s, as foundation support dried up, obtaining financial resources and other forms of material support would be a major "side-task" for Morheuser in pressing the case. After reformers finally prevailed on the merits in *Abbott* in 1990, the ELC started drawing substantial resources from poorer, urban school districts (in the form of allocations for "fees for services rendered"). These allocations now account for about half of the ELC's annual budget.

58 Of course, Morheuser's tactical approach did not come out of nowhere. One influence was the NAACP's long history of "point-by-point" comparisons of educational resources and programming available to racially segregated or racially identifiable schools. See Kluger (1976); see also, *Hobson v. Hansen* (265 F. Supp. 902 [D.D.C., 1967]); modified, and, as modified, affirmed sub. nom. *Smuck v. Hobson* (408 F.2d 175 [D.C. Cir. 1969]). Another influence was certainly the inclusion of elements of this approach in the New York State school finance case. For the latter point, see *Eisdorfer Interview*.

59 McCann often uses the term "refigure" to denote "meaning-making activity" fashioning new claims out of the legal materials given from the past. As noted in the text above, a final conceptual element of Morheuser's case involved maintaining "a clear focus on race." Race and racism had also dropped out of *Robinson*, in her view. The simple assertion of a state equal protection claim would be enough to allow the presentation of evidence highlighting the "racially disparate impact" of the finance system. Although not likely to succeed, "disparate impact" could constitute grounds for an equal protection violation under state constitutional law.

60 Kean was the scion of wealthy New Jersey political family. After graduating from Princeton, he taught for three years at the same private boarding school he had attended in his youth. He then went on to obtain a master's degree in education from Teacher's College before following his father's footsteps into New Jersey politics. In Jencks's terms, Kean and Cooperman favored a moralistic, or meritocratic, conception of "equality of educational opportunity," grounded upon rewarding effort. These themes also run through Kean's comments about his educational experiences and views in his political autobiography. Kean (1988, 208-239). After the National Commission on Excellence in Education issued its report, *A Nation At Risk* (1983), Kean and Cooperman issued their own "Blueprint for Educational Reform." Over the next several years, the Kean Administration not only did everything it could to resist reformers' challenge in *Abbott*, it also successfully pursued its own broad education reform agenda.

61 McCann's *Rights At Work* demonstrates the importance of looking at the role that litigation activities themselves (what is involved in "doing" the case)

can play organizationally and politically. Here, the ELC's extensive process of interviewing hundreds of potential witnesses from some 25(rich as well as poor) probably helped to establish Morheuser's and her colleagues' authority as the representatives of poorer children. To some extent, this process had to be repeated after *Abbott I*, in preparation for trial in 1987. As noted above, these lawyer-reformers had come to the conclusion that ordinary political activity offered them no hope at this point; they were simply overmatched by the raw power of suburban interests and the white majority's hostility to their goals.

However it is worth asking—and with the benefit of hindsight it is easy to ask—whether reformers' assessment of their prospects in politics was correct, and whether they missed opportunities for broader political mobilization. One can't help speculating about what might have happened had reformers put some energy and resources into building some sort of organization or broader coalition to engage in lobbying and publicity, instead of being single-mindedly focused on building a winning in court. Would involving and being accountable to a wider and more diverse group of supporters have changed the goals, strategies or tactics of the reformers? Could reformers have forged alliances across race and class? Could *Abbott* have been part of a much broader, democratic reform effort? There is at least some evidence that the prospects for ordinary political action were not quite as dismal as reformers surmised. First, in putting together and making her case at trial, Morheuser sought and received significant support from administrators, teachers and others in some of New Jersey's wealthiest districts. Second, after Florio's reform measure came undone in 1990-91, some leaders of wealthy districts and other educational interest groups were willing to form a coalition with the ELC and the poorer urban districts. Still, this counter-factual about taking more risks in politics can never be answered. We can never know whether a different approach, one more attentive to building political organizations to back reform, would have yielded dividends. On the relationship between "flesh and blood clients" and lawyers' participation in networks of community support, on one hand, and "success," on the other, see Tushnet (1987).

62   The trial court's order (issued from the bench) is discussed in *Abbott v. Burke* (477 A.2d 1278 [N.J. Super., Appellate Division, 1984]).

63   *Robinson V*, the court held, had indeed contemplated just this sort of challenge to Chapter 212. *Abbott v. Burke* (477 A.2d 1278 [1984]).

64   In its conclusion, Justice Handler's opinion remanded the case for an administrative hearing. However, in doing so, he alleviated the ELC's concerns about having to make its case before Cooperman's department of education. The court ordered the commissioner to transfer the case to the state's Office of Administrative Law (OAL), and noted the appropriateness of assigning the case to an administrative judge with "special qualifications commensurate with the demands of the case itself" (*Abbott I*, 394, quoting *City of Hackensack v. Winner* [410 A.2d 1146]). The OAL was created in 1978 in order to "systematize the work of hearing examiners assigned to investigate complaints against state agencies. Administrative law judges make recommendations to

agency heads, who can accept or reject them. A complainant dissatisfied with the final agency decision can appeal to court" (Salmore and Salmore, 185).

65 Lefelt Decision, 12. *Abbott I* proved remarkably "productive" in defining the issues and structuring the presentation of evidence and the nature of the arguments at trial. Throughout, the state defendants argued that reformers' detailed, point-by-point comparisons (tax and expenditure data, resources, conditions and processes, and educational outcome) across poor urban and rich suburban districts were irrelevant to the constitutional question. The reformers' framing at the extremes was "unfair," for it ignored the vast majority of districts in the middle. Moreover, highlighting its claims about corruption and waste in the cities, the state further claimed that comparing poor, urban Jersey City to wealthy, suburban South Orange/Maplewood was like comparing "oranges to *rotten* apples" (Lefelt, 362). In response, ALJ Lefelt repeatedly pointed to *Abbott I*: "I FIND that such comparisons are not only appropriate but were expected by the Supreme Court [in *Abbott*] . . . In order to judge the school system in a State as geographically small as ours, I believe that any district within the system should be examinable and comparable with any other" (Lefelt, 27–28). ALJ Lefelt thus argued that *Abbott I* compelled him to listen to what reformers had to say about disparities across very poor and very rich districts. Having listened, he found himself won over to reformers' basic outlook. Although he did not agree with reformers' on every point, their "relative needs" orientation does inform the entire sweep of his opinion.

66 Simon also notes that with respect to law and courts, Rosenberg "shares the realist tendency to reify social circumstances as independent of the legal definitions that inscribe them—and [to reify] legal institutions as independent of the social forces that influence them" (938–39).

67 There is an additional point to make here with respect to *The Hollow Hope*: Since Rosenberg acknowledges that Montgomery was central in inspiring the civil rights movement, his claim that *Brown* and the courts were not that important in Montgomery can be seen as the linchpin of his larger argument about Brown, the courts, and "indirect effects" on the movement. We would add that we have no stake in the mythology about Brown peddled by certain legal academics and liberal lawyers since the late 1960s. Indeed, we agree with and have learned much from Rosenberg's attack upon this mythology, as well as upon larger myths of legalism.

68 The New Jersey case study presented above follows McCann mainly in adopting the standpoint of would-be reformers and in treating law as potentially "constitutive" of social and political understandings and possibilities.

69 We borrow these words from Linda Gordon's *Heroes of Their Own Lives: The Politics and History of Family Violence*. Gordon's treatment of family violence relies heavily upon analyses of "case records of social work agencies devoted to child protection." The entire relevant passage, which follows, evokes the spirit of our commentary on McCann. Gordon writes: "The interactions between client and worker which are central to my argument, central to whole

historical construction of family violence, can *only* be revealed in actual case histories. Throughout this book I have chosen to tell, as much as possible, *whole stories rather than excerpts from stories*, so that the peculiarities of every situation are inescapable, and so that my generalizations are seen for what they are: abstractions, not 'typical cases.' I also tell whole stories in order to maximize the readers' opportunity to 'see' my interpretation and to argue with it . . ." (18, emphases added). For a perceptive typology of narratives in legal studies, see Ewick and Silbey (1995). In Ewick and Silbey's terms, we are advocating the pursuit of narrative as product (narratives constructed by researchers), and also as method (attention to narratives used by actors in the world). We drafted this conclusion before McCann (1996) was available. In this response to Rosenberg's review of *Rights At Work*, McCann acknowledges and discusses some of the points we make here.

70 The four stages are: (1) "the movement building process"; (2) "the struggle to compel formal changes in official policy"; (3) "the struggle for control over actual policy development and implementation"; (4) "the transformative legacy of legal action" (McCann 1994, 11).

71 McCann's decision to proceed in this way no doubt stems from "some very conventional social scientific commitments," particularly his "intent to develop a generalizable theoretical approach" (McCann, 14).

72 This argument for thick, narrative description, we think, raises some difficult issues in the philosophy of social science, particularly with respect to conceptualizations of relationships among researchers, subject matter (including political actors), and readers. McCann has highlighted some of these issues in his discussions of "interpretivist," or "post-realist" research. Interpretive researchers "assume a rather skeptical position regarding traditional scientific goals of defining clear causal relations and developing strong predictive capacities . . . , [for] every historical moment is subject to multiple contingencies which no theory can predict. . . . Moreover, it is important to remember that social action is generated out of ever-changing processes of human conceptualization" (McCann 1994, 15). Our comments in this conclusion explore some further implications of this underlying, interpretivist conception of social research. Thus, we view our critique of McCann as a friendly one that follows from McCann's own larger theoretical commitments.

73 When in Part Three of his book Scheingold turned to "Strategist of Rights," his first words were these: "The basic message of the politics of rights to lawyers interested in altering the status quo is simple. They are directed to turn their attention, at least in part, to the mobilizing potential of litigation" (1974, 151).

74 For some recent commentary, see Kessler (1996, 790).

75 We do meet several lawyers in *Rights At Work*. However, McCann doesn't tell us much about them. Nor does he ever take up why these lawyers are "realistic" in their orientation toward law and politics. Their labor backgrounds

(and perhaps also connections with the National Lawyers Guild) might explain this. If so, then their focus on power and mobilization would be nothing new. If not, then we might have occasion to think about political learning or, more broadly, the diffusion of realist understandings in the legal culture generally and the implications of this. On this last point, see Brigham (1987).

76   On these points, see Tushnet (1987, 153–155). According to Tushnet, "What matters is not the inevitable, that lawyers have a kind of power with respect to their clients, but the variable, what disciplines them in the exercise of the power they have" (150).

77   This effort would require the researcher to enter the world of doctrine and legal practice in even more detail than does McCann, in order to get at the significance of legal arguments and doctrine for political processes and outcomes-to see "lawyer's law" from the inside, but without stopping there in the way that many legal academics concerned with legal rhetoric tend to do.

78   McCann notes that he increasingly turned to a conversational mode of interviewing as his research progressed—"a willingness to engage in friendly and responsive but substantively serious conversation" (20)—and comments that ". . . the best education about political activity comes from activists themselves" (xi).

79   A number of caveats are in order: *First*: As King, Keohane and Verba (1994) put it: "the difference between the amount of complexity in the world and that in the thickest of descriptions is still vastly larger than the difference between this thickest of descriptions and the most abstract, quantitative or formal analysis...There is no choice but to simplify." Designing Social Inquiry: Scientific Inference in Qualitative Research (Princeton: Princeton University Press, 1994). Much depends, then, upon the researcher's purposes. Our suggestions about 'whole stories' proceed from a certain conception of practical utility—of the work that thick description guided by McCann's outlook might do—which in turn involves exploring processes of "repositioning" between researchers and subjects. For an interesting discussion of "repositioning," see Harrington and Yngvesson (1990, 135, 144–45). For another fascinating example of "repositioning" examining rights consciousness among persons with disabilities, see Engel and Munger (1996, 7). *Second*: We agree with McCann that "there is a consequential world out there to study, but . . . all efforts to understand it are only partial, biased, imperfect social constructions . . .[T]here is no value-free mode of empirical research activity." (McCann 1995, 6). The sorts of interpretive accounts we have in mind are not purely phenomonological; the point is not simply to understand consciousness, but to explain events and outcomes, and critically to evaluate action in context. The problem with narrative accounts is that they "explain by way of etiology[;]" they "show by way of the enchainment of events how we got to where we are" (Brooks 1996, 14, 19). The risk, of course, is that causal claims will be made, but without the internal and external checks and balances that follow from commitments to formalization, operationalization, falsifiability, and the like. We think the price paid is worth it, but we wouldn't go so far as to

claim that nothing is lost in the decision to go with thick description (to tell whole stories). *Third*: Our suggestions about cause lawyering and reflexivity would seem to require the elaboration of possible orientations toward law and politics on both sides of the researcher/subject divide. Ideal-typical possibilities might be "legalists," "realists," and "postrealist" (or "constitutive") views about a range of law/politics issues (e.g., beliefs and behaviors with respect to: lawyer-client relations; how normative visions and policy goals get translated into legal claims and arguments; the "articulation" between the "legal" and "political" dimensions of a reform effort, and so on).

80 While various scholars have defined new institutionalism differently, Robert Putnam has succinctly laid out the area of agreement:

1. *Institutions shape politics*. The rules and standard operating procedures that make up institutions leave their imprint on political outcomes by structuring political behavior. Outcomes are not simply reducible to the billiard-ball interaction of individuals nor to the intersection of broad social forces. Institutions influence outcomes because they shape actors' identities, power, and strategies.

1. *Institutions are shaped by history*. Whatever other factors may affect their form, institutions have inertia and "robustness." They therefore embody historical trajectories and turning points. History matters because it is "path dependent": what comes first (even if it was in some sense "accidental") conditions what comes later. Individuals may "choose" their institutions, but they do not choose them under circumstances of their own making, and their choices in turn influence the rules within which their successors choose (7–8).

See also, Pierson (1993); and Smith (1988).

81 In this light, it is interesting that McCann tends to place very different law and courts scholars, such as Horowitz (1977) and Rosenberg (1991), in the same "neo-realist gap studies" camp. (McCann 1994, 177; 288–93). McCann does this in order to make some important points about the differences between his view and these and many other "realist-informed" studies. Further, McCann does distinguish between two somewhat different claims made by neorealists: First, that courts lack power and resources to see things through (Rosenberg); and second, that courts lack capacity to make 'effective' policy (Horowitz). *However*, we think McCann tends to collapse these two strands into a broad claim that courts are "insignificant" or "ineffective." The problem here is that, for Horowitz and others following him (e.g., Melnick 1994), "ineffective" does not mean "insignificant." For these neo-conservative scholars, courts play a very important and often decisive role in politics and policy, but, as a general matter, the processes are "antidemocratic" and the results are perverse. Students of law and change embracing a mobilization perspective might do well to emulate the close, descriptive work of scholars like Horowitz and Melnick. Compared to such neoconservative, realist approaches, of course, left-liberal mobilization views would evaluate legitimacy and capacity (policy results) from a different normative baseline.

Works Cited

Abernathy, Ralph David. 1958. "The Natural History of a Social Movement: The Montgomery Improvement Association" Pp. 99–172 in *The Walking City: Montgomery Bus Boycott, 1955–56*. Brooklyn: Carlson Publishing.

———. 1989. *And the Walls Came Tumbling Down*. New York: Harper & Row.

Barrett, George. 1956. "Montgomery: Testing Ground," *New York Times Magazine* (December 12):48.

Berke, Joel and Margaret Goertz. 1984. *Politicians, Judges and City Schools* (New York: Russell Sage).

Branch, Taylor. 1988. *Parting the Waters: America in the King Years 1954-1963*. New York: Simon & Schuster.

Braun, Robert. 1978. "Study Finds Wide Gap in School Aid Formula" *Newark Star-Ledger* (April 30): 1.

———. 1979a. "School Aid Revise Could Add $53 Million" *Newark Star-Ledger* (July 26): 1.

———. 1979b. "Coalition Plans Legal Action in Attempt to Overturn T & E" *Newark Star-Ledger* (November 4): 1.

Brigham, John. 1987. *The Cult of the Court*. Philadelphia: Temple University Press.

Brooks, Peter. 1996. "The Law as Narrative and Rhetoric." Pp. 14–22 in *Law's Stories*, ed. Peter Brooks and Paul Gerwitz. New Haven: Yale University Press.

Coons, John, E., William H. Clune, and Stephen C. Sugarman. 1970. *Private Wealth and Public Education*. Cambridge, MA: Harvard University Press.

DePalma, Anthony. 1990. "About New Jersey" *New York Times*. (June 24): 21.

Dove, Ronald G., Jr. 1991. "Acorns in A Mountain Pool: The Role of Litigation, Law and Lawyers in Kentucky Education Reform" *Journal of Education Finance* 17 (Summer) :83.

Engel, David, and Frank Munger. 1996. "Rights, Rememberance, and the Reconciliation of Difference" *Law and Society Review* 30: 7.

Ewick, Patricia, and Susan S. Silbey. 1995. "Subversive Stories and Hegemonic Tales: Toward a Sociology of Narrative" *Law and Society Review* 29: 197.

Feeley, Malcom. 1992. Hollow Hopes, Flypaper, and Metaphors. Review of *The Hollow Hope. Law and Social Inquiry* 17: 745–763.

Firestone, William, and Margaret Goertz. 1994. New Jersey's Quality Education Act: Fiscal, Programmatic, Curricular and Intergovernmental Effects. Paper presented at annual meeting of the American Education Research Association, Nashville, TN (March).

Galanter, Marc, 1983. "The Radiating Effects of Courts." Pp. 117–42 *Empirical Theories of Courts,* ed. Keith D. Boynum and Lynn Mather. New York: Longman.

Gambitta, Richard L.L., and Marlynn May and James C. Foster, 1981. *Governing Through Courts.* New York: Sage Publications.

Garrow, David J. 1986. *Bearing the Cross: Martin Luther King Jr., and the Southern Christian Leadership Conference.* New York: Morrow.

———. 1989. "The Origins of the Montgomery Bus Boycott of 1955–56." Pp. 607–622 *The Walking City: Montgomery Bus Boycott, 1955–56,* ed. David J. Garrow. Brooklyn: Carlson Publishing.

Giddens, Anthony. 1990. *The Consequences of Modernity.* Palo Alto: Stanford University Press.

Glennon, Robert Jerome. 1991. "The Role of Law in the Civil Rights Movement: The Montgomery Bus Boycott, 1955–1957" *Law and History Review* 9 (Spring): 69.

Gordon, Linda. 1988. *Heroes of Their Own Lives: The Politics and History of Family Violence.* New York: Penguin Books.

Handler, Joel F. 1978. *Social Movements and the Legal System.* New York: Academic Press.

Harrington, Christine B., and Barbara Yngvesson. 1990. "Interpretive Sociolegal Research" *Law and Social Inquiry* 15: 135.

Horowitz, Donald. 1977. *The Courts and Social Policy.* Washington, D.C.: The Brookings Institution

Jencks, Christopher. 1988. "Whom Must We Treat Equally for Educational Opportunity to Be Equal?" *Ethics* 98 (April): 518–533.

Kaden, Lewis B. 1983. "Courts and Legislatures in a Federal System: The Case of School Finance" *Hofstra Law Review* 11: 1213–25.

Kean, Thomas H. *1988. The Politics of Inclusion.* New York: Free Press.

Kennedy, Randall. 1989. "Martin Luther King's Constitution: A Legal History of the Montgomery Bus Boycott" *Yale Law Journal* 98:999.

Kessler, Mark. 1996. Lawyers and Social Change in the Postmodern World. Review of *Lawyers in a Postmodern World* and *Rebellious Lawyering. Law and Society Review* 30: 796.

King, Gary, Robert Keohane, and Sidney Verba. 1994. *Designing Social Inquiry: Scientific Inference in Qualitative Research.* Princeton: Princeton University Press.

King, Martin Luther, Jr. 1956. "The Montgomery Story" Speech delivered June 27. Reprinted in *U.S. News and World Report* (August 3).

———. 1958. *Stride Toward Freedom: The Montgomery Story.* New York: Harper.

———. 1959. "Yale University Address" *Martin Luther King Papers,* Boston University. (January 14).

———. 1986. A Testament of Hope: The Essential Writings of Martin Luther King Jr., ed. James Melvin Washington. San Francisco: Harper and Row.

———. 1994. The Papers of Martin Luther King, Jr.: Volume II: Rediscovering Precious Values, July 1951–November 1955, ed. Ralph E. Luker, Penny A. Russel, and Peter Holloran. Berkeley: University of California Press.

Kinkaid, John. 1993. Introduction to *New Jersey Politics and Government: Suburban Politics Comes of Age,* by Barbara G. Salmore and Stephen A. Salmore. Lincoln, NE: University of Nebraska Press.

Klarman, Michael J. 1994. "How Brown Changed Race Relations: The Backlash Thesis" *Journal of American History* (June):81.

Kozol, Jonathan. 1991. *Savage Inequalities.* New York: Crown Publishers.

Lehne, Richard. 1978. *The Quest for Justice: The Politics of School finance Reform.* New York: Longman.

Luker, Ralph E., Penny A. Russel, and Peter Holloran, eds. 1994. *Introduction to the Papers of Martin Luther King, Jr.* Volume II: *Rediscovering Precious Values,* July 1951-November 1955. Berkeley: University of California Press.

March, James G., and Johan P. Olsen. 1989. *Rediscovering Institutions: The Organizational Basis of Politics.* New York: Free Press.

McCann, Michael W. 1986. *Taking Reform Seriously.* Ithaca: Cornell University Press

———. 1992. Reform Litigation on Trial. Review of *The Hollow Hope. Law and Social Inquiry* 17: 715–743.

———. 1994. *Rights At Work: Pay Equity Reform and the Politics of Legal Mobilization.* Chicago: University of Chicago Press.

———. 1995. It's Only Law and Courts, But I Like It. . . . Paper presented at annual meeting of American Political Science Association.

———. 1996. "Causal versus Constitutive Explanations (or, On the Difficulty of Being So Positive...)" *Law and Social Inquiry* 21: 457.

McLarin, Kimberly J. 1994. "At the Bar" *New York Times.* (July 22): B9.

Melnick, R. Shep. 1994. *Between the Lines: Statutory Interpretation and the Politics of Entitlements.* Washington, D.C.: The Brookings Institution.

National Advisory Commission. 1968. *Report on Civil Disorders.* New York: Bantam.

Olson, Susan M. 1984. *Clients and Lawyers: Securing the Rights of Disabled Persons*. Westport, CT: Greenwood Press.

Pierson, Paul. 1993. "When Effects Become Cause: Policy Feedback and Political Change" *World Politics* (July).

Putnam, Robert. 1993. *Making Democracy Work: Civic Associations in Modern Italy*. Princeton: Princeton University Press.

Rabin, Robert l. 1976. "Lawyers for Social Change: Perspectives on Public interest Law." *Stanford Law Review* 28:207, 228–229.

Reock, Ernest C. Jr. 1993. "State Aid for Schools in New Jersey, 1976–1993." Center for Government Services, Rutgers.

Robinson, Jo Ann Gibson. 1987. *The Montgomery Bus Boycott and the Women Who Started It: The Memoir of Jo Ann Gibson Robinson*, ed. David J. Garrow. Knoxville: University of Tennessee Press.

Rosenberg, Gerald N. 1991. *The Hollow Hope: Can Courts Bring About Social Change?* Chicago: University of Chicago Press.

———. 1992. "Hollow Hopes and Other Aspirations: A Reply to Feeley and McCann" *Law and Social Inquiry* 17: 761–778.

Salmore, Barbara G., and Stephen A. Salmore. 1993. *New Jersey Politics and Government: Suburban Politics Comes of Age*. Lincoln, NE: University of Nebraska Press.

Scheingold, Stuart A. 1974. *The Politics of Rights*. New Haven: Yale University Press.

———. 1981. "The Politics of Rights Revisited," in *Governing Through Courts,"* ed. Richard L.L. Gamitta et al. New York: Sage Publications.

Schorr, Lisabeth B. 1988. *Within Our Reach: Breaking the Cycle of Disadvantage*. New York: Doubleday.

Schuck, Peter. 1993. Public Law Litigation and Social Reform. Review of *The HollowHope*. *Yale Law Journal* 102 (May): 1763.

Simon, Jonathan. 1992. The Long Walk Home to Politics. Review of *The Hollow Hope*. *Law and Society Review* 24: 923.

Skocpol, Theda. 1992. *Protecting Soldiers and Mothers: The Political Origins of Social Policy in the United States*. Cambridge, MA: Harvard University Press.

Smith, Rogers M. 1988. "Political Jurisprudence, the 'New Institutionalism,' and the Future of Public Law" *American Political Science Review* 82 (March): 89.

Sternlieb, George and James W. Hughes. 1986. "Demographic and Economic Dynamics" Pp. 27–44 in *The Political State of New Jersey*, ed. Gerald M. Pomper. New Brunswick: Rutgers University Press.

Tarr, Alan and Mary Cornelia Porter. 1988. *State Supreme Courts in State and Nation*. New Haven: Yale University Press.

Taylor, William L., and Dianne M. Piche. 1990. *Shortchanging Children: The Impact of Fiscal Inequity on the Education of Students at Risk*. A Report Prepared for the Committee on Education and Labor, U.S. House of Representatives, 101st Cong., 2nd sess. Committee Print.

Thornton, J. Miles III. 1980. "Challenge and Response in the Montgomery Bus Boycott of 1955–56" *Alabama Review* 33 (July):163.

Tushnet, Mark. 1987. *The NAACP's Legal Strategy Against Segregated Education*. Chapel Hill, NC: University of North Carolina Press.

Underwood, Julie K. 1994. "School Finance Litigation: Legal Theories, Judicial Activism, and Social Neglect," *Journal of Education Finance* 20 (Fall).

Zarate, Vincent R. 1979. "Council Told Gap is Growing Wider Between Rich and Poor" *Newark Star-Ledger* (October 5): 21.

Chapter 3

The Pro-Choice Legal Mobilization and Decline of Clinic Blockades

Robert Van Dyk

Introduction

Abortion clinic blockades were the most common form of civil disobedience in the 1980s, and they rank among the largest cases of civil disobedience in American history. From 1987 to 1992 at least 40,000 arrests were made at abortion clinics, with over 15,000 in 1989 alone.[1] After the high point of the blockade movement in the late 1980s and early 1990s, however, clinic blockades significantly declined. There were only a handful of arrests in 1994. In this essay I examine the decline of clinic blockades in light of two related, yet distinct, academic literatures. The first theoretical discourse that informs this work is the literature on legal mobilization. The second is the more general explanatory framework used to understand participation in social movements. I think there are fruitful insights to be gained by exploring the connections between these veins of inquiry.

My argument has three parts. First, I argue that a central factor in the decline of clinic blockades was a legal mobilization by supporters of abortion rights. Much of this paper is devoted to describing the creative and novel ways that legal advocates for women's groups and abortion providers used the law to deter blockaders. Second, I argue that this mobilization is a good example of the potentially desirable "radiating effects"[2] of litigation in promoting a progressive political cause. There has been much skepticism of late as to the importance of the courts in promoting social change, and the effect of litigation on clinic blockaders provides an instructive, if limited, case of success. Third, I argue that the nature of the radiating effects and their success in deterring blockades is made clearer when considered in the light of social movement theory. Abortion defenders' success in the courts undermined the blockade movement at both the mezzo (organizational) and micro (individual) levels. At the mezzo-level it debilitated the central blockade organization, Operation Rescue, and it undermined the movement's base of support in churches. At the micro-level it raised the costs of participation to such an extent that otherwise supportive movement participants were deterred by the fear of high sanctions. I will briefly describe some of the pertinent issues from the legal mobilization and social movement perspectives before moving to the evidence regarding the mechanics of the legal counter-assault against the clinic blockade movement.

There are good reasons to be skeptical of the value of a legal mobilization in deterring clinic blockades. Much recent scholarship urges caution against a turn to the law in search of progressive social change. This skepticism comes from a variety of disciplinary approaches, ranging from the critical legal studies' criticism of the inherent biases of the liberal legal form, to expositions of the problematic relationship between litigation and grassroots mobilization (Kairys 1982; Kelman 1987; McCann 1986). The most recent and emphatic voice of skepticism comes from Gerald Rosenberg (1991) in *The Hollow Hope*. The general theme running through these works is that litigation may carry more costs than benefits for social movements. As Rosenberg puts it, "not only does litigation steer activists to an institution that is constrained from helping them, but also it siphons off crucial resources and talent, and runs the risk of weakening political efforts" (339). Popular protest and legislation are offered as a more promising use of resources.

In this essay I wish to draw attention to the legal mobilization against clinic blockades as a case in which litigation *was* a relatively successful political strategy. The success of the pro-choice turn to litigation does not directly contradict these skeptics' claims about the efficacy of the courts in promoting social change. In many ways the legal mobilization by abortion defenders was about protecting the status quo. Defeating the clinic blockade movement did not create a libertarian social democracy, and Rosenberg readily recognizes that a turn to courts can be useful in this limited role (Rosenberg 1991, 33). Thus the success of the legal mobilization against clinic blockades should not be entirely surprising. Turning to the courts can supply "leverage" with which to move political opponents (McCann 1994, ch. 5). This leverage, in turn, can have a number of radiating effects far beyond the immediate litigation in which the legal mobilization takes place. While the reasons the legal mobilization had a strong negative effect on the blockade movement is made clear by social movement theory, the reason for success in the courtroom is a bit less clear. In the conclusion I consider the reasons the pro-choice legal mobilization enjoyed success in the courtroom, and I offer some general comments on the implications of this case for theories regarding the conditions in which courts are effective avenues for promoting a progressive agenda.

Below I briefly elaborate some of the central concepts in social movement theory to lay the groundwork for understanding the effects of the legal mobilization on clinic blockaders. I then present a thumbnail account of the germination of the clinic blockade movement, before moving to the details of pro-choice legal mobilization.

Social Movement Theory

Social movements do not rise spontaneously from masses of isolated individuals with a common grievance. Recent theories and empirical studies direct attention to the importance of resources and organizations as prerequisites for social movement development.[3] When a committed core of activists is able to gain the support of preexisting social networks and organizational resources, widespread social mobilization is far more likely (Snow, Zurcher, and Ekland-Olson, 787–801). Preexisting social networks serve as the basis for coordinated action in a number of ways. When movement activists succeed in mobilizing a preexisting group, they gain not only access to the group's material resources, but movements also gain benefit of a leadership structure and the potential to transfer allegiance from a pre-existing group to the movement. The most salient and well-studied example of this dynamic comes from the role of the churches in the civil rights movement (McAdam 1982; Morris 1984).

Underlying these recent mezzo-level accounts of mobilization, with their organizational emphasis, is a micro-level account of individual participation that relies, in part, on a vision of movement participants as rational actors. This vein of theorizing posits that movement participants are attentive to the importance of costs and benefits when deciding to join a collective action.[4] When costs of participation are high, fewer people will be willing to participate than when costs are low. Resources and organizations reduce the costs of mobilization, enhance the likelihood of success, and provide ready informational conduits and authority structures through which ideologically committed leaders can recruit and rally participants.

The organizing *for* clinic blockades was dependent on both the successful mobilization of preexisting social networks and the ability to provide opportunities for participation with relatively low costs for participants. The legal mobilization *against* clinic blockades was particularly successful because it affected the blockade movement adversely at both the organizational and individual levels. The sanctions helped incapacitate the central movement organization, Operation Rescue, and frightened the organizational base of the movement in the conservative Protestant churches. The mobilization also increased the costs for individual participants to such an extent that many formerly willing participants were no longer interested in participating.

Clinic Blockades
The clinic blockade movement did not receive widespread media attention until 1988, but the movement had roots in a core groups of activists who advocated and participated in blockades dating to the mid-1970s. The initial advocates of direct action at clinics were primarily Catholics, and this remained true through the mid-1980s. After several years of sporadic activity at disparate locations across the country, connections developed between these small local groups, and organizational ties coalesced in the Pro-Life Action Network (PLAN). Early leaders included Joseph Scheidler in Chicago, John Ryan in St. Louis, and Joan Andrews, a roving blockader hailing from Tennessee.

The key factors for the expansion of clinic blockades into a widespread movement came in two related developments. First was the entrance of a charismatic Protestant leader in the person of Randall Terry. Terry forged links between the predominantly Catholic PLAN and conservative Protestant churches. Through the mobilization of a core of PLAN supporters, together with new recruits from conservative Protestant churches, including many young pastors, the newly formed Operation Rescue (OR) orchestrated a series of massive blockades.[5] Second, the protests at the 1988 Democratic Convention in Atlanta drew not only national media attention but also support from leading elites in the Christian right. Jerry Falwell, Pat Robertson, James Dobson, and Dr. James Kennedy all endorsed the movement. Terry appeared on Robertson's television program and Dobson's radio show where he explained the blockade philosophy and appealed for recruits and money. Participation and contributions skyrocketed. The support of a preexisting network in the conservative churches and the access to a mass audience through the endorsement of leaders in the Christian Right provided the organizational and resource base for widespread action. Over two hundred blockades took place in eighty metropolitan areas in 1989 alone (see figure below).

The growth of these blockades was dependent on the ability of blockade organizers to successfully mobilize an ideological message that presented clinic blockades as the logical extension of participants' Christian faith, but it was also reliant on the relatively low level of sanctions that met the clinic blockaders. In most blockades participants could count on a minor fine and no more than several hours in jail. Randall Terry informed potential participants that the consequences of blockades were not likely to be great. In his first book, *Operation Rescue*, he announced to potential recruits, "In most cases, you will be released a short time after your arrest. It may take an hour or a few hours. The inconvenience and time is a small price to pay for saving lives . . ." (Terry 1988, 237). Some protesters referred to the citations they received at the larger events as "toilet paper tickets." Here is how one protester described the consequences of large blockades.[6]

In NYC they have what they call toilet paper tickets for demonstrations. They're souvenirs. They give you a ticket and when you leave town they just tear up their copy. We did one rescue outside the actual city of New York City, and I have gotten a couple of notices from them, way back when this happened. I was supposed to do this, and I was supposed to do that. I told them, if I can get back there I'll do it, if not then tell me what my community service is and I'll do it over here. But I am not going to fly back to New York for a misdemeanor or a violation or something. And then I did pretty much the same thing in Philadelphia. And of course, Washington, D.C., they never follow those tickets up, those are toilet paper tickets, too (C.H. [pseud], interview by author, 12/5/92).

In some cases, especially those involving large national events, blockade leaders approached local police prior to the blockade in order to make their intentions known and to negotiate the penalties protesters would incur. In exchange for cooperation at the time of arrest, and agreement to provide names and plead guilty, the police would agree to levy only a minor fine. This promise of a low fine was then used to encourage participation.[7] While the decision to participate in a clinic blockade was clearly one of considerable gravity for most participants, the hesitation to participate probably came from reservations about intentionally breaking the law more than it came from a fear of punishment.

In terms of social movement theory, the clinic blockade movement flourished from the combined support of the network of long term activists (PLAN) and church-based social networks, including those accessed through media elites (Pat Robertson, James Dobson). Together with the promise of a relatively low level of sanctions for participants, the movement grew. The legal mobilization against clinic blockades, however, succeeded in both undermining the organizational basis of the movement and in dramatically increasing the cost of participation.

Pro-choice Legal Mobilization

The Need for Legal Mobilization

Clinic blockaders were clearly breaking the law. Blocking streets without a permit and closing entrances to buildings are not activities protected under the First Amendment. Despite the illegality of their behavior, the criminal justice system was decidedly inconsistent in its treatment of blockaders. The lack of a consistently vigorous pursuit of significant charges against protesters necessitated a response by the pro-choice community.

The reasons for the inconsistency of the responses by law-enforcement officials were varied. As with any criminal activity, discretion on the part of law-enforcement officials resulted in wide variation in the responses to blockades. In some cases police delayed removing blockaders for hours, either because of sympathy with the protesters or because of the lack of resources to conduct a mass arrest. At blockades in Buffalo in 1988, the police lingered for hours, despite the demands of the clinic operators for action. Clinic operator Marilynn Buckham said, "For two full days, the police have dragged their feet. The protesters will probably be back. Why should they go anywhere else if they have such a great host like the Buffalo Police? It's a disgrace." One reason for the inaction was probably the influence of Buffalo's mayor, James Griffen. After the protests he declared, "I think everyone knows how I stand, I'm against abortion, I've got signs up in my office concerning the right to life" (quoted in Likoudis 1988, 6). A similar dynamic unfolded in Wichita during the massive blockades in 1991. Initially, police dealt harshly with the blockaders, but after unfavorable news coverage and pressure on local law-enforcement officials, the mayor reportedly ordered the police to be more accommodating (Thomas 1991, D3). At a massive blockade of a clinic owned by Dr. George Tiller, police allowed protesters to take "baby steps" on the way to waiting buses. Each arrest took up to twenty minutes, and the clinic was closed for almost two days. Long delays in making arrests allowed the blockaders to achieve their goal of keeping the clinic closed.[8]

Similarly, the responses of prosecutors and judges to blockades varied enormously. As mentioned above, protesters sometimes faced only a violation, little more than a traffic ticket. In other cases they were prosecuted for more serious crimes, such as trespass, or charges of resisting arrest were added for 'going limp' and refusing to walk to police vehicles. Judges have wide discretion in setting bail for the protesters, and at trial some judges went so far as to find blockaders not guilty under a defense of necessity.[9] Some prosecutors and judges were also hesitant to hold clinic blockaders in jail. Not only is the criminal justice system overburdened everywhere, but thorough prosecution of demonstrators is costly. Clinic blockaders were generally the kind of law-abiding middle-class citizens whom prosecutors and judges see little purpose in holding in jail. Blockaders sometimes tried to intentionally overburden the prison system in order to negotiate a lower sentence, and this has occasionally been successful in winning a quick release from jail.

In short, the criminal justice system was not a dependable source of sanctions against clinic blockaders. Enforcement of existing law was sporadic and penalties often low or nonexistent. Moreover, prosecution of individual protesters for trespass, loitering, and nuisance did little to undermine the organizational base of the movement. Blockaders moved to other clinics, or crossed state lines and thereby avoid facing the same judges or prosecutors more than once. Thus defenders of abortion clinics took the initiative and launched a counterattack against clinic blockaders. A primary vehicle for counterattacks was through the courts.[10]

The Pro-Choice Litigators

The pro-choice mobilization against clinic blockades was composed of a number of different groups, all of which had deep roots in defending abortion rights. Among the prominent players were the National Organization for Women (NOW), the NOW Legal Defense and Education Fund, the Center For Constitutional Rights, and the American

Civil Liberties Union. Planned Parenthood held a clinic-violence conference and was a party of several cases. The National Abortion Federation and National Abortion Rights Action League also provided support and joined litigation. Other actions were initiated by private attorneys for clinics or individual doctors, while some suits were brought forward by local women's groups, such as the Northwest Women's Law Center, which handled litigation in Washington State. The American Civil Liberties Union Reproductive Freedom Project published a text advising clinic operators how to deal with direct action against clinics (Reproductive Freedom Project 1986). The text included both practical advice regarding the immediate encounter with protesters at the clinic, as well as suggestions about available legal remedies. Among the legal remedies were injunctions and civil damages. The work also outlined state and federal causes of action and criminal prosecutions. These progressive groups sometimes won support from government attorneys, too. For example, the Town of West Hartford, Connecticut pursued a civil suit against the blockaders, seeking damages in the amount of the overtime expenses for the police *(Town of West Hartford v. Operation Rescue,* [915 F. 2nd 92]), and the Atlanta, Georgia, sought and obtained an injunction prior to protests in 1988 *(Hirsch v. City of Atlanta,* [261 Ga. 22]).

The Legal Weapons
Pro-choice attorneys mobilized legal claims to ensure that stiff penalties would face clinic blockaders and to undermine the organizational base of the blockade movement. They advanced a number of different legal claims. Some arguments were relatively straightforward, such as claims that blockaders harassed clinic staff and interfered with contractual relations. Other claims required more creative use of existing laws. The most innovative legal arguments against clinic blockaders were developed as part of the effort to find a federal cause of action that could move legal proceedings into the federal courts.

Federal courts hold several advantages over state courts. First, the successful development of a federal claim allows similar claims to be made across the United States. Instead of having to formulate new arguments to fit the nuances of each state's laws, attorneys can use federal claims to make similar arguments in federal courts across the country. Model briefs and precedents established in parallel cases can serve as guides for future legal actions, reducing the time and effort needed to develop a case. Second, federal courts are often more expeditious. This was especially important because the plaintiffs were seeking temporary restraining orders in the face of imminent blockades. Third, federal courts can command enormous resources in the form of federal marshals to enforce their orders and can send protesters to federal prisons. Local officials are often overwhelmed by large protests; they often turned to neighboring jurisdictions for assistance and even resorted to housing protesters in gymnasiums and garages.

Pro-choice proponents faced problems finding a federal cause of action for their suits. There was no federal prohibition on blocking entry to clinics until 1994.[11] Pro-choice attorneys developed two main lines of attack on clinic blockades through federal law. One, the Klan Act, was eventually found to be an inappropriate legal vehicle by the Supreme Court, (*Bray v. Alexandria Women's Health Clinic*, [113 S. Ct. 753]), and a second, RICO, was upheld (*NOW v. Scheidler*, [No. 92-780]). Suits were also pursued through the state courts. The basis of each of these claims is briefly reviewed below.

The Klan Act

One key vehicle for moving claims to the federal courts was volume 42 of the U.S.Code, sections 1985(3), the *Ku Klux Klan Act*. The Klan Act was part of the Civil Rights Act passed shortly after the Civil War. Its purpose, as elaborated in subsequent cases, was to prevent conspiracies "for the purpose of depriving, either directly or indirectly, any person or class of persons of the equal protection of the laws, or of equal privileges and immunities under the laws" (*NOW v. Operation Rescue*, [726 F. Supp. 1492]). Defenders of abortion clinics argued that clinic blockaders were part of a conspiracy directed toward denying women as a class their constitutional rights to abortion and the right to travel.[12] The Klan Act requires that there be some class-based animus behind the behavior, that is, that the conspirators be motivated by a desire to deny rights to a specific class of people. Pro-choice attorneys argued that clinic blockaders were animated by a desire to deny rights to women as a class. Clinic blockades, they argued, were organized conspiracies directed against women as a class with the purpose of denying their constitutional rights to travel and their right to obtain an abortion.

The Klan Act was used in federal court to request injunctions against clinic blockaders. An injunction is a command by the court for someone to refrain from some activity or perform some action. They are generally issued in cases where existing laws are not adequate to prevent or remedy some illegal activity. Thus judges can issue an injunction prohibiting named and unnamed persons from blocking clinic entrances, and they can further impose fines upon the persons should they violate the court order. This gives an added disincentive to persons considering the prohibited activity. Enforcement of contempt charges in such civil suits comes when the plaintiff demonstrates that the defendants knowingly violated the terms of the injunction. If contempt is successfully demonstrated, the plaintiffs may also move to have the defendants pay legal fees incurred in bringing forward the case for contempt. The ability to obtain attorneys' fees under the Klan Act was another reason for emphasizing the federal civil rights statute. State tort actions do not provide for recovery of attorneys' fees.

RICO

The Racketeer Influenced and Corrupt Organizations Act (RICO) [18 U.S. 1961–1968] as amended 1988] was passed as part of the Organized Crime Control Act of 1970. In 1985, the Supreme Court decided the statute should be read broadly to allow application beyond cases involving organized crime (*Sedima, S.P.R.L. v. Imrex Co., Inc.* [473 U.S. 479]). Since then it has been used in a variety of contexts, from a public utility rate controversy to a Michigan hospital-union dispute. RICO allows for civil suits to be brought against a person or group that "has employed a pattern of racketeering activity or the proceeds thereof . . . so as to affect an interstate enterprise" in a variety of ways prohibited by the act (Moretti 1991, 1368). In a private civil suit, the plaintiff must show that the racketeering activity resulted in injury to their business or property (Moretti 1991, 1368). RICO allows any person or group whose property or business is injured through racketeering activity to sue to recover attorneys' fees and triple damages (Gale 1990, 1345).

Racketeering activity is defined in the statute as including a number of acts, and abortion clinics based their suits on a claim that the blockaders were engaging in extortion, as defined by the federal *Hobbs Act of 1988*.[13] Abortion clinics claimed that the activities of abortion clinic protesters, including clinic blockades, harassing patients and staff, and making false appointments constituted extortion and that the repeated nature of these actions met the requirement that the acts be part of a pattern. On this basis they sued abortion clinic protesters in the federal courts, seeking triple damages and attorneys' fees under the statute's guidelines for punitive damages.

In addition to the attraction of the triple damages, civil suits under RICO have several advantages over criminal prosecutions. No indictment is necessary, and the plaintiffs need not rely on prosecutor's discretion to bring a suit. Further, as Andrew Califa summarizes:

> To prevail in a civil RICO action, plaintiffs must prove their claims by a preponderance of the evidence, a certainly less demanding level of proof than 'clear and convincing' or the normal criminal standard of 'beyond a reasonable doubt.' RICO denies the defendant criminal law's heightened burden of proof and its procedural protections.. For example, the pleading requirements under civil RICO are more liberal than a criminal law indictment. Also, if a civil RICO defendant invokes the fifth amendment privilege against self-incrimination, a negative inference may be drawn at trial. Furthermore, civil RICO does not require a conviction of the underlying predicate activities (1990, 814–815).

Together these factors made RICO an attractive legal route for opposing the clinic blockaders.

State Law

Many claims against clinic blockaders were also pursued through state courts. The ACLU Reproductive Freedom Project outlined five general categories of state civil claims that could be used against abortion protesters: intentional infliction of emotional distress, invasion of privacy, assault and battery, harassment, and tortious interference with contractual relations. Evidence of each of these was used against abortion protesters as the basis of civil suits for damages and to support requests for injunctive relief.

Into the Courts

Using the Klan Act

While arguments relying on the Klan Act in cases involving anti-abortion activists appeared as early as 1985,[14] pro-choice attorneys did not gain their first great success until 1988. An early and prominent use of the Klan Act came against Operation Rescue at their first major action in New York City.

In early 1988, Randall Terry announced the first official nationwide event for Operation Rescue. Following a successful 'test run' in Cherry Hill, New Jersey, during Thanksgiving weekend in 1987, Operation Rescue targeted New York City for the first week of May in 1988. In response to the announcement of upcoming blockades, the pro-choice community responded with a legal mobilization. Attorneys for the NOW Legal Defense and Education Fund as well as the Center for Constitutional Rights filed suit in state courts seeking an injunction.

The suit was filed on April 25, and the blockades were scheduled to begin on May 2. The New York state court issued a temporary restraining order (TRO) on April 28, but the order did not specifically prohibit blocking entrances to clinics. On May 2, the clinic blockades began as scheduled. A blockade in midtown Manhattan resulted in 503 arrests. That afternoon state court Judge Cahn held a hearing and modified the TRO specifically to prohibit blockading clinics. The next day, May 3, several hundred more protesters blocked entrance to a clinic in Queens. Terry was presented with the judge's order, but he did nothing to encourage the blockaders to obey the order. On the afternoon of May 3, the suit was moved to federal court after the plaintiffs asserted a claim based on the Klan Act.

On May 4 federal district court judge Ward continued the TRO but modified it to include substantial penalties for violators. Violators of the TRO were subject to a $25,000 fine for each day they disobeyed the order as well as being held liable for excess costs incurred by the city. Blockades nonetheless took place on May 5 and 6. On May 31 the pro-choice attorneys sought contempt sanctions against Terry and OR. They also requested financial information regarding the assets and income of the defendants. Terry's lawyers refused to produce the requested documents, claiming that this information was protected by the First, Fourth, Fifth, and Fourteenth amendments. In August, Judge Ward found the constitutional claims for withholding the information were not "substantially justified" and awarded the pro-choice attorneys $16,142.75 to cover the costs of the motions compelling discovery. In September, New York City was awarded $19,141 to pay for the costs of policing the protests, and in October Judge Ward announced more fines for the violation of his injunction. Not only was a $50,000 fine levied against Terry and OR, but Judge Ward also directed that the fine be paid to NOW.[15] Terry responded, "That's like asking civil rights leaders to pay $50,000 to the Ku Klux Klan," and he called the judge a "tyrant" (quoted in Kurtz 1989, A3). Ten other protesters were subsequently fined a total of $450,000 for later violating the injunction (Lewin 1990, A16).

The success in obtaining an injunction and fines against blockade participants in New York bolstered efforts to do the same in other sites of blockade activity. An injunction was obtained before the major actions of Operation Rescue in most of the major cities that they targeted. In Philadelphia an injunction based on the Klan Act was obtained before the blockades in July of 1988 (*Roe v. Operation Rescue* [710 F. Supp. 577 {E. D. Pa. 1989}]). Operation Rescue's next target was Atlanta, and there the City of Atlanta itself got an injunction from a Fulton County judge (*Hirsh v. City of Atlanta* [261 Ga. 22]). The 'D.C. Project' of November 1989 also arrived to face a preliminary injunction. This injunction prohibited the actual act of blockading as well as the encouragement of blockades. Federal district court judge Oberdorfer in Washington D.C. ordered, among other things, that movement leaders such as Terry, Mahoney, Foreman, the Brays, and McMonagle be

> enjoined and restrained from inducing, encouraging, directing, aiding, or abetting others in any manner, or by any means, to trespass on, to blockade, or to impede or obstruct access to or egress from any facility at which abortions, family planning, or gynecological services are performed in the District of Columbia (*NOW v. Operation Rescue* [747 F. Supp. 771 {D.D.C. 1990}]).

This meant that blockade leaders could not avoid contempt charges by simply avoiding arrest themselves.

In Los Angeles, the ACLU sought and obtained a statewide injunction from U.S. district court judge Wallace Tashima. After OR personnel violated the injunction in the Los Angeles Area in 1989 he ordered the defendants to pay $10,000 in fines each as well as $110,000 to the ACLU to cover attorneys' fees (Times News Services 1989, A2). Tashima did, however, lift the injunction in early 1990, finding that the Klan Act did not provide a federal cause of action. Following protests in the Seattle and Spokane areas in 1988 and 1989, the Northwest Women's Law Center led the legal mobilization in Washington State. Again acting on the basis of the Klan Act, Federal Judge Barbara Rothstein issued an injunction that placed fines of $500 on violators. The fine was later raised to $5,000 (Times Staff 1989, B2).

The most noteworthy incident of the use of the Klan Act for intervention by a federal judge came in the series of abortion clinic blockades in Wichita in the summer of 1991. In what movement participants called the "summer of mercy," thousands converged on Wichita for blockades. The protests began as a week-long affair, and initial success brought many blockade enthusiasts from around the country as the protests stretched on for weeks. At one point protesters managed to block entry to one clinic for over 26 hours straight, with 672 eventual arrests occurring on July 23rd and 24th. While this massive blockade was taking place, federal district court judge Patrick F. Kelly relied on the Klan Act to issue a TRO at the request of the lawyers for Dr. George Tiller and his clinic, Women's Health Care Services. Judge Kelly included fines of $25,000 for a first violation and $50,000 for each violation thereafter. Blockade leaders Terry and Mahoney were arrested and incarcerated when they refused to promise Kelly they would stop participating in blockades. As in other cases in which injunctions were granted, clinic blockades did not immediately cease, partly because federal marshals did not immediately enforce the injunction. Over a thousand more arrests took place in Wichita in the weeks following the injunction.[16]

Hundreds blockaded in New York, Philadelphia, Washington, Los Angeles, Wichita, and elsewhere despite the injunctions. The injunctions did, however, provide a basis for plaintiffs to seek a finding of civil contempt against violators. "Clinic defenders," such as members of the well-organized Washington Area Clinic Defense Task Force, relied on plants within pro-life groups to warn them of the time and location of blockades. Clinic employees and volunteers hoping to keep them open gathered evidence by wielding video cameras that captured the blockades on film. These would then be introduced as evidence at hearings in which civil sanctions were sought. In time, the injunctions began to have an effect as pro-choice attorneys pressed their cases.

Not all attempts to obtain injunctive relief through the federal courts with the use of the Klan Act were successful. In some circuits the courts found that the Klan Act was inapplicable because of the absence of a class-based animus on the part of the blockaders, a position that was eventually endorsed by the Supreme Court in *Bray*.[17] But Justice Scalia's *Bray* decision did not come until 1993, so the injunctions were in place long enough to influence the blockade movement. Pro-choice efforts brought both the threat and reality of fines and incarceration.[18]

Using RICO

The use of civil RICO suits against abortion clinic protesters first came in the case *Northeast Women's Center, Inc. v. McMonagle* (670 F. Supp. 1300 [E.D. Pa. 1987]). This suit was an attempt to stop the local activity at the Northeast Women's Center, Inc. in Philadelphia. The Center provides health services, including abortions, and it was the focus of several clinic blockades and invasions in late 1984 and 1985. On December 8, 1984, 31 protesters entered the clinic and refused to leave. They were arrested and charged with defiant trespass. Subsequent arrests at the clinic in August and November of 1985 helped bolster the center's claim that it was the target of a systematic effort to close it down. The RICO suit commenced in August 1985, and after extensive legal maneuvering finally resulted in a judgment for the center in May 1987. The jury found 22 protesters in violation of various sections of RICO and awarded the clinic almost $100,000 in compensatory and punitive damages (Melley 1988, 308).

In a second victory for the use of RICO, a U.S. district court jury in Washington State awarded $279,500 in damages to the Everett Women's Health Center. The center was the target of repeated arson attempts in 1983 and 1984 by Curtis Beseda, who was sentenced to twenty years in prison for the crimes. Beseda was fined $268,500 and two others were fined $11,000 each (UPI Wire, 1989). This case dealt not with clinic blockades, but with arson, and these acts predated Operation Rescue. The case did establish, however, another precedent in the use of RICO against anti-abortion activists.

In the mid-1980s Patricia Ireland, who would later become president of NOW, joined Morris Dees and the Southern Poverty Law Center in their suit against anti-abortion activists Scheidler and Ryan. Ireland suggested the use of the civil RICO statutes, but Dees insisted on basing the case on the Sherman Antitrust Act. Dees thought that proving the necessary predicate acts in a RICO suit would be too difficult. "There is no way to prove that Joe Scheidler and John Ryan burned any buildings anywhere," said Dees (quoted in Kornhauser 1990, 1). The suit originally was an attempt to go after those associated with clinic bombings and arson, but it soon became an attempt to strike at the leaders of the direct action movement as a whole. As bombings and arson attacks declined in the mid to late 1980s, Dees withdrew from the suit, but NOW and Ireland decided to push RICO.

NOW pursued the claim in the United States District Court for the Northern District of Illinois. Rather than seeking damages relating to actions by specific persons at an individual clinic, NOW sought to implicate the most active leaders of the national clinic blockade movement, focusing on the central figures in the Pro-Life Action Network (PLAN), including Joseph Scheidler, Randall Terry, and John Ryan. NOW claimed that these anti-abortion activists "engaged in a conspiracy to close all women's health centers providing abortions through a pattern of illegal activity." The suit alleged that the defendants engaged in a wide variety of illegal activities with the purpose of closing clinics, activities including

> extortion; physical and verbal intimidation and threats directed at health center personnel and patients; trespass upon and damage to center property; blockades of centers; destruction of center advertising; telephone campaigns designed to tie up center phone lines; false appointments to prevent legitimate patients from making them; and direct interference with centers' business relationships with landlords, patients, personnel, and medical laboratories (*NOW v. Scheidler* [968 F. 2nd 615 {7th Cir. 1992}]).

NOW spent several years gathering information through the process of discovery to build their case. However, the district court rejected NOW's RICO claim, finding that the acts in question required a showing of an economic motivation. The circuit court of appeals upheld the lower court decision, finding "that RICO requires either an economically motivated enterprise or economically motivated predicate acts" (*NOW v. Scheidler*, 614). The circuit court recognized their interpretation conflicted with that in *McMonagle,* but nonetheless found for the defendants. NOW appealed to the Supreme Court, which, in a unanimous decision written by Chief Justice Rehnquist, held that RICO does not require an economic motive, thereby clearing the way for a trial in district court (Greenhouse 1994, A1).

A large judgment was also granted against the clinic blockade group active in the Fort Wayne, Indiana area. A permanent injunction was granted under the Klan Act, and defendants were found criminally liable under RICO.[19] The leader of the movement in Ft. Wayne, one of the defendants in the lawsuit, lost his home as a result of the decision. He subsequently went to Wichita to participate in the summer of 1991 blockades (Brown interview, 8/16/92).

Similarly, Portland, Oregon, activists sustained a blow in a RICO suit. The blockaders reached an out of court settlement agreeing to the terms of a permanent injunction and to allow the filing clinic to seek up to $50,000 in attorney's fees (AP 1991, F4; de Parrie 1991, 3–4). Burdened with these enormous judgments, the blockade movement in Portland dwindled.

Mobilizing State Law

Some civil suits in state courts were remarkably successful in obtaining large judgments against blockade activists. In February 1991, the core of blockade activists in Portland, Oregon, including Andrew

Burnett, publisher of the *Life Advocate*, the leading periodical of the direct action movement against abortion, were dealt a massive blow in the form of an $8 million judgment in a civil trial. Three leaders of the local direct action movement were fined $500,000 each, and 31 other defendants were ordered to pay $200,000 each (Leeson 1991, A1).

State criminal prosecutions were an added weapon, but they were more dependent on a sympathetic police force and enthusiastic prosecuting attorneys. Some state criminal charges were pursued vigorously by local prosecutors, resulting in diverse jail sentences and fines, especially for repeat offenders. One judge even sentenced three blockaders, (including one pastor), in Sarasota, Florida, to a road gang for sixty days after they violated the probation terms for a trespassing conviction (Life Advocate 1990, 14).

The Effects of Legal Mobilization

The pro-choice campaign to rain sanctions on the clinic blockade movement sent shocks through every level of the movement. The general effect of their campaign was to increase costs to participants. For individual participants, this meant that in many cases clinic blockades would no longer be a one day affair with little or no cost. Instead, fines, court dates, and incarceration loomed. For the leadership, especially those identified by name in injunctions, massive fines accrued. The movement was further crippled when its organizational base in the churches began to withdraw support, fearing they too would be drawn into a legal imbroglio. Not only was the increased threat of penalties a deterrent, but the clinic blockade movement had to spend more and more time and resources fending off legal assaults, thus draining its energies. Below I consider each of these effects in turn.

Raising the Costs

Blockade proponents declare that abortion is murder. As such, they argue, it must be opposed with the same fervor and sacrifice warranted by the killing of innocent born persons. The consequences of inaction are said to be God's judgment against the United States and the prospect of eternal damnation for the feckless Christian. Despite these moral imperatives and dire consequences, many participants were still not willing to endure high costs for the movement. As the legal mobilization progressed, penalties increased, and participation declined.

Let me begin with some examples from rank and file members of the movement. Consider B. C., an upper middle class woman in her early forties. She was arrested four times in clinic blockades in Wichita in 1991. Her first three arrests resulted in only brief incarceration and appearances before a county judge over a video link. After her fourth arrest, however, she faced federal charges because of the injunction. B. C. did not return to Tiller's clinic after her fourth arrest because a condition of her release on bond was to refrain from further activities.

> One of the things that really, when I got out of jail I really had a hard time, I hadn't expected this. But I really had a hard time going back out to Tiller's. Because I was on probation and then I would have lost my bond money which was a thousand dollars. If I had got arrested I would have lost it. It was hard to go down there for prayer and watch the rescues going on and not be involved. It's probably bad to say but what kept me was the material things, or the time that, you know, was I willing to give up everything to do that again? You know I lead some Bible studies and I had made a commitment as far as that. I mean am I willing to give everything up? And I guess I'm not (author interview, 9/10/92).

Some movement participants were even able to put a dollar value on the price they are willing to pay. For example, S. M., a school bus driver, found her threshold at $200. "Once it got up to $200 that was it. I would sidewalk counsel, but no more arrests" (author interview, 9/4/92).

M. R., a rank and file activist from Portland who traveled to blockades around the country, was hit with a judgment for $200,000 in the civil suit filed by the Lovejoy clinic. He also attributed the movement's decline to the raising of costs.

> See, once you start to try and beat the system you learn that you can't beat the system. It can't be beaten. They will kill you before they will allow you to beat them. . . . I think the system is fairly effective at breaking the rescue. There are much fewer rescues, maybe it is just in Portland. But we are unwilling to pay the price. The price keeps going up, and it has reached the point where, well there is two things happening. It is harder and harder to be willing to pay that price. And there is another group arising, Missionaries to the Unborn, Lambs of Christ, that are saying 'ok, we will pay that price.' And as long as I have got young kids, I am doing what I can do, but I am not paying that price. That's my decision. After my kids are grown, I'm not sure (author interview, 12/6/92).

The demands of job, family, and home came to outweigh the moral imperative to 'rescue' as the price of blockades increased.

Leadership figures, too, found the increase in sanctions to be the primary reason for the movement's decline. F. M., one of the primary organizers of the Wichita Rescue Movement, found an easy and direct explanation for the end of clinic blockades in Wichita.

> Cost, cost. . . . And it's just like, why am I not up there getting arrested? Well, I know that Boeing would fire me. That one summer when I did get arrested with the loitering charge I knew the risk was relatively small, hundreds of people were getting arrested, Boeing's not apt to do something. Because there is a First Amendment right, Boeing would have to be pretty stupid to go after you, they don't want the publicity. But now if I got put away in jail for an extended period of time and I don't have vacation to cover it...So I have kept out of the eye of the media for quite a few years now. I felt I could be a lot stronger doing other things (author interview, 9/9/92).

A local Catholic Priest active in organizing in Wichita likewise had a simple answer for the decline of blockades in Wichita: "The stakes are much higher. Practical reasons, people can't afford it" (C.J. [pseud.], author interview, 9/9/92). Or consider B. D., who served as the director of communications for a local direct action group in Wichita. She too attributed the decline of the movement to the increase in penalties.

> *Question:* Why do you think it has declined lately? Why are there fewer rescues?
> *Response:* Because it's not a one day thing anymore. People are losing their jobs over this and not everyone is willing to do that. The Lord says to consider the costs before you run into battle.
> *Question:* Do you find that in the scriptures?
> *Response:* Oh, yes. The Lord says 'what king would go out to war without first considering, basically the size of the other troops.' Basically implying that it is better to consider it, meditate on it, and if you know that you can't pay that cost then not to. Instead of getting into the middle of it and saying 'Ahhh, I got to get out of here.' It's a real unknown right now. Everything is in transition (author interview, 9/9/92).

L. D., a pastor for a large evangelical church in Wichita, also attributed the movement's decline to raising costs. "For the rescuers who continue to rescue in a seasoned location, like Wichita, NYC, Houston, well the prices have gotten so high that no one is prepared to pay them" (author interview, 9/1/92).

The legal sanctions against participants in blockades clearly took a toll on the movement's national organization as well. By late 1989, Terry was in jail in Atlanta, refusing to post a bail bond of $2,000.

This was a critical period for the movement. Not only did Terry's incarceration deprive the movement of his charismatic leadership, but it also served as a sign of the consequences of complete commitment to the movement's doctrine. In a mass mailing dated October 10, 1989, from the Fulton County Jail, Terry explicitly acknowledged the effect of increasing legal sanctions.

> I am deeply troubled by what I see happening to the Rescue Movement nationwide. In city after city (with a couple of exceptions), the number of rescuers are shrinking, and the average number of rescue missions per week is dropping. *Why*? Why this downhill trend? *The cost.* People are starting to ask, "Is this worth it? Can I afford to keep rescuing children? Am I willing to risk this or that in order to stop this holocaust?". . . . I fear we have become just like them. I am afraid we aren't willing to pay the price to end child-killing . . . . We would rather have the status quo—our current jobs, homes, no long jail sentences, etc. (Terry [emphasis in original] 1989, 2).

The impact of Judge Ward's fines against OR was also clearly manifested in the changing character of the blockade leadership's appeals. While Terry was still in prison, the Reverend Joseph Foreman became acting director of Operation Rescue. In the December newsletter and fundraising appeal to supporters, the sanctions from the NOW suit loomed. Operation Rescue, as a formal organization, was approaching its end. Foreman wrote:

> The New York Federal Prosecutor's office has said that it would take the steps necessary to collect this money unless we posted a $50,000 bond while we appeal to the Supreme Court. If we do not post, they will try to collect against us. If we do post a bond and lose our appeal, they automatically collect the $50,000. If we do not past a bond, just picture a bounty hunter with all the power of the IRS—and you will begin to see what a Federal Prosecutor can do to us. . . . Our lawyers guarantee that they will come, during our appeal, and shut us down. December 8th will be when they can begin to padlock us and seize everything we have (Foreman 1989, 1).

Foreman asked that all future donations be sent to an Atlanta address instead of to Binghamton, lest the donations be seized by the government. Just before Christmas, federal marshals seized Operation Rescue bank accounts in an effort to satisfy the $50,000 contempt judgment. Shortly afterward, Terry was released from jail in Atlanta after an anonymous person paid his fine. The central OR office in Binghamton, New York, was forced to cut its staff from 23 to 3 after the accounts were seized (Terry 1990a, 130). Shortly thereafter Terry announced OR was closing due to debt (Los Angeles Times 1990, A 24).

RICO suits have in a like manner played a role in deterring participation. An organizer in Washington State, H. D., was well aware of the use of RICO against anti-abortion groups.

> [T]he other side is trying to make broad sweeps and pull people in for actions. It's pretty serious the way they throw a broad net. What we say as an individual citizen, 'we've done this, this, this'—they take and make a broad umbrella and say 'look, she was over here,' . . . and they pull you in. . . . For example, the groups that were picketing up in Everett in the early eighties, just picketing. And there was one person, unknown to any of the pro-lifers, that firebombed. So then there is big court action and the initial net that went out was every pro-life group practically in the state, on this side, was pulled into the court action. Most of them were released, because they had done nothing. And these were just picketers, this was before rescue (author interview, 8/10/92).

As a result of her fear of being implicated in RICO, she was hesitant to identify even her perfectly legal anti-abortion activism. She preferred to say, "I do this as a citizen, and all of these areas are pro-life work," rather than identifying with a particular group or institution.

National leaders also expressed their fear of the consequences of RICO suits. After the ruling in *NOW v. Scheidler*, national leader Pat Mahoney said that "people will be afraid to let us have rallies . . . or to come to our events." He further feared that people would even be afraid to contribute, lest they be called part of a conspiracy (quoted in UPI 1994). While there still must be a trial against the national leaders implicated in the NOW suit, it can hardly encourage others to step forward.

Pro-choice advocates tried to take news of their legal victories directly to protesters at the clinics. According to the *Life Advocate* magazine, pro-choice activists took news of the judgment against the Oregon blockaders directly to pro-life picketers and "sidewalk counselors" in other cities around the country. A flyer describing the size and targets of the large judgment with the words "Be Advised: You May Be Next" was distributed to protesters at clinics in order to inform them of the penalties others had faced (Advocates for Life 1991, 4). A clinic in Minneapolis added the charges of nuisance and harassment in order to parallel the successful Lovejoy suit. The Minneapolis clinic asked for a total of $34 million, including $4.2 million from each of two churches, the Minneapolis Christ Center and the Bethlehem Baptist Church.

Scaring off the Churches and Other Potential Allies

The conservative Protestant churches were integral to the growth of clinic blockades. As recounted above, the growth of clinic blockades came with the rise of a new leader, Randall Terry, and the support from innumerable Christian churches. Sanctions available to clinic blockaders through civil suits and injunctions had the effect of forcing many churches to withdraw their support. This withdrawal eroded one of the key bases of support for the blockade movement.

One problem that arose for the movement as churches withdrew support was a difficulty finding places to hold the 'prayer rallies' that precede blockades. For example, at the "D.C. Project II" in the fall of 1990, Terry said that the rallies had originally been scheduled to be held at a local Christian Bible college. After a phone call from NOW, however, in which they threatened to draw the college into ongoing legal action, the college refused to allow use of their facilities. Blockade leaders had to scramble at the last minute to rent other space at considerable expense (Terry 1990b). At the national meeting of clinic blockaders in the Washington D.C. area in January of 1993, leadership overtly complained about similar problems. Meetings for the group were held in a rented auditorium in a hotel in Virginia. This rental over four days also entailed a considerable expense, and leaders again complained of the lack of support from churches. Terry noted that there were hundreds of churches in the D.C. metropolitan area, none of which would allow OR to hold meetings because of fears their assets would be at risk in lawsuits (Terry 1993). Before a large wave of blockades planned for the Los Angeles area in August 1989, the Catholic archdiocese rejected the announced plans of OR in Catholic churches, citing fear of injunctions as the main reason (Los Angeles Times, 1989, A5).

Local activists echo the experience of church withdrawal. Consider R. C., a longtime activist with Advocates for Life in Portland.

> *Question:* Are there any parts of your work you find burdensome?
> *Response:* . . . Probably the most burdensome thing that I have ever gone through with regard to rescue, is that I went to a church for a while that was not supportive. Well they started out being supportive at that October high, we'll call it, when Dobson and everybody was out there. And then as the hype died down, they became less and less and less supportive to the point where they told me they didn't want me to say anything about rescue from the pulpit. And they stopped talking about abortion from the pulpit. And then they told me that they thought it was a sin to rescue in general, but that God

had, that since I was so sincere, God was allowing me to rescue, as if sincerity means anything. And then, it went to the point where we had a bulletin board in the back hallway, which was the only place you could get abortion information in the church . . .
Question: Why do you think so many churches have backed away?
Response: . . . We are human beings. And apart from God divinely raising us up to do something above and beyond what we are normally capable of, people get exhausted. They get worn out of going to jail. They get weary of all of the politics and the judges. So unless God builds us up to help us tolerate the next four years, rescue may not continue (author interview, 12/5/92).

Another active blockader from Portland, E. R., also saw the churches backing off because of the fear of lawsuits. She says,

I think its a lack of caring on the church's part. And sometimes they put a lot of emphasis on the buildings. And we have big buildings and lots of money we put into them. And then they see us with these big lawsuits, and then they take two steps backward saying 'we want to distance ourselves, these people are obviously radical and violent. Plus they have lawsuits, it's very, very risky.' And so some of the ones with the big buildings are the worst (author interview, 12/7/92).

Without the support of the institutional base in the churches, widespread organizing became more difficult.

Operation Rescue had never drawn public support from the largest of anti-abortion groups, the National Right to Life Committee (NRLC). The NRLC never even mentioned clinic blockades in their nationwide publication, despite the high profile of blockades in the national media. There are undoubtedly many reasons for this, including the belief that clinic blockades in effect identify all opponents of abortion with civil disobedience. Another contributing reason, according to former NRLC president Wilke, is fear of RICO. "There is a perception that Right to Life opposes rescue. We don't oppose it at all, but . . . there is such a thing as RICO statutes, and those RICO statutes, which are aimed at racketeering, have been used against rescue people. If we were in any way connected to the rescue groups, our whole organization could be paralyzed." The NRLC even goes so far as to ask potential employees if they have ever participated in rescues in the past and if they have any inclination to do so in the future. If they do, they will not be hired (quoted in Rubin 1991, 247). Thus RICO has driven a wedge directly between the largest anti-abortion group in the nation and Operation Rescue.

Diverting the Movement into Court

Another effect of the legal mobilization against clinic blockades was that it forced the blockade movement to spend increasing amounts of time and resources in court. Movement activists, especially the leadership figures named in injunctions across the country, were under constant requests to attend hearings, to appear at trials, and to give depositions as part of the process of discovery. Spending time in court detracted from time that could be spent elsewhere and involved considerable expense. The slew of civil suits and criminal charges drew opponents of abortion into lengthy and expensive legal proceedings. Joseph Scheidler reports that his battles with NOW and others have cost him $90,000 in legal fees (Shribman 1990, A22). Terry's attorney was forced to pay $16,000 out of his own pocket to cover NOW legal fees related to the ongoing litigation in New York City (Terry 1990a, 129). Rev. Mahoney spent $26,000 defending himself in litigation related to *Bray* (Lawler 1992, 120). One abortion opponent with an interest in computers even designed a program called 'Res-Q-Ware' to help blockaders keep track of their court dates (Lawler 1992, 70).

Movement literature became increasingly focused on the legal ramifications of clinic blockades and the purported bias and impropriety of many judicial actions. The central publication of Operation Rescue-National, *The National Rescuer*, increasingly focused on the courtroom battles and less on actual blockades. A major part of every newsletter was the section "From the Bench," which chronicled the movement's major legal skirmishes. Trials became a common form of participation and blockades less and less frequent. The movement's rhetoric also became focused on the courts, as Terry launched ever more blistering attacks on the judiciary. At the 'D.C. Project' rallies in November of 1990, with blockades in decline, Terry lashed out at judges, calling them "godless anti-christs" (Terry 1990b). Terry's 1990 book, *Accessory to Murder*, devoted an entire chapter to "The Courts: A New Breed of Tyrants." He suggested that "judges who have issued injunctions against rescuers and presided over these massive lawsuits should be sentenced to jail terms and fined in the amounts of the huge awards which they have ordered pro-lifers to pay to abortion mills" (Terry 1990a, 135).

Higher Costs Did Not Stop Everyone

The infliction of heavy fines against clinic blockaders has definitely not deterred all activists. Some, anticipating further activities that could make them liable for fines, undertook to make themselves "judgment proof." This involved transferring all of their assets out of their own names, usually to a spouse or relative, so that they would be able to avoid loss of these assets in the event of future penalties. Divesting themselves of all assets, however, could not protect them from having future wages garnished. Thus some took to either hiding their assets as well as possible or avoiding employment in which wages would be lost. A small splinter of the clinic blockade movement became increasingly vociferous in their defense of the use of overt violence against clinics (Bray 1994). For most participants, however, such measures were clearly unacceptable. Far more withdrew from blockade activity than persevered despite fines.

Conclusion

The legal mobilization against clinic blockades was an important factor in initiating the blockade movement's decline. Through a concerted effort at mobilizing legal tools, defenders of abortion struck blows against the leadership, rank and file, and institutional base of the blockades' support. The increased threat of sanctions produced by the pro-choice mobilization forced many potential blockaders to reconsider their willingness to participate. When costs were low, participation seemed reasonable in light of the potential good it could produce. The desire to express opposition to abortion through civil disobedience appeared attractive to some, especially in light of the support from local churches and the apparent effectiveness of the tactic. However, as sanctions from injunctions and civil suits raised the price of blockading, costs came to outweigh the benefits of participation. Churches became hesitant to lend their institutional support to the blockade movement, thereby undermining the movement's organizational base. Stiff fines from civil contempt charges forced the central organization, Operation Rescue, to close. And the movement was forced to expend ever increasing amounts of time and money on litigation. The success of the pro-choice legal mobilization provides an opportunity to consider the conditions that led to the pro-choice attorneys' effectiveness and, more broadly, the conditions conducive to the effective use of the courts by progressive social movements. Below is a cursory examination of these theoretical concerns.

The most recent and salient theory that describes conditions under which courts are a likely venue for promoting a progressive agenda comes from Gerald Rosenberg (1991) in *The Hollow Hope*. Rosenberg considers many of the prominent examples in which the courts are thought to have had an important effect in advancing progressive social reform—civil rights, abortion policy, the rights of the accused—and argues for a relatively constrained view of the courts. Rosenberg argues that courts are likely to be responsive to attempts to promulgate social change only when several conditions are met. First, a turn to the courts is likely to fail unless "litigators can find strong precedents on which to base their claims" (31). Second, when there is "elite support" for the goals of movement litigators then courts may more readily support movement claims (31). Third, the ability of a court-centered strategy to produce results is more likely when there is support from some citizens (or lack of opposition) *and* when one of several other conditions are met: a) the courts can offer positive or negative incentives for action, or b) when judicial decisions can be implemented by the market, or c) when court decisions create opportunities for sympathetic officials to push for the goals sought by movement attorneys (32–35).

The legal mobilization against clinic blockades does not clearly fit into the type of legal action for which Rosenberg's theory is directed; it did not produce significant social reform and was more of a defensive action to maintain hard-won terrain.[20] Despite this difference, Rosenberg's generalizations about the conditions for court efficacy nonetheless provide a good framework from which to begin analyzing the conditions that facilitated the pro-choice success. If Rosenberg's conditions are a prerequisite for more significant change, then it stands to reason that litigants seeking less ambitious goals would be successful either because Rosenberg's conditions were fulfilled or because the litigants' goals obviated the need for the conditions to be met.

The first condition, clear and supportive precedent, was not necessary for the pro-choice success. While the pro-choice litigators did enjoy some important advantages in relation to precedent, the two core legal avenues along which they advanced were neither obvious nor well settled. The Klan Act and RICO were not recognized as appropriate vehicles for responding to the likes of clinic blockaders. And what is more, the Klan Act was eventually struck down as an avenue for prosecuting blockaders in *Bray*. In this way the pro-choice legal mobilization presents a case similar to that documented by McCann (1994) regarding comparable worth. While neither the abortion defenders nor the proponents of comparable worth were finally vindicated in the courts, both movements enjoyed important benefits from pursuing a legal strategy on the way to eventual defeat. On the other hand, many of the local claims that centered on the protection of property rights to repel blockaders certainly relied on well-established precedent.

The second condition of court efficacy, elite support, was also uneven. The Bush administration opposed abortion, but it did not lend vocal support to clinic blockaders. Federal legislation to thwart blockades was moribund through the core years of activism by blockaders. The Freedom of Access to Clinic Entrances Act (FACE) did not win support in Congress until several doctors were shot in 1994. By the time FACE passed, the clinic blockade movement was largely defunct. Thus there was little elite support for the goals of the pro-choice litigants. On the other hand, such support was less important than in those cases where groups sought more significant social reform because the powers allied with the clinic blockaders were not so formidable, and the goals sought by the pro-choice community were not transformative.

The third condition for court efficacy was clearly fulfilled. Public opinion in general opposed the blockades at clinics, and what is more the court had the power to levy sanctions, as we have seen. The ability of the court to directly levy sanctions against blockaders and blockade organizations was a vital component in the success of the pro-choice mobilization.

While Rosenberg's conditions for court efficacy do shed some light on the reasons for success by the pro-choice community, there was another vital element. Rather than focusing on the broader social and political conditions that face movement attorneys, much can be learned about the reasons for success in this case by directing attention to the well-known advantages that accompany those who enjoy superior legal resources. Galanter's (1974) well-known article on "Why the 'Haves' Come Out Ahead" is revealing in this regard.

Galanter differentiates "one-shotters" (OS) from "repeat players" (RP) in the legal system. When RPs have institutional and organizational support, they enjoy tremendous advantages. ". . . RPs (tending to be larger units)...[who] can buy legal services more steadily, in larger quantities, in bulk (by retainer) and at higher rates, would get services of better quality...Not only would the RP get more talent to begin with, but he would on the whole get greater continuity, better record-keeping, more anticipatory or preventive work, more experience and specialized skill in pertinent areas, and more control over counsel."

The pro-choice network of legal talent clearly provided these institutional advantages, especially over rank and file blockaders. The pro-choice litigators generally stood as "the claimant with information, ability to surmount cost barriers, and skill to navigate restrictive procedural requirements" (Galanter 1974, 114, 116).

Galanter adduced corporations as the archetypal repeat players, but in the context of the blockade movement it was the attorneys supportive of clinics who occupied the privileged position. The staffs of NOW, the NOW-LDF, the ACLU, et al. had lawyers from some of the best law schools readily available to pursue litigation. Many had years of experience in litigation related to abortion. Some of the most prestigious firms in the country, such as Covington and Burling in Washington D.C., did pro bono work for the abortion clinics. In some cases the pro-choice attorneys also had allies from another important "repeat player," government attorneys. Clinic blockaders, on the other hand, had a far weaker pool of legal resources from which to draw. Although some organizations, such as the Rutherford Institute and Jay Sekulow's Christian Advocates Serving Evangelism (CASE), provided attorneys to leadership figures at little or no cost, many local activists had simply to obtain the best local attorney they could afford. There was no NAACP readily available to protect rank and file blockaders, and without institutional support the readily looming costs kept potential participants away.

Thus the dearth of precedent in the Klan Act and RICO was offset by the superior quality of pro-choice attorneys, and the absence of support from elected leaders was made less important by the fact that the pro-choice attorneys pursued civil claims against private individuals instead of claims that asked for a substantial change in governmental action or the reshaping of powerful private institutions. While the courts clearly present a variety of well-known constraints and costs to progressive reformers, one clear product of a past emphasis on legal strategies has been the cultivation of an institutional apparatus well equipped for rapid and highly skilled responses to attempts to limit and roll back hard won victories. Such resources hardly guarantee success, but they certainly enhanced the chances of victory in this case.

Notes

1. The exact number of arrests at clinic blockades is difficult to discern. Operation Rescue leaders claim as many of 60,000 arrests, though they provide no specific sources and obviously have an interest in inflating the number. The National Abortion Federation (NAF) also keeps track of clinic blockades on the basis of information reported by member clinics. Many clinics, however, are not members of the NAF. Further, their data show no blockades before 1987, perhaps because they were simply not reported as such before 1987. The data used in this work were compiled by the author from a number of sources that included the following: NAF data, police records, newspaper reports, and reports from blockade movement periodicals. Contact the author for more information.

2. This term comes from Galanter (1983). Galanter writes, "[L]aw is more capacious as a system of cultural and symbolic meanings than as a set of operative controls. It affects us primarily through communication of symbols—by providing threats, promises, models, persuasion, legitimacy, stigma, and so on" (127). This paper explores the effect of legal decisions on people and groups far beyond the immediate litigants in the courtroom.

3. For a review of developments in the field that points toward this evolving consensus see McAdam, McCarthy, and Zald (1988).

4. Olson (1965) and Taylor (1987) explicitly develop the theory of collective action. Chong (1991) applies the theoretical framework to the civil rights movement. Fireman and Gamson (1979) develop the connection between resource mobilization and the theory of rational action.

5. The importance of conservative Protestant churches to OR's mobilization is reflected in the fact that almost all of OR's leaders were Protestant pastors. Terry even insisted that no blockaders should participate without the permission of their pastors, Terry (1988, 225).

6. As part of a larger inquiry into the direct action movement against abortion, I conducted thirty intensive interviews with clinic blockaders from around the country. The interviews were granted on the condition of anonymity, and thus the respondents are not identified by name. The interviews ranged from one to three hours in length and were primarily composed of open-ended questions. Subjects were selected through a snowball method. Interviews were conducted in Washington State, Oregon, Kansas, Washington, D. C., Virginia, and Maryland in 1992 and 1993.

7. At the 'prayer rally' *before* clinic blockades in Washington, D.C., in January 1993, movement leaders announced that police had agreed to the charge of 'incommoding,' which carries only a small fine.

10 Abortion proponents also responded by directly confronting blockaders at clinics and by seeking legislation that sanctioned blockading. While clinic defenders did make some blockades less effective by helping patients enter clinics, they neither raised the cost of blockading nor attacked the organizational base of the movement. Some legislation was passed, but the most important law that targeted clinic protests, the Freedom of Access to Clinic Entrances Act (FACE), went into effect long after the blockade movement had crumbled. FACE will unquestionably help to deter renewed widespread action.

11 The Freedom of Access to Clinic Entrances Act (FACE) was passed in 1994, partly in response to murders and attempted murders at several clinics.

12 The right to abortion is protected only against state action. Courts and plaintiffs therefore came to rely on the right to travel, which is protected from both purely private and governmental interference, in order to pursue Klan Act claims. See, for example, *NOW v. Operation Rescue* (726 F. Supp. 1492–1494).

13 *Hobbs Act* of 1988. The Hobbs Act defines extortion as "the obtaining of property from another, with his consent, induced by wrongful use of actual or threatened force, violence, or fear, or under color of official right" (Sec 1951 [b] [2]).

14 See brief of amici curiae ACLU in *Roe v. Abortion Abolition Society,* No. 85-0577 (N.D. Texas. dated October 7, 1985).

15 Judge Ward's decisions can be found at *New York State NOW v. Terry* (697 F. Supp. 1324 [SDNY 1988]), (732 F. Supp. 388), and (737 F. Supp. 1350). His injunction and the fines were later upheld in *New York State NOW v. Terry* (886 F 2d. 1339 [2nd Cir 1989]). The Circuit Court did, however, direct that the fines be paid to the court, not NOW.

16 Judge Kelly was so infuriated by the disregard for his orders that he appeared on Nightline and the CBS morning news to denounce the protesters.

17 See, for example, the Fifth Circuit opinion in *Mississippi Women's Medical Clinic v. McMillan* (866 F. 2d 788).

18 *Bray* overturned the lower court decisions that had found the Klan Act applicable.

19 *Fort Wayne Women's Health Organization v. Windell Brane, Bryan Brown, Ellen Brown, Northeast Indiana Rescue, et al.,* unreported decision, (N.D. Indiana. May 1990).

20 Rosenberg recognizes that courts are likely to be more efficacious as a place to *defend* a progressive movement, but he does not elaborate on the reasons such success is likely.

Works Cited

Advocates for Life. 1991. "Oregon Update." *Life Advocate* (July): 4.

Associated Press. 1991. "Abortion Foes, Women's Center in Settlement," *Seattle Times* (13 February): F4.

Boxerman, Arlene. 1990. "The Use of the Necessity Defense by Abortion Clinic Protesters." *Journal of Criminal Law and Criminology* 81: 677-712.

Bray, Michael. 1994. *A Time to Kill*. Portland, Oregon: Advocates for Life Publications.

Califa, Andrew J. 1990. "RICO Threatens Civil Liberties." *Vanderbilt Law Review* 43: 814-815.

Chong, Dennis. 1991.*Collective Action and the Civil Rights Movement*. Chicago: University of Chicago Press.

deParrie, Paul. 1991. "Abortuary Awarded $8.2 Million, Rescuers Vow To Continue," *Life Advocate* (April): 3-4.

Fireman, Bruce and William A. Gamson. 1979. "Utilitarian Logic in the Resource Mobilization Perspective." in *Dynamics of Social Movements*, ed. John D. McCarthy and Mayer N. Zald. Cambridge: Winthrop.

Foreman, Joseph. 1989. "Operation Rescue." newsletter of 5 December: 1.

Galanter, Marc. 1974. "Why the 'Haves' Come Out Ahead: Speculations on the Limits of Legal Change." *Law and Society* (Fall): 95-160.

Galanter, Marc. 1983. "The Radiating Effects of Courts." Pp. 117-142 in *Empirical Theories of Courts*, ed. Keith D. Boynum and Lynn Mather. New York: Longman.

Gale, Adam D. 1990. "The Use of Civil RICO Against Antiabortion Protesters and the Economic Motive Requirement." *Columbia Law Review* 90 (June): 1341-1375.

Greenhouse, Linda. 1994. "Abortion Clinics Upheld By Court On Rackets Suit." *New York Times* (25 January): A 1.

Hobbs Act. 1988. U.S. Code. Vol. 18, sec. 1951.

Kairys, David, ed. 1982. *The Politics of Law: A Progressive Critique*. New York: Pantheon.

Kelman, Mark. 1987. *A Guide to Critical Legal Studies*. Cambridge: Harvard University Press.

Kornhauser, Anne. 1990. "An Activist to Her Bone: NOW Strategist Pushes Limits." *Legal Times* (9 July): 1.

Kurtz, Howard. 1989. "Operation Rescue: Aggressively Antiabortion." *Washington Post* (6 March): A 3.

Lawler, Philip F. 1992. *Operation Rescue* . Huntington, Indiana: Our Sunday Visitor Publishing.

Leeson, Fred. 1991. "Lovejoy protesters face fines." *Oregonian* (12 February): A 1.

Lewin, Tamar. 1990. "With Thin Staff and Thick Debt, Anti-Abortion Group Faces Struggle" *New York Times* (11 June): A 16.

Likoudis, Paul. 1988. "Buffalo Hosts Largest Rescue Operation." *The Wanderer* (6 November): 6.

Los Angeles Times. 1989. "Catholic Archdiocese Rejects Operation Rescue." (5 August): A 5.

Los Angeles Times. 1991. "Operation Rescue Closes Due to Debt." (1 February): A 24.

McAdam, Doug. 1982. *Political Process and the Development of Black Insurgency* . Chicago: University of Chicago Press.

McAdam, Doug, John D. McCarthy, and Mayer N. Zald. 1988. "Social Movements." Pp. 695–737 in *Handbook of Sociology* , ed. Neil J. Smelser. Beverly Hills: Sage.

McCann, Michael. 1986. *Taking Reform Seriously* . Ithaca: Cornell University Press.

McCann, Michael. 1994. *Rights at Work*. Chicago: University of Chicago Press.

Melley, Anne. 1988. "The Stretching of Civil RICO: Pro-Life Demonstrators Are Racketeers?" *UMKC Law Review* 56: 308.

Moretti, Michelle R. 1991. "Using Civil RICO to Battle Anti-Abortion Violence." *New England Law Review* 25 (Summer): 1363.

Morris, Aldon. 1984. *The Origins of the Civil Rights Movement* . New York: Free Press.

Olson, Mancur. 1965. *The Logic of Collective Action* . Cambridge: Harvard University Press.

Project Rescue. 1990. "Project Rescue Sarasota and Manatee Counties." *Life Advocate* (March): 14.

Reproductive Freedom Project. 1986. *Preserving the Right to Choose: How to Cope with Violence and Disruption at Abortion Clinics* . New York: ACLU Foundation.

Rosenberg, Gerald N. 1991. *The Hollow Hope: Can Courts Bring About Social Change?* Chicago: University of Chicago Press.

Rubin, Alissa. 1991. "Interest Groups and Abortion Politics in the Post-*Webster* Era." In *Interest Group Politics,* 3rd Edition, ed. A. J. Cigler and B. A. Loomis. Washington D.C.: Congressional Quarterly.

Shribman, David. 1990. "NOW's use of RICO Against Attacks by Groups on Abortion Clinics Stirs Debate on Law's Intent." *Wall Street Journal* (22 May): A 22.

Sipchen, Bob. 1990. "Pain, Politics, and the Police." *Los Angeles Times* (8 January): A 1.

Snow, David A., Louis A . Zurcher, and Sheldon Ekland-Olson. 1980. "Social Networks and Social Movements: A Microstructural approach to Differential Recruitment." *American Sociological Review* 45: 787–801.

Taylor, Michael. 1987. *The Possibility of Cooperation* . Cambridge: Cambridge University Press.

Terry, Randall. 1988. *Operation Rescue*. Springdale, Pennsylvania: Whittaker House.

Terry, Randall. 1989. "Operation Rescue." newsletter of 10 October: 2.

Terry, Randall. 1990a. *Accessory to Murder* . Brentwood, Tennessee: Wolgemuth and Hyatt.

Terry, Randall. 1990b. "D.C. Project II—11/15," Tape recorded speech obtained at clinic blockade rally.

Terry, Randall. 1993. Speech at Crystal City, VA., recorded by author. (21 January).

Thomas, Judy Lundstrom. 1991. "Abortion Protests Bring 200 Arrests." *Wichita Eagle* (24 July): D 3.

Times News Services. 1989. "Abortion Protesters Found in Contempt." *Seattle Times* (30 August): A 2.

Times Staff. 1989. "Abortion Clinic Blockaders Face $5,000-A-Day Fines." Seattle Times (21 July): B 2.

United Press International Wire. 1989. "RICO Decision in Seattle." (11 August).

United Press International Wire. 1994. "Operation Rescue Says RICO Decision Chills Dissent." (25 January).

Chapter 4

Legal Functionalism and Social Change: A Reassessment of Rosenberg's *The Hollow Hope**

David Schultz
Stephen E. Gottlieb

Introduction

Functionalism has been fundamental to American law since the latter's inception.[1] James Madison's comments in *Federalist Papers* 10 and 51 (1937, 53–62, 335–341) express faith in using constitutional norms to channel interests and power to mitigate the threat of majoritarian factions. Chief Justice Marshall followed a common law tradition by interpreting law according to its purposes.[2] Justice Cardozo (1964) defended that approach as an implication of the purpose of law itself to promote the decency of existence. Functionalism was and is deeply ingrained in the realist movement and continues to influence our judgment about how to employ legal norms to achieve social change.[3]

More contemporary commitments to legal functionalism may be traced to litigation arising out of *Brown v. Board of Education* (347 US 483) in 1954. Since *Brown*, various groups and individuals have increasingly turned to the federal courts as a forum for bringing about social reform of various institutions, including schools, *San Antonio Indep. Sch. Dist. v Rodriguez* (411 US 1) in 1973, prisons, *Rhodes v Chapman* (452 US 337) in 1981, mental institutions, *Wyatt v Aderholt* (503 F2d 1305 [5th Cir]) in 1974, and malapportioned legislatures, *Baker v Carr* (369 US 186) in 1962; *Reynolds v Sims* (377 U.S. 533) in 1964; and *Wesberry v Sanders* (376 US 1) in 1964. As a result of this "structural reform litigation,"[4] critics have debated both the wisdom and efficacy of turning to the judiciary to address social ills. While some have lauded these efforts as necessary to protect minority rights (e.g., Ely 1980; Brennan 1989), to keep the political process open (Ely 1980), or otherwise to address a justiciable and legitimate constitutional or statutory claim (Cooper 1988), others have maintained that this litigation is countermajoritarian (Bickel 1962; Wechsler 1959; and Bork 1971), that it undermines confidence in local legislatures (Nagel (1984), or that it is an activity ill-suited for the judiciary because the courts lack the expertise or information gathering skills necessary to fashion a remedy appropriate to the facts of the case (Horowitz 1977).

Gerald Rosenberg (1991) challenges functional claims about the law, specifically assertions that the Supreme and lower federal courts are able to effect significant social change (4, 341). However, what makes Rosenberg's claims apparently novel are his efforts to look for empirical evidence to support claims of judicial efficacy surrounding some of the most famous cases where the Court has allegedly articulated significant social reform (4, 28). To accomplish this, Rosenberg's book contrasts two models of the Supreme Court: the constrained and dynamic models (2–4). It is his claim that social reformers are wrong in that the courts cannot effect social reform unless certain conditions are met (25–6, 339). Thus, Rosenberg argues that the dynamic view of the court is wrong and that the constrained vision is more correct in its description of what the Court can do in effecting social reform (336). To support his claim, Rosenberg looked at different types of evidence to see if the Supreme Court had direct or indirect influence in the areas of race (*Brown v. Board of Education*), gender and abortion (*Roe v. Wade*, et al.), reapportionment (*Baker v. Carr*), the environment and criminal due process. He claims evidence is lacking to support any indication of influence and that Congress and other social trends can more account for change than the judiciary alone (56, 63, 81).

Rosenberg concludes that "U.S. Courts can *almost never* be effective producers of significant social reform" (338, emphasis in original) and that the Court can only bring about change in some limited conditions. Moreover, Rosenberg, in commenting upon scholarship in his field, boldly states that "[t]he findings of this study also suggest that a great deal of writing about courts is fundamentally flawed." (342) *Hollow Hope* thus trumpets the two-pronged pronouncement that there is no evidence to support scholarship that the courts are viable

Legal Functionalism and Social Change 171

forums to press social grievances (338–9), and that the author has produced a book that rights previous wrongs in studies of the courts and social change.

Both claims are weighty, and reviews of Rosenberg's book by political scientists seem enamored by his arguments. For example, Harry Stumpf states that "[t]his book is long overdue" (1993, 256), and that "we are all indebted to Rosenberg for a superb examination of the critical issue of law, and social change concerning the exercise of judicial power in America," (1993, 258). Susan E. Lawrence in the *American Political Science Review* (1992, 812), uncritically describes *Hollow Hope* as a "tremendously important book" (813), while Samuel Krislov describes it as "an exciting and challenging volume which contests contemporary liberal over-valuation of courts as instruments of social change," even though the data and conclusions of the book are "unconvincing," (1992, 367, 369).

Despite these laudatory reviews, law review commentary has been less flattering, arguing that the book fails to say anything new (Schuck 1993, 1763, 1765), fails to discriminate among different types of litigation ("Grand Illusion" 1992, 1135, 1138–39), fails to consider counterfactuals as ways to assess judicial efficacy (Devins 1992, 1038–39), and that it otherwise confuses the goals of the litigants with those of social reformers (Schuck 1993, 1772). Overall, while social scientists generally laud the book, the legal community has been less enthusiastic.

These reviews of Rosenberg's book are as interesting as the book itself. They provide a kaleidoscope of the philosophical and empirical traditions in the academy, speaking eloquently of the breakdown of communications among social scientists and lawyers as well as upon efforts to criticize Rosenberg's positivism and assault on the courts. Each review, however, accepts Rosenberg's positivism and focuses on whether he is correct or whether his data supports his conclusions. These approaches circle around two central questions. First, what is the role of the courts in society? How do they interact and affect society? Second, does it make sense to use the law and the courts instrumentally to create rules that have goals, and should the law be interpreted by those goals?

Law need not be functional. It could be symbolic, or arbitrary, or pluralist, or imminent. Ultimately the issue posed from all of the perspectives, including Rosenberg's, is why use the law, especially the courts? Challenging functionalism is the much broader question which

Rosenberg's book raises, but only in the context of the courts. Whether positivist or otherwise, whether we approach law from the bottom up or the top down, does it make sense to interpret or create law functionally—that is, according to objectives which rules are designed to accomplish? In part, this is the question we intend to address.

We try to clarify the functionalist issue with three propositions. Law matters. But intentions do go awry. And it is not clear that law without intent would achieve similar or better results.

The significance of law is partly concealed in Rosenberg because his version of positivist methodology may be inappropriate for the questions he wishes to ask. Specifically, he applies different standards of proof and causality to the courts than to other institutions when looking for evidence of social change; he overstates his claims given the methodology and evidence that he has; and the methodology Rosenberg employs is either inappropriate or is a poorly constructed and manipulated use of social science research methods for the study of historical causation.

The significance of law is closely connected to a proper understanding of the role of law in society. Rosenberg misunderstands the nature of judicial policymaking as well as the impact of the courts and law upon American society. Ignored is how the courts and the law define or redefine structures, institutions, and expectations, and how such redefinition may be critical to any assessment of functionalism and judicial policymaking.

Intentions go awry of course. To that extent functionalism is weakened. But it is not true only of courts. To the extent that Rosenberg's claims about the law are true, then not only should the courts lack efficacy, but so should Congress and the President as well. Once we admit that the law can secure goals, then Rosenberg has failed to specify how functionalism incorporates two of three branches of the national government while excluding the judiciary. In short, Rosenberg's challenge to functionalism is either over- or underinclusive.

Finally, Rosenberg's attack forces one to examine the null hypothesis that he does not consider. Rosenberg points out that it is difficult to test what would have happened had the courts acted differently. But Rosenberg's approach goes only half way. He considers the relative impact of other branches of government. But the impact of a course of judicial action is precisely how different things have become from what they would have been had the courts adopted another course of action or nonaction. Thus the null hypothesis for Rosenberg's thesis would be a court that did not attempt to alter society. What would law do if it were constructed without an intention to affect behavior? Some theories do privilege the "invisible hand" as is best known in economics. But each such invisible hand is organized and protected by very intentional efforts. Thus his attack on legal functionalism is inadequate.

This review considers Rosenberg's inappropriate methodology, his misunderstanding of law and society, and his attack on functionalism in law.

Rosenberg's Argument

Two Models of Judicial Efficacy

Hollow Hope opens the functionalist debate by asking the question "To what degree, and under what conditions, can judicial processes be used to produce political and social change[?]" (1). To answer that question, Rosenberg articulates two models of judicial behavior and social change that he sees in the scholarly literature. The first, which he labels the "dynamic model," refers to an activist court that is functional and can bring about change (2). The second model is the constrained court, which stresses the limited ability of the court to bring about change (3). Once developing these two models, Rosenberg states that the book has a different aim. Relying heavily on empirical data, I ask under what conditions can courts produce political and social change? When does it make sense for individuals and groups pressing for such change to litigate? (4)

Rosenberg's project is not one that simply asserts that the courts can or cannot bring about change, but instead one designed to explain under what conditions, if at all, the judiciary is able to effect significant social change. Moreover, the book seeks to test empirically both the dynamic and constrained models, looking for evidence supporting one over the other.

Critical to Rosenberg's empirical analysis is his definition of "social reform." On page four he states that social reform refers to

> reforms that affect large groups of people such as blacks, or workers, or women, or partisans of a particular political persuasion; in other words, *policy change with national impact.* (emphasis in original) (Rosenberg 1991).

Rosenberg also states that his study concentrates on the U.S. Supreme Court, although he issues a disclaimer indicating that he is not ignoring state and lower federal courts (7). By definition, Rosenberg only tests and looks for social reform initiated by the Supreme Court that has a national impact. Such a definition, we will argue later on, is problematic insofar as it ignores how real social change occurs, and how implementation of Supreme Court decisions occurs through local courts.[5]

Rosenberg's definition of social change serves as a hypothesis to test the dynamic and constrained models of the courts. For supporters of the dynamic model, the Court has both direct and indirect effects.[6] Supporters of the dynamic view claim that the Court has the independence that the other branches lack to engage in social reform, (see Grand Illusion 1992, 25-26). However, Rosenberg finds little empirical support for the dynamic model (28), and therefore proposed three constraints on the courts that compromise the functionalism of the dynamic model:

1. The bounded nature of constitutional rights prevents courts from hearing or effectively acting on many significant social reform claims, and lessens the chances of popular mobilization.
2. The judiciary lacks the necessary independence from the other branches of government to produce significant social reform.
3. Courts lack the tools to develop appropriate policies readily and implement decisions ordering significant social reform (10–21).

These three constraints demonstrate that the Court can sometimes make a change, but only under certain conditions (5). Hence, Rosenberg argues that there is more evidence to support the constrained model, and that only under certain conditions may the Court's efficacy be enhanced. These conditions are:

1. Courts may effectively produce significant social reform when other actors offer positive incentives to induce compliance.
2. Courts may effectively produce significant social reform when other actors impose costs to induce compliance.
3. Courts may effectively produce significant social reform when judicial decisions can be implemented by the market.
4. Courts may effectively produce social reform by providing leverage, or a shield, cover, or excuse, for persons crucial to implementation who are *willing to act*. (33–35; emphasis in original).

As described below, however, he then treated evidence that these conditions existed as evidence for the very different proposition that the Court had no influence upon events.

Testing Judicial Efficacy
To support his thesis that the dynamic model is flawed and that the constrained model is a more accurate picture of judicial efficacy, Rosenberg devotes the major portion of his book to analysis of the impact of the Court's *Brown v. Board of Education* decision upon the desegregation of schools. The time frame for this analysis is the first ten years after *Brown* was decided. Given this time frame, he asserts that it was not *Brown*, but the 1964 Civil Rights Act that had a major impact on school desegregation (1991, 47). As Rosenberg states:

> If the courts were effective in desegregating public schools, the results should show up before 1964. However, if it was Congress and the executive branch, through the 1964 Civil Rights Act and the 1965 ESEA [Elementary and Secondary Education Act of 1965, vol. 20 U.S. Code, various sections], that made the real difference, then change would occur only in the years after 1964 or 1965. (Rosenberg 1991, 49)

In reviewing data on the number of black children attending schools with whites (51), Rosenberg finds little evidence of increased integration occurring as a result of *Brown*. At best, the Court made major contributions in border states, yet none in southern ones. It was not until 1964 and 1965, after the 1964 Civil Rights Act (vol. 42 U.S. Code sec. 2000d), that the real desegregation occurred (51). This demonstrates that it was the action of Congress and the Executive that helped desegregation, not the courts (56, 63).

In addition to looking at the percentage of black children attending school with whites, Rosenberg turns to other indices to measure impact. For example, to see what type of indirect impact the *Brown* decision may have had, Rosenberg looks to news reports, magazine articles, and other forums of popular discussion to see if the *Brown* case is discussed (Rosenberg, 1991, 111). Again, he finds little influence, if influence can be defined as the number of articles discussing the *Brown* decision. Neither press coverage nor textbook treatment of Blacks provide evidence of a dynamic Court (117). According to Rosenberg, the paucity of coverage of this decision should be enough to show that the *Brown* decision contributed little to public discussion surrounding segregation and desegregation.[7] However, to test and see if *Brown* influenced the debate on civil rights, Rosenberg also examines reference to this decision during congressional debate of the 1964 Civil Rights Act. Again, he notes few comments by members of Congress about *Brown* (120). Overall, Rosenberg finds no evidence for the extra-judicial-effects thesis (with *Brown*) (131).

Lack of media and congressional discussion of *Brown*, as well as the relative absence of change by 1964 in the percentage of Blacks attending school with whites, prompts Rosenberg's conclusion that on a national scale "*Brown* and its progeny stand for the proposition that courts are impotent to produce significant social reform" (Rosenberg 1991, 71, 93, 105). For Rosenberg, the courts contributed little to civil rights when acting alone (81). This is so, in part, because groups can drag out changes for years (88), and because there were no financial or market incentives to integrate. At best, *Brown*'s legacy was simply "reinforcing the belief in a legal strategy" (156).

Having questioned the evidence available to support a dynamic view of the Court in the *Brown* case, Rosenberg proceeds to offer an alternative set of hypotheses for the integration that occurred after 1964–65. As noted above, the author sees a greater impact on integration coming from the 1964 Civil Rights Act and the 1965 Elementary and Secondary Education Act. Both created financial and other incentives to desegregate. In fact, for Rosenberg, Department of Health, Education, and Welfare (HEW) funding for schools had more impact on desegregation (Rosenberg 1991, 98) than did the judiciary. Rosenberg also points to changes in economic and other social forces that brought about pressure for civil rights as directly affecting school desegregation (157–69). These changes included improvement in black employment, migration, and growing electoral strength of black voters. As far as influencing political debate as well as other institutions such as Congress to act, "[f]ear of violence, not the inspiration of Court action, was most clearly a major impetus for federal action" (123). Hence, enough alternatives to explain social change are presented (in Rosenberg's mind), that attributing civil rights debate and desegregation to the Court is problematic.

Besides examining civil rights, Rosenberg also turns to abortion, the environment, criminal due process, and legislative reapportionment in search of support for the dynamic court model. In all instances, he concludes that there is insufficient evidence, either direct or indirect, of judicial efficacy. For example, in looking at *Roe's* direct impact, Rosenberg looks to the number of abortions performed per year (Rosenberg 1991, 190, 194). Here he finds that the number of abortions in the United States was already increasing before *Roe* and that the decision does not appear to have made any real change in the curve of the number of abortions being performed (179–80). As far as *Roe's* extrajudicial impact, Rosenberg counts the number of articles covering abortion and related topics (230–31), finding no "sharp increase in press and magazine coverage of abortion and women's rights after the major Court decisions" (230). Similarly, he notes little shift in public support for abortion, although he downplays the impact on anti-abortion reaction/opinion (237). As a result of *Roe*, Rosenberg finds no significant change in the membership in organizations such as the National Organization of Women (241).

In the areas of the environment, criminal law, and reapportionment, he similarly indicates that the Court played a secondary role and that it did not have a major impact in improving environmental quality (Rosenberg 1991, 276) or attitudes on the environment (292). Important Court decisions failed to deter illegal searches (318) or significantly affect other issues relating to prisoners' rights or rights of the accused. Finally, the Court's reapportionment decisions had little impact, failing, among other things, to bring about significant legislative turnover (296). In sum, the Court had little impact in securing compliance with its directives in these areas of law (270).

For each of the policy areas Rosenberg selects, he finds little evidence for the dynamic model of the Court and much to support the view that the constrained vision more accurately describes judicial efficacy. Additionally, Rosenberg asserts that other institutions, such as Congress or the presidency, had a greater impact on reforms, or that other social forces brought about changes in the policy areas examined. Hence, Rosenberg concludes that perhaps the strategy of going to the courts for social reform is flawed, and that groups would be better advised to spend their resources on other activity besides litigation (Rosenberg 1991, 339).

The Courts and Causal Influence

Crucial to Rosenberg's claim that the dynamic vision of the Court is flawed and that the Court is unable to bring about significant social reform is his definition and depiction of causality. Rosenberg devotes several pages to discuss his causal model and how to measure extrajudicial influence of Supreme Court opinions (Rosenberg 1991, 107–10). He notes here how difficult it is in the social sciences to control the environment and undertake controlled experiments as in the natural sciences (108). Despite this difficulty, Rosenberg specifies that three types of information need to be known to assess social change.

> First, the mechanisms or links of influence must be clearly specified. One needs to be told, for example, that Court decision A influenced President B to win legislation C that improved civil rights. Once the hypothesized links are specified, then, second, the kind of evidence that would substantiate them must be presented. . . . Third, other possible explanations for the change must be explored and evaluated. . . . For it is possible that even though President B acted after Court decision A, the action was taken because of pressure from other actors who acted independently of the Court (108–09).

Slightly reformulated, Rosenberg's causal model is to: 1) specify a hypothesis of causality; 2) look for evidence to support that hypothesis; and 3) look for counter-hypotheses and see if that evidence better explains the phenomenon than the originally hypothesized link.

There are some additional qualifications to this simple model. First, Rosenberg offers a discussion of what counts as evidence to support causality.

> While there are no precise and exact measures that can be applied, there are a number of indicators than can be examined. One is *attribution*. Using the example above, if President B states that action was taken because of Court decision A, that would be good evidence for the link. Similarly, if President B's *actions changed* in such a way to conform with the Court, regardless of what was said, this might be evidence too. If one of the links involved the public, then *opinion change* would certainly be an important measure. Further, if one of the links involved *salience*, bringing issues to the forefront of elite and public attention, measures of media coverage could be obtained [emphasis in original] (Rosenberg 1991, 109).

What counts as evidence of causality is: 1) admission of influence by an important actor, or 2) change in attitudes or behavior to cohere with judicial pronouncements. Finally, temporality of events is also an important variable for Rosenberg. By that, the closer in time two events are, the greater the likelihood of their connection, whereas the further apart in time, the more likely other events may have been the cause of a change. In brief, Rosenberg tells us that the "last link" between an event and some change is indicative of the first event causing the second. Hence, for example, since the passage of the 1964 Civil Rights Act and the 1965 Voting Rights Act were the last acts prior to the changes in civil rights that he notes, it must be these events that are the cause for change in behavior or attitudes in school desegregation (Rosenberg 1991, 109).

Rosenberg's fully developed model of causality and evidence thus specifies that:

1. Events are causally linked if:
   a. there is an asserted hypothesis specifying a linkage between two events;
   b. those events are temporally close enough to one another (within ten years) so that no other variables can be viewed as intervening;
   c. that one event is the last event to occur before a specified change in behavior or attitudes has occurred.
2. Evidence supports a causal link if:
   a. some actor indicates influence; or
   b. actions or attitudes of some actor or group changes to conform with the hypothesized causal force; or
   c. if the evidence does not better support a counter or rival hypothesis.

This model of causality and evidence, known as a "covering law" or nomological model, appears to be the type of causal or correlative model often employed in empirical and positivist social science work. It is a model of investigation premised mainly upon a scientific model of investigation (Bernstein 1976; Kaplan 1964) and it rests upon inductive assumptions that constant conjoining of two events in close proximity of time constitutes a causal influence. It is a very empirical model of explanation that asserts that if events are in fact connected, we merely need to look for evidence to support and describe the nature of that connection.

The Court and Society

Rosenberg's model fundamentally misstates the Court's role in social change. It obscures how the Court exerts power and how it makes policy.

The Nature of Influence

In order to measure the power of the Court, it is first necessary to define it and figure out how it can be measured. These are not trivial problems and they have created tremendous problems with Rosenberg's study.

Rosenberg's definition of influence ignores the power of silence and mishandles the significance of numbers and assumptions. He assumes that influence is public, expressed, and visible: People say they are influenced. Or we can trace the sequence of influence by tracing statements and pressure. Or their behavior reflects it by alteration to follow precedent. Influence can be watched. Yet many people have strong incentives to mask the patterns of influence in order to show that they have been right on this issue from the beginning—that they did not get their beliefs from the courts or from anyone else. Politicians are not big on footnotes.

Perhaps more significant, politics is often a game of inches. Small changes can be magnified politically from the impossible to the invincible. Lacking entirely in Rosenberg is the sense that politics is a game of percentages. It is simply and categorically unhelpful to be told what most people thought. The civil rights movement broke on a country in which safe districts were defined as districts in which the prevailing *party* had won 55% of the vote, and a large percentage of districts were not considered safe. Small changes in view of that context could move mountains. Expectations of small changes could be very significant. By that definition, a mere 5% of the voters holds the power. By extension, a factor of no significance to the vast majority of the population can dominate the political agenda by influencing that critical 5%. Often ethnic groups are carriers of just such political dynamite. It is not necessary that we document the power of the court on large numbers. A few will do.

In that context the perception that *Brown* reflected the law of the land could have considerable significance through a small change in the number of unbelievers who nevertheless believed that public officials should obey the law. Even a perception that people might react that way could be crucial.

The critical question is not necessarily support or opposition or salience, as Rosenberg would have it, but the way people's assumptions change in the face of critical changes in the environment. It is worth thinking about game theory in this regard and the significance of signals. Before *Brown*, people could easily treat segregation as an injustice that one has to live with because it is so strongly ingrained. *Brown* need not have changed views. It only needed to change the assumption that this was an untouchable injustice and that there was no exit or option instead of loyalty to the segregationist status quo (Hirshman 1978). In other words, Rosenberg imposes an unfriendly grid on the complexities of power. Indeed, his assumption that since power is an empirical concept it can be measured is demonstrably incorrect. Dahl tried to define power some years ago and found himself hopelessly entangled in assumptions (Dahl 1957b; MacRae and Price 1959).

What is critical about *Brown, Roe, Baker*, and other similar decisions is how they reshaped choices, expectations, institutions, and structures. In this respect, American politics was significantly different the day after these decisions because the Court granted legitimacy to certain claims, attached legal support or approbation to certain actions, or otherwise defined new roles for itself of for other institutions to follow. In short, it created alternative political options for groups (e.g. blacks), as well as previously unrecognized expectations that were henceforth part of the status quo. As Ronald Coase has noted, the law does impose social costs (1960) and it does have an impact upon the market. Milton Friedman (Friedman 1962, 25) has argued:

> These then are the basic roles of government in a free society: to provide a means whereby we can modify the rules, to mediate differences among us on the meaning of the rules, and to enforce compliance with the rules on the part of those few who would otherwise not play the game.

For Friedman, government definition and enforcement of contracts and property rights, and otherwise articulating and enforcing the rules of a free market constitute the primary role of the state (1962, 25–27). Two Nobel Prize winning economists see something that Rosenberg misses: namely, that law serves functional goals in structuring the market and in forging preferences and relations that might not exist had the law not defined them. As Bachrach and Baratz note (1970, 7), decision making not only favors one group, but it excludes others from the political agenda. Viewed in this context, *Brown* and other decisions both recognized one set of preferences (integration) as legitimate while also labeling another set of hitherto legitimate preferences (segregation) as illegitimate. In so doing, the Court created the legal framework and incentives to do certain things that might not have been forthcoming had the decisions gone the other way (i.e., the

Court opened the door to additional court cases, public protests against segregation, and so on). Perhaps the more appropriate way to assess Court decisions, then, is by looking to the more complex but also more important structural changes that the law can effect. It is here that the true importance of *Brown* and other similar decisions reside.

Rosenberg's assumptions about time and process are similarly puzzling. Part of the response of the political process involves a sequence of steps that includes ascertaining whether a problem needs to be dealt with, developing a coalition, and determining what steps will prove useful and will be supported (Jones 1977, 25–80). There is a good deal of testing of the waters, not over a single up or down proposition, but about methods. That process, legislatively involving 535 people in Congress formally, and many more informally, cannot be performed instantly. Yet Rosenberg's chronological assumptions depend on the absence of what Coase and game theorists would term transaction costs associated with certain courses of action. Again, decisions such as *Brown* altered if not reduced the costs for individual members of Congress to act and speak out on segregation because the decision created a framework in which such discussion could even take place.

Still another issue regarding the functional effectiveness of the Court concerns Rosenberg's criteria for the channels of communication that will count as influence. He wrote that the "concerns of clear attribution, time, and increased press coverage all cut against the thesis [of judicial power]" (1991, 156). Rosenberg noted that press coverage was worst in the South and then seemed to evaluate coverage exclusively based on its southern weakness (111–116). Yet part of what needs to be explained is northern behavior. Moreover it is hard to imagine southerners any less aware of *Brown* than of sex, despite the poor coverage of sex in the press, especially in the 1950s. It was not necessary that *Brown* be specifically identified. Much discussion of the issues raised by *Brown* could go on without express mention of the case and yet depend absolutely on the unspoken assumption that people knew about *Brown* and that the discussion would make no sense except for *Brown*. That would be the case with almost any discussion of desegregation after 1954. Indeed, the use of the term hardly existed before 1954.[8] To look for *Brown* is to miss the story. *Brown* and its progeny affected discourse so deeply that its mention was unnecessary.[9]

Rosenberg assumed that if the courts had an impact, discussion of civil rights should have increased. But that is unnecessary. All that needed to change were the assumptions made in the discussions that took place. Indeed one is forced to question Rosenberg's research methods—if he were correct, a young teenager when *Brown* was decided should have remained unaware of the case, the consequences, the efforts, and the failures at desegregation. In fact, if Rosenberg is correct, it would be remarkable if any one at all should have been aware of *Brown* or desegregation even today! However, many of us in the 1950s were well informed about *Brown*, even if we did not mention the case by name. *Brown* was a major fact of life, and the fact that there was so much adverse reaction to it in the South, despite Rosenberg's inability to find media coverage, is a testament to its public impact.

Rosenberg's criteria for influence also depend on the majority. He argues that the Court did not influence legislation because other reasons were important, or more important, or crucial (Rosenberg, 1991, 118–119). But this is a peculiar definition of influence. Lawyers are most familiar with a notion of causality in which we argue that an event would not have happened but for a particular act or event. That notion of "but for," or necessary, causality does not postulate anything about percentages of influence. Necessary causality might well be much too little to bring a result about in any reliable fashion. Thus it is a concept of cause that is inadequate for social scientists seeking to determine "laws" of behavior. To say an event will come about in 5% of the cases is to say it usually will not come about. Statistical tests for the confidence of predictions screen out many such findings as too unreliable to justify the statistical conclusion that the act or event under scrutiny is a "cause" for the result being examined. But that statistical lack of confidence is not equivalent to a finding that the preceding event was not a cause of the following event. Indeed, the reliability of those findings is a function of the sensitivity of our measurements. Thus we can establish, reliably, many much more modest relationships simply by increasing the size of the sample.

Thus the lawyers' "but for" cause and the social scientists' statistical confidence are tools for very different tasks. They are not mutually contradictory but they are not fungible either. In a given case we know that the preceding event did bring the result about, that it was a necessary or "but for" cause, even though the actual pattern of events is not one which would always take place in the same way or even take place sufficiently often that it is reliable. The case for the Court is actually much stronger. We do not have a bizarre chain of events. We have instead a quite foreseeable and expected direction of influence despite unanticipatible details. The question is not whether Congress acted because of the election results alone, but whether it would have acted differently without *Brown*. The question is not whether a majority of the members of Congress acted as they did because of *Brown* alone, or even whether *Brown* was at least a necessary cause of the behavior of a majority. The question is whether *Brown* was a necessary ("but for") cause for the behavior of a sufficient number of congressmen whose behavior in turn was a necessary element in the decisions of Congress. In effect, had *Brown* not occurred, other items, such as the Cold War, McCarthyism, or some different set of issues would have filled the agenda. *Brown* put something on the agenda and made it acceptable and legitimate to criticize segregation. It was a "but for" cause of steps in the process leading to desegregation.

The Nature of Policy Making and Evaluation

A second set of concerns with *Hollow Hope* is related to the nature of judicial policymaking. Specifically, Rosenberg misstates how courts and policymaking work and, in the process, divides the question of functionalism according to one set of standards for the judiciary and another set of standards for other institutions. One cannot have it both ways.

In placing his emphasis on the direct impact of Supreme Court decisions upon social change, he ignores how lower courts do much of the implementation work of enforcing Supreme Court decisions. Cases the Supreme Court handles are almost always appellate cases where, once the Court has acted, the case is turned back to lower courts or other agencies for implementation. The Supreme Court is not an implementing agency but a policy maker, and like any other policymaking institution, we should look to those who have the real responsibility of implementation to find the direct impact Rosenberg wants.

Lower courts are like street-level bureaucrats or administrative agencies undertaking the enforcement work of Congress or a legislature (Weatherly and Lipsky 1977). The policy implementation literature stresses that once a law is made, the real implementation and battles over enforcement occur as officials seek to ascertain and implement what Congress intended (Bardach 1977; Pressman and Wildavsky 1973; "Symposium on Successful Policy Implementation" 1980; Weatherly and Lipsky 1977; Ripley and Franklin 1986; Ripley and Franklin 1976; Jones 1970; Moynihan 1969; Lindblom 1968); Van Horn 1979; and Van Horn et al. 1989). Parity, then, suggests that

Rosenberg not assess Court efficacy and legal functionalism differently from the standards he applied to other policy institutions. In the same way that congressional mandates are locally implemented, Supreme Court decisions are also locally implemented.[10] We should look to lower courts, local battles, and discussions of issues, lower court opinions, and articles on the lower court cases to appreciate what is going on as far as the impact and influence of a decision is concerned.

This suggests that Rosenberg has overlooked the most important places to find influence of judicial impact. In part, we should look at *Brown, Roe,* and other cases for their precedential impact, citation, and implementation in future litigation and ask both if these decisions were controlling in lower court decisions as well as what happened ultimately in those cases. Conversely, we might ask if *Brown* had not been decided, would subsequent cases have been brought or would there have been precedent for lower courts to decide the way they did? These are important questions to ask when assessing the import and impact of a specific Court decision.

Rosenberg's omission masks power. Examining the chain of influence would also pierce the arbitrary time scale Rosenberg created for presuming whether influence existed. By following the courts we could watch the chain of events in real time for somewhat better evidence of the actual power of the courts' orders.

Rosenberg's omission of the process of implementation also leads to a false comparison between judicial and other institutions. His study of judicial policy making submits that the Court faces many problems implementing its orders, and, therefore, the efficacy of the Court as a dynamic institution is questionable. Biased judges (Rosenberg 1991, 91) and foot-dragging by interest groups can stymie judicial change for years (88) yet Rosenberg seems to ignore that Congress, too, is hampered by implementation difficulties that include lower state and federal officials opposing policy changes (see, e.g., Van Horn 1979; and Van Horn et al. 1989). Similarly, groups like the National Rifle Association, the American Medical Association, and the Tobacco industry,[11] among others, can close down the legislative arena and delay change for years (see, e.g., Cigler and Loomis, eds. 1991; Hrebenan and Scott 1982; and Ornstein 1978). In short, there may not be any institution that lives up to the dynamic model Rosenberg describes in the beginning of his book, and to set such a model up for the Court is setting up and burning the proverbial straw man. Courts, then, may be no better or worse than other branches in policymaking.

Rosenberg's study not only misses the large-scale implications of litigation, but his abstract approach to assessing judicial efficacy and impact also ignores the different goals of litigation as well as the diversity of the types of decisions issued by the Court. In the policy evaluation literature, one problematic point is how to compare the intentions of the policy-makers versus the outcomes (see e.g. Van Horn 1979; Van Horn et al 1989). When assessing the policy impact of the Court, is it the intentions of the Court, the litigants in the case, or someone or something else we need to consider when judging whether or not the case had the impact desired? What Rosenberg appears to be doing, then, is confusing precedent, implementation in instances not before the Court, compliance, and impact. The Court did have an impact in many ways, as we noted above, but general compliance with announced principles may not always have been forthcoming and is not appropriate as an exclusive measure of judicial efficacy.

We should not necessarily ask whether decision X had a particular kind of significant social impact, because the goal of bringing that case was not necessarily to achieve that type of reform. Instead, merely bringing the case and having it heard in itself might constitute a victory. This is clearly true in the case of *Baker v. Carr* (369 U.S. 186) of 1962, where an issue previously denied a judicial forum and standing[12] was now granted both. Rosenberg gets it wrong on both the small and large scales. To say that *Baker* had no impact misses the way it restructured American politics and the ability to challenge legislative activity.

Litigants may be bringing a case primarily to address the particular concerns of a specific case involving litigant Y, and not to secure large-scale social reform. Looking at what a specific litigant wanted and then seeing if that was secured might be a better way to assess the impact of a case. Alternatively, asking what the Court actually said in a case and then comparing its stated policy with what occurred might also be a better way to measure impact. After all, it may not be true that the Court intended to bring about significant social reform (along the lines spelled out by Rosenberg) when deciding a particular case.

The "all deliberate speed order" of *Brown* II was not a fully worked out remedial decree. The Supreme Court did not clarify implementation orders until after 1964 and into the 1970s. In fact, in the two *Brown* decisions the Court specifically ordered other institutions to devise plans to remedy the discrimination ("Grand Illusion" 1992, n.4 1138–40). Hence, the Court eschewed for itself the role of direct supervision and implementation of its decision. In short, the orders in *Brown* were not directed towards immediate large-scale social reform overseen by the Court. The real decision was much more modest, and perhaps evidence to assess judicial impact here should be made in terms of the actual order given in the case. It was in *Green v. County School Board* (391 U.S. 430) in 1968 and *Swann v. Charlotte-Mecklenburg Board of Education* (402 U.S. 1) in 1971 (after the 1964 Civil Rights and 1965 ESEA Acts), that the Court entered more deeply and forcefully into the arena of desegregation by mandating affirmative orders and steps to integrate (Devins 1992, 1043). It was also during this time period that some of the most pronounced changes in integration occurred. Perhaps, then, the cases that ought to be examined are the cases in the late 1960s and early 1970s, and Rosenberg's ten-year time frame ought to be adjusted accordingly.

The Court's or the litigants' goals may have been more modest, and either of them seem more appropriate benchmarks for assessing efficacy than whether (unintended but putatively post-hoc assigned) social goals were secured (Devins 1992, 1040; Schuck 1993, 1772). As Nathan Hakman, one of our constitutional law mentors, used to say, "Courts first decide cases and not causes."

Hollow Hope appears also to treat all litigation the same. For example, it ignores that *Roe* was private litigation that did not ask for a large-scale remedy or social change, only for the more modest decision to invalidate Texas' abortion laws. ("Grand Illusion" 1992, n.35, 1138). Similarly, the Court's decisions in desegregation generally did not contain detailed remedial decrees; instead local officials were ordered to come up with their own plans to desegregate. ("Grand Illusion" 1138–39). *Brown*, as well as other decisions, quite clearly placed the burden of social reform on other institutions. The Court did not itself seek to bring about reform; it used other institutions to undertake implementation. ("Grand Illusion" 1139). This suggests that the Court did not see itself as trying to be the sole implementor, but that it needed assistance from other agencies or institutions.

As these examples demonstrate, it is misleading to criticize the Court for failing to do something it did not intend to do.[13] It is appropriate to ask about the large-scale implications of these individual decisions. But that is a very different question from asking whether the Court or the litigants can achieve their purposes.

In each of these ways the actual path of influence and judicial role is far more complex than Rosenberg allows. He has failed to situate the

Court within a social context that implements and gives meaning and point to judicial decisions.

Structural Model of Judicial Efficacy

Rosenberg tells us that there are four conditions that may obviate these constraints. (Rosenberg 1991, 33–35). In conceding that the Court may be able to bring about social change when other incentives or actors reinforce its decisions, Rosenberg is actually ascribing a quite powerful model of efficacy to the Court—one that is similar to the necessary-cause model we described in the section entitled *The Nature of Influence*, above.

For example, Rosenberg lists as condition number 4 that the Court may produce social reform by providing a "leverage, or a shield, cover, or excuse, for persons crucial to implementation." (Rosenberg 1991, 35). Under this condition, the Court can be used as an excuse by local officials or lower court judges to act. For example, local school boards committed to desegregation, yet afraid of local popular sentiment, can blame the Supreme Court for their choice to desegregate. Similarly, local federal judges can order busing to achieve desegregation, despite their personal opposition to this option as a remedy, by stating that they are confronted with an Article III constitutional duty mandated by the Supreme Court (Cooper 1988). In both cases, the attitudes of local officials can be crucial to persuading local sentiment to obey the Supreme Court and support their efforts to comply with the law. Moreover, in both cases, the Court serves as a mobilizer of attitudes and opinions about an issue, placing an issue on the political agenda that local officials must react to.

In describing the role of the Court as an agenda setter that shields local officials willing to act, Rosenberg has actually described an important role for the judiciary. Within a government characterized by separation of powers, the Court's judgments provide both the political cover and basis for other branches of government exercising their will to implement its decisions. Under this model of judicial efficacy, a model that seems to approximate the one described by Hamilton in *Federalist 78*, the Court renders judgments on what the law means, while other branches serve to create policies and incentives to encourage political compliance with the law. Such a division of labor fully recognizes the efficacy that the Court has upon the other coordinate branches of the national government as well as upon local governments and judges forced to confront opinions rendered by the Supreme Court.

What this means is that far from describing the role of the Court as being constrained, Rosenberg offers a vision in which the judiciary resides in the center of politics and political change in the United States. He depicts a judiciary not as constrained but as capable, under the right conditions, of forcing items on to a political agenda that might not otherwise be addressed were elected officials left to act on their own to confront hostile public opinion. Following E. E. Schattschneider's (1960) claims, the Court is able to socialize local conflicts into the larger arena of national politics. What this does is to change the calculus of political power in a community that may be stacked against political change. By entering the field of debate, the Supreme Court can change the terms of the political dialogue, alter assumptions about politics and power, and offer political support and power to local officials or groups who otherwise might be politically impotent to fight for social change. To use the fight analogy that Schattschneider employs, the Supreme Court is the friend one brings in to help when losing a fight and in need of some added muscle to help out. Under this model of the judiciary, then, the Court serves to educate and to persuade public officials and opinion. Hence, in the same way that Neustadt (1960) argued that the president's power resides in the power to persuade, the same can be said of the model of the Court implied by Rosenberg.

In sum, Rosenberg's distinction between the dynamic and constrained models of the Court is premised on an incorrect depiction of how the Court actually does operate in our political system. Instead of looking to the Court as an institution that acts alone to bring about social change, we need to look at it much like we do Congress and the presidency. We should look at each branch as one of three institutions that must work together to secure certain goals in our society. Within that framework of checks and balances and separation of powers, the judiciary may be unique in its capacity to address issues and change background norms, assumptions, and opportunities for changes that other institutions and actors may be unable to suggest themselves. However, once the Court has acted, and facing the claim of a constitutional duty, these other institutions and actors may be more free to act on civil rights or other issues than they were in the past.

This model of the Court, then, as opposed to being labeled constrained, is perhaps more suitably called the "agenda-setting" or structural model of the Court whereby the Court is able to articulate major decisions that effect paradigmatic changes in political and legal discourse in America. In the process of changing that discourse, the

Court is effectuating political change.[15] Hence, what *Hollow Hope* may actually prove, is not that the Court is not an agent of social change, but that instead it is often an important and powerful force in our political system.

Social Science and Historical Positivism

Rosenberg's study forces one to come to grips with the question how we would ascertain the Court's impact. Assuming that Rosenberg had specified appropriate models to test that impact, there are nevertheless numerous methodological errors in his efforts to assert causal connections between judicial pronouncements and the behavior and attitudes of other actors and institutions. These problems include the use of inappropriate methodology, misuse of methodology, and evidentiary problems. But perhaps the most glaring error is that Rosenberg employs neither a scientific nor a historical model of analysis.

The central problem is correlation. Just because one phenomenon preceded another does not mean the former is necessarily the cause of the latter. (Kaplan 1964, 368). These two events may be discrete and not at all connected or related to one another except that one event precedes another. For example, people tie shoes in the morning before eating dinner that night. In fact, this relationship seems to occur everyday. However, no one would argue that tying one's shoes causes one to eat dinner. The two events, instead of being causally linked, are merely correlated to one another.

To assert a causal connection, according to Miller (1987, 101), we would need some type of explanation that shows some connection between these two events deeper than a temporal relationship.

As William Dray (1964, 93) argues:

> One important difference between causal candidates which merely satisfy the test of invariable correlation, and those which also meet the practical test, is this. Having observed that whenever x then y, if I merely know that from an occurrence of x it is safe to predict a y, without knowing the nature of the 'connection' between them, then I must always be prepared to entertain the hypothesis that both x and y are effects of something else.

Merely placing events temporally prior to another does not indicate that the former is the cause of the latter (Dray 1964, 94). Temporal placement may show a correlation, but it does not establish a deeper connection.[16] Mere temporal sequence is a "hunch" of such connection until a deeper explanation (as suggested also by Miller above) is established and shown.

There are two fundamental alternatives.

Social Science Explanation

Social science deals with this problem by requiring a theory connecting the events, an appropriate sample, and an opportunity to check the null hypothesis. Theory helps to define the direction of cause. A proper sample minimizes the intrusion of chance. And the null hypothesis allows social science to investigate whether the hypothesized variable matters. Such methods are basic to all forms of social science. Even historians are beginning to use such methods when large categories of events allow.

Rosenberg gives us none of this. His is an explanation of unique events. He clothes a variety of factors with the paraphernalia of science—charts, figures, statistics, and the like. But there are no samples of issues that might have been brought to the courts, no cases of judicial inaction. It is simply not possible to test the consequences of alternative courses of judicial conduct in Rosenberg's method.

Even if Rosenberg's covering-law model of explanation is the proper one to use to illuminate the impact of specific Court decisions, his methodology is inconsistently applied and undeveloped to generate the conclusions he wishes to support. For example, Paul Burstein argues that Rosenberg employs too few case studies to make his claim that the Court "almost never" effects social change (1992, 231–3). To look at only a half dozen or so major cases and to extrapolate from them the conclusion that the dynamic model is false and the constrained one true forces his scant evidence to support conclusions that are far too broad. At best, what Rosenberg can conclude is that in X cases and under Y conditions the Court was unable to bring about Z types of social change.

If Rosenberg really wishes to generate broader conclusions about judicial efficacy to bring about social change, he needs to do several things in addition to what he has done. One, as noted above, more cases are necessary so that the data can be aggregated to justify inductive claims. Two, more attention to *cateris paribus* assumptions is required. In other words, we need to hold or find some constant environmental or initial conditions if we are going to aggregate a series of cases to make some type of inductive claim about judicial impact. Three, Rosenberg should select cases where there is some consensus or hypothesis that the Court had no impact and then test them. Better would be some sampling of social controversies only some of which were taken to court. Looking at cases which had no impact and cases which were not taken to court could tell us something about impact and causality—i.e., whether these cases are really different from the ones he examines. Though sampling eliminates many observer biases, some closer looks can advance understanding. But, as other critics have noted, in taking a closer look at a few cases, Rosenberg should have considered counterfactuals in his study (Devins 1992, 1038; Scheppele 1992, 465-6). In other words he should have asked what would have happened had *Roe* or *Brown* not been decided.[17] Even better would be to look at cases in which alleged liberal causes failed. Despite the difficulty of exploring counterfactuals, they are central to confronting the null hypothesis given the small number of cases studied. Exploring both of these counterfactuals might tell us what history or future Court litigation might have looked like had these cases not served as precedent for future lower court cases, congressional debate, or civil rights or anti-abortion protests. Moreover, considering these counterfactuals would help Rosenberg test and clarify issues surrounding judicial primary and secondary impact.

The Nature of Historical Explanation
The alternative is the investigation of single events with the methods of history. Focus on a single event, like a Supreme Court decision, is not normally possible by the scientific methods described above. Large categories of isolatable events needed for comparison may not be generally available. Thus historical explanation cannot generally proceed by means of nomological employment of general covering laws that link events in a correlation. Instead, historians generally use a hermeneutical or interpretative process or model to assess the significance and relationship between events as we see and construct them (Kaplan 1964, 368-9).

Major twentieth century historians and social scientists support this claim. Historians argue that historical generalizations are different from the generalizations made in other forms of inquiry. Patrick Gardiner (1952, 92-3) contends that historical generalizations are so loose and porous that they do not admit precise correlations premised on covering-laws. Further, Gardiner argues that historical explanations do not represent "sequences of events as instantiating cases of laws which can be exhibited tidily and comprehensively and for which there exist precise rules of application" (1952, 96). Similarly, Isaiah Berlin (1957,

54) critiques the search for laws in history and for the use of a scientific covering law model. Berlin states that historical generalizations differ from those in science because historians must make evaluative connections and statements to support historical connections, and not rely upon the search for more a priori-like facts found in science. Finally, Hans-Georg Gadamer (1986) argues the case for the hermeneutical approach to the study of history, arguing against the covering law model that is employed by Rosenberg.[18]

There are several major reasons for this conclusion. First, historical events are complex. Historical explanation requires a depth, a discussion of connection or significance that the covering law model lacks (Walsh 1976, 98–102). Historical studies are narratives of relationships which thread through the historical record, selected on the basis of the historians' theories of what might be connected. They are always partial, never complete. For example, Rosenberg's theory of media impact is plausible, but lack of mass-media coverage and carriage of the message of *Brown* and *Roe* is only one narrative or story of impact as it might develop.

Complexity is a problem for Rosenberg. His inattention to the richness of history is evident in his failure to see that changes and interrelations in initial conditions make it difficult to isolate impact or cause. As we stated above, *Brown* and *Roe* changed history and attitudes when they were decided, and we do not know and cannot separate these decisions from other events that were occurring at the same time. This means that a covering-law model would have difficulty measuring causality adequately along the lines developed in *Hollow Hope*, because major Court decisions redefine social and historical relations enough that there is no direct, straight-line historical trajectory from point A to point B. Rosenberg compounds the problem by searching for a single isolated cause for an event (civil rights changes in the 1960s, for example), when historians tell us that such a search is inappropriate to historical understanding. Most historians would not try to pin causality down to one isolated event, but to several phenomena occurring together.

Partly as the result of complexity, history is always and unavoidably a selection created by the historian. Historians may have been the first postmodernists. E. H. Carr (1967, 6) contends that positivist history (involving the type of explanation that Rosenberg uses) is simply the search for, or accumulation of, facts, entailing the belief that historical facts simply exist "out there."[19] Instead, historians know that facts or relationships are not given (Hume 1980, 103), but that what facts are,

are part of constructing a theory that shows how certain incidents are facts within a certain explanation. Hume tells us that historians deal with many causes and that it is foolish to believe that events are caused by one cause (1980, 89, 91). Historical research is the process of trying to show how we see things connected, not in showing how things are in themselves are connected. R. G. Collingwood similarly questions whether history exists "out there," awaiting the simple unmediated reconstruction of "how it was back then," by simply discovering facts from the past. Instead, historical knowledge is a series of inferential judgments where historical connection is a reenactment of an order that a historian has in her mind. Here, she seeks to substantiate with evidence connections that have been stipulated. History is reenacted in the historian's mind of a stipulated chain of events; it is a reflective activity; and historical knowledge is mediated and indirect because historical understanding is contextual (Collingwood 1980, 240–258, 302, 308, 282).

History is interpretive, hermeneutic, and reflective partly because people intentionally use and alter the meaning of historical events. Historical events are not static, having determined results. Instead they interact with their human environment in such a way that small changes can make large differences, as in the theory of chaos.

Rosenberg's limitation of cause and effect to a ten-year time period, for example, is quite artificial when it comes to historical explanation (Scheppele 1992, 466). Events such as the French Revolution, the invention of the printing press or the computer, the defeat of the Spanish Armada, or even the death or crucifixion of Socrates or Jesus have historical import that far distance a ten-year time line. To say that none of these events are the "cause" of other changes in the world years down the line is to use the term cause in such a restricted sense that it would render the occurrence of any of these historical events quite meaningless. Instead of confining cause to the narrow notion employed by Rosenberg, historians use "cause" in a broader sense that allows for a proper understanding of the context and meaning of these events within a larger flow of history.

Reflecting the complexity of history, the necessity of selection, and the ability of history to remake itself, Michael Oakeshott (1993, 3) describes history this way:

> History is an activity in which we attempt to make past happenings intelligible to ourselves. The intelligibility sought is not that which comes from understanding events as examples of the operation of general laws or as the

effects of general causes, but that which appears when particular events are seen in the contexts of various dimensions.

Richard W. Miller (1987, 101) reinforces this point, arguing that "[i]n the social sciences, the hermeneutic approach is the most important alternative to the covering-law model."

Because of all of those factors, including the complexity, and the ability of history to reshape itself, historical materials are generally insufficient to support strict scientific generalization. It is not possible to test, prove, or defend generalizations scientifically based on insufficient material.

As Oakeshott points out, the history of individual events cannot yield a generalization of preexisting causal links between phenomena. Instead, the history of individual events seeks to understand these events within some type of context. It is within its context that we can look to understand an event's historical significance and impact. Hence, ascribing causality to an event in historical explanation is much more difficult than in most of the sciences and social sciences.

Without a scientific basis for comparison, there is no standard against which to measure the import of each element in bringing unique occurrences about. Therefore, it is essential to explore all likely available relationships in order to assess why and how events have taken place.

Rosenberg simplifies where history demands a fuller accounting. To return to Rosenberg's model of causation, his limitation of causality to a ten-year time period drastically oversimplifies very complex events. Rosenberg fails to consider, for example, that the connection between the 1964 Civil Rights Act, the 1965 ESEA, and school desegregation may be the effects of something else, i.e., Supreme Court case law. To evaluate the connections among these events, much more is needed than a set of facts about public opinion and specific reactions. The issue is how the cases affected the calculations of those involved. Needed instead are plausible theories of how events are related, along with evidence to demonstrate those connections or their absence.

The upshot of these last criticisms is that well-respected historians would argue against the application of the type of positivist methodology used in *Hollow Hope* to ascertain judicial impact. What Rosenberg is seeking to do is to apply methods and techniques of behavioral and quantitative research to an object of inquiry ill-suited for the tools of such analysis. These may not always be the most appropriate ways to address how the law and the courts are functional. Historical explanation, instead, is much more interpretive, seeking to assess from our vantage point what a particular event means to us in terms of how our world, ideas, or assumptions had changed. An interpretivist approach to the law and the courts would look to see how decisions changed expectations, redefined social relations, or arose from and worked towards redefining specific assumptions about life. Describing and evaluating *Brown* in this way elicits far more engaging and profound questions to explore than merely counting articles in newspapers, and it also yields a more profound sense of efficacy than that stipulated by Rosenberg.

Evidentiary Errors
In addition to failing to set up his methodology to test judicial impact properly, several other errors are worth discussing. First, Rosenberg's definition of "significant social reform" for measuring judicial impact is too imprecise (Burstein 1992, 231–33). How many children, women, workers, etc., must be affected, and in what way, for social reform to have occurred? Rosenberg's silence reflects his unarticulated choice of a nonscientific approach to the evidence.[20]

Second, Rosenberg seems to adopt a different standard of proof and causality for the Court vis-à-vis other institutions and socio-economic forces. In pointing to Congress, the president (Rosenberg 1991, 56, 63), or to changing market forces and incentives as the real causes for bringing about civil rights changes in the 1960s (157–169), Rosenberg does not apply the same rules of evidence regarding searches for changes in public opinion and attitudes as he does with the Court. Instead, he is more prepared to ascribe causality to Congress and the president than to the Court based on sheer sequence in time (109) without applying his own rules of what evidence supports a causal inference. In positing changing market and economic forces in America after World War II as the impetus for changes in civil rights (157–59), Rosenberg makes events more than ten years old serve as the cause of changes in the 1960s. He offers as counter-causes events more distant in time than *Brown* was from the changes in the 1960s. This counter-hypothesis seems to contradict the rules he laid down for measuring the Court's impact.[21] If Rosenberg were to argue that the socio- economic events were cumulative forces building up over periods of time, and that these events are the links establishing causal connections to changing social conditions (169), then he is still ascribing a claim for causality different than established for the Court. In sum, his claims for proving judicial impact are more stringent than for showing causality elsewhere and partly for that reason it is hard for him to show judicial efficacy.

Another level of investigatory problems occurs with the evidence Rosenberg uses to bolster claims that Court decisions did not change attitudes or behaviors. For example, when looking for the secondary impact of Court decisions, Rosenberg looks to Congress and notes the existence of few comments or references to *Brown* by congressmen in their debates on the 1964 Civil Rights Act (Rosenberg 1991, 120). While this may be true, it does not go far enough. The records of congressional debates in the 1950s should also have been checked for references to *Brown*. In fact Congress did pass civil rights legislation in the 1950s after *Brown*, so that the debates on civil rights legislation proposed or enacted between 1955 and 1964 should prove fertile territory for discussion of *Brown*. Historians have chronicled the conflict in Congress over *Brown* throughout the 1950s and its influence on the treatment of many issues before the Congress including large areas of social policy apparently distinct from civil rights (see Murphy 1962).[22]

In looking at *Roe*'s impact, Rosenberg looks to the number of abortions performed per year, contending that the number was already increasing prior to this decision (Rosenberg 1991, 190, 194). For Rosenberg, this is evidence that *Roe* did not have an impact. Counting the number of abortions performed during those years does not, however, measure change in the *availability* of abortion before *Roe*; rather, it reflects the changing demographics in the baby boom era— the increasing youth and size of the population in general and women of childbearing ages in particular. The problem is to separate *Roe* from other underlying (and not necessarily constant) trends. Perhaps one appropriate measure of *Roe*'s impact might be to look at pre- and post-*Roe* measurements of the number of women who could not obtain legal abortions. Another measurement might be to compare the number of women who contemplated abortion prior to *Roe* but could not obtain one because of legal restrictions in the first trimester with the number of women in the same situation after *Roe*. Looking at this change in access might be a better assessment than the actual number of abortions performed. Also, the changing mortality rates as a result of legal abortions performed might be an even better way to assess *Roe*'s impact (Devins 1992, 1058). In either case, looking simply at the number of abortions performed might be a more suitable measurement of other demographic changes and not of the impact of the Court's landmark decision on abortion. Trajectories are also misleading because they assume continuity in background conditions. The trajectory of abortions, however, reflected the liberalization of abortion rules state by state, and we do not know which of the states that had not already liberalized their posture before *Roe* would have slammed or kept their doors shut but for *Roe*.

There are many other evidentiary questions that could be raised. Without carping, enough has been noted here to suggest that Rosenberg does not offer the appropriate proof to support the claims he raises. Instead, his "evidence" may not be evidence for what he is seeking to measure, but for other types of phenomena.

Functionalism

As noted above, functionalism has been a part of America law since the founding and indeed has roots in the common law, if not before (Powell 1985). Despite its long history both in England and America, functionalism has been under stress. There are strong proponents of treating law as a study in semantics, extending concepts according to linguistic meaning. There are others who treat law as purely historic, elaborating what another generation decreed, although this view can blend with functionalism in some variants.

These issues are a part of the struggle among positivists, rights theorists, utilitarians, and other functionalists. Simplifying considerably, positivists see law as the command of a sovereign to be implemented by obedient courts. Rights theorists see law as a protection for inherent states, although we would argue that much of the rights literature is in fact functionalist. Utilitarians and other functionalists are more overtly teleological in approach.

One can also imagine law as largely symbolic. Symbols have large consequences, and to that extent the symbolic impact of law may be taken into account in a blend of a symbolic and functional view of law, but need not be.

For a variety of historical reasons, these positions have become politicized in the modern American context. They are not treated as more or less appropriate tools as context warrants but as aspects of legitimacy. For examples on both sides of the political spectrum, to consider the impact of the exclusionary rule or of affirmative action makes the resulting opinion either an example of "government by judiciary" (Berger 1977) or thoughtful decision making.

Rosenberg's study has to be understood in that context. It is an argument that law may be understood semantically, logically, or historically, but not teleologically. When the Court reasons with a goal in mind it is largely doomed to fail.

To examine judicial efficacy, Rosenberg concentrates upon pairing specific Court decisions with certain changes or goals in society. In doing that, *Hollow Hope* concludes that the dynamic model of the Court lacks support. Yet the policy outcomes in the cases that Rosenberg selects have been very much affected by structural decisions in other cases that have allocated rights, property, and other resources with which the very areas under Rosenberg's microscope have been contested. One might dismiss these impacts as "unintended consequences" and stick to the antifunctional implication of the Rosenberg study, or one might maintain fidelity to functionalism by attacking those allocating decisions for their mindless failure to assess impact.

Our hypothesis about assessing judicial functionalism is at once more modest, more realistic, and more powerful than the one offered by Rosenberg. It is more modest because it does not insist that influence exists if and only if it overwhelms the majority of actors. It is more realistic because it grapples with a complex world of conflicting agendas in which small events can leverage larger ones—a world which behaves in the way Rosenberg sometimes claims, in which the success of an event depends on other forces. The problem, of course, is that Rosenberg first claims that the Court can be influential only when others support it and then uses the support of those others to claim that the Court made no difference. It is an internally contradictory procedure. Finally our understanding of cause is more powerful because it recognizes the chains of causality, and, therefore, the actual influence of the Court. The claim that courts cannot influence events is far too strong. Even the claim that courts are less able to influence events than other actors may be hard to sustain, with the exception of war.

A true evaluation of functionalist jurisprudence would require that we be able to define and compare nonfunctionalist jurisprudence. There are studies purporting to examine nonfunctionalistic periods in judicial history. Robert Cover's *Justice Accused* (1975) which explores the positions of abolitionist justices on the antebellum Court, is one of the finest. Many studies of the pre-1937 Supreme Court are attacks on what seems to have been the formalism of that period.

Yet neither period was so pure. Justice Story, analyzed in detail by Cover, was concerned about the survival of the Union. His views are not clearly formalist. The early twentieth century Court was driven by a conception of judicial fairness and neutrality that may not be properly described as formalist. Dahl, in a famous study (1957), argues that the impact of the Supreme Court is largely a result of intergenerational conflict, as judges appointed for life serve during many succeeding administrations. That suggests that each generation rationalizes its own objectives. In effect, regardless of formal method, functionalism may be inherent in the human condition.[23] Rosenberg may not have been able to examine that null hypothesis because it may not exist.

Conclusion

Rosenberg's book is important in many respects. As noted throughout this article, it prompts the reader to question functionalism as well as the assumptions that differing interpretations brings to the law.

If Rosenberg is correct, then functionalism appears false. Instead, law and the courts would have to be treated as epiphenomena, with market forces, public opinion, and other institutions operating as the engines of social change. To assume law is not functional, that it does not mold preferences or influence institutional design, would be to live in a world where we assume no goals to the law or otherwise insist that the law matters. Yet law, like any institution, does constrain, influence, and otherwise alter our behavior by influencing how we think and the choices we have to select.[24]

The important question about the Court's role in society that *Hollow Hope* should have developed more is not whether the Court is constrained in terms of matching decisions to specific outcomes, but how the Court realigns political, economic, and social preferences. It is here that the true power of the Court is exercised. The Court serves as an agenda setter and excuse for policy makers to act. To understand the sources of judicial power is what *Hollow Hope* and other books on the judiciary should be directed towards.

Scientific and historical methods matter both in examining the impact of the courts and in judicial decision making. *Hollow Hope* shows the limits of seeking to use nomological and other types of positivist social science research to understand the impact of Court decisions. Assessing the impact of the Court requires proper methods either of science or of history. We need to move beyond methods that seek to isolate the Court from the larger flux of change in history if we wish to understand its impact and efficacy. Instead, we need to study the Court and the law more structurally and institutionally, and not necessarily by counting articles that refer to one of its specific decisions. We should start by asking what its decisions meant to us and to other actors and institutions that had to react to a specific decision. This means, in part, that our methods for understanding judicial efficacy need to rely more upon an institutional analysis that recognizes that the Court is embedded within a political context. The Court was designed to be one of three branches of the national government, and its real power may be in its power to socialize conflict, or set political agendas for others.

In many ways, perhaps, Alexis De Tocqueville (Tocqueville 1969, 270) was correct when he wrote in 1840: "There is hardly a political question in the United States which does not sooner or later turn into a judicial one." This claim is true because of the close association between the languages of politics and law. The net result of this for De Tocqueville was that "Americans have given their courts immense political power." What De Tocqueville recognized, and what *Hollow Hope* hints at, is that the judiciary's real power and efficacy lies in how its decisions influence our political language and the way we think about political and social issues. The Court's decisions have tremendous sway over the way we think about politics, providing the opportunity and impetus for action.

Rosenberg's book should also caution us to be more careful in assessing Court cases. We should look to the lower courts if we wish to understand links between judicial efficacy and social reform. And we must look at the differences among parties and orders in specific cases. Not all litigants have the same interests, and orders in one case are primarily meant to address that case and not be the basis of large-scale social reform. Cases may become causes or rallying cries for a movement, and that may have import for society well beyond what the litigants or the Court intended. However, to judge a case or decision by standards we have imposed upon it retroactively, at least the way Rosenberg did, risks seriously misunderstanding what these cases stood for at the time they were litigated and decided. What an event may have stood for at a particular time in history is a very different question from what it means to us today, and the two questions and should not be confused. We need, then, to be clear how decisions are social "triggers" of action (Cooper 1988, 16–18), prompting others to address the issues brought up by the Court.

Finally, we need to recognize that even if the judiciary did not produce all the results that we have attributed to them, or do all that the litigants or the Court hoped, the judiciary may have been the only game in town at a time when the political process may have been closed to some groups. At a time when other social institutions were perhaps deaf to the needs of minorities, women, prisoners, or others, the judiciary did its best to address the grievances with which it was presented and to provide legitimacy to both claims and claimants in public discussion. The litigation and decisions that Rosenberg discussed were part of a still ongoing effort to bring about social and policy change which, perhaps unfortunately, is incremental at best (Lindblom 1959), and was designed by our framers to be that way (Dahl 1965, 4–34).

Notes

*Earlier versions of this paper were presented at the 1995 American Political Science Association Annual Convention, August 30—September 3, 1995, Chicago, Illinois, and published at 12 J. L. & Pol. 63 (1996). The authors would like to thank Frances Zemans of the American Judicature Society and Marie Provine of Syracuse University for their thoughtful comments. The authors would also like to express their appreciation to Thomas M. Bevilacqua and Christina M. Bookless for excellent research assistance.

1 See Horwitz (1977) 1-31, where the author notes the emergence of an "instrumental" view that sought to use the law to reform property and contract laws in order to achieve economic growth and prosperity. Similarly, Horwitz (1992) continues a similar argument regarding the use of the law in the Post-Civil War, Progressive Era, and in the twentieth century. Nelson (1975) also notes the relationship between legal norms and social goals. Finally, Gillman (1993) offers an extended analysis of legal ideology and functionalism in American law from the 1970s to the New Deal.

2 White (1988). One of the clearest indications of Marshall's functionalism may be seen in *McCulloch v. Maryland*, 17 U.S. 316 in 1819. In ascertaining the meaning of the "necessary and proper" clause in article 2, section 8, clause 18 of the Constitution, Marshall states that it means granting Congress the discretion to use the law to serve "any means calculated to produce the end" that Congress has in mind (413-14). The scope of judicial review of constitutional norms, for Marshall, then, was to grant broad discretion to employ the law to serve social goals.

3 See MacKinnon (1989); Unger (1986); and Posner (1992) for feminist, critical legal studies, and law and economics appeals to legal functionalism.

4 See, generally Chayes (1976); Fiss (1982); Perry (1982); Ely (1980).

5 See the section entitled *The Nature of Policy Making and Evaluation*, below.

6 In setting up these distinctions, Rosenberg fails to provide any evidence about who in fact supports or believes in the dynamic model. It is not clear that anyone believes (at least today) that the Court by itself can bring about social change along the lines depicted by Rosenberg. *Hollow Hope* (81), argues that there is no evidence that the courts, acting alone, contributed directly to civil rights. Of course, what it means to "contribute directly," is vague. While Rosenberg does cite several scholars and some dicta from Court opinions claiming that the Court may have some resources or advantages that other institutions do not when it comes to articulating social change (21-26), these references do not indicate that these sources believed that the Court was capable of totally removing itself from politics, or that it was architectonic and

solely capable of initiating and implementing social change along the lines of the dynamic model sketched out by Rosenberg. For example, Chayes (1976, 1307) argues that one advantage that the judge has over legislatures in reforming social institutions is that his "professional tradition insulates him from narrow political pressures." Chayes does not state here that the judge is insulated from *all* political pressures, only "narrow" ones, i.e., the biases of powerful interest groups. Moreover, Chayes also is sensitive to the potential of interest group conflict and political pressures limiting the ability of the judge to act (1310–1313). Finally, nowhere in this discussion does Chayes suggest that the judge or judiciary is able to go it alone in undertaking structural reform of social institutions. In short, while Chayes does indicate some advantages that the courts may have to make policy, he also notes some of its weaknesses and his claims certainly do not rise to the level of judicial power described in Rosenberg's dynamic model.

There are also no references to public opinion studies or litigants to support the assumptions standing behind the dynamic model. At best, his dynamic model is a caricature of disparate assumptions and statements made about structural reform litigation that have been taken out of context.

Even if scholars or others once believed in the dynamic model, as Peter Schuck (1993, 1764–65) has noted, Rosenberg's assertions about the limits on judicial independence and efficacy are neither novel nor new. After reviewing some of the scholarly literature on judicial policy making that has previously reached conclusions similar to Rosenberg's, Schuck states that *Hollow Hope* "exhibits the common scholarly conceit of uniqueness" (1764). Numerous books and articles, dating at least from Scheingold (1974), and Horowitz (1977), have indicated the limits to judicial independence and ability to articulate social reform. There is also a supply of political science and public law literature addressing the topic of judicial compliance and impact that has anticipated many of the distinctions made in Rosenberg's book. See, e.g., Krislov, et al., ed. (1972); Wasby (1970); Cooper (1988); and Hansen (1980), among other sources. Hence, even if there was once a belief that the Court operated along the lines implied by the dynamic model, such a belief was already discredited before Rosenberg's book. This makes the dynamic model either dated or some type of straw figure that can easily be burned by Rosenberg.

There is no credible source that thinks that the Court is not contextually constrained in some way by political or social forces. In fact, the very nature of checks and balances and separation of powers was meant to place limits upon judicial power. As Alexander Hamilton stated in *Federalist 78*, the judiciary would have neither "FORCE nor WILL, but merely judgment," and would need to depend upon the other branches of government for the enforcement of its decisions. (Hamilton, Madison and Jay, 1987, 396).

There is also no evidence that the judiciary itself sought to act according to the logic outlined in the dynamic model. In fact, as we discuss below, the Court adopted a stance in its desegregation decisions that recognized limits to its own efficacy by mandating that other institutions take responsibility to formulate integration plans. See Grand Illusion (1992, 1138–40).

7   This of course assumes that we can equate the visibility of Court decisions with their social efficacy and impact. Such a claim, given empirical research that suggests that the Court has many different types of audiences that pay varying levels of attention, may be contested. See, e.g., Baum (1992, 136–40).

8   See Eisler (1993, 153–4), noting that not until *Cooper v Aaron,* 358 U.S. 1 in 1958 did the Court use the word desegregation. Eisler comments that even in 1958 Brennan used desegregatopm because of the anxiety and anger the use of the word integration carried in the South.

9   See Schultz (1993, 467), for a discussion of how some political terms can "define[] the climate of opinion" regarding the discussion of specific legal issues and terms. Similarly, Kuhn (1970, 43-52), makes similar claims about how certain unstated but generally accepted assumptions and paradigms can affect and dominate scientific research until such time as a new prevailing paradigm displaces the existing one. Oftentimes, Kuhn argues at 136–144, the displacement of one paradigm by another appears unnoticed or invisible. For our purposes, we can view *Brown* or other similarly significant cases as instances where the dominant legal paradigm or assumptions changed, resulting in a new way to view racism or other social ills.

10 See, e.g., Van Horn (1979); and Van Horn et al. (1989).

11 See Fritschler (1989) for discussion of the influence of the tobacco upon the development of legislation regulating tobacco.

12 See *Coleman v Miller,* 307 U.S. 433 (1939), where the Court declared challenges to the apportionment of State of Kansas' legislature to be a political question and, hence, not a issue for the courts to decide. *Baker v. Carr* effectively overturns Colegrove by granting standing to challenge legislative apportionment schemes.

13 When Rosenberg looks to printed news and reports for signs of indirect influence, he searches only for references to major Supreme Court decisions. (Rosenberg, 1991, 111). However, many newspapers may have opted not to refer to *Brown* or other Supreme Court cases. Instead, the papers may have discussed local litigation or controversies without reference to the Supreme Court, or they may have discussed issues implicated by Court decisions in terms of local issues and concerns that may not appear in the word searches that Rosenberg performs. Additionally, Rosenberg's study is not a true content analysis of the articles, and it misses possible changes in tone of articles, and so on, that may have occurred as a result of the changing climate on abortion, civil rights, and other fields.

14 See, e.g., Muir (1967) for a discussion of this point on how public reception of Supreme Court decisions affects people in different ways and how the attitudes of local officials are important to the way people view the legitimacy of Court decisions.

15 See White (1984); Ball (1988, 3–6); Farr (1989, 24, 25); and Farr (1988, 13, 15), for discussions of the relationship between changes in language and conceptual meaning and social and political change.

16 Even empirical social science tells us that mere correlation if not a necessary and sufficient condition to prove causality. See, e.g., Simon and Burstein (1985, 299–309); Nachmias and Nachmias (1987, 309–408); and Healey (1984, 267–271). High correlation coefficients are indicative of a relationship between two or more phenomena, yet some deeper explanation is needed to assert or demonstrate that the correlation is perhaps causal. Moreover, to assert that two variables are correlated, we also need some minimum number of cases to lend statistical significance to the correlation. Since Rosenberg is only able to study one instance of *Brown* being decided and civil rights changes transpiring in the 1960s, we hardly have enough cases to try to establish a correlative connection along the way specified in *Hollow Hope*.

17 Rosenberg (1991, 169) dismisses this tactic, claiming that he is not interested in "historical speculation." In fact, that *is* exactly what his book is, especially when seeking to find alternative explanations for the social reforms he is assessing.

18 Additionally, Walsh (1976, 197) concludes at one point in his book on historical explanation that "my aim has been limited to showing that history, so far from being through and through scientific, should be seen rather as an enquiry perused in a practical setting and sustained in important respects by practical interests." For Walsh, history and science differ in that the former does not admit of explicit generalizations but is concerned with the uniqueness of events (39). History is "colligation" or the search for explanations by tracing "intrinsic relations to other events and locating it in its historical context" (59). Defining the context is the first step in historical explanation, followed by the use and definition of evidence to help situate and further define the context as well as to support the connections asserted.

19 See also Hume (1984, 99–101); and Kant (1966), for discussions on the limits of epistemological and cognitive arguments that premise human knowledge and causality on the correspondence of ideas to events occurring outside of us. Hume (1980, 82–173), represents one of the most important and sustained assaults on the search for causes and causal knowledge along the lines developed by Rosenberg.

20 Rosenberg's definition of social reform also does not specify that reform has to be in the direction of compliance with stated Supreme Court policies. Instead, it is merely policy change with national impact (4). By his definition, even negative action or efforts to thwart compliance with the Court counts as impact (155–6, 182, and 342, among other places, note a negative or adverse impact as a result of Court decisions). Compare Van Horn (1979); and Van Horn, et al. (1989). Rosenberg appears to confuse judicial impact with compliance. Nevertheless he fails to consider adverse impact. We think that a mistake since part of the chain of cause leads through resistance toward eventual reaction and resolution. Indeed that was Dr. King's strategy.

Legal Functionalism and Social Change 207

21 Rosenberg (1991, 56, 63) argues that Congress and the presidency had more impact in desegregation than the Court. On page 98 he makes a similar claim about HEW. If we use Rosenberg's "last link" thesis for ascribing causality, then Congress was not the cause of desegregation but rather HEW or any other implementing agencies. The point here is that if we separate Congress from its implementing agencies in the same way that Rosenberg separates the Supreme Court from perhaps the lower courts which were responsible for implementing Court precedent, then one could equally argue that Congress was not the cause of social reform. Obviously Rosenberg does not say that of Congress, thereby applying a different standard of analysis to the judiciary versus other institutions.

22 In addition, when seeking to measure impact, Rosenberg never looks to number of demonstrations held, letters written to Congress or local elected officials, or letters to the editor as a result of particular Court decisions. Granted that gathering evidence of all this would be difficult, but there may have been significant changes in behavior here that have been ignored in *Hollow Hope*.

23 One of the authors has elaborated that conclusion elsewhere. See Gottlieb (1994).

24 See, e.g., March and Olsen (1984); March and Olsen (1989); Lane, ed. (1990); Schultz (1994, 413); Schuck (1993, 1772) for various discussions of how institutions influence choices and behavior.

Works Cited

Bachrach, Peter and Morton S. Baratz 1970. *Power and Poverty: Theory and Practice*. New York: Oxford University Press.

Baker v Carr 1962. 369 *U.S.* 186.

Ball, Terrence. 1988. *Transforming Political Discourse: Political Theory and Critical Conceptual History*. New York: Blackwell Publishing.

Bardach, Eugene. 1977. *The Implementation Game*. Cambridge, Mass: MIT Press.

Baum, Lawerence. 1992. *The Supreme Court*. Washington, DC: Congressional Quarterly Press.

Berger, Raoul. 1977. *Government by Judiciary*. Cambridge, Mass: Harvard University Press.

Berlin, Isaiah. 1957. *Historical Inevitability*. New York: Oxford University Press.

Bernstein, Richard J. 1976. *The Restructuring of Social and Political Theory*. San Diego, Cal: Harcourt, Brace, Jovanovich, Inc.

Bickel, Alexander. 1962. *The Least Dangerous Branch: The Supreme Court at the Bar of Politics*. New York: Macmillan Pub.

Bork, Robert H. 1971. "Neutral Principles and some First Amendment Problems." *Indiana Law Journal* 47:1

Brennan, William J. Jr. 1989. "Why have a Bill of Rights?" *Oxford Journal of Legal Studies* 9:425

Brown v. Board of Education 1954. 347 *U.S.* 483.

Burstein, Paul. 1992. "Review of The Hollow Hope," *American Journal of Sociology* 98:231.

Cardozo, Benjamin N. 1964 *The Nature of the Judicial Process*. New Haven, Conn: Yale University Press.

Carr, E.H. 1967. *What is History?* New York: Knopf Publishers.

Chayes, Abram. 1976. "The Role of the Judge in Public Law Litigation." *Harvard Law Review* 89:1281.

Cigler, Allan J. and Burdett A. Loomis, eds. 1991 *Interest Group Politics*. Washington, DC: Congressional Quarterly Press.

Civil Rights Act of 1964, *U.S. Code*. Vol 42, sec. 2000d.

Coase, Ronald H. 1960. "The Problem of Social Cost." *Journal of Law and Economics* 3:1.

Coleman v Miller 1939. 307 U.S. 433.

Collingwood, R.G. 1980. *The Idea of History*. New York: Oxford University Press.

Cooper, Phillip J. 1980. *Hard Judicial Choices: Federal District Court Judges and State and Local Officials*. New York: Oxford University Press.

Cooper v Aaron 1958 358 U.S. 1.

Cover, Robert. 1975. *Justice Accused: Antislavery and the Judicial Process*. New Haven, Conn: Yale University Press.

Dahl, Robert A. 1957a. Decision-Making in a Democracy: The Supreme Court as a National Policy Maker. *Journal of Public Law* 6:279.

Dahl, Robert A. 1957b. "The Concept of Power." *Behavioral Science* 2:201–15.

Dahl, Robert A. 1965. *A Preface to Democratic Theory*. Chicago: University of Chicago Press.

Devins, Neil. 1992. "Judicial Matters." *California Law Review* 80:1027, 1038–39.

Dray, William. 1964. *Laws and Explanation in History*. Westport, Conn: Greenwood Press.

Eisler, Kim Isaac. 1993. *A Justice for All: William J. Brennan, Jr., and the Decisions that Transformed America*. New York: Simon and Schuster.

The Elementary and Secondary Education Act of 1965. *U.S. Code*. Vol. 20, various sections.

Ely, John Hart. 1980. *Democracy and Distrust: A Theory of Judicial Review*. Cambridge, Mass: Harvard University Press.

Farr, James. 1988. "Conceptual Change and Constitutional Innovation." Pp. 13–34 in *Conceptual Change and the Constitution*, ed. T.Ball and J.G.A. Pocock, *Conceptual Change and the Constitution*. Lawrence, Kansas: University Press of Kansas.

Farr, James. 1989. "Understanding Conceptual Change Politically." Pp. 24–49 in *Political Innovation and Conceptual Change,* ed. T.Ball, J. Farr, and R. Hanson. New York: Cambridge University Press.

Fiss, Owen M. 1982. The Social and Political Foundations of Adjudication, *Law and Human Behavior* 6:121.

Friedman, Milton. 1962. *Capitalism and Freedom*. Chicago: University of Chicago Press.

Fritschler, A. Lee. 1989. *Smoking and Politics: Policy Making and the Federal Bureaucracy*. Englewood Cliffs, NJ: Prentice Hall.

Gadamer, Hans-Georg. 1986. *Truth and Method*. New York: Crossroad Pub Co.

Gardiner, Patrick. 1952. *The Nature of Historical Explanation*. New York: Oxford University Press.

Gillman, Howard. 1993. *The Constitution Besieged: The Rise and Demise of Lochner Era Police Powers Jurisprudence*. Durham, NC: Duke University Press.

Gottlieb, Stephen E. 1994. The Paradox of Balancing Significant Interests, *Hastings Law Journal* 45:825

"Grand Illusion" 1992. *Harvard Law Review* 105:1135.

Green v. County School Board 1968. 391 *U.S.* 430.

Hamilton, Alexander, James Madison and John Jay 1987. *The Federalist*. Max Beloff, ed., 2d ed. New York: Modern Library.

Hamilton, Alexander, James Madison and John Jay 1937. *The Federalist*. New York: Modern Library.

Hansen, Susan B. 1980. "State Implementation of Supreme Court Decisions: Abortion rates since Roe v Wade." *Journal of Politics* 42:372.

Healey, Joseph F. 1984. *Statistics: A Tool for Social Research*. Bellmont, Cal: Wadsworth Pub. Co.

Hirshman, Albert O. 1978. *Exit, Voice and Loyalty: Responses to Decline in Firms, Organizations, and States*. Cambridge, Mass: Harvard University Press.

Horowitz, Donald L. 1977. *The Courts and Social Policy*. Washington, DC: Brookings Institution.

Horwitz, Morton J. 1977. *The Transformation of American Law, 1780–1860*. New York: Oxford University Press.

Horwitz, Morton J. 1992. *The Transformation of American Law, 1870-1960: The Crisis of Legal Orthodoxy*. New York: Oxford University Press.

Hrebenan, Ronald J., and Ruth K. Scott 1982. *Interest Group Politics In America*. New York: Prentice Hall.

Hume, David. 1984. *An Enquiry Concerning Human Understanding*. LaSalle, Ill: Open Court Pub Co.

Hume, David. 1980. *A Treatise of Human Nature*. New York: Oxford University Press.

Jones, Charles O. 1970. *An Introduction to the Study of Public Policy*. Boston, Mass: Duxbury Press.

Kant, Immanuel. 1966. *The Critique of Pure Reason*. New York: Achor Books.

Kaplan, Abraham. 1964. *The Conduct of Inquiry: Methodology for Behavioral Science*. San Francisco, Cal: Chandler Publishing Co.

Krislov, Samuel et al., ed. 1972. *Compliance and the Law*. Beverly Hills, Cal: Sage Publications.

Krislov, Samuel. 1992. Book Review. *Constitutional Commentary* 9:367.

Kuhn, Thomas S. 1970. *The Structure of Scientific Revolutions*. Chicago: University of Chicago Press.

Lane, Fred. ed. 1990. *Current Issues in Public Administration*. New York: St. Martin's Press Inc.

Lawrence, Susan E. 1992. Review of Hollow Hope, by Rosenberg. American Political Science Review 86 (September):812

Lindblom, Charles E. 1968. *The Policy-Making Process*. Englewood Cliffs, NJ: Prentice Hall.

Lindblom, Charles E. 1959. "The Science of Muddling Through" *Public Administration Review* 19:79

MacKinnon, Catharine A. 1989. *Toward a Feminist Theory of the State*. Cambridge, Mass: Harvard University Press.

MacRae and Price 1959. "Scale Positions and 'Power' in the Senate," *Behavioral Science* 4:212-18.

March, James G. & Johan P. Olsen 1984. "The New Institutionalism: Organizational Factors in Political Life." American Political Science Review 78:735.

March, James G. & Johan P. Olsen 1989. *The Organizational Basis to Politics*. New York: Free Press.

McCulloch v Maryland 1819. 17 U.S. 316.

Miller, Richard W. 1987. *Fact and Method: Explanation, Confirmation, and Reality in the Natural and Social Sciences*. Princeton, NJ: Princeton University Press.

Moynihan, Daniel P. 1969. *Maximum Feasible Misunderstanding: Community Action in the War on Poverty*. New York: Free Press.

Muir, William K. Jr. 1967. *Prayer in Public Schools: Law and Attitude Change*. Chicago: University Chicago Press.

Murphy, Walter F. 1962. *Congress and the Court*. Chicago: University of Chicago Press.

Nachmias, David & Chava Nachmias 1987. *Research Methods in the Social Sciences*. New York: St. Martin's Press.

Nagel, Robert F. 1984. "Controlling the Structural Injunction." *Harvard Journal Law and Public Policy* 7:395.

Nelson, William E. 1975. *Americanization of Common Law: The Impact of Legal Change on Massachusetts Society, 1760-1830*. Cambridge, Mass: Harvard University Press.

Neustadt, Richard. 1960. *Presidential Power, the Politics of Leadership*. New York: Wiley Inc.

Oakeshott, Michael. 1993. "The History of Political Thought" Pp. 3–16 in *Michael Oakeshott: Morality and Politics in Modern Europe,* ed. Shirley Robin Letwin. New Haven, Conn: Yale University Press.

Ornstein, Norman J. 1978. *Interest Groups, Lobbying, and Policymaking.* Washington, DC: Congressional Quarterly Press.

Perry, Michael J. 1982. *The Constitution: the Courts, and Human Rights.* New Haven, Conn: Yale University Press.

Posner, Richard A. 1992. *Economic Analysis of the Law.* Boston, Mass: Little, Brown and Co., 4th ed.

Powell, H. Jefferson. 1985. "The Original Understanding of Original Intent." Harvard Law Review 98:885.

Pressman, Jeffrey L. and Aaron Wildavsky 1973. "Implementation" in "Symposium on Successful Policy Implementation." *Policy Studies Journal* 8:531.

Reynolds v Sims 1964. 377 *U.S.* 533.

Rhodes v Chapman 1981. 452 *U.S.* 337.

Ripley, Randall B. and Grace A. Franklin 1986. *Policy Implementation and Bureaucracy.* Pacific Grove, Cal: Brooks, Cole Publishing Co.

Ripley, Randall B. and Grace A. Franklin 1976. *Congress, the Bureaucracy, and Public Policy.* Pacific Grove, Cal: Brooks, Cole Publishing Co.

Rosenberg, Gerald. 1991. *The Hollow Hope: Can Courts Bring About Social Change?* Chicago: University of Chicago Press.

San Antonio Indep. Sch. Dist. v Rodriguez 1973. 411 *U.S.* 1.

Schattschneider, E.E. 1960. *The Semi-Sovereign People.* New York: Holt Rinehard and Winston.

Scheingold, Stuart A. 1974. *The Politics of Rights: Lawyers, Public Policy, and Political Change* New Haven, Conn: Yale University Press.

Scheppele, Kim Lane. 1992. "Review Essay." *Contemporary Sociology* 21:465

Schultz, David. 1993. "Political Theory and Legal History: Conflicting Depictions of Property in the American Political Founding." *American Journal of Legal History* 37:464.

Schultz, David. 1994. "Supreme Court Articulation of the Politics/Administration Dichotomy." Pp. 413–430 in *Handbook of Comparative and Developmental Public Administration,* ed. Ali Farazmand, New York: Marcel Dekker, Inc.

Schuck, Peter H. 1993. "Public Law Litigation and Social Reform." *Yale Law Journal* 102:1763.

Stumpf, H. P. 1993. "Book Review." *Journal of Politics* 55 (Feb.):256.

Simon, Julian L. and Paul Burstein 1985. *Basic Research Methods in Science*. New York: McGraw Hill.

Swann v. Charlotte-Mecklenburg Board of Education 1971. 402 *U.S.* 1.

De Tocqueville, Alexis 1969. *Democracy in America*. Garden City, NJ: Doubleday Co Inc.

Unger, Roberto Mangabeira. 1986. *The Critical Legal Studies Movement*. Cambridge, Mass: Harvard University Press.

Van Horn, Carl E. 1979. *Policy Implementation in the Federal System: National Goals and Local Implementors*. Lexington, Mass: Lexington Books.

Van Horn, Carl E. et al., 1989. *Politics and Public Policy*. Washington, DC: Congressional Quarterly Press.

Walsh, W.H. 1976. *An Introduction to Philosophy of History*. Westport, Conn: Greenwood Press.

Wasby, Stephen L. 1970. *The Impact of the United States Supreme Court: Some Perspectives*. Homewood, Ill: Dorsey Press.

Weatherly, Richard and Michael Lipsky 1977. "Street-Level Bureaucrats and Institutional Innovation: Implementing Special-Education Reform." *Harvard Educational Review* 47:171.

Wechsler, Herbert. 1959. "Toward Neutral Principles of Constitutional Law." *Harvard Law Review* 73:1.

Wesberry v Sanders 1964. 376 *U.S.* 1.

White, G. Edward. 1988. *The American Judicial Tradition: Profiles of Leading American Judges*. New York: Oxford University Press.

White, James Boyd. 1984. *When Words Lose Their Meaning: Constitutions and Reconstitutions of Language, Character, and Community*. Chicago: University of Chicago Press.

Wyatt v Aderholt 1974. 503 *F2d* 1305 (5th Cir.).

Chapter 5

The Supreme Court and Policy Reform: The Hollow Hope Revisited*

Bradley C. Canon

Introduction

Before the U.S. Supreme Court existed, Alexander Hamilton predicted that it would be "the least dangerous branch" because it possessed "neither the purse nor the sword." Less than two decades later, however, John Marshall seized the power of judicial review for the Court. Since that time, people have wondered in one form or another: To what extent can the U.S. Supreme Court command major changes in public policy?

For a long time this question was hypothetical because the Court did not seek much major policy change. It tended rather to defend the status quo against efforts to significantly alter public policy. It initiated little policy change itself. This is not to say that the Court was unimportant to policy-making. Decisions such as *U.S. v. E. C. Knight Co.* (156 U.S. 1) in 1895 and *Lochner v. New York* (198 U.S. 457) in 1905 certainly had an impact on national economic policy. Indeed, then as now, there were numerous proposals to curb the Court's reach in one way or another, culminating in President Franklin Roosevelt's famous "court packing" plan in 1937. But they were motivated by frustration with the Court's blockage of policy reforms, not because the Court was requiring policy reforms.

In the second half of the twentieth century, the Court changed course and initiated some highly visible policy changes by rendering new or expanded interpretations of the Bill of Rights and the equal

---

* I thank my colleague Jennifer Segal for helpful comments in drafting this chapter.

protection clause. Many such decisions were quite controversial and scholars began directly investigating the extent to which the Court could impose policy changes on the nation.

Robert Dahl (1957) made the first serious macrolevel attempt. In a pioneering article, he looked at the follow up to Court decisions that declared an act of Congress unconstitutional and concluded that on important issues Congress almost always got its way eventually. With rare and short-lived exceptions following realigning elections, the Court was dominated by members who shared the policy preferences of the reigning majority political coalition. Dahl thus concluded that the Court played at best a secondary role in shaping public policy. Research by Adamany (1973) and Funston (1975) seemed to supplement Dahl's conclusions.

Other researchers have questioned these conclusions. Led by Jonathan Casper (1976), they do not argue that the research by Dahl and others is wrong, although they do note that the conclusons rely disproportionately on the 1930s cases where the Court fought the New Deal (e.g., Canon and Ulmer 1976; Gates 1992). Rather they argue that Dahl and others cover only a fraction of the Supreme Court's policy output (finding acts of Congress unconstitutional) and ignore other types of Court decisions, e.g., finding state laws unconstitutional or statutory interpretation. Dahl does not tell the whole story, Casper argues. The Court *might* well have considerable impact on public policy. *Might* is stressed because there is no systematic macrolevel research examining the Court's policy impact in such areas.

Beginning in the 1960s, social scientists conducted considerable microlevel research into the impact of Supreme Court policies. This research usually involved empirical investigation of the consequences of controversial decisions where active or passive resistance might be expected, e.g., desegregation, schoolhouse religion, criminal justice, sexually oriented material and the First Amendment. The literature is too voluminous to discuss here. Suffice it to say that the findings are mixed. Researchers certainly found situations where Court decisions changed public policy considerably and, more important, changed public thinking and expectations about what the policy should be. But they also found resistance, "going through the motions" type compliance and limited use by those whom the Court's policies benefited.

Going beyond immediate policy change, some social scientists have looked at judicial impact from a different perspective, asking not so much whether public policy changes as a result of a court decision, but whether people's norms about what is legally right and expectations about what opportunities the law affords them change following a court decision. The works of Michael McCann (1994), Stuart Schiengold (1974) and Martha Minow (1990) particularly exemplify this approach. Much of this literature is broadly discussive, although McCann's *Rights At Work* is a thorough case study. The argument is that judicial policy changes that expand rights reinforce the sense that these rights are morally and constitutionally correct. Such decisions change the political language and alter the sense of what is politically possible. As Minow phrases it, "rights pronounced by the courts become possessions of the dispossessed" (1990, 310). Indeed, as court decisions enhancing rights disseminate through reform groups and everyday channels of communication, they can inspire persons feeling otherwise deprived to perceive themselves further endowed with rights than a court decision actually articulates. As McCann puts it, "judicially articulated legal norms take a life of their own as they are deployed in practical social action" (1992, 733).

The Hollow Hope

The three approaches—macrolevel, microlevel, and changed expectations—to the Supreme Court's impact on public policy in the United States constitute the background for my discussion of Gerald Rosenberg's landmark 1991 book *The Hollow Hope: Can Courts Bring About Social Change?* His title aside, Rosenberg focuses exclusively on the U.S. Supreme Court's impact. His fundamental conclusion is, simply put, that the Court cannot produce significant social reforms, "policy change with nationwide impact." The Court is basically "constrained", he argues, not "dynamic" and, except in conjunction with the other branches of government, effectuates only minor policy changes.

The Hollow Hope considers the impact of some controversial Supreme Court cases or series of decisions requiring or seeking social reform rendered during or shortly after the chief justiceship of Earl Warren. The greatest attention is focused on *Brown v. Board of Education* (347 U.S. 483) in 1954. The impact of *Roe v. Wade* (410 U.S. 113) in 1973 is also considered at some length. Rosenberg also discusses the Court's decisions in the criminal justice, reapportionment, environmental protection and women's rights areas. At the book's end, Rosenberg concludes that "U.S. courts can *almost never* be effective producers of significant social reform" (1991, 338, emphasis in original). The nature of "significant social reform" is not much elaborated, but from his focuses, I infer that he has in mind the most sweeping social changes in the second half of the twentieth century with which government is involved.

Rosenberg reaches his conclusion largely by considering the evidence in only one stream of research, microlevel studies of judicial impact. Although I quarrel with some of the inferences he draws from these studies, his evaluation is rich and detailed. The macrolevel studies are not much discussed in *The Hollow Hope*, but they would not contradict Rosenberg's assertion that the Supreme Court is nearly impotent. As noted, Dahl and others have advanced a somewhat similar conclusion while those skeptical of the impotence hypothesis have not built a strong case that the Court possesses policy-changing strength. While Rosenberg pays little attention to the changed expectations literature, he recognizes that Court decisions can have inspirational possibilities. To this end, he conducts his own research to test the inspirational impact of two decisions, *Brown* and *Roe*. He concludes that these cases did little to inspire blacks or women to either greater consumption of newly won rights or further mobilization. For reasons I will discuss later in this chapter, I find Rosenberg's methods of testing the inspirational hypothesis problematic. But he certainly deserves credit for being one of the first to attempt a systematic empirical investigation of decisions' inspirational possibilities.

The Hollow Hope is the first work to impose a broad conclusion on the plethora of empirical studies about the Court's impact. Previous summaries offered piecemeal conclusions. And as of this writing, no other broad study of the Court's impact on American life has been published. Moreover, its theme was pretty much unmitigated. The Court is politically impotent; its contribution to public policy is minimal, perhaps only a notch above that of Great Britain's House of Lords. Of course sweeping assertions attract professional and even public attention. *The Hollow Hope* is no exception. The book has been discussed in judicial process textbooks, been the subject of some lengthy essay reviews (McCann 1992; Feeley 1992; Simon 1992; Schuck 1993; Powe 1992; Schultz and Gottlieb 1996), and was the focus of several panels at professional meetings. *The Hollow Hope* is sufficiently well known to deserve analysis.

The Hollow Hope offers three reasons, or constraints as Rosenberg terms them, why the Supreme Court cannot generate significant policy reform:

Constraint I: The bounded nature of constitutional rights prevents courts from hearing or effectively acting on many significant social reform claims, and lessens the chances of popular mobilization (p. 13).

Constraint II: The judiciary lacks the necessary independence from other branches of the government to produce significant social reform (p. 15).

Constraint III: Courts lack the tools to readily develop appropriate policies and implement decisions ordering significant social reforms (p. 21).

The book then offers four conditions under which Court-produced reforms can be implemented successfully (overcome the constraints), all but one of which (Condition III) seem to require the assistance of other governmental actors:

Condition I: Courts may effectively produce significant social reform when other actors offer positive incentives to induce compliance (p. 33).

Condition II: Courts may effectively produce significant social reform when other actors impose costs to induce compliance (p. 33).

Condition III: Courts may effectively produce significant social reform when judicial decisions can be implemented by the market (p. 33).

Condition IV: Courts may effectively produce significant social reform by providing leverage, or a shield, cover, or excuse, for persons crucial to implementation who are *willing to act* (p. 35, emphasis in original).

In one sense it is hard to disagree with Rosenberg. Few would argue that the Supreme Court, standing alone, can produce significant, non-incremental social reform overnight. Indeed, as scholars of the presidency and Congress make clear (e.g., Neustadt 1960; Ripley and Franklin 1984), these branches are rather constrained when they act alone, and especially in the face of opposition from the other branches. In this sense, *The Hollow Hope*'s message hardly challenges the conventional scholarly wisdom.

Rosenberg seems to be arguing against reformers' optimism in an earlier era. In the 1960s liberal activists and some scholars argued that fundamental social reform could be achieved through litigation—even in the face of political opposition buttressed by public opinion (e.g., Chayes 1976; Rabin 1976). With the passage of time, however, experience considerably tempered this optimism. Scholars evaluating the impact research attributed only modest impact to Supreme Court decisions (e.g., Johnson and Canon 1984, chap. 7). Even the Critical

Legal Studies movement had lost enthusiasm about using the law to achieve social change.

It is the seeming extremity of Rosenberg's conclusions that has made *The Hollow Hope* controversial. Although he pays little attention to institutional interaction, Rosenberg argues that the Court is much weaker than the other branches—indeed, almost impotent—because (1) as an unelected body it lacks popular support, and (2) as a court, its social reform policies (as opposed to strictly legal policies) lack legitimacy. Thus many Court reform policies are seriously evaded or modified by those charged with enforcement. The Court, then, is not even a full partner in producing social reform policies; at best it is useful only for "mopping up" operations or conferring legitimacy on the other branches' policies.

Rosenberg's denial that the Supreme Court, acting alone, has any meaningful impact on political or social change in the United States seems to contradict the basic assumptions held by political scientists and others who study the Supreme Court and judicial politics generally. After all, they devote a lot of attention to the Supreme Court. Political scientists do not normally allocate energy and resources to studying institutions (or their actions) that do not affect society. Beyond that, even those who are opposed to the Court's reform policies attribute considerable impact to them (e.g., Bork 1990; Graglia 1976). For that matter, politicians, the media, and the attentive public do not behave as if the Supreme Court is the "paper tiger" that Rosenberg depicts. Why else would there be media speculation and bitter political controversy over nominees to the Court? In sum, scholars, politicians, and others, while recognizing that much judicial policy making interacts with that of the other branches, act as if Rosenberg has significantly underestimated the Court's policy making impact (e.g., O'Brien 1996, 359-360; Baum 1995, 270-271).

The controversy surrounding *The Hollow Hope* inspires me to explore further Rosenberg's "impotence conclusion"—the finding that, except with the assistance or at worst the indifference, of other governmental branches the Supreme Court has little real success in generating reform policies that affect American society. I will revisit four areas of reform that Rosenberg discussed (desegregation, abortion, criminal justice, and reapportionment). In addition, I will explore three Court-generated reforms that Rosenberg did not not discuss (schoolhouse religion, sexually oriented material, and advertising by professionals). The discussion of each reform will necessarily be brief. Thus my focus will be particularly on the degree to which Constraints II

The Supreme Court and Policy Reform

(lack of independence) and III (absence of tools) apply to Court generated reform. (As a general proposition, Constraint I concerning the limited nature of constitutional rights seems pretty self-evident and will not be further discussed in this chapter.) Beyond that, when Court reforms seem reasonably successful, I will discuss whether one or more of the four conditions for success existed. The chapter will conclude with a more general evaluation of Rosenberg's constraints and conditions as limitations on the implementation and impact of the Supreme Court's significant reforms in public policy.

Dimensions of Impact Analysis

I will analyze Rosenberg's findings about the Court's impact on two dimensions. One dimension pertains to who has to act to "implement" a decision: governmental agencies or those "consumers" actually or potentially affected by the decision. That is, must a government agency act to give effect to the Court's policy or can consumers accept or reject the policy directly (without government as an intermediary)? The other dimension pertains to how the public, especially the affected public, reacts to a Court decision. Decisions can produce behavior that ranges from grudging and/or uninterested compliance (or even defiance) to enthusiasm and inspiration to see that the policy is successful. In Figure 1, I depict the two dimensions and their interactions in a four-cell pattern. I do not consider the dimensions as di-

Figure 1: Placement of Reforms on Two Dimensions of Impact Analysis

Who Acts?	Type of Reaction	
	DIRECT	INSPIRATIONAL
IMPLEMENTATION REQUIRED	Criminal Justice Reapportionment Schoolhouse Religion	Desegregation
CONSUMER CHOICE	Advertising by Professionals Sexually Oriented Material	Abortion

chotomous, but it is easier to visualize and discuss them in a four-cell pattern. Figure 1 also locates each of the Supreme Court's policy reforms discussed in this chapter on the dimensions.

The "Who Acts?" Dimension

In *Judicial Policies: Implementation and Impact* (1984), Charles Johnson and I wrote of four populations that are concerned with the implementation or impact of judicial policies. The first is the interpreting population. Judges in courts below the policy-making court are its most influential members. Next is the implementing population. Its members are charged with making the policy work. Most commonly this involves persons in government agencies, e.g., police departments or school systems. Then comes the consumer population. These are the people who receive the advantages or disadvantages of a court decision, e.g., children who will attend desegregated schools or pregnant women who can obtain abortions. Finally there is the secondary population. These are people who are not directly affected by the decision, but who have an interest in it, e.g., politicians or male pro-life activists. For purposes of this chapter, the distinction between the implementors and the consumers is particularly important. Rosenberg made no distinction between implementors and consumers, but doing so facilitates my analysis of his findings.

Many judicial policies such as desegregation, especially busing, require government implementing agencies to make considerable changes in behavior and policy before anything happens. But some reform decisions such as abortion simply remove authority to make a policy from the government, thus allowing members of the consumer population to act in a previously forbidden manner.

The former are *implementation-required policies*. There are more obstacles to making reform policies effective when government has to act. Reforms by definition alter the status quo and thus are subject to lower court and bureaucratic inertia when implementation is required. Reforms also have opponents, so considerable political and social pressure will be brought on bureaucrats to ignore or minimize the impact of reform decisions. Often, in fact, the implementors themselves are strong opponents of reform, e.g., prosecutors and police in criminal justice reforms.

Consumer-choice policies are at the other end of the dimension. Arguably, reform decisions will be more effective when consumers can take advantage of them without the necessity of governmental implementation. Their opponents no longer have the machinery of government working for them; successful opposition must rely on the power of persuasion. This is not to say that such reforms always produce widespread change. For one thing, the new policy may not be very popular among consumers and few will take advantage of it. In a similar but more complex vein, many consumer-choice policies require two steps to be effective: the willingness of entrepreneurs to provide a previously prohibited service (e.g., abortions, sexually oriented books or videos) and an interested consumer population. Obviously, unless there are willing providers, a reform will not be effective. Social or economic pressures may limit providers; abortion clinics are rare in America's rural counties. Finally, government can discourage providers or consumers through various actions such as zoning regulations regarding adult bookstores.

It should be noted, however, that implementation-required policies that are effectively administered may well have a greater impact than consumer-choice policies. Consumers cannot easily avoid the former. For example, poorer white parents may have little choice but to send their children to desegregated schools (Giles and Gatlin 1980). By contrast, if few people take advantage of consumer choice reforms, their impact may be minimal.

Types of Reaction

The second dimension of judicial impact centers on reactions to policy reform. At one end, there is *direct compliance*. Here members of the implementing population, who presumably would not do so otherwise, change their behavior to comply with a Court generated reform. Normally implementors comply because they have a sense of professionalism, law abidingness or they fear punishment or stigmazation. But as considerable research shows (Johnson and Canon 1984, chap. 3), people can be ignorant of the policy, skirt its edge at times, avoid, or even defy the policy or at best comply indifferently. Obviously the fewer people who comply with a policy, the less impact it will have.

Indirect impact is at the other end of the dimension. Here the implementing population acts in accord with a reform policy, not because of a sense of professionalism or law abidingness, but as a consequence of interest group or public demands for its implementation. The route to implementation is indirect: the new policy inspires relevant consumers to put pressure on the perhaps reluctant legislators and implementors before they will act. Thus implementation takes longer, perhaps a decade or more. I will term the indirect end of the dimension *inspirational impact*. The policy reform inspires people to act socially (especially politically) in ways they would not have done in the absence of the new policy. When such actions are successful, they change the social and political environment sufficiently to obtain implementation from legislative bodies and governmental bureaucracies. As Marc Galanter (1983, 126) puts it, court decisions often "work through the transmission and reception of information rather than by concrete imposition of controls."

Inspirational impact is not usually a result of the Court changing minds. Initially, at least, a reform decision largely preaches to the choir. But like an inspirational new minister, a reform decision may put a new perspective on what can be accomplished. It opens new tactical options. Leaders can use it as a call to action because action may now produce the desired policy results, whereas before it would have been futile and even counterproductive. Indeed, the inspiration may stimulate persons to goals well beyond those specified by the Court. Few may be familiar with or even know about the Court's particular opinion, but many can be infected by its general direction and seek reforms that go beyond the Court's holding. Moreover, the decision does more than add a tactical weapon—it also supplies an institutional imprimatur to the call to action: "This is not just us talking, this is an agency of the United States government saying that we are right; we have the authority of the federal government behind us." In short, the judicial articulation of values can take on a life of its own as it inspires efforts to achieve social reform.

Seven Court Generated Reforms
My analysis of Rosenberg's "impotence" thesis will focus on seven Supreme-Court-generated policy reforms. They are ones where the casual observer might well believe that the Court's decisions dramatically changed national policy that subsequently caused a notable change in our political or social behavior. The reforms are placed in the appropriate cell in the cross-dimensional analysis depicted in Figure 1. The reforms are: (1) legislative reapportionment, (2) criminal justice (added rights for defendants), (3) schoolhouse religion, (4) desegregation, (5) greater availability of sexually oriented material, (6) advertising by professionals, and (7) abortion. *The Hollow Hope* addresses four of them (1, 2, 4, and 7), but not the other three. While the importance of social reforms is a matter of judgment, I believe these seven

are the most important ones in the second half of the twentieth century for which it can reasonably be argued that the Supreme Court played a major if not central role in their achievement. In fact, the key decisions in these policy areas occurred before 1980, so there is sufficient time to assess their impact.

Five of the Court's reforms were largely accomplished (to the extent that they were successful) directly; they did not seem to inspire any significant degree of organized political or social action demanding implementation or encouraging consumption. Two, *Brown* and *Roe*, seemed to inspire or have the potential for inspiring political pressures and greater consumption and *The Hollow Hope* considers their inspirational impact at some length.

Four of the seven were implementation-required reforms. Some required fairly complex actions (e.g., desegregation) while others simply called for the cessation of an existing policy (e.g., prayers in schools). But each needed some type of governmental action to be implemented. Three are consumer choice reforms; no government action was necessary.

I do not include two policy areas that were covered in *The Hollow Hope*. One is environmental protection. Rosenberg does not argue that the Supreme Court either initiated or inspired the environmental movement. The movement found a strong political ally in President Nixon and obtained its policy charter in the National Environmental Policy Act of 1970. The Court has rejected all efforts to create constitutionally-based environmental guarantees; its decisions in this area have largely involved statutory construction or procedural issues. Rosenberg focuses on these decisions and notes that environmentalists have been disappointed with the Court's overall record. It seems to me that there is no plausible argument that the Court has been "dynamic" concerning environmental reform and that almost all observers conclude that its role has been the "constrained" one that Rosenberg argues the courts actually follow.

The Hollow Hope also discusses women's rights. Its focus on abortion is a major part of this coverage, and I do discuss the Court's role in shaping abortion policy. In 1971 the Court did extend the equal protection clause to cover gender in *Reed v. Reed* (404 U.S. 71) and elaborated on the coverage in subsequent cases. But none of the cases singularly or together seem to call for major reform. The Court's interpretation of the Equal Pay Act of 1963 or Title IX of the 1964 Civil Rights Act may have greater consequences on society, but this illustrates that the Court is following the Congressional (and executive) lead. In my judgment, the Court was not the prime governmental mover in the struggle for gender equality. It has played the subordinate role that Rosenberg posits for the Court generally.

Having made the distinction between implementation-required and consumer- choice and between direct and inspirational impact reforms, I will now discuss the seven cases in their appropriate cells.

Direct Impact/Implementation Required Reforms

Reapportionment

In *Baker v. Carr* (369 U.S. 186; 1962) and follow up cases, the Supreme Court clearly commanded a major political reform through imposition of the "one person, one vote" rule on state legislatures and the national House of Representatives districts. The decisions clearly called for implementation by requiring legislatures to reapportion themselves and their state's House districts. As there were only 50 legislatures and numerous plaintiffs ready to bring lawsuits, judicial monitoring and insurance of compliance were not difficult. Legislatures were significantly reapportioned by the late 1960s and in many cases earlier. Nor did the Court later back off this reform. While the Burger and Rehnquist Courts modified some reforms initiated by the Warren Court, they did not retreat from the "one man, one vote" doctrine. State legislative and House districts today vary by less than 5% in population, and usually by only one or two percent.

Little inspirational impact occurred, nor was it necessary. The mass public "was generally supportive of, but essentially oblivious to the 'Reapportionment Revolution'" (Rosenberg 1991, 299). People probably perceived few real or psychic benefits from it. Few were inspired to pressure the legislature; indeed, such pressures were structurally foredoomed in the absence of a judicial threat. Only direct impact could accomplish this reform.

Rosenberg readily acknowledges that legislative reapportionment took place. He argues, however, that it did not accomplish the reformers' policy goal of changing partisan control of legislative chambers or of producing more urban oriented legislation. He cites several studies to this effect and concludes that "reapportionment . . . did not always, or even often, achieve the goals the reformers desired" (Rosenberg 1991, 301). It is not clear, however, what reformers Rosenberg is talking about and what goals they desired. In studies of the impact of the Supreme Court, the measure of success should not be based upon the policy desires of myriad reformers with various goals, but should be measured against the goals of the Supreme Court justices who established the reform. There is no evidence that the justices were motivated by particular policy preferences in *Baker* or its follow-up decisions, or that they would have decided the cases differently had malapportionment discriminated against rural interests. Reforms usually center on a principle. Here the Court adopted the reform principle and made its implementation stick.

The Court did this despite its seeming lack of independence and absence of tools (Constraints II and III). That is, it acted independently of Congress and in opposition to the state legislatures and it had sufficient tools to accomplish its purpose. Nor were any of the conditions Rosenberg posits for overcoming the constraints present. State legislatures were the only bodies that could comply with *Baker* and its progeny, and the courts were the only actors that threatened and sometimes imposed costs on the legislatures.

Criminal Justice

The Warren Court is perhaps most famous for its decisions reforming criminal due process such as *Mapp v. Ohio* (367 U.S. 643) in 1962, *Gideon v. Wainwright* (372 U.S. 335) in 1963, *Miranda v. Arizona* (384 U.S. 436) in 1966, and *In re Gault* (387 U.S. 1) in 1967. These decisions clearly required implementation, mostly by police, prosecutors and trial court judges. (While trial judges are in the judiciary, their interests here, especially at the state level, are often tied to prosecutors and police; they are often subject to reelection or retention considerations.) Moreover, the Court's criminal justice decisions must be directly implemented. They certainly did not give voice to a mass reform movement, not did they inspire one. Congress and state legislatures did take some implementory actions after Court decisions such as provision of counsel for indigents and bail reform, but they were of the less controversial type. *Miranda* and to a lesser extent *Mapp* met great resistance in legislative bodies and Congress's Omnibus Crime Control and Safe Streets Act of 1968 purported to limit *Miranda* (Schmidhauser and Berg 1972, 164–71). Richard Nixon's successful 1968 campaign focused on "law and order" as he aligned himself with the so-called peace forces as opposed to the criminal forces. Even as I write three decades later, President Bill Clinton is championing anti crime legislation so as not to appear "soft" on crime.

The criminal justice decisions also inspired intellectual debate. There was little legal and academic discussion of how the system did or should work prior to the 1960s. Such discussion has been common since then, which may stem as much from the rise in crime, especially narcotics crime, as from *Mapp, Miranda* and other cases. Nonetheless, it has helped secure judicial and public acceptance of certain principles the Court has articulated in these cases (e.g., curbing illegal searches, informing suspects of their rights, counsel for indigent adults and juvenile defendants), core accomplishments that have changed the framework if not the ambience of the criminal justice system.

Rosenberg reviews research about the impact of the criminal justice decisions and concludes that they had some impact on the criminal justice system, but that police and trial courts have engaged in much behavior that minimizes this impact. He calls the Court's decisions "The Revolution That Wasn't" (1991, 334). The problem is partly systemic: *Gideon*'s promise of the right of counsel is subverted because the overload on public defenders reduces their effectiveness. It is also partly one of suspects' or defendants' habits: despite receiving Miranda warnings, most suspects answer police questions rather than remain silent. And, of course, it is partly because the police and trial courts engage in behavior that minimizes the impact of *Miranda*, and especially the exclusionary rule, through such devices as routinized delivery of the warnings, police perjury, routine issuance of search warrants, and the admission of questionably obtained evidence.

In sum, the Court's decisions, accompanied by some degree of support from public officials and people at large, have curbed the more flagrant abuses, but they have induced little support for fundamental changes in the criminal justice system. Indeed, the Burger and Rehnquist Courts, reflecting public skepticism of further reforms, largely discontinued efforts to reform the criminal justice system and in some areas, such as the death penalty, have retreated somewhat. Arguably, criminal justice is such an essential function to society that when any significant degree of crime exists, the system cannot help but be an assembly line (Blumberg 1979). The criminal justice decisions certainly made some changes in the process, but they did not and could not revamp the system. To a considerable extent, Rosenberg's Constraints II and III prevailed here. Other government actors did assist the Court in accomplishing the reforms to the degree they were carried out, but the limited nature of the assistance limited the scope of the reforms.

Schoolhouse Religion

In two 1960s cases, *Engel v. Vitale* (370 U.S. 421) and *Abington Twp. v. Schempp* (373 U.S. 203), the Court found formal prayers or

Bible reading in public schools unconstitutional, practices then occurring in about two thirds of the nation's school systems. *The Hollow Hope* does not address the Court's schoolhouse religion cases, but they are worth considering. Some might argue that *Engel* and *Schempp* do not constitute a significant reform because the changes they require are more symbolic than real. No doubt great symbolism is associated with these cases, but the behavior at issue was highly valued by large numbers of people (and intensely disvalued by a small minority). The Court's decisions required implementation, albeit the minimal one of ending organized prayer or Bible reading in public schools. But implementation was not really that simple (e.g., Johnson 1967; Muir 1967; Dolbeare and Hammond 1971). Even when not held dear, these exercises were ingrained by habit and inertia. Moreover, because teachers are not directly supervised, many could continue brief religious practices in an atmosphere of indifferent administrators. Nor did *Engel* and *Schempp* inspire support for the reform (except in the sense of giving a green light to lawsuits). No mass movement or militant minority pressured legislators or took to the streets to get rid of prayers. Yet, while we still hear of occasional instances of religious exercises in public schols, by and large they no longer occur systematically.

The Court's rulings against organized religion in the schools did, however, inspire those fervently favoring its continuation to mobilize politically. Thus pressured, neither legislative bodies nor executive agencies helped to implement the demise of schoolhouse religion. To the contrary, this was bitterly opposed by most legislators. Over the years, in fact, there has been sufficient strength in Congress that one house or the other has approved a constitutional amendment to allow prayers in the schools, and this proposal remains a part of the Republican platform. Often school board policy changes, if adopted at all, occurred only under threat of a lawsuit. Nor did *Engel* and *Schempp* eventually change minds. Public opinion polls a third of a century later continue to show majority support for prayers in the public schools. Indeed, it is difficult to think of another judicial reform that has been so widely opposed for so long. Yet the Court not only held to its initial rulings, but expanded them to bar such activities as the posting of the Ten Commandments in school rooms and non denominational prayers at graduation exercises (*Stone v. Graham,* 449 U.S. 39, 1980, and *Lee v. Weisman,* 505 U.S. 77, 1992).

Thus the Supreme Court appears to have effectuated a significant social reform in the schoolhouse religion area despite Constraints II and III. Conditions I and II do not obtain; no non judicial actors offered incentives or imposed costs on school administrators or teachers. Condition III (market incentives) is not relevant. Condition IV may have existed in some situations, but the use of *Engel* and *Schempp* as an excuse or shield to remove religious exercises from the public schools does not seem widespread.

Inspirational Impact/Implementation Required Reforms

Desegregation

Brown v. Board is the premier case of social reform in this cell. It is beyond question that desegregation is one of the greatest social reforms in American history. What is more debatable is the role the Supreme Court played in achieving it. There was some direct impact through lower court decrees or voluntary compliance, but it most certainly was not widespread. Thus Rosenberg argues that the Court's role was minor because desegregation was not achieved until Congress and the President signed on to racial equality and put sufficient incentives and punishments in place through the 1964 Civil Rights Act and other legislation or executive orders.

Certainly congressional and presidential policies produced a considerably more rapid implementation of school desegregation than lower court action alone would have done (Giles 1975; Rodgers and Bullock 1972). The next question focuses on the degree of linkage between *Brown* and later congressional and executive actions. Put otherwise, did *Brown* inspire African- Americans and sympathetic whites to engage in the sit-in demonstrations of the early 1960s, which in turn pressured presidents Kennedy and Johnson to push for and Congress to adopt the 1964 Civil Rights Act? Certainly if any Supreme Court case might be expected to generate an indirect and inspirational impact to achieve success, *Brown* is it. The decision was highly visible and deeply affected large numbers of people who had a community identity and who were blatantly being treated unequally.

I need to emphasize here that there is a distinction between desegregating the schools and desegregating society more generally. *Brown*, of course, required only the former, although the Court, citing *Brown*, soon required desegregation of other publicly owned facilities. Thus there can be two criteria for assessing *Brown*'s impact. The narrower one is desegregation of schools and other public facilities. We can be sure that this is what the members of the Court intended in 1954. We cannot be sure of the justices' broader goals or hopes. Of course, *Brown* arguably inspired efforts to eliminate non public segregation, formal or informal, in areas such as employment, housing, recreation and social life—to achieve social change well beyond that posited by the Supreme Court's decision, although perhaps consistent with the general if vague hopes of some justices. In assessing *Brown*'s impact, we must keep this distinction in mind.

Rosenberg certainly recognizes that inspirational impact can occur as a result of a governmental body's actions or pronouncements. He further recognizes that *Brown* could inspire its beneficiaries and their allies to increased action on behalf of desegregation. Moreover, Rosenberg moves beyond calling attention to inspiration as a force in achieving social reform. In chapter 4, he conducts empirical research into *Brown*'s inspirational impact (and later does so for *Roe v. Wade*). *The Hollow Hope* is the first major attempt to measure judicial inspiration to political action.

He argues that an inspirational decision should be salient to the mass public. Rosenberg compiled articles pertaining to civil rights from the periodical indices from 1940 through 1965. While coverage was up somewhat in 1954 and spiked in 1956 and 1957 (which he attributes to the Montgomery bus boycott and the violence accompanying the integration of schools in Clinton, Tennessee, and Little Rock, Arkansas), it then went down to pre-1954 levels before rising markedly in the Kennedy Administration. A similar pattern is reported for *Time, Newsweek*, and *The New York Times*, publications directed to more elite readers. Thus Rosenberg concludes "overall, there is no evidence of [increased press coverage] or major change in reporting in the years immediately following *Brown*" (1991, 111). He also notes that public opinion, as measured by responses to various questions concerning racial integration and sensitivity to the condition of blacks in America, showed little change prior to the 1960s.

When he focuses on the reactions of blacks, Rosenberg reaches a similar conclusion. He notes that except for 1956 there were few civil rights demonstrations in the United States prior to the sit-ins beginning in 1960. He uses data from various civil rights organizations to argue that their membership and income did not increase significantly following *Brown*. He buttresses his arguments with recollection-type data based upon others' interviews with leaders in black groups such as the NAACP, sit-in demonstrators, and Freedom Riders. The interviewees attributed their motivation to a general sense of injustice or frustration with the lack of progress rather than to devotion to constitutional principles articulated in *Brown*.

Rosenberg has pioneered the use of systematic data to measure inspirational impact. For several reasons, however, the data he presents do not offer much support for concluding that *Brown* had little inspirational impact upon the civil rights movement and its accomplishments.

For one thing, much of the data Rosenberg presents are not particularly reflective of changing perspectives among blacks of what is politically possible. Article counts do not inform us about their content. Moreover, nearly all the magazines were aimed at white, not black, audiences, so even a content analysis would catch few exhortations to actions furthering desegregation. Nor would general public opinion polls reveal peoples' changing perspectives—their willingness to act on behalf of a cause—as opposed to their attitudes, which may not have changed much following *Brown*. Beyond that, opinion polls asked of the general public will not reflect very well changes in attitudes among a 10% subcategory of the population.

Also, Rosenberg's conception of impact is too time-bound. He concedes that considerable change in school desegregation has occurred in the four decades since *Brown*, but he credits other actors. Ideas and perspectives, however, are central to inspirational impact. History and experience teach that minds or perspectives are not changed overnight; sometimes a decade or even a generation will pass before a major effect occurs. Often the young, with their more flexible mindsets and social niches, are more inspired than are the middle-aged or elderly. Thus Rosenberg's conclusion that *Brown* had little impact because the real push for racial integration did not begin until the 1960s is not in itself convincing. Although the 1960s "sit-inners" may have been in junior high school when *Brown* came down and some perhaps could not cite the case by name as they sat at dime store lunch counters, it is quite possible and perhaps likely that the decision was a vital part of the inspirational linkage producing their behavior.

My skepticism about the utility of some of Rosenberg's measures is not meant to denigrate the systematic collection of data relevant to inspirational impact. To the contrary, it is important that we do so. But we have to recognize two things. One is that good measures of changing perspectives on what can be accomplished are difficult to come by. Second, the measures that are used need to be relevant to the inspirational impact problem under study. We should not allow our frustration over the difficulty of obtaining good measures of inspirational impact to induce us to accept measures that do not bear on our hypotheses.

Clearly, desegregating schools and other public facilities required the assistance of other governmental actors, most notably Congress in the 1960s and the departments of Justice and Education subsequently. Constraints II and III (lack of independence and tools) were operative here. Likewise, Rosenberg's Conditions I, and II were present; other actors offered incentives and imposed costs to achieve desegregation. (Condition III, free market incentives, is not relevant and Condition IV, use of the decision as an excuse, seldom occurred.) I argue, however, that to some considerable extent, these actors' assistance resulted from political pressure inspired by *Brown*. Rosenberg acknowledges the importance of political pressure in motivating other actors, but believes that *Brown* was only marginally relevant to mobilizing it. Our differences might be resolved if relevant data were available for analysis, but such data are difficult to collect under the best of circumstances and all the more so from 30 or 40 years in the past.

Direct Impact/Consumer Choice Reforms

There are two issue areas in this cell where the Supreme Court arguably accomplished significant social reforms: making sexually oriented material widely available and permitting various types of commercial advertising, particularly by professionals, that previously was forbidden. These reforms are not discussed in *The Hollow Hope*. Concededly, these reforms do not quite rank with desegregation or abortion. Both, however, considerably broadened the scope of constitutional protection for freedom of speech and press. While neither was at the core of liberalism, both were generally favored by liberals (at least before the feminist attack on pornography) and opposed by conservatives. Moreover, the greater availablity of sexually oriented material appears to have changed the social ambience in this country. Indeed, assertions that the widespread availability of such material undermines the moral fiber of the citizns have been repeatedly asserted by the Christian Coalition and their sympathizers to this day.

Sexually Oriented Material
The breakthrough ruling in sexually oriented material was *Roth v. U.S.* (354 U.S. 476) in 1957 where the Supreme Court held that such material was protected by the First Amendment unless the dominant theme of the work, taken as a whole, appealed to prurient interests and lacked redeeming social value. The 1960s was the decade of the "sexual revolution." Books focusing on sex became widely available

and not just at adult bookstores, but in regular bookstores and even in supermarket book racks. Films with nudity and sexual scenes moved out of art houses or seedy theaters and into suburban malls. Topless dancers and go-go bars proliferated. The Court reinforced this trend in some 1960s decisions, e.g., *Jacobellis v. Ohio* (376 U.S. 254), *Memoirs v. Massachusetts* (383 U.S. 413) and *Redrup v. New York* (386 U.S. 767). While *Miller v. California* (413 U.S. 15) in 1973 put some boundaries on what was permissible, it was hardly a call for returning to Victorian morals. Indeed, it was a kind of "peace treaty" ratifying all but the excesses of "the grapes of *Roth*."

It is clear, however, that this reform has prevailed, that sexually oriented material was far more prevalent after *Roth* than before it. As Johnson and Canon (1984, 250) noted:

> A Rip Van Winkle who had gone to sleep in the mid-1950s would truly be astounded upon awakening today. Best selling novels then almost never focused on sex directly and did not use dirty language. On the non-fiction side, it was easier to find a guide book to climbing the Himalaya mountains than to find one on the physical aspects of sex. . . . [M]ovies were 'squeaky clean'; even married couples slept in separate beds.

Thus an important question is what role did the Court have in facilitating this reform? The answer is that the Court was the only body with any authority or political clout to pursue this reform. As far as governmental agencies' actions go, the Court initiated it. No president or governor ever urged the greater availability of sexually oriented material and neither Congress nor most state legislatures enacted any laws to make such material more available. In fact, most public officials looked askance at such a policy. Outside of government, while the ACLU might defend those charged with selling or showing obscene material, there was not a visible reform movement lobbying legislators or stirring up public opinion to change the nation's obscenity laws or even pushing litigation. Indeed, the opponents of any real change were more visible and respectable. By all appearances, the Court's *Roth* decision enabled major social reform to take place on a pervasive basis. It did this without any implementation or imposition of costs on other actors by nonjudicial government agencies, and the reform was achieved within a few years of the decision. Supreme Court decisions making sexually oriented material more available seem to belie Rosenberg's argument that the "dynamic" Court does or can not exist.

In consumer choice situations, however, Court-generated reforms (or those by any agency) can only be effective if enough consumers do in fact choose to take advantage of the reform. To some extent this is a matter of numbers, but it is not strictly measured in numbers. A change in community ambience or willingness to accept different behavior can mark a successful reform even if only a small portion of the population actually chooses the newly available option. But some visible change is necessary to account a judicial reform as effective. For example, if the Court had decided 1986's *Bowers v. Hardwick* (478 U.S. 748) in the opposite manner—striking down state sodomy laws—the case would not have initiated a significant social reform. It would, of course, have symbolic importance, but it is difficult to believe that people would start engaging in homosexual activities because of the Court's decision.

As discussed earlier, sometimes consumer choice reforms require two levels of choice to be effective. First, someone must choose to provide the materials or services that the Court has said the government cannot forbid. Normally providers will do this if they sense a sufficient demand. This was the case following *Roth*. There is always a demand for sexually oriented material, but the public appetite for this material increased markedly in the 1960s compared to the 1950s. Basically there are two explanations for this increase. One is that the Court's *Roth* decision inspired providers (authors, publishing houses, film makers, producers, store owners, and so on) to write or stock things they previously would have avoided, and the greater visibility and availability of sexually oriented material induced greater public interest in it. The other is that the public, particularly the younger portion of it, was shedding its rigid Victorian moral code and was ready for a change in policy. I speculate that both explanations contributed to the proliferation of sex material in the 1960s, but that the second has more potency that the first. *Roth* itself did not likely inspire many authors or filmmakers, although it may have led publishers or producers to signal an acceptance of more racy or graphic material. On the other hand, many persons' morality and tolerance were changing independently of judicial action and in this sense *Roth* and *Miller* did not themselves reform the nation's sexual mores; the ultimate consumer interest was already rising. But the Court did enable the change. It made the creation, distribution, and sale of sexually oriented material much less risky legally and imbued it with a legitimacy and acceptability it would not otherwise have possessed.

In sum, the Supreme Court was a crucial actor in achieving this reform and no other governmental body played any role. Neither its seeming lack of independence nor its lack of tools (Constraints II and III) forestalled success. The absence of other government actors in the implementation process made these constraints irrelevant. Thus the conditions necessary to overcome them were not relevant. It is worth noting, however, that Condition III (market incentives) helps explain why sexually oriented material is so much more widely available since the 1960s. Publishers, film and video makers, and retail stores saw a market demand for such material and filled it. But market incentives are a universal explanation for changes in behavior and are applicable to all policy changes that give the consumer population a choice; it is hardly limited to the Supreme Court or to courts in general.

Advertising by Professionals
Prior to the 1970s, the First Amendment provided no protection for commerical speech. The question, in fact, was not much litigated. Of course, advertising is essential to twentieth century commerce, so neither the states nor the federal government regulated it to any great extent, but advertising by those in the licensed professions (e.g., physicians and attorneys) was commonly prohibited. In the 1976 case of *Virginia Board of Pharmacy v. Virginia Consumers Council* (425 U.S. 748), the Court, with only one justice dissenting, ended this prohibition. The case involved pharmacists, but a year later the Court extended its logic to attorneys and by implication to all professionals.

Two small and politically marginal interests sought professional advertising. Consumer activists (who were behind the *Virginia Pharmacy* case) saw the ban as a device to enhance professionals' income by discouraging price shopping. Second, younger or economically more marginal members of professions quickly becoming overcrowded (particularly attorneys) saw advertising as a means of enlarging their clientele. While consumer groups engaged in some lobbying activity and sought publicity, obtaining a right for professionals to advertise was but one of their numerous goals. Economically hungry professionals engaged in no non judicial efforts to overturn the advertising ban.

Thus, as with *Roth*, *Virginia Pharmacy* was neither the culmination of an intense, organized push for reform nor a ratification of a reform essentially brokered by legislatures or executive agencies. Professional advertising was not a burning issue in the public mind; most people gave little thought to the matter and only a handful of consumer activists pursued it. The change was largely opposed by state and national professional associations such as the American Bar Association, groups from which legislators normally take their signals. Yet the Court adopted this reform and went on to expand the scope of permissible advertisements in such cases as *In Re Primus* (436 U.S. 412) in 1978 and *Edenfield v. Fane* (507 U.S. 761) in 1993.

It is unlikely that professionals will advertise unless they think it will generate additional clients. This is seen in the fact that attorneys who advertise are almost always ones whose practice necessitates a turnover in clients, e.g., bankruptcies, drunken driving, divorce, and auto accidents. There is no need for blue ribbon law firms with established corporate clients to advertise. This economic consideration limits the proportion of professionals who will choose to advertise.

Certainly *Virginia Pharmacy* and its progeny have had an impact. One can hear pitches for lawyers, accountants (especially at income tax time), dentists, and others on the radio from time to time and occasionally they appear on television (especially from managed health care plans and lawyers). Newspapers carry ads from professionals, and the telephone books are replete with their box ads. There are also direct mail solicitatons. Nonetheless, the floodgates have not opened. We are not saturated with professional advertising and many who might be economically advantaged by doing so nevertheless think it is unprofessional. A recent survey (Bowen 1995) shows that only about a third of those attorneys whose practice depends upon high turnover have actually advertised.

Thus the Supreme Court has been reasonably successful in initiating and securing social reform regarding advertising by professionals. The Court's immediate goal was to give potential clients greater information about their fees and specialties, and enough professionals have taken advantage of this option to make this a reality, at least in more populated areas. However, the availability of this option has not turned the professions into significantly more commercial enterprises. But it is doubtful the Court intended this.

As with sexually oriented material and other consumer choice reforms, Constraints II and III (lack of independence and tools) are irrelevant to implementation. Thus the conditions for overcoming them are inapplicable. Once again, however, market incentives help explain the consumer response. In this policy area, however, many professional decided that the costs of advertising was not worth the benefits.

Inspirational Impact/Consumer Choice Reform

Abortion

Legal abortion is the chief social reform in this cell. Unlike many women's rights decisions which required implementation to be effective—e.g., *Frontiero v. Richardson* (411 U.S. 677) in 1973 or *Johnson v. Santa Clara County* (480 U.S. 646) in 1987, *Roe v. Wade* is basically a two-tier consumer choice decision. It removed the legal prohibitions against early term abortions and allowed a woman to choose whether to terminate the pregnancy or carry the fetus to term. The former choice, however, is premised in the availability of a provider; some physicians must choose to perform abortions.

I have some reservations about placing the abortion decision in the inspirational impact category. Abortion rights, of course, is a central belief to the women's movement. But there was no overt, visible campaign following *Roe* that urged women to terminate an unwanted pregnancy. However, it is likely that *Roe* and the publicity surrounding it inspired clinic counselors and friends to advise some women to obtain an abortion who otherwise would not have done so. But we do not know how many women this might be. Still, *Roe* seems to have produced more inspiration to action than *Roth* or *Virginia Pharmacy*. Moreover, Rosenberg discusses the possible catalytic effects of the abortion decision. So I treat it here as a decision that inspired action. But unlike Inspirational Impact/Implementation Required reforms, the inspiration *Roe* gives is not to political action—lobbying, rallies and other mobilization tactics—but toward acceptance of abortion as a personal-choice possibility by women who previously would not have considered it.

Because it was a consumer choice decision, the post-*Roe* situation differed from the post-*Brown* one. There was no reason to expect *Roe* to inspire women (or anyone) to renewed effort to achieve legal abortion as a social reform. *Roe* accomplished this in itself. The struggle was seemingly over and women's groups turned their attentions to gender equality issues (Epstein and Koblyka 1992, chap. 6). There was no need to lobby, rally or mobilize voters to pressure legislatures or executive agencies. Only after the pro-life forces mobilized did pro-choice groups become politically active—defending and and not trying to overturn the status quo.

Thus if *Roe* was inspirational, it was not a call to group action to continue a struggle, but to the two tiers of consumers to exercise the newly won right. Such inspiration is not easy. It is socially and politically awkward to advocate abortion in any general sense. All *Roe* did and all its supporters can do is to argue that a woman should have a choice. The Court's declaration that choice is a constitutional right may have inspired a few women to consider the abortion alternative who would not have done so in a pre-*Roe* situation, but pregnant women are not primarily guided by constitutional values. Such inspirational impact as *Roe* had was more circuitous. It probably encouraged groups (from Planned Parenthood to feminist counseling clinics) to make their services known and to advise pregnant women about their options and to recommend abortion to women in many situations. A good number of pregnant teenagers whose parents and other relevant adults opposed abortion sought advice from such groups. All this occurred in the face of considerable hostility. Social pressures along with occasional violence have discouraged many hospitals and physicians from performing abortions. Few abortion clinics are located in rural areas. Often state or local policies discourage abortion. Thus some inspiration is necessary for counseling groups and pregnant women to offer and consider abortion as an alternative. But *Roe* is not the only inspirational factor and may or may not be a major one.

As he did with *Brown*, Rosenberg considers the possibility that *Roe v. Wade* could inspire an increased number of pregnant women to obtain an abortion. Thus he compiles some of the same data regarding publicity about abortion. He finds that periodical articles about abortion were not as numerous in the three years after *Roe* as they had been in the three years preceding it. *New York Times* coverage peaked in 1972, one year before the decision. While membership in organizations such as the National Organization of Women rose rapidly after *Roe*, it was on a dramatic upswing before *Roe* as well. But these data are not particularly relevant to measuring inspiration. Periodical or newspaper coverage tends to focus more on the struggle and, especially with newspapers, rises and falls with the occurrence of particular events. Once victory is achieved, coverage declines, especially if no implementation is necessary. Membership in feminist organizations can be affected by many goals, not just abortion. After *Roe*, in fact, it is likely that fewer women would join NOW and other women's groups to help achieve abortion rights.

There is no doubt that the number of legal abortions rose rapidly after *Roe*, reaching about 1.6 million in 1980 and remaining remarkably steady afterward (Rosenberg 1991, 178–180; 1995, 394). This contrasts with about 500,000 legal abortions in 1972, the year before *Roe*. What is arguable is whether the Court decision contributed to this increase to any significant degree. Rosenberg and others note that the rapid increase in legal abortions began in 1970, three years prior to *Roe*, and contend that the post-1972 increase may well be a continuation of that trend and largely unaffected by the Court's action. On the eve of *Roe*, four states allowed abortion on demand and another dozen had eased their abortion restrictions to the point where a woman determined to have an abortion could most likely obtain one. Legal abortions, thus, were an available option to women in many geographical areas. Rosenberg concedes that without *Roe* few additional states might have followed the trend and that some might even have reinstated their abortion restrictions—that the Court's impact was more than negligible. But the thrust of his argument, to use Susan Hansen's (1980, 375) phrasing, is that the Court "was reflecting social change rather than legislating it."

But a Court decision reflecting social change can be an important one. As discussed earlier, social reforms seldom originate in government agencies, but government is often necessary to promulgate and secure the changes. This is all the more true when strenuous opposition to the reform exists. And it is beyond argument that abortion is vigorously opposed by politically potent and emotionally sustained groups. The early easing of abortion laws took place before this opposition jelled. But once the pro-life forces came together, abortion reform received far more grief than assistance from legislative and executive bodies, state or federal. Congress passed the Hyde Amendment (with Carter administration support) which severely restricted federal funding for abortions, and it came close to sending a constitutional amendment prohibiting abortion to the states. A number of states passed laws that discouraged women from obtaining an abortion.

The Supreme Court is the one governmental body that has sustained abortion rights. It has continually reiterated the constitutionality of abortion against strong challenges. Abortion opponents, realizing the Supreme Court's crucial role, have lobbied hard and sometimes successfully for the appointment of new justices with pro-life inclinations. Indeed, when it appeared that the Court would abandon *Roe* in *Webster v. Reproductive Health Services* (492 U.S. 490) in 1989 and *Planned Parenthood v. Casey* (505 U.S. 833) in 1992, the pro-choice camp was full of gloom and panic because it had nowhere else to turn.

In sum, the Supreme Court was and remains an important player in the achivement of abortion reform. It did not literally initiate the reform and there is some question about how much *Roe* and other decisions inspired women to obtain abortions. Abortions would most likely be available in some jurisdictions regardless of *Roe*. But the Court made it a nationwide option and, almost alone, has protected it against frequent and intense challenges. Legal abortion has had some support in the other branches of government, but in the main it has met opposition. The freedom of choice policy has prevailed despite Constraints II and III (absence of independence and tools). Other branches have occasionally given incentives or imposed costs on public agencies administering Medicaid to both comply with and *resist* the Court's abortion decisions, but Conditions I and II probably affect the frequency of abortions in America only to a minor degree. Condition III offers some explanation for the rapid rise of abortion providers following *Roe*, although some abortion services are not inspired by profit. Reflecting the public's divisiveness, some public officials no doubt support freedom of choice and have used *Roe* as a shield for their actions (Condition IV), but others are fiercely pro-life.

Conclusion

In *The Hollow Hope* Rosenberg paints a picture of a Supreme Court that is almost impotent, a government appendage that acts in minor ways or is occasionally helpful in securing major policy change, but has little important policy-making capacity. The Court is not independent, he argues, and cannot successfully implement major policy reform except in conjunction with the political branches.

By contrast, my portrait of the Court is one of significant policy-making independence and capacity. The justices were largely successful in establishing four or five of the seven policies I discussed without much assistance from other branches of government. In reforming criminal justice procedures, it is arguable that the implementing agencies muffled the reforms' effect. It is also arguable that too few professionals are engaging in advertising to conclude that *Virginia Pharmacy* and subsequent cases led to widespread change. And certainly desegregation received considerable implementation assistance from the other branches of government. What is less clear is the extent that *Brown* inspired the political pressure to get Congress and the executive to act. But I argue that both *Roe v. Wade* and *Baker v. Carr* were successful Supreme Court reforms and that the Court also accomplished reforms in two areas (the availability of sexually oriented material and removing religion from the public schools) not addressed in *The Hollow Hope*. Obviously, Rosenberg and I paint quite different pictures of the Supreme Court's policy-making capacity.

Part of this difference is a function of our perspectives. Rosenberg sometimes attributes goals to the justices that go well beyond what they say in their opinions. This is particularly noticeable with *Brown* and the reapportionment cases. Then when America does not achieve complete desegregation and racial harmony in all aspects of life or when reapportioned legislatures do not pass liberal, urban-oriented policies, Rosenberg asserts that the Court's goals were never met. More broadly, Rosenberg tends to look at the frustrations of the implementation process (e.g., there are no abortion facilities in 75% of America's counties) and to conclude that reform is failing. He sees the glass as half empty. By contrast, I see the glass as half full. If legislatures are apportioned upon the "one person, one vote" principle and abortions can be generally obtained (albeit with some inconvenience for rural women), I treat the reform as basically successful. History teaches that reforms are not achieved universally and instantaneously. This is true of legislative reforms (e.g., the Fair Housing Act or Americans with Disabilities Act) as well. It is unrealistic to expect otherwise.

But the difference in our conclusions is based upon more than our perspectives. Rosenberg writes as if full implementation is required of all reforms. His Constraint III states that the Court lacks the tools to develop appropriate implementation policies for achieving significant reform. He does not distinguish between gradations of implementation or note that some reforms need no implementation. Yet we would expect that a reform's success would be related to the nature of its implementation. The easier the implementation, the more likely its achievement. My review of seven policy areas seems to bear this hypothesis out. No tools are necessary for achieving the three consumer choice reforms. Two, sexually oriented material and abortion, are now widely available in this country despite intense opposition. Professionals' use of advertising is visible if not overwhelming and it may be on the increase. The Court can be quite dynamic in changing society by instituting consumer choice reforms.

Two other reforms, reapportionment and ending schoolhouse religion, required minimal implementation in the sense that no bureaucratic planning, training exercises, monitoring, and so on, were necessary. Reapportionment was easily achieved. By and large schoolhouse religion has been eliminated or minimized. The fact that occasional exceptions get considerable publicity illustrates how much our expectations have changed since *Engel* and *Schempp*.

Desegregation and criminal justice reforms required a more complex implementation process, and Constraint III is more applicable to them. Desegregation was achieved through complex and often painful implementation processes and certainly with active federal assistance. The Court's decisions in *Mapp, Miranda*, and other cases have changed the behavior of participants in the criminal justice process somewhat but have probably had just a modest overall impact on arrests and conviction rates.

The Court's success in achieving these social reforms is all the more impressive because it occurred in the face of sometime indifference and more often strong opposition from Congress, the president, and state governments. This flies in the face of Rosenberg's Constraint II, which says that the judiciary lacks the necessary independence from the other branches of government to produce significant social reform. Sexually oriented material epitomizes the fact that Constraint II is only a sometime barrier to major Court-generated policy change. Congress has always resisted the proliferation of such material; even as I write, it is trying to stop "indecency" on the Internet. Similar resistance inheres in state legislatures. Sexually oriented material has few public defenders (although apparently many consumers). Likewise, legislatures resisted reapportionment fiercely. It was the courts and not the president or the governors that overcame this opposition. Further, it is certain that the Court's decisions on religion in the schools were not popular with either legislative bodies or the public. And clearly the Court's abortion reform has received more opposition than assistance from the other branches of government. Although both presidents Carter and Clinton took pro-choice positions, the Reagan and Bush administrations acted to discourage abortions. Through the Hyde Amendment and other laws, Congress has shown hostility to therapeutic or elective abortions. Most state legislatures are similarly hostile, although some have supported the pro-choice position. In sum, Constraint II is simply not as strong or universal a constraint as is claimed in the *The Hollow Hope*.

As noted above, the inapplicability of Constraints II and III to consumer choice Supreme Court policy reforms means that the conditions Rosenberg sets forth for overcoming the constraints are not applicable as explanations for the policy's success or failure. Neither legislative bodies nor executive agencies offered inducements for people to purchase sexually oriented material, for women to obtain abortions, or for professionals to advertise. However, Condition III (market incentives), although not an explanation for overcoming the constraints, does help explain variance in the Court's consumer choice reform.

In the reforms where a minimal degree of implementation must occur, no non judicial actors offered inducements or threatened sanctions to legislators following *Baker v. Carr* or *Schempp*. Similarly, there is little evidence showing that malapportioned legislators were just waiting for *Baker* so they could apportion themselves out of office or that school administrators were eager to use *Schempp* to get rid of prayers or Bible readings. Constraints II and III simply did not nullify the courts' abilities to implement these reforms and the explanation for this does not lie in the conditions Rosenberg lays out for overcoming the constraints.

Rosenberg portrays a weak policy-making role for the Supreme Court, an institution whose attempts at major social change often fail or which are largely dependent upon other governmental agencies to suceed. *The Hollow Hope* is a good read and full of interesting observations and ideas, but unfortunately its picture of the Court's role is badly skewed; it is reminiscent of those reflections seen in carnival mirrors that make one appear taller or wider or grossly exaggerate the head or arms or legs. The Court's image is recognizable, but clearly distorted. Certainly "American courts are not all powerful institutions" as Rosenberg reminds us (1991, 343), but it does not follow that they are impotent at changing public policy. The Supreme Court, at least over the last half century, has instituted or had a crucial role in securing a number of major policy reforms in the United States. It is not a bit player or supporting actor, but a major player with both an independent and interdependent role on the public policy stage.

Notes

1. For summaries see Johnson and Canon (1984), Wasby (1970), and Canon (1991).

2. See, e.g., McCann (1994), Schiengold (1974), and Minow (1990). The approach of this focus is not so much on the impact of court decisions as it is on how reform oriented disputes are settled.

3. The preface (p. xi–xii) indicates that his analysis applies only to recent liberal decisions. Most major Court decisions in the last 50 years fall in this category.

4. Rosenberg (1992) did contribute to macro-level literature.

5. Of course there is plenty of argument about how much the Court should expand or constrict constitutional rights guarantees.

6. We can also discuss consumer population compliance, e.g., did drivers reduce their speed when the 55 mile per hour speed limit was imposed or do parents send their children to desegregated schools, but this chapter does not focus on consumers' reaction to judicial decisions perceived as adverse to their interest.

7. Of course, well-crafted and eloquently phrased Court opinions may have some long run intellectual persuasive power. The famous 1943 flag salute case, *West Virginia Board v. Barnette* (319 U.S. 624), is a good example. Most opinions of the Court don't reach such eloquence. Even the decision's defenders concede that the opinion in *Roe v. Wade* is poorly written. Most opinions that are accounted as memorable and eventually persuasive are dissents.

8. Some reform decisions, particularly those banning schoolhouse religion, enhancing criminal defendants' rights, or allowing the sale of pornography inspired considerable organized negative pressures on legislatures and government agencies. However, negative inspirational impact will not be considered in this chapter.

9. Upon legislative failure, federal courts would reapportion the districts themselves. This happened only occasionally, due less to overt legislative resistance than to members' inability to agree on new lines.

10. There is an element of consumer choice in these decisions in that suspects or defendants can choose not to exercise their Miranda rights or to waive counsel, etc. But in any real sense, they get this choice only after governmental implementation.

11. See Feeley's (1982) comparison of late nineteenth century and late twentieth century trial courts processes.

12. Rosenberg is not alone in this conclusion. See, e.g., Bradley (1993).

13 Long standing separationist and civil liberties groups sometimes lobbied defensively. That is, they sought defeat or modification of bills that would restore prayer to schools.

14 Johnson (1967) found a superintendent in one of his two case studies willing to end prayer. Neither of the other two major studies (Muir, and Dolbeare and Hammond) of the implementation of the prayer cases found any system interested in complying the the Court's decisions.

15 Rosenberg also cited studies of public school textbooks and concluded that no change in authors' attitudes towards blacks' role in society was noticeable.

16 Some of Rosenberg's measures are relevant to *Brown*'s inspirational impact, e.g., number of civil rights demonstrations and changes in contributions to and membership in civil rights organizations. In my view, Rosenberg's data about contributions and memberships are indicative of *Brown*'s impact. See McCann (1992, 723) for an argument that Rosenberg misanalyzes these data.

17 I use this phrase rather than a term like obscenity or pornography because the latter are more legally oriented terms whose meaning has changed over time. Most of the material at issue in Supreme Court cases of 30 and 40 years ago would not raise mainstream eyebrows today.

18 *New York Times v. Sullivan* (376 U.S. 254) in 1964, which is on almost everyone's list of landmark Warren Court decisions, might also go in this cell. It brought the First Amendment into libel law and was intended to let editors be more critical in commenting on public affairs. I do not include it here because government agencies (except for the courts as forums) were not involved in policing or prosecuting publications before *Sullivan*. There is almost no research concerning the impact of *Sullivan* and other libel decisions on what appears in the media.

19 Expressing frustration with the Court's decisions, a few legislatures repealed their statewide obscenity laws and let local governments handle the matter.

20 While several professions, most notably law and medicine, have become more commercialized since the 1970s, the ability to advertise makes only a minor contribution to this trend.

21 While pro-choice political mobilization activities diminished markedly once the goal was achieved with *Roe*, they hardly disappeared. Subsequent mobilization tactics, however, were largely defensive. They were designed to counteract the pressures pro-life groups were putting on federal, state and local policy makers.

22 *Roe* might be credited with catalyzing abortion opponents to political action, but as noted earlier this chapter is limited to inspiration to action that accords with the Supreme Court's decisions.

Works Cited

Adamany, David. 1973. "Legitimacy, Realigning Elections and the Supreme Court." *Wisconsin Law Review* 1973: 791–846.

Baum, Lawrence A. 1995. *The Supreme Court, 5th ed.* Washington: CQ Press.

Blumberg, Abraham. 1979. *Criminal Justice, 2nd ed.* New York: New Viewpoints.

Bork, Robert. 1990. *The Tempting of America.* New York: Macmillan.

Bowen, Lauren L. 1995. "Do Court Decisions Matter?" Pp. 376–389 in *Contemplating Courts*, ed. Lee Epstein. Washington: CQ Press.

Bradley, Craig. 1993. *The Failure of the Criminal Procedure Revolution.* Philadelphia: University of Pennsylvania Press.

Canon, Bradley C. 1991. "Courts and Policy: Implementation and Impact." Pp. 435–466 in *The American Courts: A Critical Assessment*, eds. John B. Gates and Charles A. Johnson. Washington: CQ Press.

Canon, Bradley C. and S. Sidney Ulmer. 1976. "The Supreme Court and Critical Elections: A Dissent." *American Political Science Review* 70: 1215–1218.

Casper, Jonathan. 1976. "The Supreme Court and National Policy Making." *American Political Science Review* 70: 50–63.

Chayes, Abraham. 1976. "The Role of the Judge in Public Law Litigation." *Harvard Law Review* 89: 1281–1316.

Dahl, Robert A. 1957. "Decision Making in a Democracy: The Supreme Court as a National Policy Maker." *Journal of Public Law* 6: 279–295.

Dolbeare, Kenneth and Phillip Hammond. 1971. *The School Prayer Decisions: From Court Policy to Local Practice.* Chicago: University of Chicago Press.

Epstein, Lee and Joseph F. Koblyka. 1992. *The Supreme Court and Legal Change: Abortion and the Death Penalty.* Chapel Hill: University of North Carolina Press.

Feeley, Malcolm. 1992. Hollow Hopes, Flypaper and Metaphors. Review of *the Hollow Hope. Law and Social Inquiry* 17: 145–160.

Feeley, Malcolm. 1982. "Plea Bargaining and the Structure of the Criminal Process." *Justice System Journal* 7: 338–355.

Funston, Richard Y. 1975. "The Supreme Court and Critical Elections." *American Political Science Review* 69: 795–811.

Galanter, Marc. 1983. "The Radiating Effects of Courts." Pp. 117–142 in *Empirical Theories of Courts*, ed. Keith D. Doyum and Lynn Mather. New York: Longman.

Gates, John B. 1992. *The Supreme Court and Partisan Realignment* Boulder, CO: Westview.

Giles, Micheal. 1975. "HEW Versus the Federal Courts." *American Politics Quarterly* 3: 81-90.

Giles, Micheal and Douglas Gatlin. 1980. "Mass Level Compliance with Public Policy: The Case of School Desegregation." *Journal of Politics* 42: 722-746.

Graglia, Lino. 1976. *Disaster by Decree: The Supreme Court Decisions on Race and Schools*. Ithaca, NY: Cornell University Press.

Hansen, Susan. 1980. "State Implementation of Supreme Court Decisions: Abortion Since *Roe v. Wade*." *Journal of Politics* 42: 372-392.

Johnson, Charles A. and Bradley C. Canon. 1984. *Judicial Policies: Implementation and Impact*. Washington: CQ Press.

Johnson, Richard. 1967. *The Dynamics of Compliance*. Evanston, IL: Northwestern University Press.

McCann, Michael W. 1994. *Rights at Work*. Chicago: University of Chicago Press.

McCann, Michael W. 1992. Reform Litigation on Trial. Review of *The Hollow Hope*. *Law and Social Inquiry* 17: 715-743.

Minow, Martha. 1990. *Making All the Difference: Inclusion, Exclusion and American Law*. Ithaca, NY: Cornell University Press.

Muir, William. 1967. *Prayer in the Public Schools: Law and Attitude Change*. Chicago: University of Chicago Press.

Neustadt, Richard E. 1960. *Presidential Power: The Politics of Leadership*. New York: John Wiley and Sons.

O'Brien, David. 1996. *Storm Center: The Supreme Court in American Politics*, 5th Ed. New York: W. W. Norton.

Powe, Jr., L. A. 1992. The Supreme Court, Social Change and Legal Scholarship. Review of *The Hollow Hope*. *Stanford Law Review* 44: 1615-1641.

Rabin, Robert. 1976. "Lawyers for Social Change: Perspectives on Public Interest Law." *Stanford Law Review* 28: 207-261.

Ripley, Randall and Grace Franklin. 1984. *Congress, the Bureaucracy and Public Policy*. Homewood, IL: Dorsey Press.

Rodgers, Harrell and Charles Bullock III. 1972. *Law and Social Change: Civil Rights Laws and Their Consequences*. New York: McGraw Hill.

Rosenberg, Gerald N. 1991. *The Hollow Hope: Can Courts Bring About Social Change?* Chicago: University of Chicago Press.

Rosenberg, Gerald N. 1992. "Judicial Independence and the Reality of Political Power." *Review of Politics* 54: 369-398.

Rosenberg, Gerald N. 1995. "The Real World of Constitutional Rights: The Supreme Court and the Implementation of Abortion Rights." Pp. 390–419 in *Contemplating Courts*, ed. Lee Epstein. Washington: CQ Press.

Schiengold, Stuart. 1974. *The Politics of Rights*. New Haven: Yale University Press.

Schmidhauser, John R. and Larry Berg. 1972. *The Supreme Court and Congress: Conflict and Interaction, 1945–1968*. New York: Free Press.

Schuck, Peter. 1993. Public Law Litigation and Social Reform. Review of *The Hollow Hope*. *Yale Law Review* 102: 1763–1786.

Schultz, David and Stephen E. Gottleib. 1996. "Legal Functionalism and Social Change: A Reassessment of Rosenberg's *The Hollow Hope*." *Journal of Law and Politics* 12: 63–91.

Simon, Jonathan. 1992. 'The Long Walk Home' to Politics. Review of *The Hollow Hope*. *Law and Society Review* 26: 923–941.

Wasby, Stephen L. 1970. *The Impact of the United States Supreme Court: Some Perspectives*. Homewood, IL: Dorsey Press.

Chapter 6

Knowledge and Desire: Thinking about Courts and Social Change

Gerald N. Rosenberg

Introduction

Since the mid-twentieth century, courts in the United States have been involved in many of the most important, difficult, and emotional issues of modern politics. From racial and gender equality to abortion to reform of the criminal process to physician-assisted suicide, to name just a few, court decisions have been an important part of the history and politics of the mid- and late-twentieth century United States. The chapters in this book all start with this premise. All the authors believe that courts matter, that what they do is important to understanding law and social change. They differ, however, in two key respects: first, in their assessment of the ability of courts to further social change, and second, in their approach to understanding the relationship between courts and social change.

Court decisions, especially Supreme Court decisions interpreting the Constitution, hold a particular fascination for many academics. Unlike legislative and executive bodies, which deal in the realm of partisan politics, courts work with principles. While a legislator or an executive is likely to ask questions like, "Is this a good policy?" or "Is this a policy my constituents want?" or "How will my position on this issue help or hinder my re-election?," these questions are anathema to judges. Rather, judges in constitutional cases must ask whether the challenged act violates the Constitution, regardless of its policy outcome. That is, judges deal in principles, not partisan policy outcomes.[1] For many academics, whose work is about abstract ideas, the judiciary's commitment to principle makes it a fascinating branch of government.

But because principled beliefs are deeply held, it also makes the judiciary the object of heated debate.

The deeply contested nature of the constitutional issues with which courts sometimes deal, combined with their commitment to principle which stokes the fires of ideological debate, can lead to heated and passionate defenses and criticisms of the courts. McCloskey notes that historically debate over controversial Supreme Court decisions often is "a contest between those who happen for the moment to like the Court because it serves their purpose and those who traduce it because it does not" (1994, 206). Controversial Court decisions tend to be evaluated substantively, by whether one agrees or disagrees with the outcome. It is uncommon, if not rare, to find scholars or political activists who support the outcome in a case but believe the case is wrongly decided.[2] In other words, ideological belief filters understanding. One *desires* a particular outcome, and if the Supreme Court reaches such an outcome, it is to be praised. Historically, this has often been the case. Until the New Deal, for example, it was conservatives who supported an activist Court and urged it to strike down the "excesses" of legislative majorities. Progressives, in contrast, argued that the Court was antidemocratic, acting against the will of the people, and was a tool of capital.[3] In the wake of the New Deal, when the Court essentially switched sides, so did its supporters and critics. Conservatives lambasted the courts for allegedly carrying out the desires of an unrepresentative liberal elite, while progressives praised the judiciary for its moral vision. In understanding the role of the courts in social change, ideological belief or desire often is determinate.

One of the main aims of social science is to lessen the likelihood of desire controlling understanding. The tools of social science, although clearly resting on a host of epistemological beliefs, provide a way of analyzing events without desire holding sway. One such tool, for example, is the insistence that claims be supported by evidence, that they be falsifiable. The collection of relevant evidence is particularly useful for deciding between competing claims. If a claim cannot be falsified by empirical evidence, then one has no way of judging its accuracy. Without such evidence, desire is unchecked and ideology reigns supreme. With the tools of social science, persuasion is possible and opinions can change. Social science holds forth the possibility of knowledge; ideology only the fulfillment of desire.

Much of the material in this book appears based on desire, not knowledge. That is, several of the authors seem to believe that the Court made an important contribution to changes they support. But since these are beliefs rather than hypotheses to be tested, the authors do not provide evidence that might persuade others that they are right. As I will illustrate in this chapter, a good deal of the criticisms of *The Hollow Hope* contained in this book, and a good deal of the methodology on which they are based, is driven by desire. This can be seen in mischaracterization of the argument of *The Hollow Hope*, lack of evidence to support claims, contradictory arguments, and implausible claims. While there is much for which *The Hollow Hope* can be criticized, criticisms driven by desire only demonstrate that people disagree. They offer little guidance in sorting out how to study courts and social change, and how to decide between competing claims.

My aim in this chapter is not to reargue *The Hollow Hope*, nor to respond to each and every critical point raised by others. Rather, I will focus on broader points of methodology as exemplified by particular criticisms or claims made by others in this book.[4] I argue that the most useful approach to the study of courts and social change is based on careful empirical work combined with historical sensitivity, methodological awareness, and broader normative concerns. However, in so arguing, I will sometimes go into a good bit of detail. As a result, some readers may feel that on the one hand I am indeed re-arguing *The Hollow Hope*.[5] But to ignore *The Hollow Hope*, which is, after all, the target of the criticism, would be to ignore the brunt of the chapters. On the other hand, in selecting only some critical points to respond to, other readers may feel that I am slighting some important claims, or overemphasizing other less important ones. But to respond to each and every point with which I disagree would be tedious for both author and reader. So, in the pages that follow, I highlight both general and specific points that I believe to be important in the study of courts and social change. My hope is that this chapter will provide readers with a critical sense of the strengths and weakness of different approaches to the study of courts and law, of how I might respond to critical points I don't discuss, and with what justifications. It is an argument for using the tools of social science to help understand the world around us, for knowledge rather than desire, and for historical sensitivity and methodological awareness.

General Points

The Hollow Hope hit a raw nerve. The chapters in this book, as well as the review literature *The Hollow Hope* generated, are testimony to the importance of the issue of law and social change. But at least some of the review literature criticized *The Hollow Hope* for claims it never made, or caricatured its arguments. In particular, *The Hollow Hope* is criticized both in the chapters of this book and elsewhere for denying the importance of courts and law, and for setting up a straw person argument about the efficacy of litigation. Neither criticism is correct.

Courts Matter

The Hollow Hope is often misinterpreted as arguing that courts are irrelevant to social change and that court decisions have no impact on society. That is emphatically not the argument of *The Hollow Hope*. Of course courts matter! And they matter in a myriad of ways. Court decisions sometimes can and do change behavior. For example, changes in the common law can have important effects on all sorts of behavior, particularly in the area of legal liability (torts), contracts, and business relationships more generally. Similarly, court decisions can be an obstacle to change. As discussed below, the Supreme Court has historically acted as a barrier to social reform. In terms of social reform litigation, one of the claims of *The Hollow Hope* is that courts affect society in a powerful ideological way by drawing resources to litigation and away from political mobilization. Courts affect society in lots of ways, and their decisions make a difference.

The Hollow Hope never denied this. It focused on a *particular type of litigation* that captured the attention of a generation of lawyers and academics and seemed to mark the United States as an exception to the political practices of other capitalist democracies; litigation aimed at producing what I called "significant social reform." *The Hollow Hope* was explicit about the kinds of cases it examined, cases that involved litigation to obtain the

> broadening and equalizing of the possession and enjoyment of what are commonly perceived as basic goods in American society . . . [such as] 'Rights and liberties, powers and opportunities, income and wealth.'. . . Fleshed out, these include political goods such as participation in the political process and freedom of speech and association; legal goods such as equal and non-discriminatory treatment of all people; material goods; and self-respect, the opportunity for every individual to lead a satisfying and worthy life. Contributions to political and social change bring these benefits to people formerly deprived of them. . . . [Further, significant social reforms] affect large groups of people such as blacks, or workers, or women, or partisans of a particular political persuasion; in other words, *policy change with nationwide impact*. Litigation aimed at changing the way a single bureaucracy functions would

not fit this definition, for example, while litigation attempting to change the functioning of a whole set of bureaucracies or institutions nationwide would" (Rosenberg 1991, 4, references omitted).

It is in these and only these type of cases that I examined the conditions under which courts could produce change. And in finding that these conditions were rare, I emphatically did not conclude that courts don't matter or have no impact on the broader society. I argued more narrowly, concluding only that courts were unlikely to further significant social reform. But even here, I argued that when certain conditions were present, courts could make a major contribution to significant social reform.

This misreading of *The Hollow Hope* can be illustrated by several arguments made by Schultz and Gottlieb. For example, after correctly describing *The Hollow Hope* as examining race, gender and abortion, reapportionment, the environment and criminal due process, they write, Rosenberg "claims evidence is lacking to support *any indication of influence* and that Congress and other social trends can more account for change that the judiciary alone" (Schultz and Gottlieb, 5; emphasis added) . While in general I do give more credit to Congress, changing mores, and changing patterns of social and economic behavior than to Court decisions, I most certainly do find important judicial influence in some of these areas. In abortion, for example, the presence of Condition III, market forces for implementation, allowed the Court to have some influence.[6] Similarly, reapportionment occurred because of Condition I, the presence of non- Court actors itching to act, and prison reform and some reform of the criminal process occurred because of Condition IV, the desire of some officials key to the implementation process to make the change and their use of Court decisions as leverage and cover. School desegregation was helped along by courts in the late 1960s and early 1970s when, through congressional and executive branch action, pressure from economic interests, and changing beliefs among local school board officials, Conditions I, II, and IV were present. So, when Schultz and Gottlieb note that the "claim that courts cannot influence events is far too strong" (Schultz and Gottlieb, 60), of course they are right; that's not a claim *The Hollow Hope* makes. Courts influence events all the time. The claim *The Hollow Hope* makes is that only under certain specified conditions can courts further significant social reform. Without the presence of those decisions, court influence will still be felt, but it won't contribute very much to producing significant social reform.

Similarly, in discussing my fourth condition,[7] Schultz and Gottlieb argue that "Rosenberg has actually described an important role for the judiciary" (Schultz and Gottlieb, 38). They go on to note that Condition IV "depicts a judiciary not as constrained but as capable, under the right conditions, of forcing items on to a political agenda that might not otherwise be addressed were elected officials left to act on their own to confront hostile public opinion" (Schultz and Gottlieb 39). I agree. Where I suspect we disagree is in my conclusion that those conditions are rare[8] and, when present, reflective of change already far along. As I noted in *The Hollow Hope* (338)

> when the constraints are overcome, and one of the four conditions is present, courts can help produce significant social reform. However, this means, by definition, that institutional, structural, and ideological barriers to change are weak. A court's contribution, then, is akin to officially recognizing the evolving state of affairs, more like the cutting of the ribbon on a new project than its construction. Without such change, the constraints reign.

I can think of no explanation other than the power of desire for this mischaracterization.

Another example of mischaracterization of my argument is found in Zalman's chapter where I am accused of committing the crime of "juricide":

> Certain works of political scientists exhibit a mood that negates the existence of law, a phenomenon labeled 'juricide.' Examples include Gerald Rosenberg's position that Supreme Court cases have had no impact on social policy. . . . (Zalman 1)

As I have argued, this is certainly not my position. Similarly, and almost as colorfully, Zalman also claims that

> Rosenberg . . . argues that the Supreme Court, perhaps like the English monarchy, is an irrelevancy, at least insofar as people look to it as a guarantor of rights as a forum where political ends can be attained. The implication is that public law, at least, is dead, but no one seems to notice. (Zalman, 349–350).

As I hope is now clear, the "irrelevancy" of courts and the death of public law is not now, nor ever was, my argument or its implications.

The importance of courts to law and social change, and the strength of a careful empirical approach to studying it, is illustrated in Van Dyk's study of how pro-choice groups used courts to stymie the use of abortion clinic blockades by anti-abortion activists. Van Dyk demonstrates that through the use of injunctions and the imposition of fines, pro-choice lawyers raised the cost of participation in abortion clinic blockades sufficiently high to deter many participants. Further, legal action against the organizations leading the blockades, like Operation Rescue, essentially bankrupted them. Van Dyk is persuasive in arguing that the legal mobilization against clinic blockades is a case in which litigation was successful in ending certain activities of a social movement and protecting abortion clinics. Courts mattered in effectively ending clinic blockades by anti-abortion activists.

Why was litigation successful? In part it was because pro-choice litigants were protecting the status quo. They brought suits not to challenge and change the status quo, but rather to preserve it. The protection of private property is a cherished foundation of American law, and pro-choice lawyers were arguing for it. Legal concepts of trespass and nuisance are deeply embedded in the law. Thus, as Van Dyk correctly understands, pro-choice lawyers worked out of an essentially conservative legal position. Their aim was not to produce significant social reform as I defined it in *The Hollow Hope*, but rather to allow the pre blockade status quo to continue.

Courts can be particularly effective in preserving the status quo. This is principally because court decisions upholding status quo arrangements require little change in existing institutions and practices. In the wake of the decisions affording protection to abortion clinics, for example, the clinics and their staffs could go about their professional work in the same manner they had previously. No changes were required in organization, staffing, budgeting, bureaucratic reporting, and so on. Further, as Van Dyk notes, pro-choice lawyers were often experienced litigators, either from national pro-choice groups (e.g., the ACLU, the NOW Legal Defense Fund), from elite law forms (Covington and Burling), or government prosecutors. It is often the case that those preserving status quo arrangements have access to top legal talent. To the extent that such "hired guns" make a difference, litigation preserving the status quo is privileged.

There is nothing new about using the law to preserve the status quo. Famous cases include, for example, the successful efforts by Alabama to keep the NAACP out of the state for nearly a decade in the late 1950s and early 1960s; *Buckley v. Valeo* (424 U.S. 1 [1976]), in which the U.S. Supreme Court gutted campaign reform legislation, guaranteeing that corporate wealth would continue to exercise enormous influence on politics; and the two cases in which the U.S. Supreme Court invalidated congressional legislation banning child labor—*Hammer v. Dagenhart* (247 U.S. 251 [1918]), and *Bailey v. Drexel Furniture Co.* (259 U.S. 20 [1922])—decisions which stood for several decades. None of this runs counter to anything in *The Hollow Hope*.

Van Dyk, in contrast to Schultz and Gottlieb, and Zalman, offers careful empirical support for his conclusions. Through his case study he focusses on one aspect of the relationship between courts and social change, the defensive use of litigation to preserve status quo arrangements. The sweeping generalizations that come from desire are not found here. Rather, the reader is reminded that courts can do many different things. Van Dyk's study is an example of the kind of work that can further understanding.

Straw Persons

One of the criticisms of *The Hollow Hope* found in several of the chapters of this book as well as in many other reviews is that I have set up a straw person argument. The criticism is that nobody believes that courts, acting alone, can change society. Therefore, I have set up a straw person that is relatively easy to knock over.

I must confess to never fully understanding this objection.[9] Since the 1950s the United States has witnessed numerous organizations, acting without close links to organizations pursuing political mobilization strategies, invest enormous resources in litigation. Given the scarce resources social reformers possess, this was a costly strategy. Their leaders argued important cases, gave speeches, wrote books and articles, and were covered in the press. In an early review of *The Hollow Hope*, Feeley (1992, 749–50), in a rough count, found attributions to 42 different supporters of judicial efficacy in *The Hollow Hope*. I believe they are leading lawyers, legal academics, and social scientists. Thus, I am baffled by Schultz and Gottlieb's comment that "Rosenberg fails to provide any evidence about who in fact supports or believes in the dynamic model [that courts can produce significant social reform]" (Schultz and Gottlieb, 223, n.5). All one has to do is look at the enormous amount of resources poured into litigation by social reformers, effectively curtailing or ending other strategies for change. Studying how people actually behave does not create a straw person argument.

The straw person argument sometimes takes a narrower form and claims that there is no serious academic literature that supports the singular importance of courts. But this is demonstrably false. There is a good deal of literature, written by both legal academics and social scientists, that argues for the unique importance of litigation as an instrument of social reform.[10] Indeed, the arguments of Schultz and Gottlieb, Zalman, and, in part, Canon, stress the importance, if not the necessity, of litigation for social reform. I have always found it somewhat contradictory for critics to argue that no one believes that courts have singular importance and then argue for the singular importance of a particular case, usually *Brown*. But the real point of the criticism may be that there is also a literature that questions judicial efficacy and that *The Hollow Hope* slighted it. If so, it was an act of omission rather than commission, for the argument in *The Hollow Hope* is clearly built on the scholarly work that preceded it, work that is explicitly acknowledged in *The Hollow Hope*.

Finally, if *The Hollow Hope* is based on a straw person argument, I wouldn't have expected it to have generated the kind of scholarly interest that it has. Something peculiar is going on. As I suggested in the introduction, and will illustrate below, I have come to believe that many (but not all!) critics of *The Hollow Hope* share the hopes and desires of the idealistic legal reformers. Their animated response to *The Hollow Hope*, and the mischaracterizations of its arguments that many of them present, may be partly explained by its critique of their deeply held ideological beliefs.

Evidence

Although I am not from Missouri, I have always admired the "motto" of that state, "show me." A good deal of the criticism of *The Hollow Hope* developed in this book simply asserts that courts made a crucial contribution to producing significant social reform. How do the authors know this? They assert it without ever telling the reader. Their arguments are somewhat akin to the remark attributed to Justice Stewart in discussing pornography, "I know it when I see it." The problem with assertions, in "knowing" the importance of the Court in producing significant social reform without needing supporting evidence, is that one has no way of knowing whether they are accurate or not. For centuries most people believed the earth was flat. It was a matter not merely of faith but of the prevailing cultural understanding of the world. Assertions about Court importance by academics who study courts have much the same flavor. They are unexamined, taken for granted. The argument of *The Hollow Hope*, for all its faults, is supported by a wealth of data. I challenge those studying the courts to avoid unsupported claims about the importance of courts and do the empirical work.

It would be more tedious than useful to list each and every unsupported assertion. I will highlight only a very few of them. I suggest that in rereading the chapters, or going over notes on them, or thinking about them, readers be alert for unsupported claims. Perhaps thinking about how they could be examined might further our understanding. Court decisions and social change are not merely abstract notions; they are also actual events. If the aim of scholars is to understand the actual world in which we live, empirical investigation must be a central part of every investigation.

The lack of supporting data for assertions runs through each of the critiques of *The Hollow Hope*. Canon, for example, focusses on the inspirational effect of Court decisions, particularly *Brown*. But he doesn't support his claims. How, then, is the reader to judge them, other than by a pre-reading commitment to a particular understanding of the role of the Court? The trouble with Canon's approach is it lets him off the hook too easily. His argument seems to be something like this: 1. the Supreme Court has inspirational impact; 2. we can't measure its impact in *Brown* because it happened too long ago and we lack sufficiently honed measures; 3. therefore *Brown* had inspirational impact. But this is argument by assertion, with point 3 being merely a particularized restatement of point 1 with no support from point 2. As Canon graciously notes, I developed an array of indices in Chapter 4 of *The Hollow Hope* to try to measure this claim of inspirational effect (only some of which he discusses). Readers are, of course, free to criticize them but the burden is on those who believe in the Court's inspirational effects to depart from the realm of assertion and find support for the claim. In his chapter, at least, Canon does not do this.

Problems of lack of empirical support are fundamental in the Schultz and Gottlieb chapter. An important thrust of their argument is the claim that

> What is critical about *Brown, Roe, Baker* and other similar decisions is how they reshaped choices, expectations, institutions, and structures. In this respect, American politics was significantly different the day after these decisions because the Court granted legitimacy to certain claims, attached legal support or approbation to certain actions, or otherwise defined new roles for itself or for other institutions to follow (191).

As with Canon, this is argument by assertion with unsupported claims, repeated throughout the chapter, about structural changes, beliefs of elected officials, unspoken assumptions, attitudes, agenda-setting, and so on. In a trivial sense they are correct that after the action of the Court some things, like the technical state of the law, were different. But that doesn't get one very far in exploring whether and how the changes mattered. Rather, it assumes the importance of the Court by definition. They could be right, but how do they know? What is their evidence?

Zalman faces the same challenge. A crucial part of his critique of *The Hollow Hope* is the claim that, "Without *Brown* it is unlikely that the limited Civil Rights Act of 1957 would have been passed or that the spirit of suppressed African Americans would finally be stirred to sustained and successful action" (344). He also argues, with less qualification, that "the [*Brown*] decision made a seismic impact on the psyche of most African Americans and thus planted seeds of hope and revolt against segregation" (345). This is plausible. Indeed, I specifically investigated the potential effect of *Brown* on civil rights legislation and as inspiration within the African-American community.[11] I found little evidence to support these claims. Perhaps I am mistaken, but without evidence the reader must fall back on understandings developed prior to reading Zalman's chapter. This means that either one adopts a position of general skepticism or one agrees or disagrees depending on one's prior beliefs.

Overall, a general notion that many critiques of *The Hollow Hope* seem to have goes something like this: "Look, *Brown* happened; it had to matter." The problem with this critique is that many events happen in the world that exert little or no causal influence on later events. Of course *Brown* mattered, but it doesn't automatically or necessarily follow that it furthered the cause of civil rights. Such a claim assumes the importance of a particular institution, and a particular outcome of that institution, rather than treating the importance of that institution and outcome as a question for investigation.

The examples I have presented here illustrate the problematic nature of studying the courts and social change, and making claims about them, without providing empirical evidence to assess them. It is quite possible that the claims discussed above are correct, and that they further our understanding. But one has no way of assessing this other than by ideological belief. And when ideological belief influences not only the questions one asks but also the approach one takes to answering them, little may be learned.

History

Court decisions don't happen in the abstract. They come from an institution situated in time and space, in a particular political, social, economic, and cultural setting. One of the more interesting puzzles I find in the critiques is the abstraction of the Court from the broader society in which it exists. On the one hand, several authors offer the claim that *The Hollow Hope* focuses too narrowly on the Court. On the other hand, they do so in critiques that have a narrow focus on the Court! This is puzzling for two reasons. First, it is contradictory, with authors doing exactly what they criticize *The Hollow Hope* for. Second, and more importantly, it is wrong. *The Hollow Hope* squarely places the Court in broader context. Indeed, one of the strongest messages of *The Hollow Hope* is that it is intellectually indefensible to examine the effects of the Court on significant social reform without clearly placing it in the broader historical context.

This ahistoricism is most pronounced in the chapters written by lawyers. Zalman, for example, makes the following claim: "Rosenberg thus paints a picture of History Immaculate—inevitable and triumphant—regardless of the intervention of human agency" (343). How does Zalman reach this position? He does so by virtually exclusive focus on the Court, abstracting it from the world around it. In civil rights, for example, his argument seems to be that since *Brown* was decided, and change did occur, to question the power of the Court in producing significant social reform is to be ahistorical! But only if I am guilty of "juricide," as Zalman charges, and only if courts are crucial to social reform, as Zalman believes, can such a position be arrived at. In other words, only through an ideological belief in a powerful Court can this view be taken. However, the argument I made in *The Hollow Hope* has lots of human agency. In civil rights, for example, from the massive migration of African-Americans out of the rural South to the courageous actions of those involved in the civil rights movement to the actions of President Johnson and members of Congress, human agency abounds. I do not give much credit to the Court for producing change, but that hardly reduces my argument to one devoid of human agency. Indeed, Zalman's views are closer to that position, positing a powerful Court without exploring the conditions under which it operates.

Schultz and Gottlieb, also lawyers, devote considerable space in their chapter to criticizing *The Hollow Hope* for assigning causal importance too narrowly. "Historical events are complex," (206) they argue, and thus "We need to move beyond methods that seek to isolate the Court from the larger flux of change in history if we wish to understand its impact and efficacy" (217). I emphatically agree, and that is precisely what I did in *The Hollow Hope*! I examined a whole host of historical and contextual factors, as well as Court action. Thus, it is not *The Hollow Hope* that is making a narrow causal argument; it is Schultz and Gottlieb who are singling out the Court as playing a crucial role. When they argue, "Most historians would not try to pin causality down to one isolated event, but to several phenomena occurring together" (207), they describe my argument for the causal importance of a whole host of factors. In contrast, Schultz and Gottlieb privilege the Court. In so doing, they are lead away from the historical setting.

The ahistoricism of Schultz and Gottlieb is buttressed by their theoretical position. Their position is put clearly and repeatedly; historical causation can't be specified. Thus, they argue, "*Brown* and *Roe* changed history and attitudes when they were decided, and we do not know and cannot separate these decisions from other events that were occurring at the same time" (207); and "[Rosenberg's] inattention to the richness of history is evident in his failure to see that changes and interrelations in initial conditions make it difficult to isolate impact or cause" (207). Schultz and Gottlieb terminate inquiry by definition. They assert judicial efficacy and then claim, as a matter of epistemology, that their assertion can't be investigated. But the admitted difficulty in separating out causal influence does not license scholars to make any claim they want. *The Hollow Hope* devotes a great deal of space to the "richness of history" in an attempt to separate out different strands of influence. For example, much of the data gathered in chapter 4 on the indirect influence of *Brown* starts in 1940, nearly a decade and a half before *Brown*. In addition, chapters five and eight are *entirely devoted* to investigating historical factors that may have led to social change, ranging from migration patterns to the influences of World War II and the Cold War to family structure to income patterns to access to higher education, and so forth. Schultz and Gottlieb ignore history in making an essentially monocausal claim for judicial efficacy.

By positing an important role for the Court, *a priori*, Schultz and Gottlieb remove it from its historical context. Clearly, not every act of every institution at all times and all places carries the same level of importance. My general point is that unless one places an institution in historical context, one has no way of addressing relative importance. By failing to do so in their critique of *The Hollow Hope*, Schultz and Gottlieb's charge of ahistoricism is misdirected. But it does highlight the need for scholarly examination of the relationship between law and social change to carefully situate the events being examined in the broader historical context.

Causation

Discussions of evidence and historical understanding are based on theory of causation. In *The Hollow Hope*, I briefly sketched one, essentially arguing that asserting causation requires specifying mechanisms by which a prior event A "caused" a subsequent event B, specifying the kind of evidence that would support a finding of causal influence, investigating whether such evidence supports the claim, and investigating alternative explanations. I also noted that because social scientists do not understand well enough the dynamics of influence and causation to state with certainty that the claims of Court influence (or any other causal claims) are right or wrong, finding little or no evidence would not necessarily rule out causal influence (Rosenberg 1991, 107-108). But because claims of causal influence are claims about the real world, finding little or no evidence should shift the burden on those making a causal claim to find persuasive evidence supporting it. Otherwise, they run the risk of substituting desire for knowledge.

Schultz and Gottlieb invest the most space critiquing *The Hollow Hope* for its causal theory. For example, they argue that the "assumption that since power is an empirical concept it can be measured is demonstrably incorrect. Dahl tried to define power some years ago and found himself hopelessly entangled in assumptions" (190-191). Whether this is a correct description of Dahl's work is debatable, but clearly measurement is distinct from definition. Power relations may have many different and subtle facets, but this does not preclude all measurement. We have no trouble assigning causation and power to relations in much of our lives, and in much of our politics. Most of the authors in this book, including Schultz and Gottlieb, readily assign causal power to the Court. I do not find these causal claims persuasive because they don't specify mechanisms, don't provide evidence and don't consider alternative explanations. But this is not because power is an unmeasurable concept. And if Schultz and Gottlieb are correct, then they have no grounds for their numerous assertions of the power of the Court. If power can't be measured, then any argument about causal influence is as good as any other. It all depends on one's desires.

My guess, however, is that Schultz and Gottlieb are trying to make the narrower point that many facets of power are too subtle for the crude measurement tools of social science. I have some sympathy with this point, but it doesn't help Schultz and Gottlieb very much for two main reasons. First, subtlety is often neither noticed nor effective. Subtle effects, by their very definition, can be lost in the myriad of other factors at work in shaping behavior. That is, any influence they might exert is simply not felt and acted upon because other, more powerful forces, are exerting power. Second, if evidence is unobtainable, then one is pushed back to what I have been calling desire, the substitution of ideological preferences for knowledge. Schultz and Gottlieb clearly fall into this trap in several places.

The most illustrative example of desire is Schultz and Gottlieb's argument about silence. They write, "Rosenberg's definition of influence ignores the power of silence. . . ." (189) A few pages later, they claim that "*Brown* and its progeny affected discourse so deeply that its mention was unnecessary" (193). The claim seems to be that merely because no one talks about an alleged causal event it does not follow that the event lacks causal influence. A stronger version of the claim is that the fact that people don't discuss an alleged causal event is testimony to its importance. But how plausible is this? On the one hand, it seems to concede *The Hollow Hope*'s argument that *Brown* was not frequently mentioned. But, on the other hand, it is deeply troublesome. For those of us who lived through the Vietnam War, it is reminiscent of President Nixon's reliance on the "Silent Majority" in the wake of antiwar demonstrations and growing disenchantment with his policies. The crux of Nixon's argument was that the war had majority support but that the majority, unlike the antiwar minority, was keeping its opinions to itself. The problem is that with no evidence on what the "Silent Majority" is thinking, its silence could be used to support any position. So it is with Schultz and Gottlieb's argument about *Brown*. Silence can be interpreted in any way an author wants. But Schultz and Gottlieb's interpretation strikes me as nonsensical. It requires that either the case was so awesome that it left all of America speechless, or there was a "conspiracy so immense" that it affected everyone. The appeal to silence is not persuasive. It is an appeal based on desire, not knowledge.

Schultz and Gottlieb make the appeal to silence in part to criticize *The Hollow Hope* for focussing too narrowly on mentions of *Brown* itself rather than on broader indications of changing attitudes. But this is a misreading of *The Hollow Hope*, for much of the evidence it assessed looked at broader claims. In addition, they overlook the fact that it did not take *Brown* to give politicians, the press, and the public a vision of equality. There was the Fourteenth Amendment to the Constitution, the Declaration of Independence, the recent horrors of the Holocaust, and the general claim of equality before the law. What it did take to bring these visions to the fore was the vivid picture of the ugliness of segregation that southern repression of the civil rights movement, particularly in places like Birmingham and Selma, provided.

Another example of causal arguments from desire is to base them on personal experience. Schultz and Gottlieb argue that "many of us in the 1950s were well informed about *Brown*, even if we did not mention the case by name" (193). One of the telltale signs of an argument from desire is the appeal to personal experience. "If me and my friends believe X," the argument goes, "then X must be true." How often have many of us thought that if only everyone thought the same way we did, the world would be a better place? But, alas, it usually turns out that we are not representative of many more than our small group of friends. I have no doubt that both Schultz and Gottlieb were well informed about *Brown*, but I have grave doubt this tells us much more than an interesting bit of personal history.

From silence to personal experience, Schultz and Gottlieb then expand their causal argument to courts and lawyers: "Rosenberg has overlooked the most important places to find influence of judicial impact. In part, we should look at *Brown*, *Roe*, and other cases for their precedential impact, citation, and implementation in future litigation. . . ." (196). Their argument seems to be that much of the battle for civil rights was fought in lower courts and that looking only at *Brown* misses this important aspect of judicial influence. That is, *Brown* may have permitted lower courts to serve as reform institutions. But examining the use of Supreme Court cases in lower courts is not very useful information if what is to be explained is significant social reform. Lawyers arguing cases, and lower court judges writing opinions, can cite cases and issue orders until they are blue in the face, or suffer from carpal tunnel syndrome, but that will tell us precious little about how behavior changes. It is tautological to study the use of precedents as a way of asking how courts affect society. All the study of precedents shows is how courts affect courts. If the question to be answered is the ability of courts to produce significant social reform, examining precedent is the wrong track.

Yet another example of Schultz and Gottlieb's desire overwhelming the search for knowledge is found in their unexamined assumptions. In discussing *Brown*, they write that "the critical question is . . . the way people's assumptions change in the face of critical changes in the environment" (190). The problem here is what made *Brown* a critical change? They assume its importance rather than testing it. What is their evidence? Similarly, they argue that "the important question about the Court's role in society that *Hollow Hope* should have developed more is . . . how the Court realigns political, economic, and social preferences. It is here that the true power of the Court is exercised" (217). Again, Schultz and Gottlieb want scholars to start from a normative position that the Court has power in such and such a way. This is an argument from desire, not knowledge. Instead, I argue that scholars should start from a prior position, investigating whether, and under what conditions, the Court has such power. The great advantage of the approach I am suggesting is that it is perfectly possible that it will end up with conclusions similar to Schultz and Gottlieb's. Indeed, when I started the project that became *The Hollow Hope* that is where I expected it to lead. But the fact that it didn't suggests Schultz and Gottlieb's approach is flawed because it pre-commits them to an answer. They are precluded, by definition, from finding that in some cases that Court doesn't have much influence in realigning political, economic, and social preferences.

Zalman takes a similar approach, assuming rather than investigating a causal role for the Court and then criticizing others who don't adopt the same position a priori. Zalman's main critique of *The Hollow Hope*, as discussed earlier, is that it is premised on the "*implicit* jurisprudential position" that "law does not exist." Thus, it is "fundamentally incorrect" (332). Of course such a position is incorrect, and *The Hollow Hope* never argued it. Zalman reaches this position by conflating law with Supreme Court decisions, some Supreme Court decisions with all Supreme Court decisions, and the post-World War II era of decisions, essentially the Warren Court, for the Court's whole history. Therefore, for Zalman, to raise questions about the contribution of some Warren Court opinions to producing significant social reform is understood as denying the existence of law! The problem with Zalman's analysis, as well as with the analysis of Gottlieb and Schultz, is that it substitutes desire for knowledge. Because these authors appear to like many of the substantive outcomes of the Warren Court, any questioning of its efficacy is conflated with an attack on the courts. This leads them to attribute wild claims to those like me who remain skeptical of certain alleged abilities of the Supreme Court.

Another critical point raised by Schultz and Gottlieb is what they see as the failure of *The Hollow Hope* to examine alternative explanations. They write, "Rosenberg should have considered counterfactuals in his studies. By that, he should have asked what would have happened had *Roe* or *Brown* not been decided" (205). I agree that counterfactuals are useful and can be important. That is why *The Hollow Hope* has two chapters that explicitly explore alternative explanations! In Chapter Five, "The Current of History," I write that the claim of *Brown's* lack of importance in producing significant social reform

> runs so counter to the accepted wisdom that one might be tempted to sympathize with a skeptical reader who might say : 'But the Court did act, and change did occur—what else could have accounted for it?' In this chapter, I will marshall evidence suggesting that pro-civil-rights forces existed independent of the Supreme Court and could plausibly have accounted for eventual congressional and executive branch action as well as for Court action. While we can never know what would have happened if the Court had not acted as it did (if *Brown* had never been decided or had come out the other way), the existence and strength of pro-civil-rights forces at least suggest that change would have occurred, albeit at a pace unknown (Rosenberg 1991, 157).

Similarly, in Chapter Eight, "The Tide of History," I examine possible alternative explanations for changes in access to legal abortion and lessening gender discrimination. The chapter, I note, is "designed for the skeptical reader" whose reaction to my argument about the uneven contribution of the Court to these changes may be, "What else could have possibly caused changes other than Court action?" (Rosenberg 1991, 247). Clearly, *The Hollow Hope* explores alternative explanations.

It is important to point out, however, that counterfactuals are useful but not definitive. While it is impossible to know what would have happened absent a particular event, it is often easy to tell a plausible story. The problem is that Schultz and Gottlieb could tell one story and I could tell another. In civil rights, theirs might stress how Congress refused to act and segregation remained, and mine would stress how the civil rights movement pressured Congress to act, resulting in pretty much the same story as occurred. My story would have the Court invalidating school segregation in a minor case, probably in the late 1960s, as some southern school district brought suit, finding itself caught between its state law requiring segregation and a termination of federal funds under Title VI of the 1964 Civil Rights Act.[12] The Court, in a case like those upholding the 1964 Civil Rights Act, might have invalidated the state law in a case that would quickly fade from view. The challenge, then, becomes bringing evidence to bear in order to determine which counter factual is the more plausible. While I believe that the wealth of evidence makes the counter factual *The Hollow Hope* offers more plausible, I expect Schultz and Gottlieb would disagree.

Finally, there is a confusion of impact with contribution to producing significant social reform. Actions of governmental institutions can have impact without furthering social reform goals. Schultz and Gottlieb conflate the two, arguing that "*Brown* was a major fact of life, and the fact that there was so much adverse reaction to it in the South...is a testament to its public impact" (193). While there was a great deal of adverse impact to *Brown* in the South, and this is evidence of its impact, it is most decidedly not evidence of its furthering the cause of significant social reform.[13]

Understanding causal relations is difficult. In critiquing the arguments of Schultz and Gottlieb and Zalman, I have emphasized the importance of paying attention both to the causal theory one adopts and to the kind of evidence that supports it. Because neither Schultz and Gottlieb nor Zalman do this, their arguments are weakened by assertions without evidence, and claims about the effects of Court decisions without any empirical testing of those claims. In the end, they have no way of knowing the importance of *Brown*, other than by belief prior to any sustained analysis and assertion of that belief. This is the mark of desire, not the quest for knowledge. I do not find it a useful or productive way to understand the relationship between courts and social change.

Evidence, History, and Causation— The Montgomery Bus Boycott

In examining the origins and the success of the Montgomery bus boycott, and the contribution that *Brown* may have made to it, McMahon avoids many of the problems discussed in the last few sections. In particular, he looks to data to support his argument. Where he and I part company, however, is that he neglects to place the boycott in its historical setting, and his interpretation of evidence is not based on an explicit theory of causal significance. Thus, while his empirical approach is useful, it demonstrates that empirical work alone is not sufficient to understand the relationship between courts and social change.

McMahon's argument is that "*Brown* figures prominently in [the boycott leaders'] discussions of why the bus boycott took place in 1955–56, as does the federal judiciary in their (especially King's) accounts of the events surrounding the busing campaign" (10). He argues that the boycott was a "dual campaign, one in the streets and one in the courts . . . a campaign to press for the fulfillment of *Brown's* promise by bringing a test case to court and confronting white leaders with the reality of the Court's landmark decision" (11). And, it was a Court decision in the end, McMahon argues, that brought victory to the boycotters.

McMahon's analysis conflates two distinct groups in Montgomery. On the one hand, there was a group of NAACP activists who shared that organization's commitment to litigation. But there was also another, more radical group, the Women's Political Council (WPC), that had been planning a bus boycott for years, including, in the words of its President, Jo Ann Robinson, the preparation of "fifty thousand notices calling people to boycott the buses; only the specifics of time and place had to be added" (Robinson 1987, 39). According to both Robinson and J. Miles Thornton, III, the leading historian of the boycott, the arrest of Rosa Parks provided the opportunity for the WPC to act. Relying on its preparations, and acting on its own, the WPC mimeographed notices announcing a one-day boycott and blanketed black Montgomery with them. Contra to McMahon, they did not coordinate with the NAACP or those supporting a legal test case. Indeed, according to Thornton, by the time of the December 2 meeting of Montgomery's black leadership called by E. D. Nixon to discuss what to do, the forty or so assembled leaders "found themselves faced with a *fait accompli*" (Thornton 1980, 197). While the women soon lost control of the boycott, and their contribution to it was overlooked until recently, McMahon's argument for the driving role of litigation in the origins of the bus boycott lacks historical support.

A good deal of other evidence undermines McMahon's claims that the bus boycott can be understood as "a campaign to press for the fulfillment of *Brown's* promise by bringing a test case to court and confronting white leaders with the reality of the Court's landmark decision" (McMahon, 11). If McMahon is right, then why didn't the boycotters initially demand an end to bus segregation based on race? Their principal demand, instead, called for modified seating by race, with blacks starting at the back and whites at the front. As late as April 1956, five months into the boycott, King was still willing to settle on these terms (Fairclough 1987, 20).[14] As Thornton describes it, the boycotters were not trying to overturn the segregation law, as *Brown* might have inspired them to do. Instead, they "initially conceived their movement not so much as a direct action against bus segregation itself as rather a search for a means to manipulate the political process." (Thornton 1980, 231). This led the NAACP, the successful litigators in *Brown*, to withhold support from the bus boycott on the grounds that the demands were too "mild" (Wilkins 1984, 228). Indeed, rather than the planned test case to further *Brown* that McMahon sees in Montgomery, Abernathy writes that "at first we regarded the Montgomery bus boycott as an interruption of our plans rather than as the beginning of their fulfillment" (Abernathy 1989, 169). McMahon's argument lacks support.

McMahon also neglects the role of other bus boycotts on the events in Montgomery. The Montgomery bus boycott was not the first of its kind. In particular, the idea of a bus boycott was not new, having been used successfully by blacks in Baton Rouge, Louisiana, *prior to Brown*, during the summer of 1953. Dr. Martin Luther King, Jr., the leader of the Montgomery bus boycott, knew the leader of that boycott, Rev. T. J. Jemison, from college days, and spoke with him early in the boycott (King 1958, 75–76). From the Baton Rouge boycott, Abernathy notes, Montgomery's blacks took "considerable inspiration" (Abernathy 1989, 178; Garrow 1986, 26–27). Indeed, Morris argues that the Montgomery bus boycott was "partly inspired by the Baton Rouge effort and to some extent modeled after it" (1984, x). Similarly, Montgomery's blacks "did know that other cities in the Deep South, notably Mobile and Atlanta, had already conceded the 'first come, first served' principle" (Fairclough 1987, 12). In other words, McMahon's focus is too narrow.

In making his case for the significance of *Brown*, McMahon quotes a number of mentions of the case by King and Abernathy and then concludes that "the Court's decision had a significant impact on the thinking of the City's African American leaders" (15). But is this conclusion justified? McMahon seems to believe that if he can find reference to *Brown* as important or inspirational that the argument of *The Hollow Hope* is weakened, or even fatally flawed. It seems to me, however, that the question is not whether anyone ever mentioned *Brown*, or mentioned it in an inspirational way. Of course they did, and McMahon provides examples. The more important, and difficult question, is how important *Brown* was in originating and sustaining the boycott. Put another way, is it likely that the boycott would have originated, continued, and succeeded without *Brown*? This is the kind of counter factual that Schultz and Gottlieb urge be undertaken. The problem with McMahon's analysis is that he offers no explicit theoretical justification for concluding that mention of a prior event by leaders of a current movement means that the prior event has causal importance. Under the theory I offered in *The Hollow Hope*, asserting causal importance requires, among other factors, specifying mechanisms by which a prior event A "caused" a subsequent event B, and investigating alternative explanations. In other words, what did *Brown* add to the boycott? By not placing the boycott in the broader context of both the politics and culture of Montgomery, the South more generally, and the civil rights movement, and by not providing any guidance on how to assess mentions of *Brown*, McMahon's evidence is less useful than it could have been.

I do agree with McMahon that it was a Court decision that was the ultimate cause of the boycott's successful end. However, we agree for quite different reasons. For McMahon, once "the city's legal maneuvers [were] exhausted" (21), the buses were desegregated. But why? The 1950s and 1960s are full of examples of white officials unwilling to concede when faced with adverse Court decisions, and *nothing changing*. In the field of transportation, for example, there were several Court decisions invalidating segregation that were simply ignored,[15] as the Freedom Rides, to take the most notorious example, violently demonstrated. And *Brown*, of course, was simply ignored in almost all of the South, with barely one in one hundred African-American children in school with whites nearly a decade after the decision. Why was Montgomery different?

The Court made a difference in Montgomery because, as I argue in *The Hollow Hope*, the Court's decision in *Gayle v. Browder* provided the city with a way out of a situation that had turned into both a domestic and an international nightmare. Elected white politicians could concede without "giving in" to the black boycotters. That is, these officials could argue that they had no choice but to follow the ruling of the Supreme Court. Thus, they could both retain white support and end the boycott. This is Condition IV of *The Hollow Hope*. But it is crucially premised on the fact that there was an organized and effective boycott in Montgomery that was bankrupting the bus company and bringing Montgomery into disrepute. Without the boycott, the Court's decision would likely have joined the long and growing list of other Court opinions ordering desegregation that were routinely and unproblematically ignored by white southern officials.

The disagreements I have highlighted are more than just quibbles about interpreting historical events. Rather, they stress two important points about scholarly work on courts and social change. First, as others have emphasized, the historical context is crucial. Court decisions and social movements must be explicitly situated in their historical settings and studied as such. By neglecting to place the boycott in its historical setting, McMahon overstates the importance of *Brown*. Second, authors must be explicit about their theory of causal significance. Otherwise, readers are left without guidance about how to judge particular pieces of evidence. So, for example, without such a theory the reader has no way of assessing the causal influence of the mentions of *Brown* that McMahon presents. While I applaud McMahon's empirical approach, in and of itself it is not sufficient to understand the relationship between courts and social change.

Particularism

These difficulties with McMahon's approach that I have highlighted illustrate the trouble with particularized history. McMahon and Paris argue for "the construction of thick, 'conflict and policy narratives' guided by McCann's model. . . ." (Chapter 2, 75). The problem with this approach is several-fold. On the one hand, by its narrow focus it can miss the larger picture (as I argue McMahon did in his study of Montgomery). But, as I pointed out in my critique of McCann and interpretivist approaches (Rosenberg 1996), any level of description can always be criticized on interpretivist grounds for being too general and missing the crucial details. Of most importance to me, however, is that without a commitment to the kind of positivist social science that McMahon and Paris criticize, "thick, narrative description" will not lead to generalization. It may lead to a more detailed and nuanced understanding of the *particular events described*, but it cannot, as an epistemological matter, lead to generalization. In studying courts and social change, what is the point of nongeneralizable studies in and of themselves? I am not satisfied with answers like, "this is an interesting case," or "I want to know more about this." Unless scholarship is a totally narcissistic calling, then it is fair to ask, why is this an interesting case? or why do you want to know more about it? When I ask this question, the answer inevitably involves a claim of generalization, that the case is illustrative or representative of a larger theoretical question. Before accepting the call for narrative work, I need to be persuaded that there is space between narcissism on the one hand and the kind of positivism for which I have argued.

One possible argument for narrative work might be constructed from the state of knowledge about particular relationships. It may be, for example, that when little is known about a particular relationship, a collection of narratives will be most useful for gathering crucial information. Such a collection might then be used to suggest patterns and generate hypotheses for testing. As a field progresses, narratives might also be useful to further test and refine theoretical understandings. But "thick, narrative description" for its own sake is not the best way to understand the relationship between courts and social change.

Agenda-Setting

In their chapter on agenda setting, Flemming, Bohte, and Wood ask an important question and approach it in a sensible way. Their question is what influence, if any, the Supreme Court may have on agenda setting, on influencing the issues the media consider. They consider several possibilities, ranging from "no significant expansion in media coverage" following a "politically significant Court decision" to "short-lived" attention to "systemic attention that persists for long periods of time" (11, 13). To assess these alternative hypotheses, they turned to the *Readers' Guide to Periodical Literature* and collected and coded 7,799 references to school desegregation (2,700), freedom of speech/censorship (3,075), and church/state relations (2,024) over an approximately 45- year period. Using a somewhat complex set of statistical tools, they conclude that while "*Brown* produced a lasting impact on media coverage of school desegregation issues, raising it by about 41% over the long term" (16), "the other two decisions were best modeled as temporary changes, producing only transitory shifts in media attention to school desegregation issues" (17).

The approach exemplified by Flemming, Bohte, and Wood is the kind of work that I think offers the best chance of furthering our understanding. This is not because it is quantitative, for as they Wood point out, *The Hollow Hope* does not use statistical tools. Rather, Flemming, Bohte, and Wood's approach is driven not by desire but by knowledge. It considers a number of possibilities, including one that the Court has little long-term impact. It is based on empirical data, testing its hypotheses. And it even concludes that in two of its three cases the hypothesis of little Court influence is confirmed! That being said, I believe there are three distinct weaknesses in the analysis that make its conclusion about *Brown* less persuasive than might originally appear. Underlying them is a lack of historical sensitivity and inattention to the theoretical underpinnings for their claims of causal influence.

Flemming, Bohte, and Wood base their analysis on *Readers' Guide* categories specifically dealing with education. In contrast, *The Hollow Hope* used a much broader civil rights measure. In a long footnote (number 4), Flemming, Bohte, and Wood argue that the "heterogeneity" of *The Hollow Hope's* broad measure "reduces its sensitivity to events directly affecting school desegregation" (33). This means that

> Rosenberg may have undercounted media attention regarding school desegregation because he overlooked or ignored a related, highly relevant *Readers' Guide* category. Under the heading 'Public Schools in America there is a subcategory entitled 'Public Schools—Desegregation.' Over time, this subcategory grows so large that it swamps the number of articles in the two school-related subcategories from the 'Negroes in America' category. In short, most stories on school desegregation in the *Readers' Guide* are found under a heading that Rosenberg does not include in his analysis (33–34).

Thus, Flemming, Bohte, and Wood suggest that *The Hollow Hope's* finding that *Brown* had little impact on media coverage is an artifact of its choice of measure.

The reason *The Hollow Hope* uses the broader measure, and the reason I think it is the better one, is that *Brown* is not just about education. Both its supporters and its critics saw it, and see it, as a decision about race relations, about desegregation in all aspects of American life. And in the (mostly *per curiam*) cases that followed *Brown* in the 1950s, the Court used it to strike down segregation in areas far from education. Flemming, Bohte, and Wood demonstrate that there was a good deal more media coverage of school desegregation in the years after *Brown* than in the seven years preceding it. But that needs to be assessed in the broader context of overall change in civil rights coverage. In other words, the inclusive, broader measure is the key one because it focuses not on shifts among sub categories but on overall coverage. And interestingly, the overall data are not that different than Flemming, Bohte, and Wood's data, showing rather large increases in coverage in 1956 and 1957, as well as in the 1960s. My disagreement, then, is both with Flemming, Bohte, and Wood's data, and with the conclusions they draw from them. When placed in the larger historical context through which *Brown* was understood, the broader measure makes more sense.

The second problematic aspect of Flemming, Bohte, and Wood's methodological approach is their use of months as the temporal unit of analysis instead of years as I used in *The Hollow Hope*. Their justification for doing so was the seemingly sensible one that "[t]he longer the time period the greater the number of potentially confounding influences we can expect to find surrounding the time of particular Supreme Court cases" (6). The problem with this approach, however, is that it implicitly assumes a particular model of media effects, that the public pays attention to short-term changes. The analysis in *The Hollow Hope* was based on an explicit model that shifting public attention in a *sustained* way requires consistent, long-term change. In the real world, in contrast to the world of statistical models, political decisions, be they Court opinions, congressional acts, or presidential decrees, often are overtaken by events. Students of the relationship between courts and social change should focus on where Court decisions fit in the context of a dynamic political system. In other words, while it may be the case that Court decisions have an impact on media coverage in the short run, this doesn't tell us very much about their ability to contribute to social change in the long run. Thus, using year as the unit of analysis is the more appropriate measure.

The third problematic aspect of Flemming, Bohte, and Wood's argument is in many ways the most important, for it directly challenges their interpretation of the data. To start, at least one of their conclusions simply doesn't follow from their data: "For the most controversial of decisions, the Supreme Court's voice in the national dialogue is obviously heard, and its views shift the focus of national discourse" (23). Their data don't show this. As noted above, in two of their three cases the Court had little lasting impact. Also, since they offer no discussion of how much media coverage is required for the Court's voice to be heard and to shift the focus of national discourse, their conclusion is unsupported. Data without theory shed little light.

In presenting their statistical model, Flemming, Bohte, and Wood note that a threat to its validity is "history," meaning that the "rival hypothesis exists that not X but some more or less simultaneous event produced the shift" in media coverage (14). In examining their data, they note that a "large spike occurred immediately after *Brown*, reflecting contemporaneous media attention to the decision, but while attention to school desegregation issues then receded somewhat it remained significantly higher than during the pre-intervention portion of the series" (16). The key question this suggests is what kept it higher? Their response is to look to history: "The reaction to the decision, of course, kept the issue of school desegregation in the limelight" (17). But how can they tell? How do they know that it wasn't the civil rights movement, independent of *Brown,* that kept the issue in the limelight? They assume that post-1954 changes are due to the Court and not to the activities of the civil rights movement. *The Hollow Hope* produces a wealth of data that argues otherwise. This challenge becomes particularly acute in their argument that the Court's decision in the Little Rock crisis (*Cooper*) "independently prompted additional media coverage of school desegregation" (18). An alternative hypothesis is that it was the threat of violence and the presence of federal troops that motivated the coverage. That's what I found in *The Hollow Hope*. Flemming, Bohte, and Wood have convincingly demonstrated that media coverage of school desegregation increased in the years after 1954. What they have only asserted is that this increase was due to Court decisions.

At the end of the chapter, Flemming, Bohte, and Wood offer a somewhat different take on what determines whether a Court decision will change media coverage. They write that "it is the magnitude or scale of the political opposition to the decisions and the issues they raise that matters most" (23). Although they give no reasons for why opposition matters while support doesn't, this starts the work of placing Court decisions in the political context which receives them. For its overall point is that the needs and beliefs of political actors are key to the agenda-setting role of the Court. While many litigators, as well as commentators, seem to believe that a Court decision finding a constitutional right will influence the political agenda, Flemming, Bohte, and Wood suggest that this depends to a large extent on how much political energy is dedicated to the substantive issue. And this is all that *The Hollow Hope* argued. Its claim was not that Court decisions supporting significant social reform couldn't lead to increased media attention, but rather that they were unlikely to do so without sustained political agitation. And the resources and skill it takes to win a Court case differ from the ones it takes to sustain a political movement.

Overall, then, by not focusing on the historical setting of the 1950s and 1960s, and by not offering an explicit theory of how and how much media coverage influences events, Flemming, Bohte, and Wood's impressive empirical work doesn't further understanding as much as it could. While they do make a strong case for the potential impact of Court decisions on media coverage, they do not make a convincing case for the contribution of Court decisions to furthering significant social reform.

The Success of Litigation

Both Canon and Schultz and Gottlieb criticize *The Hollow Hope* for asking too much of courts. For Canon, "In studies of the impact of the Supreme Court, the measure of success should not be based upon the policy desires of myriad reformers with various goals, but should be measured against the goals of the Supreme Court justices who established the reform" (251) Thus, *The Hollow Hope* is faulted because it "sometimes attributes goals to the justices that go well beyond what they say in their opinions" (60). Similarly, Schultz and Gottlieb argue that "it may not be true that the Court intended to bring about a significant social reform..." (34). Thus, "it is misleading to criticize the Court for failing to do something it did not intend to do" (36–7).

The Hollow Hope does not criticize courts. It does criticize litigators seeking significant social reform for litigating when the Court is constrained from helping them and when conditions for overcoming those constraints are not present. Further, it criticizes scholars for paying insufficient attention to the actual effects of litigation for significant social reform. It is not *The Hollow Hope* which asks too much of courts but rather social reform litigators. Their policy goals in bringing litigation are the appropriate measure for the question *The Hollow Hope* asks.

But what if one wants to study the impact of Supreme Court decisions rather than the efficacy of litigation to further significant social reform? This is a different but fine question, deserving of research. But it is also a difficult one, particularly if one wishes to judge the "success" of the Court in having its decisions implemented. In that case, as Canon suggests, presumably the goals of the justices are the right measure for a baseline measurement of success. However, Canon must be wary of pitfalls in positing "the goals of the Supreme Court justices." Normally, the only "data" justices provide for discerning goals are written opinions. Intuiting what goals lie behind those opinions, without the help of speeches, press conferences, interviews, election campaigns, and all the tools available with other political officials, is tricky. If discerning legislative intent is difficult, the difficulties are appreciably greater with discerning justices' goals.

There is also a question about what is required to conclude that significant social reform has been achieved. Canon criticizes *The Hollow Hope* for arguing "as if full implementation is required of all reforms" (61). Similarly, Schultz and Gottlieb argue that "general compliance with announced principles . . . is not appropriate as an exclusive measure of judicial efficacy" (34). They point out that "merely bringing a case and having it heard in itself might constitute a victory" (34).

There are two difficulties with this line of reasoning. First, it deemphasizes litigants' goals, which are to produce significant social reform. In the cases I examined, having a case heard was not the goal of the litigants and was not in and of itself considered a victory by them. In general, it seems highly unlikely that social reform lawyers would be willing to have their cases heard by the Supreme Court, even if they lose, on the ground that just getting into Court is a victory. Further, social reformers who litigate are result oriented, believing that the finding of a constitutional right will produce the substantive results they desire. If, for example, nearly 99% of African-American children in the 11 southern states that required segregation before *Brown* remained in segregated schools a decade after *Brown*, I don't understand, as a substantive matter, why it is problematic to conclude that *Brown* failed to further significant social reform.

Second, this argument treats constitutional rights more as bureaucratic regulations than as fundamental commitments. The theory behind the Constitution is that fundamental rights do not vary from place to place, leave no room for discretion, and have immediate applicability. The entire defense of judicial review, the power of an unelected and unaccountable branch to invalidate the actions of the democratically accountable branches, is premised on the claim that constitutional rights, as the supreme law of the land, are imbued with heightened legitimacy. When the United States is said to be a nation of laws and not people it is in part because discretion is limited by constitutional rights. If constitutional rights requiring significant social reform are understood as little more than bureaucratic regulations, enforced unevenly depending on political support, then the defense of judicial review, and the argument for the importance of constitutional rights, is critically weakened. Thus, because litigators want results, and because the theory of constitutional rights requires that implementation follow constitutional decisions, it is appropriate to use full implementation as a baseline for assessing success.

Given this discussion, the critics' point may be that sophisticated litigators view constitutional litigation not as likely to produce change by itself but as a potential resource in the struggle for significant social reform. That is, they know that winning a constitutional right may not fully change behavior. They believe, however, that constitutional rights change notions of what is acceptable and even possible, and can be used to inspire others, leverage resources, and build momentum for their movements for change. If this is the case, then looking at full implementation may miss much of what is most useful about courts in furthering significant social reform.

I agree that looking only at full implementation may miss much, and that is why *The Hollow Hope* devotes several chapters to exploring these other possibilities. Under the rubric of "indirect effects," I looked for, but did not find, evidence supportive of each of these claims. As before, I challenge proponents of this position to produce evidence that supports it.[16]

The Canon Analysis

In his thoughtful and interesting chapter, Canon offers a gracious critical response to *The Hollow Hope*. Although I am not persuaded by much of what Canon argues, in large part it represents the kind of work I hoped *The Hollow Hope* would provoke. Since I have discussed some of Canon's arguments in earlier sections, I focus here on his more substantive claims.

Canon examines the role of the Court in legislative reapportionment, criminal justice, schoolhouse religion, desegregation, sexually oriented material, advertising by professionals, and abortion. He does so because he sees them as the "most important [reforms] in the second half of the twentieth century for which it can reasonably be argued that the Supreme Court played a major if not central role in their achievement" (248). His central argument is that the Court is a good deal more efficacious than *The Hollow Hope* admits. This is in large part because the Court is more independent and often faces less severe implementation problems than Constraints II and III of *The Hollow Hope* propose.

At the outset, it must be noted that Canon's question differs from mine. *The Hollow Hope* focuses not on reform per se but on significant social reform. Thus, in *The Hollow Hope* I examine only 4 of Canon's 7 cases (legislative reapportionment, criminal justice, desegregation, and abortion). Of the remaining three, it seems clear to me that the increased availability of sexually oriented material, and advertising by professionals, important though they may be, do not fit the definition of significant social reform. I believe the same is true of prohibiting prayer in schools, although the case is somewhat closer. In discussing Canon's arguments, then, I will focus on the substantive areas we both discuss with the exception of desegregation since I have already done so above. But I will also address the other three briefly and show why the conditions for judicial efficacy I lay out in *The Hollow Hope* are met by these cases.

It must also be noted that Canon excludes a certain kind of impact from his analysis, what he calls "negative inspirational impact." In footnote 31 (21–22) he notes that some Court decisions "inspired considerable organized negative pressures on legislatures and government agencies." It seems to me, however, that such impacts can be crucial for implementation purposes. For example, as I argue below, organized opposition to abortion choice, at least in part driven by the Court's decisions, plays an important role in limiting the success of those decisions. Similarly, Klarman (1994) argues that Court-inspired opposition is key to understanding desegregation. Thus, whether one is interested in significant social reform or a broader notion, examining opposition is important in understanding the Court's contribution to reform.

In the reapportionment area, Canon argues that since legislatures were "significantly reapportioned" (24) in response to the Court's decisions, the Court played a key role in reform. As discussed above, he argues that in assessing the success of the Court, the "goals of the Supreme Court justices who established the reform" and not "the policy desires of myriad reformers with various goals" should be the baseline (25, 26). My disagreement is not that reapportionment occurred (it did), but with Canon's baseline and with his lack of explanation for why the change occurred.

As I have repeatedly emphasized, my question is whether it makes sense for reformers to litigate. In the reapportionment arena, litigators were not political theorists concerned with abstract notions of democratic theory. Rather, they were urban interests attempting to leverage greater resources out of state legislatures which, they argued, were apportioned so as to favor rural interests. Although legislatures were reapportioned, it is not clear that urban interests benefited. Change occurred, but not the change the litigants sought.

But more importantly, Canon doesn't explore why state legislatures reapportioned. He states, rather, that Constraints II and III (lack of judicial independence and lack of implementation powers) should have stymied change. But this abstracts the reapportionment cases from the social and political context in which they occurred. For example, there was a great deal of political support for reapportionment throughout the country, in both political and academic circles, that overcame

Constraint II. On the national level both parties supported it as did leaders of national organizations. As I note in *The Hollow Hope* (1991, 298–299, references omitted),

> the lawyer who argued the reform cause in *Baker* . . . was a past president of the American Bar Association. In addition, and perhaps most important, both the Eisenhower and Kennedy administrations urged the Court to act, with the U.S. appearing in all the important reapportionment cases . . . in practice the United States was the "chief advocate" for reform. . . . In the six cases headlined by *Reynolds v. Sims*, for example, that held that both houses of the state legislatures had to be apportioned on a population basis, the U.S. filed briefs totalling over 500 pages.

As for Constraint III, lack of implementation powers, this was overcome because there were a group of political elites strongly supportive of the reapportionment decisions who were able to use them to gain leverage on increasingly isolated rural legislators. On the whole, state governors, elected statewide, supported reapportionment, as did big-city mayors. Because Canon doesn't examine the forces behind reapportionment litigation, he doesn't sufficiently credit the role that political elites played in implementing the decisions.

Canon's argument is different in the criminal justice area. Here, despite the general claim that the Warren Court revolutionized criminal process, Canon finds that the Court's decisions "have curbed the more flagrant abuses, but they have induced little support for fundamental changes in the criminal justice system" (29). This is because to "a considerable extent, Rosenberg's two Constraints prevailed here" (30). In other words, Canon supports *The Hollow Hope*'s argument in this case. It is perhaps mischievous of me to note that reform of the criminal justice process is an area where Canon has done extensive empirical work.[17]

Abortion is the third substantive area that both Canon and *The Hollow Hope* examine. Canon's argument here is that even if the Court was only reflecting social change, rather than creating it, "a Court decision reflecting social change can be an important one" (56). Examining both state and federal opposition to abortion, Canon goes further and argues that the "Supreme Court is the one governmental body that has sustained abortion rights. Indeed, when it appeared that the Court would abandon its position in *Webster* and *Casey*, the pro-choice camp was full of gloom and panic because it had nowhere to turn" (57). Thus, the "freedom of choice policy has prevailed despite Constraints II and III" (58). These claims require consideration.

Canon is right that a decision reflecting social change can be important because it codifies that change in law, giving it institutional backing. This can make it harder for opponents of the change to stop it. But the reason *Roe* and *Doe* have increased the availability of legal abortion is that Condition III, a market mechanism for implementation, is present. Although the overwhelmingly majority of hospitals in the United States, the main providers of birth services, have refused to perform abortions, this obstacle has been overcome by abortion clinics. Abortion has remained an option for women in some parts of the country, then, because they have demanded it and the Court allowed the market to respond. Where there is demand for a service, and the market can provide it, litigation may be a good strategic choice for reformers.

From a social reform point of view, however, the trouble with market mechanisms of implementation is that provision of the reform is uneven. In states where religious and cultural factors are hostile to legal abortion, it is almost impossible to obtain one today, despite the fact that the Constitution is the law of the land. This remains the case even when legislative obstacles have been overturned by federal courts. In states that have enacted such obstacles the abortion rates are well below both the national average and the rates of adjoining and similar states. Contrary to Canon, the Court only made abortion "a nationwide option" (58) in theory, not in practice.[18] If in the wake of *Webster* and *Casey* the pro-choice movement thought it had nowhere to turn, that had more to due with the poverty of its political strategy than with the role of the Court. Abortion is the most common surgical procedure performed on American women, and reportedly the most common surgical procedure performed in the United States. The failure of the pro-choice movement to win legislative support in many states for such a large-scale practice represents, in large part, its over reliance on courts and its failure to mobilize the population.

Canon also overstates opposition to legal abortion. As I detail in *The Hollow Hope*, from the time of the initial decisions (1973) onward, there was and is a great deal of political support for abortion choice. Congress did pass the Hyde Amendment, essentially removing federal funding of abortion, but is has done little else to limit access to safe and legal abortion. From at least 1970 on, a majority of Americans have supported legal abortion in most cases. While the anti-abortion minority has been more vociferous, for the last several decades it has represented 20% or less of the population. Court decisions supporting access to safe and legal abortion have been in the mainstream.

In sum, the Court contributed to widening access to safe and legal abortion because there was a political movement demanding it, there was majority support for it, and there was a market mechanism for implementation. *The Hollow Hope* argues that it is precisely in these situations that litigation for significant social reform can produce that reform, albeit in an uneven manner.

The availability of sexually oriented materials and advertising by professionals are areas that I don't believe involve significant social reform. Thus, the argument of *The Hollow Hope* is not applicable. However, the "success" of the Court in both cases can be explained in large part by *The Hollow Hope*'s Condition III, the availability of a market method for implementation.

The availability of sexually oriented material grew because the market was producing the stuff and there was (un)healthy demand for it. When that happens, Court decisions can make a difference by simply removing legal prohibitions. But one also needs to remember, as Canon notes, that these decisions came down in a rapidly changing society. There was a sexual revolution going on that was hardly Court-driven. Be it in music, literature, movies, theater, or in schools and universities, traditional notions were under siege. Writing in 1960, McCloskey noted that one "can obviously not give too much credit (or blame) to the Supreme Court; the United States as a whole was undergoing what may be described as a 'sexual revolution,' and the Court could scarcely have stopped it even had it wanted to" (McCloskey, 154). While Canon seems correct in arguing that the Court was "the only body with any authority or political clout to pursue this reform" (43), the same trend in the greater availability of sexually oriented material was occurring in other western countries bereft of the United States Supreme Court. In the end, then, the Court's decision may have increased the speed at which sexually oriented material became available, but that was because there was a market mechanism for implementation. So while I don't believe this case has much to do with significant social reform, I do maintain that it fits under the conditions of *The Hollow Hope*.

Advertising by professionals is a similar case. It is not an example of significant social reform and is an example of market demand stymied by government regulation. Remove the regulation and those professionals who wish to advertise will, limited only by their resources and their sense of its potential payoff.

Finally, Canon raises the issue of prayer in schools. His basic claim is that the Court's decisions prohibiting prayer in schools were highly unpopular with both elected officials and the public but were implemented. That is, "the Supreme Court appears to have effectuated a significant social reform in the schoolhouse religion area despite [the] Constraints. . . ." (32).

Schoolhouse religion is more difficult to assess. On the one hand, it doesn't seem to meet the conditions of significant social reform that I lay out.[19] That is, prohibiting prayer in school does not seem to involve "rights and liberties, powers and opportunities, income and wealth . . . [or] self-respect" in important ways. While one could argue that forcing children to say a prayer they don't believe in violates their rights and is an affront to their self-respect, children find endlessly creative ways to poke fun at mandatory prayers, the Pledge of Allegiance, and the like.[20] On the other hand, this response may be unsatisfying, because it negates inquiry be definition. So, assuming for the sake of argument that the Court's decisions produced significant social reform, what might possibly explain it?

Canon himself suggests that perhaps the implementation problems the decisions posed were minimal. Simply put, all that had to occur for the decisions to be implemented was for school principals and teachers to stop reciting prayers at the start of the school day. This required no expenditure of funds, no massive dislocation in students' or teachers' lives (like busing, or re-assignment to a new school), no change in curriculum, little change in the school day, etc. The ease of implementation may play an important role.[21]

A second possibility focuses on the beliefs of school personnel. As Canon points out, studies of implementation of the decisions have found uneven implementation, due in large part to strongly held religious beliefs on the part of some school personnel. This suggests that one important factor might lie in the beliefs school personnel held about prayer in school. As the cultural politics of the 1960s spread throughout the country, it is possible that those young people who became teachers and were educated in the period did not believe in the importance of prayer in school. As they replaced older personnel, the incidence of prayer in school declined.

In the end, where Canon and I disagree is in the importance of issues on which the Court can "succeed." Advertising by professionals, the availability of sexually oriented materials, and arguably prayer in schools, are not as important to most Americans as questions of civil rights and abortion. They do not fit under my definition of significant social reform. And if the Court succeeded in these areas, the reason is largely due to what I call market forces and Canon calls consumer choice. With reapportionment, we disagree about the aim of the litigants and about the social and political context in which reapportionment was decided. We more or less agree on criminal rights. On abortion, Canon overstates the availability of abortion to women outside of cities, and in many states. Finally, with desegregation, I challenge Canon and others to produce the evidence to substantiate their claims.

Conclusion

Despite the many disagreements that I have highlighted, there is also a great deal of agreement among the contributors to this book. Obviously, we all are fascinated by the role the Court can play in social reform. Perhaps somewhat less obviously, everyone seems to agree that the finding of a constitutional right is only a first step in that right having meaning in everyday life. In other words, the United States is a nation of people as well as a nation of laws. There is no guarantee that the finding of a constitutional right will translate into the practice of that right. Other factors such as institutional and bureaucratic resistance, opposition from powerful interests, prejudice, cultural practices, and simple inertia hinder and sometimes prevent constitutional rights from being respected. This says something fundamentally important about the role of courts, the Constitution, and rights in American society.

The contributors to this book disagree on how to move forward in understanding this reality. In responding to criticisms of the argument and methodology of *The Hollow Hope*, I have tried to highlight the strengths of a conventional social science approach to studying the relationship of courts and social change. In so doing, I have argued that the most useful approach to the study of courts and social change is based on careful empirical work combined with historical sensitivity, methodological awareness, and broader normative concerns. In particular, I pointed to the pitfalls of substituting ideological belief for research, desire for knowledge. For too many scholars, the allure of the Warren Court may cloud their vision with a romantic belief in the importance of the Court, in the triumph of rights over politics. A precommitment to the fundamental issues in the relationship between courts, law, and social change is not a useful way to further knowledge and understanding. It removes the most important questions and problems from investigation. As I have repeatedly emphasized, in investigating the world of practice rather than principle, that practice must be examined critically.

As interesting and provocative as the chapters of this book are, at the end of the day what has one learned? Do we know when, and under what conditions, it makes sense for those seeking significant social reform to litigate? Do we know more about the strengths and weaknesses of various approaches to studying courts and social change? I fear we have learned less then we could have because too many authors substituted desire for knowledge, arguing for a world they want, not the world they have. In so doing, they paid insufficient heed to careful readings, to the painstaking gathering of evidence, to theory, and to the place of history. In responding, I have tried to underscore the kind of research methodology I believe has the best chance to help answer such questions. Now let's get on with it!

Notes

1. For an empirically-rich argument that, despite the rhetoric of principle, judicial decision-making is driven by partisan policy interests, see Segal and Spaeth 1993.

2. There are, of course, examples of scholars who take such a position. Two prominent ones include Herbert Wechsler's famous criticism of *Brown*, a case whose policy outcome he supported, and John Hart Ely's critique of *Roe*, despite his political support for the result. See Wechsler (1959); Ely (1973).

3. For an engaging history of this battle in the late 19th century, see Paul 1960.

4. I will not respond to McCann because he and I have already had two published exchanges; McCann (1992; 1996), Rosenberg (1992; 1996).

5. Because I am using *criticisms* of *The Hollow Hope* and its approach to the study of courts and social change to make my points, some readers (and chapter authors!) may also feel that my argument boils down to the claim that I'm right and everyone else is wrong. Suffice it to say, there is much of value in each of the chapters that, because it is not on point, will not be discussed.

6. Schultz and Gottlieb miss this point entirely, incorrectly arguing that I use the increasing numbers of legal abortions prior to *Roe* as "evidence that *Roe* did not have an impact." (Schultz and Gottlieb, 56). To the contrary, I use the historical context to both help assess the extent of change, and to explain why *Roe* made a difference.

7. "Administrators and officials crucial for implementation are willing to act and see court orders as a tool for leveraging additional resources or for hiding behind" (*The Hollow Hope* 36).

8. I did find them, for example, albeit unevenly, in prison reform litigation and in litigation to reform the criminal process more generally. See *The Hollow Hope*, chapter 11.

9. I set out some of my objections to this critique in Rosenberg (1992).

10. Some of this literature is cited and discussed in *The Hollow Hope*. For a general discussion, see pp. 21–28. For discussion of specific claims for judicial efficacy in substantive areas, see the appropriate chapter.

11. In addition to *The Hollow Hope* (chapter 4, pp. 131–55), see Thress and Rosenberg (1992).

12. For my argument as to why the inclusion of Title VI in the 1964 Act owes little to *Brown*, see *The Hollow Hope* at 121–123.

13. For an argument that it was the adverse reaction to *Brown* in the South that ultimately produced significant social reform, see Klarman (1994).

14 Fairclough also points to a similar initial reticence to demand an end to segregation in the Tallahassee, Florida, bus boycott of 1956 (Fairclough 1987, 20).

15 These are discussed in chapter two of *The Hollow Hope*, pp. 64–65.

16 I also am somewhat skeptical that there is a large set of litigators for social reform who see their work merely as providing potential resources for reform. Such a position may be little more than a post hoc rationalization for Court victories that did not produce change. Given the enormous drain of resources that constitutional litigation involves, and the general lack of coordination between those who litigate and those who follow other strategies, skepticism is warranted. But, of course, empirical investigation may help resolve my skepticism.

17 See, for example, Canon (1973a); Canon (1973b); Canon (1974); Canon (1977); Canon and Kolson (1971).

18 For discussion of the difficulty women face in obtaining legal abortions in many states, see Rosenberg 1995.

19 Canon considers this possibility as well, writing that "Some might argue that *Engel* and *Schempp* do not constitute a significant social reform because the changes they require are more symbolic than real" (30). This, however, is a different use of the term significant social reform.

20 It may be that parents who are opposed to their children reciting prayers in school suffer the greater injury.

21 It might be instructive, however, to examine data on how much prayer in school occurs. Students of mine who have examined the issue in Chicago and its suburbs have found a mixed picture, with at least some public schools starting the day with prayer and many offering prayers at commencement exercises.

Works Cited

Abernathy, Ralph David. 1989. *And the Walls Came Tumbling Down.* New York: Harper and Row.

Canon, Bradley C. 1973a. "Is the Exclusionary Rule in Failing Health? Some New Data and a Plea Against a Precipitous Conclusion." *Kentucky Law Review* 62: 681.

Canon, Bradley C. 1973b. "Reactions of State Supreme Courts to a U.S. Supreme Court Civil Liberties Decision." *Law and Society Review* 8: 109.

Canon, Bradley C. 1974. "Organizational Contumacy in the Transmission of Judicial Policies:

The *Mapp, Escobedo, Miranda,* and *Gault* Cases." *Villanova Law Review* 20: 50.

Canon, Bradley C. 1977. "Testing the Effectiveness of Civil Liberties Policies at the State and Federal Levels: The Case of the Exclusionary Rule." *American Politics Quarterly* 5: 57–82.

Canon, Bradley C. and Kenneth Kolson. "Rural Compliance with Gault: Kentucky, A Case Study." *Journal of Family Law* 10: 300.

Ely, John Hart. 1973. "The Wages of Crying Wolf: A Comment on *Roe v. Wade.*" *Yale Law Journal* 82: 920.

Fairclough, Adam. 1987. *To Redeem the Soul of America: The Southern Christian Leadership Conference and Martin Luther King, Jr.* Athens, Georgia: University of Georgia Press.

Feeley, Malcolm M. 1992. "Hollow Hopes, Flypaper, and Metaphors." Review of *The Hollow Hope. Law and Social Inquiry* 17: 745–760.

Garrow, David J. 1986. *Bearing the Cross: Martin Luther King, Jr. and the Southern Christian Leadership Conference.* New York: Morrow.

King, Martin Luther, Jr. 1958. *Stride Toward Freedom.* New York: Harper Brothers.

Klarman, Michael J. 1994. "How *Brown* Changed Race Relations: The Backlash Thesis." *Journal of American History* 81: 81–118.

McCann, Michael W. 1992. "Reform Litigation on Trial." Review of *The Hollow Hope. Law and Social Inquiry* 17: 715–743.

McCann, Michael W. 1996. "Causal versus Constitutive Explanations (or, On the Difficulty of Being So Positive . . .)." *Law and Social Inquiry* 21: 457–482.

McCloskey, Robert G. [1960] 1994. *The American Supreme Court.* 2nd ed. Chicago: University of Chicago Press.

Morris, Aldon D. 1984. *The Origins of the Civil Rights Movement: Black Communities Organizing for Change.* New York: Free Press.

Paul, Arnold. 1960. *Conservative Crisis and the Rule of Law.* Ithaca: Cornell University Press.

Robinson, Jo Ann Gibson. 1987. *The Montgomery Bus Boycott and the Women Who Started It: The Memoir of Jo Ann Gibson Robinson.* Ed. David J. Garrow. Knoxville: University of Tennessee Press.

Rosenberg, Gerald N. 1991. *The Hollow Hope: Can Courts Bring About Social Change?* Chicago: University of Chicago Press.

Rosenberg, Gerald N. 1992. "Hollow Hopes and Other Aspirations: A Reply to Feeley and McCann." *Law and Social Inquiry* 17: 761–778.

Rosenberg, Gerald N. 1995. "The Real World of Constitutional Rights: The Supreme Court and the Implementation of the Abortion Decisions." Pp. 390–419 in *Contemplating Courts,* ed. Lee Epstein. Washington, D.C.: Congressional Quarterly Press.

Rosenberg, Gerald N. 1996. "Positivism, Interpretivism, and the Study of Law." Review of *Rights At Work. Law and Social Inquiry* 21: 435–455.

Segal, Jeffrey A. and Harold J. Spaeth. 1993. *The Supreme Court and the Attitudinal Model.* New York: Cambridge University Press.

Thornton, J. Miles III. 1980. "Challenge and Response in the Montgomery Bus Boycott of 1955–1956." *Alabama Review* 33 (July): 163-235.

Thress, Thomas E. and Gerald N. Rosenberg. 1992. "The Supreme Court, the Civil Rights Movement, and the African-American Press." Paper delivered at the Annual Meeting of the Midwest Political Science Association.

Wechsler, Herbert. 1959. "Toward Neutral Principles of Constitutional Law." *Harvard L. Review* 73:1.

Wilkins, Roy (with Tom Mathews). 1984. *Standing Fast: The Autobiography of Roy Wilkins.* New York, Penguin.

Chapter 7

Juricide*

Marvin Zalman

It has been more than a century since Holmes' epigrammatic opening lines in *The Common Law*—"The life of the law has not been logic: it has been experience"—set the stage for the rise of law and society scholarship ([1881] 1963). At the end of the twentieth century each of the social disciplines—anthropology, economics, history, political science, psychology, sociology—can list its post-Holmesian law and society classics and conflicting schools of thought. Jurisprudence has been influenced by law and society scholarship as well as by analytic philosophy. A politicized form of literary criticism has concerned itself with law, as have such hybrid and interdisciplinary areas of study as biography and criminal justice. Specialized journals that bridge law and other disciplines abound. Law review literature seems to be passing from the lexical analysis of cases and statutes to interdisciplinary scholarship. Ideological rifts, as well as generational, racial, and gender divides, have intensified much of this scholarship. "Political jurisprudence"—the study of law and courts with the tools and perspectives of political science—is a part of this larger movement and shares its strengths and weaknesses (Stumpf 1988). The areas of interest to political jurisprudence include: judicial decision- and policy-making; judicial selection; the interactions of courts with other political entities; courts and public opinion and interest groups; the mobilization of law; and the impact of legal and court action on society (Gates and Johnson, eds., 1991; Epstein, ed., 1995). The overlapping area of constitutional inquiry, of high interest to political scholars, is pursued via an eclectic mix of methods that include the lexical analysis of Supreme Court decisions, political theory, and American and British constitutional history.

This sketch sets the stage for this chapter's thesis. Political jurisprudence and law and society scholarship in general has added immeasurably to an understanding of the legal enterprise. The overwhelming majority of political scholars who study law and courts treat the law as a relevant and existing category of social action that influences (and is influenced by) social and political behavior. In this chapter I examine a mood among some political scholars whose research has taken a turn so hostile to the legal enterprise as to presage the "death of the law" or what I have labeled "juricide." Three recent studies of the United States Supreme Court posit, each in its own way, that law is an irrelevant or pernicious process—it either clouds understanding of what "really" happens in courts and society or retards social progress. These are Jeffrey Segal and Harold Spaeth's (1993) attempt to show that their attitudinal model completely explains Supreme Court decisions; Gerald Rosenberg's (1991) bid to show that the Supreme Court has not fostered social change in this century; and Richard Brisbin's (1993) postmodern analysis purporting to show that law is nought but "violence" or that there is fundamentally little difference between Justices Antonin Scalia and William Brennan.

There are different ways to evaluate these works. Published critiques of Segal and Spaeth and Rosenberg have argued that, although there is much to appreciate in each study, they suffer from methodological or conceptual flaws or they mistake the scope of their findings. For a review of some of these critiques, see David Schultz's introduction to this volume. In this chapter I will instead conduct a jurisprudential probe that asks what these methodologically diverse works say about the fundamental question of the meaning of law and its standard interpretive process. I will establish and examine the *implicit* jurisprudential position taken by these studies—that law does not exist—and argue that they are fundamentally incorrect in this regard. In the conclusion I will speculate on why such accomplished works take what is a minority position among political scientists. I will note that within twentieth century jurisprudence several movements, the legal realism school and critical legal studies, have announced—prematurely—the end of law. Both schools of thought were met with vigorous criticism from within the law. The similarities and differences between those episodes in jurisprudence and the antilaw studies of political scientists will be noted.

First Critique: The Attitudinal Model

When political scientists contrast the political and the legal models (George and Epstein 1992), there is a tendency to reduce the legal or doctrinal model to a straw man that is easily punctured by a demonstration that extralegal variables better explain court outcomes than explanations given in judicial opinions (Glick 1983, 3). Doctrinal legal research—the lexical analysis of appellate cases and statutes—is the staple of appellate judges, attorneys writing briefs, and law professors. This is a practical undertaking that is not without intellectual rigor or without its theories. In the grand Roman law tradition of continental Europe, it is labeled "legal science" (Wolff 1951). Although often derided by social scientists, this kind of research has real social value. By establishing relatively coherent bodies of law it contributes significantly to social stability. Indeed, nonviolent social stability is impossible without some kind of interpretive regime that we tend to call law (Levi 1949, 1-3).[1] While there may be simple and complex explanations of law, the same is the case with political explanations of human behavior. Thus, a simple version of the political model has been improved by Segal by incorporating case facts to strengthen an explanatory model of Supreme Court decision making (Segal 1984, 1986). But to advance from an improved model to a total explanation involves an exaggerated and unsustainable claim.

Segal and Spaeth aim "to scientifically analyze and explain the Supreme Court, its processes, and its decisions, from an attitudinal perspective." This is posed as a scientific method, distinct from "historical, anecdotal, legalistic, tendentious or doctrinal" approaches. Key decisions, including the selection of judges, the decision to decide, the votes on the merits, and opinion assignment, are best explained by the attitudinal model, which holds that votes of the justices can best be predicted by their personal policy preferences, defined as stable attitudes as applied to the facts of the case, using logit regression analysis. The model applies the past voting behavior of justices to predict their votes (Segal and Spaeth 1993, xv–xvii, 221–226, 229–231, 364–372).[2] When applied to 196 search and seizure cases decided between 1962 and 1989, the model correctly predicted 76 percent of the case outcomes, for a 30 percent reduction in error, and 74 percent of individual justices' opinions, a 41 percent reduction in error (1993, 216–221). Decisions on the merits were predicted by Segal and Spaeth in 116 discrete categories of cases. The model did a good job of predicting outcomes in civil liberties areas but predicted more categories incorrectly than correctly in the areas of economic activity, federalism, and federal taxation (1993, 255–260).

Much of the book is informative, and the model is a valuable addition to Supreme Court research, but two flaws are discernible. First,

Segal and Spaeth claim their model demolishes other modes of political analysis. Applying their model, the background characteristics of justices, their institutional position, public opinion, the power of Congress to sanction the Court, and the role of interest groups do not predict the Court's decisions; only the Solicitor General's position holds up as a predictive variable (Segal and Spaeth 1993, 231–237). Second, the authors trash the process of legal analysis as nothing more than postdecision rationalization designed to maintain the Court's mythic position as a symbol of impartial judging (1993, 33–62). Although judicial interpretation allows different judges to come to different conclusions, to draw from this that legal reasoning is a sham misses what is vital about the nature and the social utility of legal interpretation. Most political scientists and politically oriented legal scholars do not follow Segal and Spaeth on these points.

To reflect on the weaknesses with the first position, we should ask, "What is the purpose of Segal and Spaeth's work?" If it is to develop a refined empirical technique for analyzing cases, it achieves that goal. This is not the only politically meaningful way to study the Court, and, more to the point, it is excessively narrow to call this approach scientific to the exclusion of other methods. When it comes to explaining truly significant shifts in decisions, their model cannot point to the Court's likely direction or say anything that illuminates the important political work of the Court.

On symbolic, doctrinal, and practical levels few recent cases have been as important as *Planned Parenthood v. Casey* (112 S. Ct. 2791), the 1992 case that reaffirmed *Roe v. Wade* (410 U.S. 113 [1973]). In *Casey* the conservative justices split into a moderate and an "ultra" bloc. The moderates—Justices Sandra Day O'Connor, Anthony Kennedy, and David Souter—issued an unusual joint opinion that reaffirmed *Roe* on the institutional basis of *stare decisis*, one of the elements of legal analysis scoffed at by Segal and Spaeth as an explanation of decisions. In short, the justices said that too many women and men have come to rely on *Roe*, and that the Court had an obligation to maintain the stability of this rule. *Casey* surprised many because in the 1989 case of *Webster v. Reproductive Health Services* (492 U.S. 490 [1989]) Justice O'Connor switched to the anti-*Roe* side.

Political scientists who read the abortion opinions closely and pay attention to the nature and quality of the reasoning tell us important things about the nature of the Court's process that are not available by an application of the attitudinal model. Christopher Smith's after-the-fact analysis of *Casey* provides a plausible, if not definitive, suggestion that the styles and interactions, as well as the content of one justice's opinions, can have a real impact on another justice's vote on the merits.[3] He suggests that Justice Scalia's strident personal attack on Justice O'Connor's mild anti-*Roe* dissent in *Webster* led to her reversal and support for *Roe* in *Casey* (Smith 1993).

Smith's intriguing thesis builds on the masterful study of Lee Epstein and Joseph Kobylka that, in contradistinction to Segal and Spaeth, argues that in understanding the process of change in Supreme Court decisions, "the law and the legal arguments grounded in law matter, and they matter dearly (1992, 302)." Their book ends with the 1989 *Webster* decision, so they can offer no post-hoc rationalization of *Casey*. Nevertheless, their close analysis of *Webster* lays an excellent foundation for appreciating Justice O'Connor's switch back to support for *Roe* in *Casey*. Epstein and Kobylka pay attention first to Justice O'Connor's precise legal reasoning—which indeed recognized "some kind of constitutionally based abortion right;" secondly, to her low-keyed rhetoric compared to that of Chief Justice William Rehnquist and Justice Byron White; and finally, to the fact that her institutional position was not one of absolute deference to local government (1992, 296, 297, 294–298). They argue that the pro-choice attorneys lost Justice O'Connor's vote in *Webster* because they did not pay attention to these legal points.

Surely, if Segal and Spaeth applied their model to *Casey*, it should have predicted, on the basis of the votes ("attitudes") of seven justices in *Webster*,[4] that in *Casey*, *Roe v. Wade* would be overturned and they would have been wrong. In short, Epstein and Kobylka's close attention to legal doctrine has proven to be a far better guide to predicting and understanding the outcome in *Casey* than Segal and Spaeth's attitudinal model could have been.

Segal and Spaeth set up the legal model as a straw man but failed to indicate that among the earliest and the most powerful proponents of the idea of legal realism were the greatest of jurists and masters of case analysis, including Oliver Wendell Holmes and Benjamin Cardozo (1993, 65; Holmes [1881] 1963; Cardozo 1921). By viewing legal scholars, judges, and attorneys as if they were Victorian-era believers of the Law Immaculate, or law as the most narrowly conceived formalism, Segal and Spaeth fail to appreciate the extent to which the political model has become part of the warp and woof of constitutional law thinking by lawyers. A powerful example is the Foreword to the

Harvard Law Review's annual review of 1993–94 Supreme Court cases by law professors William Eskridge and Philip Frickey (1994, 27–108), in which they advance a more complete understanding of the Court. The Court's decisions cannot "persuasively" be understood only by the legal approach nor by the simple application of the justices' conservative values. In a richly textured argument they suggest a third, institutional, approach that offers a more powerful explanation *when combined* with the legal and attitudinal perspectives. The Court, they assert, acts strategically and purposefully as a branch of government to maintain its position vis-à-vis Congress and state governments. This "legal process" approach results in a supple, efficient, and less conflictual body of law that is shaped in large measure by a signaling process that includes, among other things, devices such as *obiter dicta* in opinions and congressional hearing reports.

Eskridge and Frickey apply their thesis to many constitutional questions. I will review one. Segal and Spaeth, along with other political and legal scholars, dismiss threats to the Court as having little or no effect on decisions. Neither impeachment, reduced jurisdiction, salary freezes, constitutional overrides—hollow threats all—nor personal ambition seriously affect or impede the justices (Segal and Spaeth 1993, 69–73). The justices, in this view, are free to pursue their personal value positions. But in Eskridge and Frickey's fine-grained analysis, the conservative Supreme Court in the 1980s and early 1990s was dealt significant congressional rebukes by a Democratically controlled Congress. "The normal political process of statute enactment can effectively override the Court when it *refuses to create* individual rights" (1994, 44, emphasis in original). Congress thus expanded rights by override legislation when the Court failed to regulate racial dilution in at-large elections, curbed employee rights under federal antidiscrimination laws, and curtailed the free exercise of religion by traditionalist Native Americans in the ceremonial use of peyote.[5] In view of these negative messages at the hands of Congress, Eskridge and Frickey offer an institutional perspective on *Planned Parenthood v. Casey*:

> The Court's legitimacy was shaken [by these Congressional overrides] but not irreparably, and the Court has been careful since 1991 to avoid the impression that its civil rights decisions are anti-minority. *Casey* can be similarly viewed as the effort by centrist Justices to position the Court as neutrally as possible on the issue of abortion. Those centrist Justices rationally understood that a position rejected by big majorities in Congress and by the public would not be regarded as legitimate" (1994, 38, footnote omitted).

It is clear, then, that not all political scientists share an unalloyed enthusiasm for the attitudinal model.[6] Whatever methodological flaws may exist in the attitudinal model, it is not a complete *political* explanation of the Supreme Court.

The second flaw discernible in Segal and Spaeth's model is the manner in which they dismiss legal interpretation. The analogy to the distinction between performance and criticism may be helpful here. Legal interpretation in appellate cases appears to explain law and thus seems akin to a purely academic enterprise. Political analysis of common law makes the claim that it can better explain the product, and this is a sustainable claim. To dismiss the style of appellate cases in the dismissive manner found in Segal and Spaeth, however, displays a lack of understanding that this method is not simply a mode of explaining but a mode of creating law. I would assert that explicit political methods cannot lead to a dynamic interpretive regime that is the system of common law. Further, this method is indispensable to any sophisticated and workable legal and governmental system. Law is not a science and makes no pretense to be one. Attempts to abolish law usually fail, as communist rulers learned once they established working governments and discovered that some kind of legal agencies were necessary (Kirchheimer 1980, 259–303; Kurczewski 1993, 69-99; see Fuller 1976). The point-supported by substantial legal history-is that law as the ruler's command or as a code that answers all questions is impossible in all but the most primitive or the most tyrannical societies.[7]

This thesis can be supported by an example from search and seizure law. A significant part of Segal and Spaeth's analysis of decisions on the merits focus on search and seizure (1993, 214–242), building on Segal's important earlier study, which expressed "pleasure" at developing an attitudinal model that displayed coherence in a legal area described by legalists as "a mess" (Segal 1984, 899, 891). What Segal failed to notice or decided to overlook was that those who described the law as a mess were liberal commentators who were appalled at the Burger Court's reasoning process (Dworkin 1973; Amsterdam 1974). That reasoning strategically injected uncertainty into Warren Court doctrines precisely for the political purpose of generating more conservative decisions. Segal's study included cases to the 1981 term. His nonnormative model could in no way predict that the Court would develop a new doctrine—the "special needs" doctrine—to allow government victories in a slew of cases where search and seizures were carried out by officials other than police officers (Dressler 1991, 207–17). It would be reasonable to predict that the Burger Court would stay on a conservative path, but the specific contours of its case reasoning were critical to the conservatives' success in the "special needs" cases. A doctrine had to be developed with enough rational weight to carry moderate conservatives such as Justice Harry Blackmun, who indeed generally supported the special needs doctrine. Without developing a feasible doctrine, the conservatives could not have advanced their agenda. To predict a conservative advance on warrantless searches of school children, or government doctors' desks, or the urine testing of customs officers (*New Jersey v. T.L.O.* [469 U.S. 325 {1985}]; *O'Connor v. Ortega* [480 U.S. 709 {1987}]; *National Treasury Employees Union v. Von Raab* [489 U.S. 646 {1989}]) , without paying attention to the particular shape of the argument used, is like assuming the North would have won the Civil War without paying attention to the configuration of the terrain and the troops at Gettysburg. What this suggests is that Segal and Spaeth's attitudinal model is a technique of postdicting Supreme Court decisions. This method is a poor predictor of legally and doctrinally significant developments in law because it applies a limited range of information about the cases. A legal scholar deeply immersed in doctrine, who participates in writing appellate briefs, is in a better position to assess the way in which important shifts in the law will develop.

My critique does not diminish the interesting and valuable contributions of *The Attitudinal Model* as much as the rather arrogant attitude of the authors, who state, echoing Chief Justice John Marshall, "we must never forget it is a *model* we are expounding—one intended to endure for years to come" (Segal and Spaeth 1993, 363, emphasis in original). Their claim to advance science, it seems to me, mistakes a technique for the rational search for truth. The search for truth (a more fundamental understanding of science) about political and social phenomena may require a combination of methods, some of which are non-quantitative. A simple and profound truth about law and politics that must not be forgotten in the search for explanation is that they are, among other things, *normative* enterprises. A "science" of law that purposively excludes values is not science, but technology at best and pseudo-science at worst (Dworkin 1986; Hall 1960, 1–5 and generally; Fletcher 1978, 454–483). Segal and Spaeth's contribution to a science of the Supreme Court has its place but claims more than it should. When the authors say that their model is intended to "endure for years to come," this seems to violate the searching and critical spirit of science and scholarship which evolves in a continuing cycle of critique and reanalysis.

Second Critique: The Supreme Court's Capacity

Political scientists have demonstrated that courts have *limited capacity* to effect social change (Horowitz 1977; Peltason [1961] 1971; Shapiro 1981). To take this important insight, which has empirical and theoretical correlates, and to assert as does Gerald Rosenberg in his widely praised and criticized volume, *The Hollow Hope,* that the Supreme Court, in contrast to popular myth, has had no effect on desegregation, voter reapportionment, women's rights, police behavior, and environmental enforcement, is not only a breathtaking challenge to legal orthodoxy—it is wrong. He goes so far as to suggest that courts *impede* significant social change by diverting the political energies and funds of groups seeking change and by mobilizing opposition (Rosenberg 1991, 341–342). He amasses an impressive volume of prior research to bolster his arguments.

His thesis, briefly, is that the "Dynamic Court" model is a myth and that a model of a "Constrained Court" better fits the data: (1) courts cannot address a full range of reform claims; (2) the Supreme Court is not institutionally as independent as the Dynamic Court model makes out; and (3) courts lack the institutional means for implementing reforms (Rosenberg 1991, 10–21). Consequently, courts can produce significant social change only when certain conditions exist: when other actors, especially Congress and the executive branch, offer positive incentives or impose costs to induce compliance; when market mechanisms profit by implementing judicial reforms; or when court rulings shield implementers who are otherwise willing to act (1991, 33–35).

Rosenberg devotes most attention to the paradigmatic case—the impact of *Brown v. Board of Education* (347 U.S. 483 [1954]) on Southern segregation. In two closely argued and data-packed chapters he proves what is well known to those familiar with civil rights history, "that before Congress and the executive branch acted, courts had virtually *no direct effect* on ending discrimination in the key fields of education, voting, transportation, accommodations in public places, and housing" (Rosenberg 1991, 70–71, emphasis in original).[8] He adequately explains and exhaustively documents the lack of southern integration in the late 1950s, compared to the period after the president and Congress acted in the mid-1960s, as support for the Constrained Court model.⁹

I part company with Rosenberg's next point. The significant question about *Brown* is whether it *indirectly* led to progress in integration by setting the stage for others—both civil rights activists and later presidents and the Congress—to act. His theoretical and methodological argument is that those who believe the Court had indirect influence have not traced the causal mechanism by which this occurs.¹⁰ He concludes that *Brown* did not have an indirect effect because of a time gap of five to eight years between *Brown* and statistically measurable social action, as measured by press coverage, textbooks mentioning *Brown*, legislative action, white public opinion, and black civil rights action (Rosenberg 1991, 111–155). Empirical measurement of these factors changed only in the mid-1960s when the federal government added legislation with teeth. He adds that "while there is little evidence that *Brown* helped produce positive change, there is some evidence that it hardened resistance to civil rights among both elites and the white public (1991, 155).

He briefly attributes the massive changes in desegregation of the 1960s and later to large scale economic, demographic, and international changes (Rosenberg 1991, 157–169). Rosenberg thus paints a picture of History Immaculate—inevitable and triumphant—regardless of the intervention of human agency. He implies, without quite saying so, that civil rights gains would have been achieved more swiftly, and with less white opposition, if the NAACP Legal Defense Fund (LDF) had never launched a legal campaign to fight segregation but had instead focused on social and political fronts. For all the heroic striving of Thurgood Marshall and the LDF lawyers, for all the social ostracism that federal judges such as Frank Johnson and his family had to face, their efforts and early rulings were a waste of time at best and counterproductive at worst (Davis and Clark 1994; Peltason [1961] 1971; Bass 1993, 128–31). It seems to me, given the entrenched "southern way of life," that Rosenberg's hint that desegregation would have melted away by political and social action is fatuous.

In a different place I critique Rosenberg's thesis that *Brown* had no indirect effect on segregation (Zalman 1996). My central argument, summarized here, is that Rosenberg was shortsighted to base his conclusion on the fact that for five to eight years after *Brown* there was no empirically measurable change in five factors: press coverage, textbooks mentioning *Brown*, legislative action, white public opinion, and black civil rights action. I pointed out that Rosenberg overlooked, in sources that he cited, a strong affinity for and inspiration by *Brown* by Martin Luther King, Jr. and many African Americans (1996, 190–91). A better view is that *Brown* stimulated a "spirit of revolt" that planted the seeds for a more activist phase of civil rights activity. *Brown* marked a monumental turning point after more than a half-century of an entrenched Jim Crow regime and a certain amount of time was needed for the message to take hold with a new generation prepared for action. It is worth noting that in the late 1950s the Supreme Court struck down a variety of segregated facilities, citing *Brown*, thus signaling to the nation that it was set on its integrationist course. Without *Brown* it is unlikely that the limited Civil Rights Act of 1957 would have passed or that the spirit of suppressed African Americans would finally be stirred to sustained and successful action.[11]

I also argued that to some extent Rosenberg's Dynamic Court view is a straw man (Zalman 1996, 189–90). While some citizens may believe that the Court is all-powerful, scholars paint a more complex picture of the Court as having influence to effect social change within limiting parameters (Adamany 1991, 5–33; Canon 1991, 435–66; McIntosh 1991, 281–301; Segal 1991, 373–93). Indeed, the civil rights lawyers, who led the NAACP Legal Defense Fund's legal assault on segregation apparently did not believe that court decisions alone would sweep away the regime of segregation.

A debate about the indirect effect of *Brown* can descend to competing subjectivities and selective sources. Rosenberg acknowledges that because civil rights activism, general changes in white views, and civil rights laws and enforcement occurred *after Brown*, that the case may have had an indirect effect. The question may indeed be methodological. But what is the correct gauge to measure the indirect effect of a landmark case? Is it the number of references in the *Readers' Guide* within five years, or is it a more sensitive reconstruction of inner histories? I suggest that Taylor Branch has it right about *Brown*: "The earth shook, and then again it did not" (1988, 112). Life went on. The case was not cited as often in the papers and textbooks as it was in later years. But the evidence strongly suggests that the decision made a seismic impact on the psyche of most African Americans and thus planted seeds of hope and revolt against segregation. For these psychic seeds to germinate, five to eight years is not a long time, given the overwhelming historic, psychological, and material obstacles that had to be overcome for action to even begin (1988, 124, 25).

Third Critique: Postmodernism

Richard Brisbin's (1993) article on First Amendment interpretation is written in a postmodern vein.[12] It may be the case that we live in a postmodern cultural world where image transcends text, where meaning is never fixed and is often contested, where the ludic and the playful outweigh the ponderous and pedantic, except in academic postmodernism (Jamieson 1991, 581; Milovanovic 1994, 67–97; Posner 1995, 317), a culture that is self-referential, decentered, and fragmented (Norton 1993). "Postmodernism in this sense is neither necessarily a good thing or a bad thing. It is a cultural moment that needs to be interpreted and understood" (Balkin 1992, 1968).

Richard Brisbin's postmodern First Amendment analysis moves beyond the strain of political science analysis, such as Rosenberg's, that examines the limits of court action. He borrows a vocabulary from Derrida and from a group of postmodern legal writers that have been powerfully influenced by the work of the late Robert Cover (Minow, Ryan, Sarat, eds., 1992; Sarat and Kearns, eds., 1992; Sarat and Kearns, eds., 1993). The clarion call of these writers is the gripping opening sentence of Cover's essay, 'Violence and the Word:' "Legal interpretation takes place in a field of pain and death" (Cover 1992, 203). On the basis of this catchphrase, Austin Sarat and Thomas Kearns sketch a "jurisprudence of violence" that, at some point, seems to argue that the consequences of legal action are so horrid that all traditional kinds of legal interpretations and analysis should be replaced by social analysis of the impact of legal acts (Sarat and Kearns 1992, 207). Inconsistently, their article does no such thing and is a highly polished jurisprudential discourse.

It seems to me that Cover's point is a useful corrective to those who play legal analytic games and forget the real-world consequences of law. But once this point is conceded, does it serve any useful purpose to stay fixated on the point that judges' sentences and opinions result in real prison sentences or death penalties? Brisbin looks to see how First Amendment opinions not only "open spaces of liberty" but also impose physical violence, symbolic violence, manipulative repression, and subjection. A liberal might argue that a conservative Supreme Court justice, placing order above liberty in virtually all cases, is more likely to repress. Brisbin, while not equating Scalia and Brennan, still finds Justice Brennan guilty of (gasp!)—administering law. Brennan's guilt seems to lie in the fact that law can "cut" (Brisbin 1993, 914). Brisbin picks this word from Derrida as if it imparts profound insight.

To know that law and legal choice creates winners and losers, that as the pie is cut some get slices and some get nothing, or very little slivers, is to know very little. This is an early lesson of political science scholarship on the judicial process, and social scientists have moved well beyond this basic point to elaborate it in many ways.

Much of Brisbin's article states the obvious in elevated and excited language. To know that a rejected First Amendment defense in a criminal case leads to prison and thus to the imposition of the physical violence of prisons is again to know very little. It does not help us decide whether the Court's decision to uphold a facially neutral drug statute over traditional Native American peyote use in a religious context (*Employment Division v. Smith* [494 U.S. 872 {1990}]) is a correct decision, to say that "Scalia would have placed their bodies in jeopardy" (Brisbin 1993, 916). Liberal judges of good conscience place the bodies of those convicted of murder or rape in jeopardy every time they sentence defendants to prison. That alone does not undermine the conceptual category of punishment, the legality of American prisons, or the legitimacy of the American polity, although it does alert us to the pains of imprisonment.

The weakness of Brisbin's attempt to apply a jurisprudence of violence to the First Amendment becomes exposed when he points out that Brennan, by imposing law on people, "exclude[s] certain forms of expression, like 'fighting words' or exhibitions of child pornography, from constitutional protection" (Brisbin 1993, 922). Child pornography? It is one thing to deal with the substantive issue head-on and to muster arguments of the Man-Boy Love Association, or cultural, psychological, and biological arguments about sexuality, to argue that laws designed to criminalize sex with children and to snuff out the commercial business of child pornography are bad laws. To chastise Justice Brennan for exercising legal discretion and legal power to uphold laws striking at "kiddie porn," however, is to say that the exercise of legal power (and therefore state power) for *any* end is inherently wrong.

A basic paradigm of law, politics, and criminal justice, so basic that it is rarely discussed in any depth, is that in many instances when state power and legal power is withdrawn, human predation, violence, humiliation, raw power, and despotism can and do flourish (Muir 1977; Haley 1991, 183–86). This has been a subtext of the movements to criminalize domestic violence, hate speech, and other forms of depredation formerly beyond the ken of organized social control. The law can be an instrument of liberation and safety. It all depends on its direction and details.

In his article, Brisbin seemed to be driving toward the truly anarchic impulse in this line of postmodern analysis. If law is violence and a mere cover for Leviathan—do away with Leviathan! But at the last moment, after castigating the law for imposing violence and repression, and stating that "the practice of rights is not a palliative for the many political pathologies of liberal regimes" (Brisbin 1993, 924), Brisbin pulls back and lets us know that the system of legal liberalism is better than all the rest.[13] It would be wise for those enamored of this approach to consider that Cover himself placed his own concern for violence in context, for after stating that "judges deal pain and death," he pauses to say, "That is not all they do. Perhaps that is not what they usually do," before moving on to elaborate his theme (Cover 1992, 213).

Brisbin's article goes to show that this stripe of postmodern analysis is gratuitous and adds little to a useful or a theoretically satisfying analysis of law and courts. An illuminating review of postmodern thought in criminology similarly concludes that while postmodern skepticism is a useful goad to forcing modernists to think through issues more carefully, it "does not provide any practical guidance on policy" because it eschews the modern-rational paradigm (Schwartz and Friedrichs 1994, 237), a point that is echoed by several other observers of postmodernism. Robert Weisberg ironically observes that postmodern scholarship has least to say about criminal law, which is "assigned perhaps the starkest, most riveting task of social regulation, [but] also suffers, justifiably, from an image of utter haplessness in the face of that assignment" in part because criminal law scholarship has not yet passed out of traditional analysis and into modern scholarship (1992, 524, 522). Even more relevant, J.M. Balkin, a leader in this area of thought, concludes that postmodern thinking has severe limits:

> Yet, when we view deconstruction and its purported enemy, logocentrism, in this light, we arrive at a paradoxical conclusion. Deconstruction, in and of itself, has nothing particular to tell us about justice, or ethics, or any questions of value. For any such conclusions we might reach would be by their nature ordering, prioritizing, evaluative—in a word, logocentric. Deconstruction thus becomes important to questions of value to the extent that it depends upon and nourishes itself upon some form of preexisting logocentric practice (Balkin 1993, 200–01; see also Racevskis 1993).

Examining the role and nature of law in a postmodern culture may, therefore, enhance understanding of the legal enterprise (Balkin, 1992). If, however, postmodern thought reflects a nihilistic, faux-romantic strain, it provides at best an opportunity to reexamine the limits of the Enlightenment model. Those who suggest that the Enlightenment paradigm has run its course,[14] have a moral obligation to consider how six billion people can be sustained on Earth without "Enlightenment" science, modern medicine, and agriculture.[15] Similarly, those who play with the idea of law as violence should soberly confront the anarchic implications of their notions and ask what a society without rights would mean to the lives of the most vulnerable (Racevskis 1993, 55–56).

Conclusion

The three studies examined jurisprudentially herein, although they differ in methodology, focus, and conclusions about the Supreme Court, seem to express a common mood that is fatally hostile to the law. Segal and Spaeth deny that what the justices say in their opinions can in any meaningful way be called law. In their view the Court and its justices exercise power based on personal preferences using the language of law to cloak domination. Rosenberg, at odds with Segal and Spaeth as to the Court's power, argues that the Supreme Court, perhaps like the English monarchy, is an irrelevancy, at least insofar as people look to it as a guarantor of rights or as a forum where political ends can be attained. The implication is that public law, at least, is dead, but no one seems to notice. Brisbin's juricide appears to acknowledge the validity of Segal and Spaeth's model (Brisbin 1993, 925, n.5), implying that the process of judicial analysis is irrelevant to the outcome. Brisbin adds a normative spin and hints that whatever a judge's attitude, liberal or conservative, the whole institution and process is rotten because law is violence and courts the purveyors of violence and repression. Although Brisbin tantalizes, by pulling back from the logic of his argument at the conclusion (perhaps confronted by the appalling reality of modern day dictatorships or anarchies), he ends with an inconsistent argument that the regime of liberal law is the worst system, except for all the rest.

My criticism of juricide—the implied jurisprudence of the three studies examined herein—rests on jurisprudential and consequentialist intuitions. The problem examined here is hardly a new one. At some point modern legal theories that draw on external sources of validity run into a juridical cul-de-sac. This problem has long been recognized as a bane of the legal realist movement of the 1920s and 1930s and seems to have run the critical legal studies movement into the same sandbar (Horowitz 1992, 169–268). G. Edward White succinctly speaks of "the destructive effects of Realism" in its attack on legal formalism, precipitating a new "legitimacy crisis. If the 'rules' of law were discredited, what was left except the arbitrary power of officials? How was law thus a cementing force in society, a repository of moral values or national beliefs? How, at another level, were certainty and predictability to be fostered by appellate judging?" (1976, 292–93). The historian Daniel Boorstin, demonstrates that the "legal immanence" of the Pennsylvania Quakers and the antebellum southern planter class led to social stagnation and political decline. He notes in contrast that "the written, technical, elaborated laws of the bibliolatrous New England Puritans—God-based though they were—proved far more flexible. . . ." and more politically successful (1971, 82). He fears that the trend to a sociolegal understanding will metastasize into a "tendency to find the immanence of the law in the supposedly inevitable tendencies of the society itself. . . . The great danger of the social-science emphasis in the training of lawyers, the great danger of finding the immanence of our law in the very processes of our society is that we should make law into a tautology." If a self-satisfied society defines itself as "good," then its laws, measured by itself, will be deprived of "the normative role which, in the common-law tradition, has made them a bulwark for each generation against the specious urgencies of its own age" (1971, 94–5). In response to the legal realist challenge, mainstream jurisprudence turned to the so-called legal process school. On the heels of this came the explosion of civil rights rulings by the Supreme Court in the 1960s and 1970s and the resurgence of property-dominated rulings today. Both the doctrinal lawyers and the jurisprudes are still trying to "clean up the mess" in a deluge of scholarship that all swirls around the legitimacy of the Court's manifest exercise of power. This has generated many new avenues of argument. To the extent that they lead to the conclusion that law as law does not exist (or may as well not exist), they will not play an important role in the public realm of the law. Were the mood of "juricide" to become a dominant mode, it would be unfortunate if the public law movement were to become inbred and theoretically irrelevant to larger legal and law and society currents. As I have argued above, the interpretive regime of law is "real," very much alive, and worthy of jurisprudential meta-analysis and standard subject matter analysis, infused with the insights and the research of the social sciences. This, I believe, expresses the mainstream view of law and society scholars.

In addition to these jurisprudential musings, I am motivated by consequentialist intuitions. Segal and Spaeth are important participants in the political science behaviorist movement. Their kind of empiricism has been interpreted as contributing to the fragmentation of political science and the withdrawal of traditional liberals from the normative tradition of political reform (Seidelman 1985). The established social science disciplines give evidence of having fragmented into subspecialties. Scholars more and more publish in specialized journals and are talking only to narrow coteries. Many empiricists of the center abandon normative issues to critics of the left or the right, and pay only lip service to a concern for policy or normative issues. This academic fragmentation occurs at a moment when the larger society is polarizing sharply, as indicated by the recent advance of right-wing politics supported by its own idea factories (Lapham 1995).

The eager, destructive energy that the authors discussed in this chapter have invested in their demolitions of law, if widely adopted, creates risks for a system of effective and humane rule in a fragmented academy and polarized society. Such studies have negative attractions that we are wise to avoid, or at least to place in a critical context. At their least destructive they lead to blind theoretical alleys and lost opportunities for meaningful research or law reform. Perhaps the "techy" fascination of Segal and Spaeth, Rosenberg's inability to see the Supreme Court's influence, and Brisbin's dalliance with postmodernism are intellectual fads or passages to a more substantial scholarship. But if they are harbingers of a crabbed empiricism or a disenchantment with a rationality-based social science, or effectively dispense with an operative sense of conventional morality, then I fear we deal with a problem of a different and more serious order.

This is not to argue against bold new lines of scholarship. Perhaps it is time, as postmodernists argue, to recognize the death of the liberal basis of the legal enterprise, and of its Enlightenment values of rationality, the search for truth, the advancement or the "privileging" of science, and the rule of law. I, for one, do not believe that these values are on death's door, nor do I believe that they should cease to be the prime organizing concepts of economic, political, social, and intellectual life. These large concepts are under pressure and compete with other world views. To the extent that critiques of modernism serve to correct erroneous or harmful tendencies within rational discourse they are essential to the rational and humanistic strain of modernism. And to the extent that other perspectives, such as the spiritual, speak to valid aspects of the human personality, they must be incorporated into the larger Enlightenment schema, under its principle of toleration.

Political scientists and law and society scholars can advance penetrating, critical, theoretically grounded, and useful studies of law and courts without getting sidetracked into "juricide." Too many important opportunities for theoretical and applied research exist to be trapped in the false science of Segal and Spaeth, the arrogant myopia of Rosenberg, or the turgid romanticism of Brisbin. To appreciate the reality of law in no way requires blind subservience to any particular rule, interpretive mode, or narrow political ideology. Such an appreciation enhances the most sophisticated scholarship, both quantitative and qualitative, that illuminates the judicial process; one that is grounded in social scientific *and* legal theory, and in a solid appreciation of the rational and valuable aspects of courts, and of the courts' regime of rule grounded in case and textual interpretation.

Notes

*An earlier version was read at a plenary session of the 1995 Academy of Criminal Justice Sciences annual meeting I wish to thank John Friedl, Richard Leo, Candace McCoy, Gerhard Mueller, Larry Siegel, Christopher Smith, and Susette Talarico for comments on earlier drafts. All infelicities, errors, and wrongheaded opinions are those of the author.

1. This statement is provisionally limited to societies in the western tradition. Law exists in East Asia, but its operation and social meaning is so different from western practice and connotation, that it is best excluded from consideration. See Haley 1991.

2. In this critique I focus only on the decision on the merits.

3. A substantial amount of biographical reportage on justices such as Brennan (Eisler 1993) and Frankfurter (Silverstein 1984) supports this thesis. Since little of this can be known at the time the justices are sitting, except through the close parsing of opinions and oral argument, and perhaps by the sort of illuminating reporting by highly skilled practitioners such as Linda Greenhouse of the *New York Times*, I suppose that this would show up in the error terms of statistical analyses.

4. Rehnquist, C.J., White, O'Connor, Scalia, Kennedy, Souter, and Thomas, JJ.

5. See the Voting Rights Act (1982) overriding *City of Mobile v. Colden* (446 U.S. 55 [1980]), cited in Eskridge and Frickey, 1994, 44; the Civil Rights Act of 1991 (U.S. Code vol. 42, secs. 2000e-2[k][1]) overruling five cases, including *Wards Cove Packing v. Atonio* (490 U.S. 642 [1989]), cited in Eskridge and Frickey, p. 38; and the Religious Freedom Restoration Act (1993), overruling *Employment Division v. Smith* (494 U.S. 872 [1990]).

6. It is possible that such enthusiasm has led to a flawed methodological critique of other analytic work, as it has led to a flawed appreciation of the Court's legal and institutional roles. See Mishler and Sheehan (1993). Compare Norpoth and Segal (1994) *to* Mishler and Sheehan (1994). A resolution of the analytic questions in this exchange must be left to methodologists.

7. Examples include: Roman Law's inventiveness supported a dynamic Empire (Wolff 1951); failure of Soviet regime to eliminate law under Marxist theory (Fuller 1976, 25–27); failure of Quakers and antebellum Southern plantation class to maintain rule based on notions of "indwelling" or unwritten law (Boorstin 1971); failure of American communities to resolve disputes by excluding law (Auerbach 1983); inevitability of judicial interpretation in code law system (Shapiro 1981, 126–156); Papal legal revolution and growth of Western centralized political power dependant on legal system (Berman 1983); chaos and incoherence of courts in the Third Reich (Müller 1991).

8   Peltason, in *Fifty-Eight Lonely Men*, made this point about the limits of court action before the advent of the 1960s civil rights legislation.

9   Lawyers were not blind to these facts. Jack Greenberg (1994, 201, 207, 401, 439, 456, 512–15), a leading civil rights lawyer, agrees with Rosenberg's point that mass behavioral changes did not occur until the 1960s and is sensitive to the limits of social and behavioral change that can be achieved by legal action. Astute lawyers are as aware of the political and institutional dynamics surrounding their areas of endeavor as are political scientists.

10 Rosenberg (1991, 108) hedges his conclusion as he must, and says: "even if I find little or no evidence of extra-judicial influence, it is simply impossible to state with certainty that the Court did not produce significant social reform in civil rights."

11 Any doubts about the incredible obstacles to successful action for African American rights before *Brown* are dispelled by Kluger (1977).

12 Although some postmodernists seem to take perverse delight in insisting that it cannot be defined, Richard Posner (1995, 315–18) has neatly described the various ways in which the term is used. He briefly skewers postmodern writing while keeping an open mind as to what may come (". . . though Balkin's article and the recent writings of Pierre Schlag and Stephen Winter hold promise of something better.").

13 "[T]he liberal practice of rights still affords some political space where the expression of some differences can occur. . . . [I]ronically, the practice of rights in liberal regimes promotes resistance-by factions, classes, and persons engaged in everyday choices-to the boundaries on liberty that are the political function of the practice. No other political arrangement, no other design for a regime, so effectively promises criticism of itself and attention to liberty" (Brisbin 1993, 925).

14 Schwartz and Friedrichs (1994, 238) are too quick to agree that "the essential justification of modernity—the opposition to the forces of feudalism—is long dead." If dealing the final blow to feudalism was the only rationale for the Enlightenment, it would long ago have withered. For example, two of the most important of the causes and products of modernity are a scientific approach to understanding the world and nonsecularism in the realm of government. Neither of these are necessarily reactions to feudalism. I am not convinced that the intellectual foundation of modern science has been undermined by postmodern thought (see Mootz 1993). I fear that those who wish to see modernity and all its products "disappear" might get their wish fulfilled by those who would be only to willing to unravel such modernistic products as secularism, human equality, individual rights, the rule of law, scientific autonomy, and the like.

15 Certainly, that these and related institutions and modes of life have caused contemporary problems. Yet, I think that solutions to the world's ecological and demographic crisis must be solved by the application of *more* rational

and scientific approaches (which encompass better understandings of how people respond to change). The alternative is a Malthusian "solution," signs of which are apparent in many places, which will be a "final solution" for many. See Kaplan (1994).

Works Cited

Adamany, David. 1991. "The Supreme Court." Pp. 5–33 in *The American Courts: A Critical Assessment*, ed. John B. Gates and Charles A. Johnson. Washington, D.C.: CQ Press.

Amsterdam, Anthony G. 1974. "Perspectives on the Fourth Amendment." *Minnesota Law Review* 58:349–447.

Auerbach, Jerold S. 1983. *Justice Without Law? Resolving Disputes Without Lawyers*. Oxford: Oxford University Press.

Balkin, J.M. 1992. "What Is A Postmodern Constitutionalism?" *Michigan Law Review* 90:1966–90.

———. 1993. "Tradition, Betrayal, and the Politics of Deconstruction. " Pp. 190-206 in *Contemporary Perspectives on Constitutional Interpretation*, ed. Susan J. Brison and Walter Sinnott-Armstrong. Boulder, CO: Westview Press.

Bass, Jack. 1993. *Taming the Storm: The Life and Times of Judge Frank M. Johnson, Jr. and the South's Fight over Civil Rights*. New York: Anchor Books/Doubleday.

Berman, Harold. 1983. *Law and Revolution: The Formation of the Western Legal Tradition*. Cambridge: Harvard University Press.

Boorstin, Daniel J. 1971. "The Perils of Indwelling Law." Pp. 75–97 in *The Rule of Law*, ed. Robert Paul Wolff. New York: Simon and Schuster.

Branch, Taylor. 1988. *Parting the Waters: America in the King Years 1954–63*. New York: Simon and Schuster.

Brisbin, Richard J., Jr. 1993. "Antonin Scalia, William Brennan, and the Politics of Expression: A Study of Legal Violence and Repression." *American Political Science Review* 87(4):912–27.

Canon, Bradley C. 1991. "Courts and Policy: Compliance, Implementation, and Impact." Pp. 435–66 in *The American Courts: A Critical Assessment*, ed. John B. Gates and Charles A. Johnson. Washington, D.C.: CQ Press.

Cardozo, Benjamin N. 1921. *The Nature of the Judicial Decision*. New Haven: Yale University Press.

Cover, Robert. 1992. "Violence and the Word." Pp. 203–238 in *Narrative, Violence and the Law,* ed. Martha Minow, Michael Ryan, and Austin Sarat. Ann Arbor: University of Michigan Press.

Davis, Michael D. and Hunter R. Clark. 1994. *Thurgood Marshall: Warrior at the Bar, Rebel on the Bench, Updated and Revised Edition*. New York: Citadel Press.

Dressler, Joshua. 1991. *Understanding Criminal Procedure.* New York: Matthew Bender.

Dworkin, R. B. 1973. "Fact Style Adjudication and the Fourth Amendment: The Limits of Lawyering." *Indiana Law Journal* 48:329-368.

Dworkin, Ronald. 1986. *Law's Empire.* Cambridge: Harvard University Press.

Eisler, Kim Isaac. 1993. *A Justice for All: William J. Brennan, Jr., and the Decisions that Transformed America.* New York: Simon & Schuster.

Epstein, Lee, ed. 1995. *Contemplating Courts.* Washington, D.C.: CQ Press.

Epstein, Lee and Joseph F. Kobylka. 1992. *The Supreme Court and Legal Change: Abortion and the Death Penalty.* Chapel Hill: University of North Carolina Press.

Eskridge, William N., Jr. and Philip P. Frickey. 1994. "Foreword: Law As Equilibrium." *Harvard Law Review* 108:27-108.

Fletcher, George P. 1978. *Rethinking Criminal Law.* Boston: Little, Brown.

Fuller, Lon L. 1976. *The Morality of Law: Revised Edition.* New Haven: Yale University Press.

Gates, John B. and Charles A. Johnson, eds. *The American Courts: A Critical Assessment.* Washington, D.C.: CQ Press.

George, Tracey E. and Lee Epstein. 1992. "On the Nature of Supreme Court Decision Making." *American Political Science Review* 86(2):323-37.

Glick, Henry R. 1983. *Courts, Politics and Justice.* New York: McGraw-Hill.

Greenberg, Jack. 1994. *Crusaders in the Courts: How A Dedicated Band of Lawyers Fought for the Civil Rights Revolution.* New York: Basic Books.

Haley, John Owen. 1991. *Authority Without Power: Law and the Japanese Paradox.* New York: Oxford University Press.

Hall, Jerome. 1960. *General Principles of Criminal Law,* 2d ed. Indianapolis, In: Bobbs-Merrill.

Holmes, Oliver W., Jr. [1881] 1963. *The Common Law.* (ed. Mark DeWolfe Howe). Boston: Little Brown.

Horowitz, Donald L. 1977. *The Courts and Social Policy.* Washington, D.C.: Brookings.

Horowitz, Morton J. 1992. *The Transformation of American Law, 1870-1960: The Crisis of Legal Orthodoxy.* New York: Oxford University Press.

Jamieson, Dale. 1991. "The Poverty of Postmodernist Theory." *University of Colorado Law Review* 62:577-95.

Kaplan, Robert D. 1994. "The Coming Anarchy," *The Atlantic Monthly* (February) 44-76.

Kirchheimer, Otto. [1961] 1980. *Political Justice: The Use of Legal Procedure for Political Ends*. Westport, Conn.: Greenwood Press.

Kluger, Richard. 1977. *Simple Justice*. London: Andre Deutsch.

Kurczewski, Jacek. 1993. *The Resurrection of Rights in Poland*. Oxford: Clarendon Press.

Lapham, Lewis H. 1995. "Reactionary Chic: How the Nineties Right Recycles the Bombast of the Sixties Left." *Harper's Magazine* (March):31-42.

Levi, Edward. 1949. *An Introduction to Legal Reasoning*. Chicago: University of Chicago Press.

McIntosh, Wayne V. 1991. "Courts and Socioeconomic Change." Pp. 281-301 in *The American Courts: A Critical Assessment*, ed. John B. Gates and Charles A. Johnson. Washington, D.C.: CQ Press.

Milovanovic, Dragan. 1994. "The Postmodernist Turn: Lacan, Psychoanalytic Semiotics, and the Construction of Subjectivity in Law." *Emory International Law Journal* 8:67-97.

Minow, Martha, Michael Ryan and Austin Sarat, eds. 1992. *Narrative, Violence, and the Law*. Ann Arbor: University of Michigan Press.

Mishler, William and Reginald S. Sheehan. 1993. "The Supreme Court As a Countermajoritarian Institution? The Impact of Public Opinion on Supreme Court Decisions." *American Political Science Review* 87(1):87-101.

Mishler, William and Reginald S. Sheehan. 1994. "Response: Popular Influence on Supreme Court Decisions." *American Political Science Review* 88(3): 716-24.

Mootz, Francis J., III. 1993. "Is the Rule of Law Possible in A Postmodern World." *Washington Law Review* 68:249-305.

Muir, William Ker. 1977. *Police: Streetcorner Politicians*. Chicago: University of Chicago Press.

Müller, Ingo. 1991. *Hitler's Justice: The Courts of the Third Reich*. (tr. Deborah Lucas Schneider). Cambridge: Harvard University Press.

Norpoth, Helmut and Jeffrey A. Segal. 1994. "Comment: Popular Influence on Supreme Court Decisions." *American Political Science Review* 88(3):711-16.

Norton, Anne. 1993. *Republic of Signs: Liberal Theory and American Popular Culture*. Chicago: University of Chicago Press.

Peltason, J. W. [1961] 1971. *Fifty-Eight Lonely Men: Southern Federal Judges and School Desegregation*. Urbana: University of Illinois Press.

Posner, Richard A. 1995. *Overcoming Law*. Cambridge: Harvard University Press.

Racevskis, Karlis. 1993. *Postmodernism and the Search for Enlightenment*. Charlottesville: University of Virginia Press.

Religious Freedom Restoration Act. 1993. 107 Stat. 1488; U.S. Code. Vol. 42, sec. 2000bb.

Rosenberg, Gerald N. 1991. *The Hollow Hope: Can Courts Bring About Social Change?* Chicago: University of Chicago Press.

Sarat, Austin and Thomas R. Kearns, eds. 1992. *Law's Violence*. Ann Arbor: University of Michigan Press.

―――. 1993. *The Fate of Law*. Ann Arbor: University of Michigan Press.

Sarat, Austin and Thomas R. Kearns. 1993. "A Journey Through Forgetting: Toward a Jurisprudence of Violence." Pp. 209-73 in *The Fate of Law*, ed. Austin Sarat and Thomas R. Kearns. Ann Arbor: University of Michigan Press.

Schwartz, Martin and David O. Friedrichs. 1994. "Postmodern Thought and Criminological Discontent: New Metaphors for Understanding Violence." *Criminology* 32(2):221-46.

Segal, Jeffrey. 1984. "Predicting Supreme Court Cases Probabilistically: The Search and Seizure Cases, 1962-1984." *American Political Science Review* 78: 891-900.

―――. 1986. "Supreme Court Justices as Human Decision Makers: An Individual-level Analysis of the Search and Seizure Cases." *Journal of Politics* 48: 938-55.

―――. 1991. "Courts, Executives, Legislatures." Pp. 373-93 in *The American Courts: A Critical Assessment*, ed. John B. Gates and Charles A. Johnson. Washington, D.C.: CQ Press.

Segal, Jeffrey A. and Harold J. Spaeth. 1993. *The Supreme Court and the Attitudinal Model*. New York: Cambridge University Press.

Seidelman, Raymond. 1985. *Disenchanted Realists: Political Science and the American Crisis, 1994-1984*. Albany: State University of New York Press.

Shapiro, Martin. 1981. *Courts: A Comparative and Political Analysis*. Chicago: University of Chicago Press.

Silverstein, Mark. 1984. *Constitutional Faiths: Felix Frankfurter, Hugo Black and the Process of Judicial Decision Making*. Ithaca: Cornell University Press.

Smith, Christopher. 1993. *Justice Antonin Scalia and the Supreme Court's Conservative Moment*. Westport, Conn.: Praeger.

Stumpf, Harry P. 1988. *American Judicial Politics*. San Diego: Harcourt Brace Jovanovich.

Voting Rights Act. 1982. Pub.L. 97-205 sec. 3, 96 Stat. 131.

Weisberg, Robert. 1992. "Criminal Law, Criminology, and the Small World of Legal Scholars." *University of Colorado Law Review* 63(3):521-68.

White, G. Edward. 1976. *The American Judicial Tradition: Profiles of Leading American Judges.* New York, Oxford University Press.

Wolff, Hans Julius. 1951. *Roman Law: An Historical Introduction.* Norman: University of Oklahoma Press.

Zalman, Marvin. 1996. "Book Review Essay: Civil Rights and Criminal Justice." *Journal of Criminal Justice Education* 7(1):177-98.

Chapter 8

Law and Political Struggles for Social Change: Puzzles, Paradoxes, and Promises in Future Research

Michael W. McCann

Introduction

The essays in this book evidence the expanding range of inquiry and debate regarding the ways in which law does and does not figure into struggles for social change. Because the authors of these other essays speak well for themselves, I will avoid the temptation to comment on or to respond directly to them. Nor is my primary concern to expand at length on the critical debates among advocates of different intellectual approaches to the subject that are featured in the previous pages. The general interpretive approach to the politics of "legal mobilization" that I embrace has been developed, illustrated, and defended at length in my writings published elsewhere (McCann 1994; McCann 1992a; McCann 1992b; McCann 1996a; McCann and March 1996).

My modest mission in this essay will focus instead on various "puzzles, paradoxes, and promises" in contemporary interpretive sociolegal research.. That is, I want to examine a variety of tensions, dilemmas, and challenges that interpretive researchers routinely confront in their studies. For some of these challenges I will offer examples of promising new research strategies or conceptual developments, while for others I can do little but begin to outline complexities that deserve consideration. In doing this, I inescapably will raise what could be construed as criticisms of work by myself and others. But my goal is less to identify deficiencies than to point out, or at least urge discussion about, new possibilities at stake in our projects. As such, this essay looks to past research mostly with an eye toward future endeavors. My aim is far more speculative and interrogatory than conclusive. And along the way the discussion will address some examples of very interesting recent work by other scholars, including some essays in this book.

What and Where is "Law"?

One of the major differences in social science analysis of law turns on whether the starting point (or unit of analysis) is "law" or some specific legal institution (such as appellate or trial courts) or specific types of elite legal officials (such as judges or lawyers). The study of courts—and especially of appellate courts, including the U.S. Supreme Court—has fairly well dominated the research agenda of political scientists in the public law subfield for decades. Among such scholars, there is a long-standing debate about how much law matters for the actions of judges and other participants in court proceedings. On the one hand, many scholars who focus on legal doctrine posit that legal norms and conventions greatly influence the cognitive processes, values, and, hence, behavior of judicial actors. But this influence is typically more assumed than conceptualized in complex terms or demonstrated through explicit empirical research exercises.

On the other hand, just as many scholars embrace the widely accepted premises of legal realism, and contend that legal norms have little effect on behavior. Indeed, the marriage of legal realism and behavioral social science has led much public law scholarship on courts to largely discount attention to law as norms, knowledges, and conventional practices (See McCann 1996a; McCann 1996b; Brigham and Harrington 1989; and essays by Paris, Schultz and Gottlieb, and Zalman in this volume). From this vantage point, law tends to be epiphenomenal; legal arguments are viewed as mostly post hoc rationalizations, tactical ploys of persuasion, or meaningless rituals. The focus of such empirical studies thus is on processes of cognition and behavior often obscured by esoteric legal argument, and hence on what judges (or other officials) "really do" rather than what they "merely say." At best, legal norms are viewed as outcomes, as dependent variables, with little independent power of their own to influence, to give structure and meaning to, social actors (whether elites such as judges or ordinary citizens). This view of law's diminutive causal stature is most evident in "attitudinal" studies of internal judicial decision making and, of greatest relevance to this essay, empirical studies of judicial "impact' on society.[1]

I have written previously about the curiously paradoxical results of the latter mainstream behavioral approaches (McCann 1996b). For one thing, such approaches purport to study a subject (law) that their own epistemology portrays as a mostly ephemeral and inconsequential ghost. Moreover, behavioral studies of law have borrowed heavily from social scientific conceptual frames and methodologies designed for study of mostly extrajudicial political phenomena. Such methods routinely have, in turn, justified the discounting of legal norms, knowldeges, and conventions in favor of other types of understandings. As a result, prevailing behavioral studies not only tend to support the view that law does not matter, but they remain highly dependent on and derivative of academic frameworks that include few conceptual and methodological tools fitting for their own juridical subject. The practices, relationships, and impacts of judicial institutions thus are predictably portrayed by such studies in ways virtually indistinguishable from those of other political institutions. In both senses, then, much behavioral study systematically downplays the distinctive character of law, legal action, and courts alike. That the study of public law—dominated by these twin traditions of formal doctrinal analysis and behavioralism/realism—remains a marginal academic project among political scientists thus is hardly surprising.

A third tradition, often labeled "interpretive sociolegal" research, provides an alternative to both of these approaches. Much of this scholarship is focused on study of courts and judges in sociohistorical framework; it is often identified within the framework of "new institutionalism (Smith 1996; see also Paris in this volume). Like some other essays in this book, my own research on legal mobilization in group struggles has largely worked within this alternative tradition of analysis. This approach is similar to formal doctrinal analysis in that it takes law seriously as a potentially influential, if variable, social force. And like positivist behavioral studies, it is committed to rigorous empirical study. But the differences among these approaches are many and significant.

My version of interpretive analysis disaggregates what we signify as "law" or "the legal" into three different but related senses—*official legal institutions*, such as courts or regulatory agencies; *official legal actors*, such as judges or lawyers; and *legal norms*, values, discourses, and knowledges manfiest in conventional practices.[2] When I write about "law" per se, it is primarily the latter phenomena to which I refer. And it is law in this sense—as norms, discourses, and conventional practices—that is the primary focus of my research. This does not mean that courts play little role in my stories of law and politics, only that they are not the center of analysis. Specifically, I am interested in how legal norms and practices at once shape (or prefigure) the terms of social relations, become (or do not become) mobilized to reshape social relations, and thus often (but not always) facilitate the construction of new meanings, relationships, and identities among subjects. In short, I am interested in the production, reproduction, and reconstruction of law in society and of society through law. As such, the study of "how law matters" for political activity requires attention to *both* behavior and meaning construction in social life, and to what goes on within courts as well as what goes on in organizational settings outside of (but interacting with) courts.

But What Is Law?

Sociolegal scholars like myself face some important conceptual problems in our quest, however. Our propensity to identify law as an inherently pluralistic, mutable, dynamic force permeating society—"law is all over," in Austin Sarat's (1990) memorable phrase—raises the question of just what we mean by, and how we identify, "law." In short, once we expand our understanding of law from determinate rules to indeterminate knowledges and conventions, and once we range beyond study of official legal institutions (courts and the like) and actors (judges) as sites of legal practice, how do we specify what counts as legal? How do we distinguish legal norms, conventions, and knowledges from other types of social conventions? And even when we are studying legal officials, how do we distinguish the uniquely legal aspects and influences in their actions? This question is important in a variety of ways. To take one specific example, scholars are often unclear as to whether the working premise that "law is all over" is a testable empirical generalization about the extent of law's causal influence or simply an evocative phrase that points to potential sites for interpretive legal research beyond courts. My own approach builds more from the latter perspective, although I am more convinced all the time about the former claim, at least in the contemporary United States. Yet most of us are relatively unclear or evasive on this point in our writings.

Our entire discussion about how law matters is confounded in similar ways. To the extent that our inquiry is about law's effects, whether narrowly or broadly construed, it is necessary to be as clear as we can about what does and does not count as law. This seems an important issue for those of us who tend to think that law matters more than realist-minded behavioralists often claim. If we want to demonstrate that legal norms figure prominently in political struggles for change, after all, then we ought to be explicit about how we identify "law" and separate it from other types of (extralegal or nonlegal) social phenomena. This is especially significant in that many of us want to argue that legal conventions can be mobilized for resistant or transformative purposes, that legal norms can be constructed in ways that diverge from and challenge official legal constructions, and that these norms can become manifest as forms of enforceable and often violent social power.[3] Although this conceptual challenge is quite fundamental, however, it has not received much attention from interpretive scholars, in part because it is so difficult to address. A quick consideration of several representative scholarly studies will illustrate some of the problems at stake and suggest a tentative position on the issue. Throughout the discussion, the key issue is how the relationships between law, society, and state are conceptualized.

Perhaps the most familiar way to address the problem is to stipulate some essential characteristics that categorically define "law" and distinguish legal norms from other social norms or forces. One of the more notable efforts to do this is Roberto Unger's classic tome *Law in Modern Society* (1976). His analysis identifies law most broadly as "any recurring mode of interaction among individuals and groups, together with the more or less explicit acknowledgment by these groups and individuals that such patterns of interaction produce reciprocal expectations of conduct that ought to be satisfied" (1976, 49). The great value of this approach is that it both encourages the study of legal norms in social interaction beyond official state institutions and facilitates recognition of quite different types of legal forms. Indeed, one of Unger's most important points is that law's specific forms vary with sociohistorical context. He thus distinguishes among "customary," "bureaucratic," and "modern rule of law" forms as ideal types.[4] The latter form captures what we in the United States and throughout the Western industrialized world have identified as essentially "legal" in nature. In this understanding modern liberal legal norms are distinguished by four specific traits: they are "public," "positive,' "general," and "autonomous." Unger's approach is especially instructive in its recognition of law's inherent plurality and relative independence from "the state" as both specific practical conventions and ideology.

But Unger's complex framework also illustrates the problem of categorical structural definitions. On the one hand, his general definition of "law" as an analytical category is so broad as to include many types of social practices and norms—customs, folkways, religious mores, and so on—that render the very concept itself of little practical value for contemporary studies of law's power and consequences. On the other hand, one of Unger's most insightful contentions is that legal practices in liberal western societies during the late twentieth century increasingly lack the fundamental traits of the familiar "rule of law" model. This development of increasingly indeterminate, particularistic legal forms of action entails both promises and dangers for social justice, he demonstrates. But more important to the discussion here is that postmodern legal forms are increasingly difficult to identify as conventionally "legal" in contemporary liberal capitalist societies. Law is alternatively everywhere and nowhere at once. For all of its analytical profundity and evocative challenge, therefore, Unger's grand scheme leaves us with inadequate conceptual terms for distinguishing among the different modes of legal and extralegal conventions in our society today.

Robert Cover's (1983) influential essay "Nomos and Narrative" is representative of another promising but problematic approach. Cover constructed the term "jurigenesis" to describe the fertile cultural processes of legal meaning-making that continually emanate from different communities and sites within society. As he portrays it, this process of creative legal production is radically unstable and destabilizing. In this sense, his vision of law falls firmly within the culturally oriented "legal pluralism" camp. Yet he boldly distinguishes this dynamic social process of proliferating legal traditions in society from forces within the official state committed to imperial control over, and containment of, legal construction. While law's meanings and forms are inherently indeterminate and plural in character, therefore, state officials work relentlessly to control and even to "kill" rivals to official state versions of authoritative law. Cover focuses in particular on the "jurispathic" role of courts in containing the ever-expanding processes of legal production.

Cover's vision is valuable in a host of ways. Its virtues include especially the emphasis on the contested and dynamic character of law, the insistence on linking law's discursive power to its inherently coercive and violent nature, and the recognition that courts rarely should be viewed as agents or even friends of egalitarian social change. But Cover's approach strikes me as unsatisfactory in the simplistic dichotomy that he draws between a pluralistic society of creative community legal traditions and a monolithic state united in its commitment to contain such legal creativity. After all, most states are complex institutions disaggregated into sectors with their own relatively autonomous traditions, conventions, and interests. To identify courts in particular as united in their jurispathic logic and bound to the singular interests and world views of other state actors seems rather simplistic. More to the point here, this framework helps little in providing a workable conception of "law." If the bulk of legal generation takes place independent of the state, how do we distinguish "law" from other social, ethical, and religious forms of normativity that sustain cultural interaction? Are the beliefs, codes, and conventions developed by each grouping without state sanction, and even often in defiance of state authorities, to be understood as law? What of the complex, dynamic interaction between, and fusing of, generically legal constructions and other social norms or traditions in actual practical life? Beyond the insightful analogy between religious and secular law drawn by Cover, for example, how can we distinguish between them as distinct forms of social practice and recognize their inherent interdependence? These are conceptual problems, I think, that many scholars attuned to legal pluralism have yet to address adequately.[5]

A different and arguably more successful approach has emerged from much recent scholarship addressing "law and everyday resistance."[6] The primary project uniting scholars who work in this tradition is to demonstrate how "ordinary" people are at once shaped by and mobilizers of the law, how legal meanings at once constitute and are constituted by routine social practices in many spheres of cultural life. In this view, citizens take part in giving meaning to law by their various resistances to official law and contests within legal arenas. This work is valuable precisely because it blurs the boundaries between state and society, and between citizens and official elites whose interactions constantly renegotiate the varied meanings of law. Barbara Yngvesson's book, *Virtuous Citizens, Disruptive Subjects* (1993), in particular demonstrates well how local courts are sites of legal contestation and construction among citizens in conflicts with one another and state officials. Neither courts nor law are outside of society, but rather both are defined in quite diverse ways by the manifold communities in which they are embedded.

Much of this scholarship is problematic as well, however. In particular, actions of individual citizens within courts or other official legal institutions receive the primary attention, thus ignoring legal "naming, blaming, claiming," and enforcing practices among subjects in various social contexts who never go to court. The ways that law shapes and is reshaped by relationships of citizens apart from direct intervolvement by courts or other state institutions—in neighborhoods, family homes, workplaces, schools, and so on—receives little attention. In short, while these studies treat courts and other official state legal institutions in a more complex way than does Cover's analysis, the latter's laudable attention to law's many manifestations and expressions outside of official arenas is not matched by most studies of everyday resistance. The resulting analyses of legal practice thus seem too closely tethered to official state arenas and actors, however "decentered" they may be in theory. The many faces of law *in* society—often in the "shadow" of official action but free from direct intervention—are slighted, as are law's variable relation to other types of extralegal norms, practices, and conventions.[7]

Yet another subtly different theoretical perspective is offered by Alan Hunt (1993, esp. chapters 12-13). His approach very clearly emphasizes the importance of distinguishing between law, or the legal system, and the state. As neo-Marxists long have put it, law is "relatively autonomous." In Hunt's words,

> "We should recognize the diversity of legal phenomena and avoid falling into the presumption of a unitary entity 'the Law,' while at the same time trying to give due recognition to the importance of both the state as a political agency and to state-law. . . . These spheres of diversification and of centralization exist in constant tension" (Hunt, 1993, 308).

In other words, Hunt recognizes the dual tendencies of legal generation and containment recognized by Cover, but locates neither primarily in state or society. Moreover, he is committed to viewing both state and society in the pluralistic terms specified by studies of everyday resistance, although he emphasizes the need for more study of the complex social contexts in which legal plurality is generated. His approach recognizes different aspects of law's plurality—as multiple traditions of governing legal conventions, as contested constructions of those legal conventions, and as interrelationships between legal and extralegal norms in social practice. Hunt avoids simplistic treatment of state, society, and law in part by reliance on Gramsci's notion of "hegemony"—those forms of discursive or ideological power which sustain the dominant terms of order throughout specific cultures (1993, ch. 10). But in all of this he stresses the need to accord atttention to law's "specificity," to its unique character as a force of governance that must be analyzed in discrete, non-self referential terms.

Hunt's framework still does not solve the problem of how we distinguish "the legal" from the extralegal or nonlegal, it is true. He neither applies his theoretical framework in a focused empirical study nor offers many clues about how to do so. Consequently, many routine issues of identifying law in practice are evaded. Nevertheless, I think that Hunt points in some useful directions. In short, his approach suggests that only those norms and discourses of "governance" that are at least generally authorized by state officials, and especially by judicial officials, should be designated as "legal" and treated as law. This does not mean that particular constructions of legal meaning must conform to official definition. But at least the general discursive terms and logics from which multiple legal meanings, constructions, and contests develop must be authorized by the state to be accorded the status of law.

For example, my *Rights at Work* (1994) focused on legal claims of women that drew on official antidiscrimination discourse but directly and resolutely challenged the particular constructions of judges, elected officials, and employers. Such a view recognized legal plurality, legal contestation, and counter-hegemonic legal action while attempting to distinguish uniquely "legal" factors from extralegal aspects of the social context, such as "technocratic norms (see ch. 6). As such, my study revealed law's power in animating social action and structuring (and restructuring) social relations within workplaces far removed from direct judicial intervention. Helena Silverstein's evocative *Unleashing Rights* (1996) pushes this type of analysis regarding the reconstruction and subversion of official legal norms even further by examining the development of animal rights discourses and advocacy tactics. Again, her analysis demonstrates the power of law outside as well as inside official legal forums. Yet, both studies also suggest that, for reasons noted above, many types of social norms, values, and discursive codes—including some authorized by state officials—should not be treated in many cases as "law" or "legal" forms of power.

Admittedly, this framework is far less precise than efforts to define law in some more mechanical, functional, or essentialist fashion. Many "hard cases" no doubt face researchers in distinguishing what types of practice should be counted as law, and in discerning how legal and extralegal forces are mutually constitutive in practical activity. It is important to recognize that the status of general norms and discursive logics as well as particular claims of entitlement often are in flux, thus either increasing or decreasing in the legal authority accorded them by various types of public officials. Moreover, the line between general social norms or discourses lacking state authorization and particularistic deviant, resistant, or even rebellious reconstructions of state-authorized legal norms often is unclear. Finally, the task of linking law's power as discursive meanings to its coercive, violent manifestations (either actual or threatened) remains a challenge that goes unfulfilled in many of our studies. But at least this emphasis on linking legal construction in society to official state authorization as law provides some guide to the enterprise of clarifying our research target. In any case, my point is less to insist on one best answer to this conceptual problem than just to highlight the problem itself. For empirical studies that stick close to courts or other official arenas, the challenge is usually less significant. Yet for those studies of how law figures into social conflict where there is little direct judicial involvement—and I do want to encourage more of such work—the issue looms larger.

A few scholars no doubt will find the concern itself to be fairly trivial, a mere matter of semantics. Others may see it as a topic best left to legal philosophers. My position holds, by contrast, that this is a critical issue that empirical sociolegal scholarship, whether positivist or postpositivist, should address directly. The imperative of conceptual clarity, coherence, and consistency in our analyses of how and how much law figures into political struggle renders attention to this issue obligatory.

Locating Law in Social Context

Beyond the above noted issues of defining and distinguishing "legal stuff," a challenge remains in assessing how much legal meanings and conventions "matter" relative to other social factors. This is especially important in that interpretive scholars tirelessly insist that law must be studied "in context" to understand its meaning, influence, and implications. Positivist scholars who focus on behavior often give similar attention to context as well, of course. They typically seek to ascertain the relative weights of various contingencies that interact with and influence law. This is achieved in judicial impact studies, for example, by investigating causal linkages between judicial decisions (the independent variables) and changes in targeted behaviors (the dependent variables) in various social settings. The promise of such approaches is parsimony and verifiability in assessing relative weights of different factors that shape behavior in different situations.[8] Yet such studies are limited, post- realist interpretivists point out, by their inability to account for the indeterminacy and plurality of legal conventions as well as for the constitutive, relational dimensions of law's power (see McCann 1996a).

At the same time, however, constitutive approaches have their own problems of specifying discrete causal significance. Consider just one basic paradox at the heart of many interpretivists' claims. The latter often proclaim that law must be studied in relation to its context, but they also routinely emphasize that law is itself part of, or is embedded in, the context of intersubjective social practice. This seeming conceptual paradox defines a significant challenge for efforts to design empirical studies capable of confident claims about how law does or does not matter in different settings. I have argued elsewhere that it misses the point to critique interpretive studies for failing to discern clear linear causal linkages among discrete factors, as that is not the project at stake for most of us (McCann 1996a). Our very goal of understanding law in more relational, interactive, and constitutive terms flies in the face of linear causal models.

But just what can interpretive scholars say about how and when law matters in different venues of social struggle among variously social groups? Most interpretive scholars—including several authors in this volume along with myself—point to the complexity, subtlety, and richness of their accounts of law in practice to answer skeptics (McCann 1996a; see also Paris, and Schultz and Gottlieb in this volume). The problems of disaggregating relevant factors in ways that facilitate conceptual generalization and comparative study remain a challenge for those of us who undertake interpretive work, however. Unfortunately, I have no easy solution for this problem except an appeal for theoretical clarity and attention to the need for developing well defined analytical frameworks that can be applied to different settings. Let me address several different aspects of this challenge that illustrate the problem and some possible responses.

I begin with a general conceptual issue. Interpretive scholars often distinguish between what are regarded as "instrumental" and (deeply) "constitutive" understandings of law's social power (Sarat and Kearns 1993). Instrumental approaches tend to view law as a resource independent of citizen agents and relationships that can, at least potentially, be wielded like a tool or weapon. Such approaches tend to focus on legal advocates' tactical uses of law and the various contextual factors that enhance or impede effective legal actions; such studies focus attention on loose causal connections among agent intentionality, behavior, and social effects. Postrealist studies that emphasize law's constitutive character, by contrast, focus far more on "the way everyday understandings, conventions, and assumptions structure legal thinking and practice," on how law is inherently so embedded in relations and practices as to be relatively unknown to citizen agents (1993, 10). The interpretive focus is on how law un-self-consciously prefigures social meaning and is reproduced or refigured in social action.

On the one hand, I think that this conceptual distinction is very important. No doubt legal scholars of all affiliations can enhance their work by explicit acknowledgment of reliance on these different logics of power in their work. On the other hand, however, I find the tendency of many interpretivists to reject instrumental analysis in favor of exclusively constitutive understandings to be a bit simplistic. For one thing, scholars who advance constitutive frameworks invariably load their studies with lots of instrumental analysis or claims, whether they recognize it or not. And there is good reason for this. As Helena Silverstein has argued, "the process of meaning making, highlighted by the constitutive perspective, is tied to instrumentalism" (1996, 215).[9] After all, law becomes meaningful through the practical engagement with legal norms, conventions, and tactics over time; while, conversely, it is the "taken for granted" status of legal knowledges that facilitates instrumental legal action by citizens. Just as avoidance of constitutive analysis of meaning strikes interpretive sociolegal scholars as limited, therefore, so is avoidance of direct, rigorous instrumental dimensions disingenuous and misleading. And if this is the case, it makes sense that interpretive studies should focus on both aspects of law's power, and employ conceptual tools and empirical methods appropriate to each logic. This was the general approach that I employed in *Rights at Work*, although my assumed project of merging instrumental and constitutive approaches was not explicitly theorized or integrated into the interpretive project.[10]

My other brief points follow from this premise. For one thing, it is just as important to distinguish conceptually among various modes of instrumental legal action as well as between uniquely "legal" tactics and other forms of political action. For example, *Rights at Work* disaggregated movement building dimensions of legal mobilization from other different types of legal action seeking to leverage concessions from opponents. In each case, the audience and character of the goal at stake was quite unique. Likewise, not only did the specific legal actions—invoking rights claims, threatening to file charges, actually filing charges, and so on—vary at different moments, but their relationship to other types of political activity—for example, different publicity efforts, financial resource development campaigns, direct legislative lobbying, etc.—varied as well. In making these connections, moreover, I was interested not only in the intentions and outcomes of my subjects' actions, but also in how these actions both expressed and altered legal meanings or consciousness among the subjects. My project did not attempt to specify in exact terms the relative significance of each tactic at every point of struggle. But specification of how different tactics interacted in multiple case study settings did permit some fairly strong claims about "context."

This same logic is operable for efforts to identify how various situational factors shape the potential for legal meaning construction and tactical action. I have borrowed heavily on sociologist Doug McAdam's (1982) "political process" model for mapping the complex terrain of political struggle. In this conceptual map, special attention is given to overall socioeconomic changes affecting disputants as well as to various elements of the specific *opportunity structure* and *resource base* available to the parties at different points in time. According to this scheme, law is targeted as both a series of discrete social factors independent of reform advocates and more generally as a constitutive force shaping these actors' very understandings, aspirations, inclinations, and imagined options. I am not eternally wedded to this specific model of contextual mapping, but it is my view that interpretive sociolegal work generally would benefit from generation of parallel analytical frameworks that can be applied to the study of law's workings in different settings. Again, theoretical clarity in the interpretive enterprise is the best way to provide a rigorous alternative to positivist studies of linear causal effects.

Finally, it is worth noting the challenge of directing analysis beyond identification of discrete contextual factors to what usually are labeled "structural" dimensions. Here I have in mind various critical traditions of conceptualizing broad patterns of hierarchical power relationships—class, race, gender, and so on—that permeate and structure social life. Much contemporary socio-legal research makes casually confident references to these modes of sociological analysis, to be sure, But the heavy attention to legal meanings, experience, and consciousness of individual subjects often obscures these types of analysis about patterns of relational power beyond individual influence and often beyond even their routine comprehension. As Carroll Seron and Frank Munger have recently written, "contemporary studies of law and society have sidestepped the capacity to explain the sources and significance of difference and inequality in terms that individuals themselves cannot employ" (1996, 208). This is especially important in that structural analysis facilitates broad generalization and comparative case study inquiry regarding the enduring legacies of inequality in society. When coupled with more poststructural attention to intersubjective knowledges and meanings, such structural analyses can generate important perspectives that transcend narrowly one-dimensional instrumental or constitutive approaches.

In all of these aspects of attention to "context," research methods should be chosen on the basis of their relevance to the conceptual mission at stake. Studies that emphasize law's constitutive meaning-making power are likely to draw heavily on qualitative methods, especially on in-depth interviews, in analyzing a small number of cases, to be sure. But other methods can be useful as well. For example, I (1994, chapter 3) and others have used simple time series graphs to demonstrate correlations between changing court rulings and shifting legal expectations or understandings among specific citizen populations. Christine Harrington and Daniel Ward (1993) have used far more extensive quantitative data to demonstrate that circuit courts, far from being passively reactive institutions, "produce" litigation by "signifying what is possible" to disputants and potential litigants. Such data can be very important parts of interpretive arguments about political experience. At the same time, both qualitative and quantitative methods can be used to show changing patterns of instrumental activity, such as filings of legal charges or threats of litigation. In short, just as interpretive scholars can benefit from mixing instrumental, constitutive, and structural understandings of law in/as context, so can methodological flexibility be a virtue as well for interpretive research.

Social Change, Political Struggle, and Identity

My inquiry so far has addressed issues of how we identify and analyze legal norms and practices in complex social relationships. I want to move now, finally, to consider the question of how we identify and assess law's specific role in generating "social change.' As noted earlier, several approaches have dominated how we researchers traditionally think about change. Many studies have examined the processes of change *within* courts and among judges at various levels, and especially at the appellate level.[11] Such studies tend to focus on whether advocates of particular causes win or lose in court; winning is assumed to be significant in itself. More attuned to my interest in social change and the themes of this book are the host of studies that have examined the "impact " or effects of judicial rulings on society. Such studies often begin with cases of more or less successful action in court, but aim to assess whether legal "victories" actually change official actions or social relationships in significant ways. Some of these studies, most notably by critical legal scholars, have focused attention on the ideological dimensions of judicial doctrine and the changing social meanings of law in society that they generate. Other behavioral studies have examined more narrowly the ways that judicial rulings do or don't affect citizen and official behavior, relying mostly on a variety of compliance-oriented indicators.

There is much merit to these studies, but interpretive sociolegal scholars tend to find them quite limited in scope. For one thing, the very focus on "change" is a bit misleading in much of this scholarship. After all, the primary thrust of most such studies is to show that little change at all results from seemingly transformative judicial rulings; the scholars conclude that law far more sustains status quo relations and hierarchies than poses effective challenges to them. This is true of both impact studies, such as Rosenberg's *The Hollow Hope,* and many critical legal studies essays. Moreover, equality-minded scholars should be at least as interested in how new legal doctrines, rulings, or statutes can be harmful for disadvantaged groups under study—for the poor, racial minorities, women, immigrants, and the like—and how such changes are resisted. Indeed, social movements and subaltern groups seeking to fend off new legal policies and practices imposed by dominant groups have been a very important dimension of political struggle in our nation's history. One need only think back to the battles opposing legal and other types of changes waged by Populist farmers and organized labor around the turn of the century or by minorities and women in the last decade to find important examples of such efforts to thwart imposed changes in legal imperatives. Such battles are about "change," it is true, but the achievement of change itself through law is hardly the standard of success that many scholars would seek.

Finally, these prior points call attention to the fact that every type of change itself also creates new forms of constraint; every transformation in relations creates new terms of order, often which ossify into new hierarchies, disadvantage, or injury for some peoples. Even what we identify as political "gains" or positive changes from legal reform action typically bring new unintended costs at they require investment of scarce resources, generate counter-mobilization by opponents, and reduce flexibility in "claiming" entitlements in other situations for variously situated subjects. For all of these reasons, therefore, I tend to identify my own general interests as focusing on "law and social struggle" rather than social change per se.

Beyond these general qualifications are the more subtle issues about just what we mean by "impacts," "effects," or "influence" and how we conceptualize useful indicators for them. The most common categorical distinction is drawn by legal scholars between "direct" and "indirect" effects (Handler 1978, Rosenberg 1991, McCann 1994). Direct effects are typically defined as those intended and achieved by the intervention of legal officials, most often judges or regulatory agents, in specific sites among contending parties. Such effects are often modeled in linear causal terms, although they surely need not be; indeed, more interactive, dialectical approaches are every bit as useful. Indirect effects, by contrast, refer to manifestations of legal meaning and action that are more diffuse and indeterminate in nature, often affecting relationships among variously situated subjects over time that were not directly targeted by the specific legal actors and actions under study.[12] This distinction was very important to my analysis in *Rights at Work*. It enabled me to show that, whereas much critical literature correctly contends that judicial victories often do not directly generate signficant degrees of desired change, legal mobilization tactics can in some cases generate many indirect effects (resources for constituent mobilization, leveraging of demands, and the like) that facilitate meaningful group struggle even in the absence of dramatic, lasting judicial victories.

These basic conceptual distinctions among effects are useful, but so are others less commonly found in the literature. One very important distinction regards the varied consequences of legal action for different types of targets. Charles Johnson and Bradley Canon (1984) made a very important, if too often overlooked, contribution by specifying different populations—variously referred to as the *interpreting, implementing, consumer*, and *secondary* populations—that may be affected by judicial actions. Their approach is primarily oriented to judicial policy implementation processes and behavioral responses, but it has potentially wide application for studies regarding how law figures interactively into social relations at multiple levels of conflict. Social movement scholars often parallel this approach in further emphasizing the distinction between outcomes of political action that involve primarily *internal movement relationships* and those *external relationships* between a movement and other (either opposing or third party) groups. One of the important insights gained by this distinction is that groups often generate a variety of changes in local associational dynamics—including development of solidarity and group identity, or new policy or ideological commitments, and of material resources—that are every bit as important as changes in the behavior or policies of targeted opponents. This is noteworthy in that it recognizes that atrophy of reform battles may signal reformer exhaustion as much as satisfaction with achievements, while expanding agendas of reform demands and escalating conflict might be viewed as significant indicators of "positive" gains. For example, I argued in *Rights at Work* (1994, chapter 7) that among the most important outcomes of legal mobilization activity were the increased psychological, associational, and material capacities of working women to wage new struggles on various workplace issues over time. Such outcomes were apparent even in cases where little success was achieved toward the initial reform goals of improving wages and job mobility opportunities for working women through legal action.

Another related distinction among studies, as noted above, is between those that tend to emphasize changes in *behavior* and those that emphasize changes in *meaning* construction, consciousness, or identity. The former often are privileged among social scientists because reliable quantifiable measures can be more successfully developed for behavioral indicators or material changes. And it is, after all, useful to know whether legal advocacy contributed to such things as new policies, new case law, changed enforcement or compliance patterns, and the like. But, at the same time, changes in both the general terms of political discourse among groups and more discrete changes in perception, understanding, attitudes, values, or commitments (often defined in terms of legal or rights "consciousness") of individuals within and beyond a specific target population can be important achievements of legal mobilization struggles that deserve analysis. Such attention to aspects of "meaning" and "identity" is at the heart of much intepretive scholarship regarding law's constitutive power. This is true especially for both "everyday resistance" and social movement studies that focus on "legal consciousness."[13] A fine example in this volume is Robert Van Dyke's study of pro-life abortion clinic blockade activists. As his fascinating study demonstrates, the individual processes of both joining and "exiting" from protest activities involve fundamental changes in personal understanding, expectatations, and association. Legally relevant action (including lawbreaking) among the subjects he studied was not the product of unitary selves calculating utilities from within a stable set of preferences and frames of reference. Rather, changing patterns of action are analyzed as a product of changes in how subjects constructed meaning through an evolving legal consciousness as well as a changing context of opportunities and costs.

Of course, as this latter example suggests, changes of these two sorts—in behavior and meaning—are often related. For example, much research suggests that groups with well defined collective identities and associational histories are easier to mobilize for concerted advocacy action that are relatively isolated, unfamiliar individuals (McCann 1994, ch. 4). Moreover, changed perceptions of problems generated by one conflict often can produce greater responsiveness (or resistance) from opponents or potential allies in subsequent struggles. But it is important to emphasize also that such relationships between changes in consciousness and behavior often are very complex and unpredictable. Actors may display similar behavior in response to alleged legal stimuli, after all, but the cognitive processes guiding those specific behaviors may be very different. These points recall again my earlier argument about the value of integrating instrumental and constitutive, meaning-oriented dimensions of study regarding legal practice.

In sum, my aim in these previous pages has been to emphasize that there are many valid ways to conceptualize the "effects' (or changes) of law in practice and many useful indicators that enable us to assess the character and degree of change that results from legal action. As a result, the task of assessing legal advocacy success or failure is always a very complex matter. Some social movement scholars thus have pressed for broad theoretical frameworks to structure such analyses across various contexts. My position agrees with this, but emphasizes that there is ample room for different frameworks, and it is the careful specification of basic concepts and theoretical frames that is most important. After all, no study can examine all the effects of legal action, or even all the important effects. As Oliver (1989, 5) writes of group struggle, "Each event in a social movement is like throwing a rock into a pond, creating ripples which eventually damp out and become imperceptible. We cannot possibly follow out all the direct and indirect effects of every action." It thus is critical to specify what types of effects one's research will examine and what specific indicators of those changes serve as evidence.

Moreover, for reasons outlined above, specification regarding how the "causal" dynamics of sociolegal relations are conceptualized should figure prominently. This is especially true for interpretive studies of legal meaning, consciousness, and relational practices, all of which are less easily conceptualized in linear causal terms. Such theoretical explicitness is important not only to provide analytical clarity and the possibility of comparative assessment among case studies but, equally important, to call attention to the limits of what any study can tell us about complex sociolegal phenomena. Finally, it is important to point out that the very focus on assessing legal actions and processes for their relative "success" or efficacy in generating change itself can divert attention from the complexities of how and how much law matters in social life more generally, which is the primary concern for many of us.

Having made the case for the importance of rigorous theoretical clarity, I want to examine briefly some different models of analysis adopted in various recent studies of socio-legal conflicts among groups. In particular, what interests me is the way in which these studies focus on specific groups of citizen subjects or relationships among groups, rather than on courts, judges, or other official entities, as the starting point and defining angle of analysis. This is important because no analysis can stand above and apart from its subject matter, surveying the whole of the reality at once. Rather, all the studies noted here assume, at least implicitly, some particularistic standpoint, some posture from where actions and their implications are viewed, interpreted, and assessed. Consequently, explicit attention to defining this interpretive angle is important to presenting a coherent and comprehensive analysis of how law matters in struggles for social position and power.[14] Three general approaches to studying groups in social conflict are outlined briefly below.

Legal Mobilization by Claimants

By far the most common, and perhaps obvious, starting point has been with the particular groups—whether a social movement, an interest group, a public interest law firm, or the like—seeking to mobilize law for their own ends, often in opposition to some more powerful organized group or popular majority. For example, I emphasized in *Rights at Work* the importance of decentering courts and focusing instead on group claimants such as unionized working women in my case studies who were attempting to restructure wage practices in and through the law. Well known studies of advocates for the physically and mentally disabled, for women's rights, for animal rights advocates, for children's rights, for the poor, and for environmental and consumer goods have adopted (more or less) this approach as well.[15]

Most studies of everyday disputing and legal "resistance" have similarly focused on small-scale actions by similarly situated individual subjects (rather than by organized groups) who solicit, defy, or subvert legal authority in courts and other arenas.[16] Finally, a narrower application of this general approach has entailed a focus on "cause lawyers."[17] The latter scholarship has zoomed in on the legal specialists—whether poverty lawyers, public interest lawyers, union lawyers, or radical lawyers—who have waged battles for various marginalized groups or causes. These studies are interesting because they often raise important questions about the ambiguous implications of legal professionalism as well as legal tactics for political struggle. In my view, this literature on cause lawyering has produced a broad array of particularly valuable scholarly arguments and evidence about the promises and limitations of legal advocacy for social justice.

There are many virtues in this general claimant-oriented approach to studying law in political struggle. In particular, by focusing on groups (and individuals) in conflict, the actual aims, understandings, and calculations of subjects seeking to mobilize law on their own behalf can be addressed in complex, empirically substantiated ways. This is important, in that many behavioral and game theoretic approaches to judicial impact take advocates' preferences for granted, assuming that their goals are relatively fixed, constant, and unitary, and self evident.[18] Much interpretive study of individual and group conflict has demonstrated, by contrast, that the aims of disputants tend to be volatile, complex, and multiple. Advocacy "often hinges on changing interests, changing opportunities and threats to interests, and changing inclinations to act on group interests" (Fireman and Gamson, 1979, 8). Again, sensitivity to such complexity in consciousness is critical to assessments of both instrumental legal 'effectiveness" and the more "constitutive" dimensions of law's meanings.

Some important distinctions among group aspirations and strategies thus are worth noting here. At a general level, we can identify at least four relational strategies that animate groups. One type of political goal is *integrationist*. In this scenario, legal advocates and claimants typically begin from a position of marginalization or exclusion; their campaigns aim to achieve a greater degree of inclusion, recognition, and power within dominant social institutions or relations. The civil rights movement in the United States and its resort to courts to authorize "equal protection" as an antidote to racial segregation is perhaps the most obvious example of this type of struggle. A second type of strategy is *transformational*. Such aspirations are most typical of groups already well integrated and positioned in society but who are desirous of changes in basic values, policies, or relations within that society. The environmental movement, which in the U.S. has relied heavily on legal tactics since the 1960s, is a good example of this movement motivation. Another example is provided by Kevin O'Brien's (1996) analysis of "rightful resisters" in China who have sought to expand and enforce existing entitlements of the central government against local elites. Of course, many struggles—against apartheid in South Africa and for feminism in many cultures—involve a mix of both integrationist and transformational designs.

A third type of legal claiming activity seeks *autonomy* for specific subjects from the dominant culture rather than fuller inclusion in it. Segregationists in the South during the 1950s and religious groups such as the Amish have sought such a goal in the United States. Many stories of everyday "resistance" by poor or otherwise marginalized citizens also fit to some degree this profile of struggles to assert dignity, to define identity, or just to achieve material survival in spaces relatively free from the imperious control of dominant groups or their official representatives. Finally, some types of legal activity are more concerned with *destabilizing* or unsettling values, representations, and relations in dominant society than achieving any binding alternative set of policies, values, or identities. A good example is Lisa Bower's (1997) very interesting research on the politics of "direct action" by gays and lesbians, who have used legal and other tactics to destabilize prevailing categories of law and morality ("official recognition") in ways that might increase sensitivity to the diverse self-identifications of citizen subjects. Again, such destabilizing aspirations often go hand in hand with other aspirations noted above in actual political struggles.[19]

Claimant-oriented studies hold the promise of identifying the complex, diverse legal *tactics* of advocates well as their variable, often changing goals. After all, both choices of specific legal tactics and the particular aims of those legal tactics tend to vary with particular situations. As I demonstrated in *Rights at Work* (1994), legal actions such as litigation often aim not to secure a final affirmative judgment from judicial offices so much as to leverage concessions from opponents; the appropriate measure of success thus might be whether a dispute was settled favorably without a full trial hearing. In similar fashion, formal legal action in courts might aim as much for publicity to build support from constituents or third parties. And the specific aims and choices of legal action often depend on the resources, alternative tactics, and experiences available to political actors at any particular time. Again, because attention to both overall advocacy goals and specific tactics are important to assessing the outcomes and effectiveness of legal actions, study of legal claimants is a promising strategy of research.

But claimant-oriented approaches are limited in various ways as well. For one thing, studies of legal mobilization activity have been overwhelmingly directed to marginalized, exploited, resource-poor groups. Far less attention has been devoted to more powerful organized actors such as business, trade, and religious organizations whose "everyday" legal practices and resistances often produce very important types of social change. Moreover, the focus on legal mobilizers tends to privilege more "instrumental" types of analysis highlighting intentional action and concrete outcomes over more "relational" and "constitutive" types of analysis. In particular, legal mobilization studies often fall short in giving due attention to the influence of law over time in shaping the context in which disputes emerge, in narrowing practical substantive options in the development of disputes, and in reshaping ongoing relations and identity formation *among* disputants. In part, the result is that the "before" and "after" of specific conflicts or advocacy actions tend to get short shrift. More important, as discussed earlier, "instrumental" modes of analysis often discount or overshadow attention to structural and "constitutive" modes of analysis regarding meaning.

In *Rights at Work*, I attempted to develop a four stage temporal model to overcome this problem. However, my study still gave greater attention to the more instrumental aspects of legal mobilization than to the ways that law constructed the intersubjective terrain in which relationships developed over time. David Engel and Frank Munger have responded to this limitation by attempting more comprehensive biographical studies of legal subjects struggling to deal with disabilities through various forms of rights claiming. By "looking through a longer lens" at life stories, the authors document in vivid fashion "the shifting, changing role of rights in individual lives" (1996, 47). My present research regarding legal mobilization efforts of Alaskan cannery workers similarly is attempting to examine how changing terms of official law over a sixty year period have shaped changing intragroup dynamics, collective political strategies, and group identities within a single local union organization (McCann, research in progress). Specifically, this historical and biographical case study will demonstrate that NLRB legal doctrines encouraged more class-oriented forms of advocacy and worker identity among union workers in the 1930s–40s, while the elevation of civil rights remedies in the late 1960s provided incentives for new types of race/ethinicity-oriented worker organization, advocacy, and legal action in the last several decades.

It is worth noting the tradeoffs in such studies as well, however. In short, efforts to recapture a deeper, more nuanced history of conflict and identity construction also come at the cost of narrowing the range of actors or groups that can be addressed in any one study. As a result, theoretical generalization and comparative study tend to become more unwieldy and limited. In my developing study of cannery workers, therefore, I am relying on additional quantitative data and case studies by others to provide a basis for theorizing more widely about how law shapes social practice generally and how law has shaped changing union politics in particular over long periods of time. I will show that union commitments to organizing minority and female workers generally in the United States have changed dramatically over the last half century largely because of various opportunities and constraints created by federal law. As such, this work will again demonstrate the value of drawing on multiple methods for studying the complexities of law. John Brigham's (1997) fascinating study of how the "intrests" of four different social movements have been differently constituted in relation to law provides yet another excellent model for comparative theoretical development.

Dominant Group Resistance to Legal Change

While studies of marginal or plaintiff group advocacy are most numerous, other types of studies are worth attention as well. A second less common but very promising approach focuses on the flip side of many disputes—e.g., on those dominant interests or majoritarian groups who oppose change waged by others through legal mobilization efforts. A recent outstanding example of this approach is *Law and Community in Three American Towns* by Carol J. Greenhouse, Barbara Yngvesson, and David M. Engel (1994). This marvelous book builds on three independent case studies by the authors regarding how denizens of different small suburban communities view law, rights, litigation, and legal mobilizers in periods of substantial socioeconomic transition. One interesting dimension of these studies is that the actions of the alleged agents of change—mostly lower-class, ethnically and racially diverse "outsiders" who recently have moved into the communities—are not collectively organized or political in aim, and actually receive little direct attention from the authors at all. Rather, each author directs attention primarily to how "insiders" view their respective communities and blame their "decline" of the excessive rights claiming, adversarialism, and litigiousness of the newcomers and outsiders. As such, efforts to preserve traditional community values and ways of life are linked to the enforcement of norms that devalue certain ways of "legalizing" relationships. The authors' intriguing accounts of disputing incidents provide a very rich analysis into the dynamics of how law and legal practices figure into the development of "community" attachments, group conflict, and strategies by dominant elites for preserving traditional hierarchies.[20]

The work described above provides an excellent model for future inquiries into law and social conflict or change. The authors not only use an impressive array of ethnographic methods in constructing their case studies, but they employ a self-conscious comparative approach that strives for rich theoretical generalization and broad application to other group contexts. Yet this type of approach is limited in important ways as well. Most obviously, the study examines the actual legal practices of "outsiders" only through the suspicious, defensive, often hostile perspectives of dominant community groups. Important questions about the relationship between newcomers' practices, social change, and increased formal legal action thus remain unanswered. Moreover, arguments late in the book regarding hierarchical stratification and conflicts among traditional "insider" groups are left underdeveloped and overshadowed by attention to the larger conflict with outsiders entering the community. But, overall, this conflict-oriented, "insider" or dominant-group standpoint is a very promising template for studies of law, political struggle, and social change in workplaces, neighborhoods, families, communities, and the like.

Toward Relational Complexity

The two approaches examined above begin from assumptions about dyadic conflict, where one party (an individual, group, or coalition) is trying to wrest concessions from another identifiable party that is resisting change. Hence we find stories of battles between employers and employees, African Americans and whites, women and men, the poor and government administrators, community insiders and outsiders, antagonistic neighbors, and so forth.

But framing conflict in dyadic or bilateral terms—especially involving superordinate and subordinate, dominant and resistant, groups—can be highly misleading or narrowing to our understandings. Commonly, conflict involves many more than two groups, whether pitting several internally diverse coalitions and alliances against each other or just involving multiple differently situated actors. Indeed, various "third parties" in government or patron groups often are critical players in political struggles (Walker 1986). Moreover, both dominant and subaltern groups of actors may become divided among themselves in discrete conflicts. For example, many battles for political reform or social change have involved subordinate groups finding allies in one sector of the state while waging battle against other sectors. The classic struggle of civil rights groups, who enlisted first federal courts and eventually federal executive and legislative officials, against recalcitrant southern state officials committed to segregation is just one prominent example of this complexity. Indeed, as I attempted to demonstrate in *Rights at Work*, much political conflict involves efforts by marginalized or disadvantaged groups to turn some dominant norms against others, or some dominant groups and institutions against other powerful actors. Kevin J. O'Brien highlights these complexities of what he calls "rightful resistance" by Chinese dissidents. "Rightful resisters know full well that instruments of domination which facilitate control can be turned to new purposes; they have an aspirational view of government measures and elite values and recognize that the very symbols embraced by those in power can be a source of entitlement, inclusion, and empowerment" (1996, 33).[21]

In all these cases, identifying a standpoint of analysis within a volatile political situation is important. It requires not only a complex understanding of law, state, and variously situated social groupings, but also a careful, complex specification of hegemonic social power and hierarchy that is not reducible to specific actors. Indeed, the resort to conceptions of structural analysis that transcend instrumental attention to specific actors is valuable in complicated conflicts of this sort. For example, invocations of Antonio Gramsci's concept of shifting "wars of position" among different actors contesting "hegemony" are common among students of social struggle (1971, esp. 229-239). Such approaches attempt to establish some analytical base line of understanding change and the constraints of change at a more systemic level apart from the aspirations and interactions of discrete actors. After all, sometimes group struggle produces immediate, proximate changes with little lasting or widespread impact for broader social relations, while some group struggles produce only modest immediate group benefits but set in motion changes in more fundamental relations. Beginning with conceptions of structural stratification and hegemony that transcend specific group viewpoints thus can produce important types of research, whether as additions or alternatives to discrete actor-centered studies.[22]

Conclusion

This essay has attempted to identify a host of questions, challenges, and tensions that confront interpretive studies of law and social struggle. If an underlying theme connects my ruminations and queries, it is that theoretical clarity and sophistication are important to do justice to the vast complexity of the subject matter that we study. Precisely because our analytical categories of law, society, state, context, change, and the like can be so variously constructed with good result, we must labor to be as clear as possible about just what we mean by the specific intellectual constructs that inform our studies. Moreover, while I am reluctant to impose my research design on others, it seems to me that interpretive studies of law and social conflict would benefit greatly from more comparative development. This could include comparative work of many types—including comparison among legal practices within different polities, among different settings within polities, among different policy issues and constitutent groups, and among different experiences in different time periods. Such comparative approaches, in my view, provide both demand and foundation for the type of analytical theorizing that has been urged in this essay. And it is quite exciting to see just this trend developing in much recent interpretive socio-legal scholarship outlined in this volume and beyond in the field.[23]

Notes

1. Discussions of various "realist" analyses can be found in essays listed in the preceding citation; Postivist approaches that take a more complex view of law's influence include Epstein and Kobylka (1992).

2. See McCann (1994), My distinction borrows in part from Thompson (1975).

3. On legal pluralism, see Merry (1988). Merry's essay covers much theoretical ground, in light of an extensive literature review, that is relevant to the questions that I raise here.

4. Unger's analysis also posits two potential directions of postliberal, postmodern legal development.

5. This points to some confusion in much discussion of "legal pluralism" literature. It is important to distinguish among different aspects of plurality, including: 1) mutiple official legal traditions that coexist in a particular polity; 2) multiple constructions of specific legal conventions, codes, or discources within the prevailing official legal order(s); 3) the plurality of normative ordering forms, both legal and extralegal, in a society.

6. For a review of works in this tradition, see McCann and March (1996).

7. One exception is Greenhouse, Engel, and Yngvesson (1994). This wonderful book makes more strides toward addressing the linkages of legal and extral legal norms in very helpful ways.

8. Gerald Rosenberg's wellknown book, *The Hollow Hope* (1991), is the best example of this work.

9. This is a central argument of this wonderfully imaginative book.

10. Robert Van Dyk's excellent article in this volume develops this point nicely. My book in progress on legal mobilization by Alaskan cannery workers over the last half century (*Law and Labor at the Margins*) will theorize in more explicit terms this relationship between instrumental and constitutive understandings.

11. Two excellent examples are Lawrence, 1990, and Epstein and Kobylka, 1992.

12. The best argument that I know of on this subject is Galanter (1983); 117–142, See also McCann (1996a).

13. For a review, see McCann and March (1996).

14. This call for consistency and explicitness in defining an angle of vision or perspective on events is not inconsistent with the call for methodological pluralism outlined above. One can use multiple tools of seeing and measuring events even while standing in one place, after all. My argument also does not

diminish the value of trying to study events from multiple angles—e.g., the perspectives of different actors in a conflict—but the challenges in achieving conceptual clarity and cooperation from antagonistic subjects implied by such approaches are significant, and beyond my concern in this essay.

15 The position is generally adopted by well known general works, such as Scheingold (1974); Handler (1978); Rosenberg (1991). Detailed case studies also include: Olson (1984); Milner (1986); 105–129; Silverstein (1996); McCann (1986). Most of the essays in this volume, including especially the empirical cases studied by Michael Paris, likewise fit this general profile.

16 For review, see McCann and March (1996).

17 A leading collection is Sarat and Scheingold, eds. (1997).

18 See, for example McCann (1992b) and the essay by Van Dyk in this volume. On the importance of linking the study of outcomes and effects to changing advocacy intentions and goals, see Pitkin (1972).

19 Cutting across these four types of reform goals is another distinction between what we might label "identity politics" and "redistributive politics." This distinction is very important, but it opens up complexities that are beyond the scope of this essay.

20 Robert Van Dyk's essay in this volume presents a different variant on this approach. While the role of pro-choice legal mobilization tactics in federal courts are prominently featured, his primary interest is in the actions and reactions among pro-life abortion clinic blockaders, whose actions, consciousness, and identity change notably over time.

21 This is an excellent example of a study employing the legal mobilization framework for anlayzing non-US cases.

22 E.P. Thompson's classic *Whigs and Hunters* (1975) provides a classic model of legal analysis pushing in these directions. See also Seron and Munger (1996) and Hunt (1993) for further discussion.

23 One of the strengths of Rosenberg's *Hollow Hope* is that he examines several different policy areas from a basic conceptual framework, even though the comparative assessments of these different studies is not developed very far. Brigham's *The Constitution of Interests* (1997) offers multiple case studies in a comparative conceptual framework. The study by Michael Paris in this volume also contrasts two different case studies.

Works Cited

Bower, Lisa. 1997 (forthcoming). "Queer Problems/Straight Solutions: The Limits of a Politics of 'Official Recognition." in *Playing with Fire: Queer Theories/Queer Politics* ed. Shane Phelan. New York: Routledge.

Brigham, John. 1997. *The Constitution of Interests: Beyond the Politics of Rights.* New York: New York University Press.

Brigham, John and Harrington, Christine. 1989. "Realism and its Consequences: An Inquiry into Contemporary Sociolegal Research," *International Journal of the Sociology of Law* 17: 41–62.

Cover, Robert M. 1983. "Nomos and Narrative" ("Forward: The Supreme Court 1982 Term"), *Harvard Law Review* 97: 2–68.

Engel, David M and Frank W. Munger. 1996. "Rights, Remembrance, and the Reconciliation of Difference." *Law and Society Review* 30:47.

Epstein, Lee and Kobylka, Joseph. 1992. *The Supreme Court and Legal Change: Abortion and the Death Penalty.* Chapel Hill: University of North Carolina Press.

Fireman, Bruce and William A. Gamson. 1979. "Utilitarian Logic in the Resource Mobilization Perspective." P.8 in *The Dynamics of Social Movements,* ed. Mayer Zald and John McCarthy. Cambridge, MA: Winthrop Publishers.

Galanter, Marc. 1983. "The Radiating Effects of Courts." Pp. 117–42 in *Empirical Theories of Courts,* ed. Keith O. Poyum and Lynn Mather. New York: Longman.

Gramsci, Antonio. 1971. *Selections from the Prison Notebooks..* ed. Quintin Hoare and Geoffery Nowell Smith. New York: International Publishers.

Greenhouse, Carol David Engel, and Barbara Yngvesson. 1994. *Law and Community in Three American Towns* . Ithaca: Cornell University Press.

Handler, Joel. 1978. *Social Movements and the Legal System: A Theory of Law Reform and Social Change* . New York: Academic Press.

Harrington, Christine B. and Daniel Ward. 1993. Rethinking Litigation: The Role of Courts in Producing Litigation. Paper presented at the annual meetings of the American Political Science Association, Washington, D.C.

Hunt, Alan. 1993. *Explorations in Law and Society: Toward a Constitutive Theory of Law.* New York: Routledge, 1993.

Johnson, Charles A. and Bradley C. Canon. 1984. *Judicial Policies: Implementation and Impact* . Washington, D.C.: Congressional Quarterly Press.

Lawrence, Susan. 1990. *The Poor in Court: The Legal Services Program and Supreme Court Decision Making.*. Princeton: Princeton University Press.

McAdam, Doug. 1982. *Political Process and the Development of Black Insurgency, 1930–1970* . Chicago: University of Chicago Press.

McCann, Michael W. 1986. *Taking Reform Seriously: Critical Perspectives on Public Interest Liberalism* . Ithaca, N.Y.: Cornell University Press.

―――. 1994. *Rights at Work: Pay Equity Reform and the Politics of Legal Mobilization.* Chicago: University of Chicago Press.

―――. 1992a. "Resistance, Reconstruction, and Romance in Legal Scholarship," *Law & Society Review* 26: 733–750.

―――. 1992b. " Reform Litigation on Trial," *Law and Social Inquiry* 17:715–743.

―――. 1996a. "Causal vs. Constitutive Explanations: Or, 'On the Difficulty of Being So Positive,'" *Law and Social Inquiry* 21:435–482.

―――. 1996b. "It's Only Law and Courts But I Like It," *Law and Courts.* (Spring, 1996).

―――, and Tracey March. 1996. "Law and Everyday Forms of Resistance: A Socio-Political Assessment," *Studies in Law, Politics, and Society* 15: 207–236 .

Merry, Sally Engle. 1988. "Legal Pluralism." *Law and Society Review* 22:868–896.

Milner, Neal. 1986. "The Dilemmas of Legal Mobilization: Ideologies and Strategies of Mental Patient Liberation," *Law & Policy* 8:105–129.

O'Brien, Kevin J. 1996. "Rightful Resistance." *World Politics* 49:31–55.

Oliver, Pamela E. 1989. "Bringing the Crowd Back In: The Non-Organizational Elements of Social Movements," *Research in Social Movements, Conflict, and Change* 11:5.

Olson, Susan M. 1984. *Clients and Lawyers: Securing the Rights of Disabled Persons* . Westport, Conn.: Greenwood Press.

Pitkin, Hanna F. 1972. *Wittgenstein and Justice.*. Berkeley: University of California Press.

Rosenberg, Gerald. 1991. *The Hollow Hope: Can Courts Bring About Social Change?* Chicago: University of Chicago Press.

Sarat, Austin. 1990. "'. . .The Law is All Over:' Power, Resistance and the Legal Consciousness of the Welfare Poor." *Yale Journal of Law and the Humanities* 2:1663–1709.

Sarat, Austin and Thomas R. Kearns. 1993. "Beyond the Great Divide: Forms of Legal Scholarship and Everyday Life." Pp. 21–62, in *Law in Everyday Life,* ed. Austin Sarat and Thomas R. Kearns. Ann Arbor: University of Michigan Press.

Sarat, Austin and Thomas R. Kearns. 1993. "Editorial Introduction." Pp. 1–20, in *Law in Everyday Life*, ed. Austin Sarat and Thomas R. Kearns. Ann Arbor: University of Michigan Press.

Sarat, Austin and Stuart A. Scheingold, eds. 1997 (forthcoming). *Cause Lawyering: Political Commitments and Professional Responsibilities*. Oxford Universty Press.

Scheingold, Stuart A. 1974. *The Politics of Rights: Lawyers, Public Policy, and Political Change*. New Haven: Yale University Press.

Seron, Carroll and Frank Munger. 1996. "Law and Inequality: Race, Gender . . . and, of Course, Class." *Annual Review of Sociology* 22:208.

Silverstein, Helena. 1996.*Unleashing Rights: Law, Meaning, and the Animal Rights Movementt*. Ann Arbor: University of Michigan Press.

Smith, Rogers M. 1986. "Political Jurisprudence, the 'New Institutionalism,' and the Future of Public Law," American Political Science Review 78:734–749.

Thompson, E.P. 1975. *Whigs and Hunters: The Origin of the Black Act*. New York: Pantheon.

Unger, Roberto . 1976. *Law in Modern Society: Toward a Criticism of Social Theory*. New York: The Free Press.

Walker, Jack . 1986. "The Origins and Maintenance of Interest Groups in America." *American Political Science Review* 77:390–406.

Yngvesson, Barbara. 1993. *Virtuous Citizens, Disruptive Subjects: Order and Complain in a New England Court* . New York: Routledge.

About the Authors

David A. Schultz teaches political science at the University of Wisconsin River Falls. He is the author of numerous articles on Justice Scalia as well as *The Jurisprudential Vision of Justice Antonin Scalia* (1996). He has published widely on land use, regulatory takings, and eminent domain; First Amendment free speech and religious freedoms; discrimination law; plant closings; and on assorted topics in legal history and judicial politics. Schultz's writings have appeared in the *American Journal of Legal History, Suffolk Law Review, Journal of Employee Ownership Law and Finance, Nichols on Eminent Domain*, and in many other law reviews. He is also the author of several books, including *Law and Politics: Unanswered Questions* (1994), *Property, Power, and American Democracy* (1992), and *The Politics of Civil Service Reform* (1997).

John Bohte is a doctoral candidate in political science at Texas A&M University. His fields of specialization include American politics, public policy, and methodology. His current research examines the interactions among Congress, the president, and the Supreme Court in the agenda setting process.

Bradley C. Canon is a professor of political science at the University of Kentucky, where he has taught for three decades. He received his Ph.D. from the University of Wisconsin Madison in 1967. He has published in the *American Political Science Review, American Journal of Political Science* and other major journals in the discipline. Much of his research focuses on compliance with and the impact of U.S. Supreme Court decisions. He is the co-author of *Judicial Policies: Implementation and Impact* (CQ Press, 1984); a second edition will be published in 1998.

Roy B. Flemming is professor of political science at Texas A&M University. His current research, supported by the National Science Foundation, focuses on agenda setting on the Supreme Court of Canada. He is the author or co-author of numerous journal articles and four books including "Punishment Before Trial" which received the Leslie Wilkins Award for best book in criminal justice in 1982. His most recent book, entitled *The Craft of Justice: Politics and Work in Courthouse Communities* is the third of a trilogy of books based on a comparison of nine trial courts, that was financed by the National Institute of Justice and the National Science Foundation. When he is not in courts, his interests turn to opera, baseball, Formula One automobile racing, and driving his Miata with the top down on the back roads of Texas.

Stephen E. Gottlieb is Professor of law at Albany Law School. He has also been Joseph C. Hostetler-Baker and Hostetler Visiting Chair in Law at Cleveland-Marshall College of Law, and in the fall of 1997 will be Robert F. Boden Distinguished Visiting Chair at Marquette University Law School. Professor Gottlieb has written or edited four books including *Jurisprudence: Cases and Materials* (1993) and *Public Values in Constitutional Law* (1993). His articles have appeared in *New York University Law Review*, *Yale Law and Policy Review*, *Hastings Law Journal*, and *Boston University Law Review*, among many others. He also spent several years in the legal services program, worked in private commercial practice, and served in the United States Peace Corps.

Michael W. McCann is professor of political science at the University of Washington. He is author of *Taking Reform Seriously: Perspectives on Public Interest Liberalism*, and *Rights at Work: Pay Equity Reform and the Politics of Legal Mobilization*. His published essays address a variety of issues regarding law and political conflict, interpretive sociolegal theory, cause lawyering, antidiscrimination law, property rights, and tort reform. McCann is currently working on a book about changes in legal tactics and group identities among unionized workers in the United States over the last half century.

Kevin McMahon received his Ph.D. from Brandeis University in 1997 and he is assistant professor of political science at Ithaca College. His reserch focuses onpresidential efforts to influence judicial interpretation during the administrations of Franklin Roosevelt, Richard Nixon, and Ronald Reagan. He also served as a visiting professor in Russia with the Civic Education Project.

Michael Paris (J.D. Columbia University, 1986; Ph.D. Brandeis University, 1997), is assistant professor of Political Science at Rutgers University, New Brunswick. He is completing a dissertation examining the significance of legal mobilization and legal rhetoric in school finance reform efforts in the United States. His current research interests include interpretive analysis of legal mobilization and social change, and the role of law and the courts in educational reform and policy.

Gerald N. Rosenberg is associate professor of political science and lecturer in Law at the University of Chicago. A member of the Washington, D.C. bar, he is the author of *The Hollow Hope: Can Courts Bring about Social Reform?*

Robert A. Van Dyk is an assistant professor in the department of politics and government at Pacific University. He received his Ph.D. from the University of Washington and he writes and teaches about law and social movements.

B. Dan Wood is an associate professor of political science at Texas A&M University. He received his Ph.D. from the University of Houston in 1987. His fields of specialization are American politics, public policy, and political methodology. He is the author or co-author of articles in the *American Political Science Review, American Journal of Political Science, Journal of Politics, Political Science and Politics, Journal of Policy Analysis and Management*, and *The Political Methodologist*. He is also co-author of *Bureaucratic Dynamics: The Role of Bureaucracy in a Democracy* (1994). Current research includes topics in executive, legislative, and judicial control of the bureaucracy in both national and federal settings. Wood is also undertaking studies of domestic and foreign policy agendasetting.

Marvin Zalman is a professor of criminal justice at Wayne State University. He is the co-author of *Criminal Procedure: Constitution and Society*, second edition, with Larry Siegel. Professor Zalman has completed a research project, supported by the Richard A. Barber Fund for Interdisciplinary Legal Research, to examine the political dynamics of the issue of assisted suicide in Michigan. "The Relationship Between Euthanasia and Suicide In the Netherlands, A Time Series Analysis, 1950–1990," co-authored with Steven Stack, will appear in *Social Science Quarterly*. Zalman is the special editor of a forthcoming issue of the *Criminal Justice Review* on "The Assault on Rights," which includes an article, "Judges in Their Own Case: a Lockean Critique of Law Enforcement Asset Sharing in Drug Forfeiture Law and Practice." Zalman is presently working on a review of social science studies of criminal procedure.

Teaching Texts in Law and Politics

David Schultz, *General Editor*

The new series Teaching Texts in Law and Politics is devoted to textbooks that explore the multidimensional and multidisciplinary areas of law and politics. Special emphasis will be given to textbooks written for the undergraduate classroom. Subject matters to be addressed in this series include, but will not be limited to: constitutional law; civil rights and liberties issues; law, race, gender, and gender orientation studies; law and ethics; women and the law; judicial behavior and decision-making; legal theory; comparative legal systems; criminal justice; courts and the political process; and other topics on the law and the political process that would be of interest to undergraduate curriculum and education. Submission of single-author and collaborative studies, as well as collections of essays are invited.

Authors wishing to have works considered for this series should contact:

Peter Lang Publishing
Acquisitions Department
275 Seventh Avenue, 28th floor
New York, New York 10001